Designing Content Switching Solutions

Zeeshan Naseh, CCIE No. 6838
Haroon Khan, CCIE No. 4530

Cisco Press

800 East 96th Street
Indianapolis, Indiana 46240 USA

Designing Content Switching Solutions

Zeeshan Naseh, Haroon Khan

Copyright © 2006 Cisco Systems, Inc.

The Cisco Press logo is a trademark of Cisco Systems, Inc.

Published by:
Cisco Press
800 East 96th Street
Indianapolis, IN 46240 USA

Printed in the United States of America 1 2 3 4 5 6 7 8 9 0

First Printing   March 2006

Library of Congress Cataloging-in-Publication Number: 2004110845

ISBN: 1-58705-213-x

Trademark Acknowledgments

Warning and Disclaimer

Corporate and Government Sales

Cisco Press offers excellent discounts on this book when ordered in quantity for bulk purchases or special sales.

For more information please contact: **U.S. Corporate and Government Sales**   1-800-382-3419
corpsales@pearsontechgroup.com

For sales outside the U.S. please contact: **International Sales**   international@pearsoned.com

Feedback Information

At Cisco Press, our goal is to create in-depth technical books of the highest quality and value. Each book is crafted with care and precision, undergoing rigorous development that involves the unique expertise of members from the professional technical community.

Readers' feedback is a natural continuation of this process. If you have any comments regarding how we could improve the quality of this book, or otherwise alter it to better suit your needs, you can contact us through email at feedback@ciscopress.com. Please make sure to include the book title and ISBN in your message.

We greatly appreciate your assistance.

Publisher	John Wait
Editor-in-Chief	John Kane
Cisco Representative	Anthony Wolfenden
Cisco Press Program Manager	Jeff Brady
Production Manager	Patrick Kanouse
Development Editor	Jennifer Foster
Copy Editor	Emily Rader
Technical Editors	Umar Shafiq, Sukento Sukirya
Editorial Assistant	Raina Han
Book and Cover Designer	Louisa Adair
Composition	Interactive Composition Corporation
Indexer	WordWise Publishing Solutions
Proofreading	Christy Parrish

CISCO SYSTEMS

Corporate Headquarters
Cisco Systems, Inc.
170 West Tasman Drive
San Jose, CA 95134-1706
USA
www.cisco.com
Tel: 408 526-4000
    800 553-NETS (6387)
Fax: 408 526-4100

European Headquarters
Cisco Systems International BV
Haarlerbergpark
Haarlerbergweg 13-19
1101 CH Amsterdam
The Netherlands
www-europe.cisco.com
Tel: 31 0 20 357 1000
Fax: 31 0 20 357 1100

Americas Headquarters
Cisco Systems, Inc.
170 West Tasman Drive
San Jose, CA 95134-1706
USA
www.cisco.com
Tel: 408 526-7660
Fax: 408 527-0883

Asia Pacific Headquarters
Cisco Systems, Inc.
Capital Tower
168 Robinson Road
#22-01 to #29-01
Singapore 068912
www.cisco.com
Tel: +65 6317 7777
Fax: +65 6317 7799

Cisco Systems has more than 200 offices in the following countries and regions. Addresses, phone numbers, and fax numbers are listed on the
Cisco.com Web site at www.cisco.com/go/offices.

Argentina • Australia • Austria • Belgium • Brazil • Bulgaria • Canada • Chile • China PRC • Colombia • Costa Rica • Croatia • Czech Republic
Denmark • Dubai, UAE • Finland • France • Germany • Greece • Hong Kong SAR • Hungary • India • Indonesia • Ireland • Israel • Italy
Japan • Korea • Luxembourg • Malaysia • Mexico • The Netherlands • New Zealand • Norway • Peru • Philippines • Poland • Portugal
Puerto Rico • Romania • Russia • Saudi Arabia • Scotland • Singapore • Slovakia • Slovenia • South Africa • Spain • Sweden
Switzerland • Taiwan • Thailand • Turkey • Ukraine • United Kingdom • United States • Venezuela • Vietnam • Zimbabwe

About the Authors

Zeeshan Naseh, CCIE No. 6838, is a technical leader in the Cisco Advanced Technologies Services Group. His primary responsibility has been supporting the major Cisco customers, including service providers, wireless service providers, large enterprises, and financial institutions. As a design consultant, Zeeshan has focused on content switching and data centers. Zeeshan has authored several white papers and design documents that have been published internally within Cisco and on Cisco Connection Online (CCO). Zeeshan has developed and presented several break-out sessions and tutorials related to data center designs at Networkers. Prior to joining the Cisco Advanced Technology Services Group, Zeeshan worked at US WEST and FORE Systems and for the Cisco Catalyst 6500 development team. He holds a bachelor of science degree in computer engineering from the University of Arizona.

Haroon Khan, CCIE No. 4530, attended the University of California at Berkeley, where he majored in cognitive science. While attending Berkeley, Haroon started his internship at Cisco Systems, working as a software developer. From 1997 to 2000, Haroon worked for the Cisco Network Security Support group as a senior network engineer. From 2001 to 2004, Haroon worked as a senior network consultant for the Cisco Data Center Advanced Services team. His main focus was on the design and architecture of data center technologies, which included content networking, security, routing and switching, and consulting with the top Cisco enterprise and service provider customers. Haroon currently is a manager for the Cisco Advanced Services Data Center Consulting Group and lives with his wife in San Jose, CA.

About the Technical Reviewers

Umar Shafiq, CCIE No. 7119, is a network consulting engineer for the Cisco Advanced Engineering Services Group, specializing in security and data center technologies. He is responsible for creating, validating, and deploying large-scale data center designs. He also works closely with the development teams and TAC support teams in Cisco to provide support on anything from troubleshooting, to quality issues, to tools. Umar has been at Cisco for almost eight years and has a MBA from California State University.

Sukento Sukirya received his B.S. and M.S. in electrical engineering from the Texas A&M University–Kingsville in 1994 and 1997. Sukento has more than 10 years experience in the computer and networking industry. He has been working on data center and load balancing technologies for the last five years. Prior to joining Cisco, Sukento worked on several data center designs and implementation projects for major wireless carriers, including Cingular Wireless and Nextel Communications. At these companies he was the lead load balancing engineer, and his designs and troubleshooting skills minimized downtime and provided network high availability.

Dedications

Zeeshan Naseh

To my parents, for inspiring and planting the love of knowledge in me.

To my wife, Naila, for her tireless support and encouragement.

To my brother, Khurram, for his support and advice throughout my career.

Haroon Khan

This book is dedicated to Abu, Ama, and Reema, for always being there. Thank you for the encouragement, support, and love.

Acknowledgments

Our thanks and gratitude goes to the following:

Faiz Khan, Director of Advanced Services, for his ideas and continuous support and encouragement.

Martin Pueblas, Vinay Gundi, Stefano Testa, and the rest of the Cisco product team members for their proposal reviews and contributions to Chapters 8 and 13.

Sukento Sukirya and Umar Shafiq for their technical reviews and for keeping us honest.

All the team members of the Cisco Advanced Services Data Center Practice for contributing in some way, shape, or form and making this project possible.

We would like to express our special thanks to John Kane, editor-in-chief; Raina Han, our editorial assistant; Jennifer Foster and Chris Cleveland, our development editors; and all other staff members at Cisco Press for making this publication possible. Raina and Jennifer, thank you for your patience and diligent reviews.

Thanks to all of our customers with whom we have worked for the past seven years. Believe it or not, our nights and weekends in the data centers with each one of you inspired this book. Hopefully, this publication should help minimize the conference calls and root cause analysis reports. All of you are greatly appreciated. Thanks.

This Book Is Safari Enabled

The Safari® Enabled icon on the cover of your favorite technology book means the book is available through Safari Bookshelf. When you buy this book, you get free access to the online edition for 45 days.

Safari Bookshelf is an electronic reference library that lets you easily search thousands of technical books, find code samples, download chapters, and access technical information whenever and wherever you need it.

To gain 45-day Safari Enabled access to this book:

- Go to http://www.ciscopress.com/safarienabled

- Complete the brief registration form

- Enter the coupon code YNGM-5WJF-9Q8Q-JRFB-FIAP

If you have difficulty registering on Safari Bookshelf or accessing the online edition, please e-mail customer-service@safaribooksonline.com.

Contents at a Glance

Table of Contents

xiv

Icons Used in This Book

Command Syntax Conventions

The conventions used to present command syntax in this book are the same conventions used in the IOS Command Reference. The Command Reference describes these conventions as follows:

- **Boldface** indicates commands and keywords that are entered literally as shown. In actual configuration examples and output (not general command syntax), boldface indicates commands that are manually input by the user (such as a **show** command).

- *Italics* indicate arguments for which you supply actual values.

- Vertical bars | separate alternative, mutually exclusive elements.

- Square brackets [ ] indicate optional elements.

- Braces { } indicate a required choice.

- Braces within brackets [{ }] indicate a required choice within an optional element.

Foreword

Having had the honor to work together with Zeeshan and Haroon for many years, it's great to know they are sharing their wealth of knowledge in the data center networking area through this brilliantly written book. This book provides answers to the day-to-day design and architecture challenges when it comes to optimizing critical application environments, disaster recovery, and integrating data center networking services. Zeeshan and Haroon have helped design and deploy some of the largest and most complex data center networking environments. The authors have taken a very practical approach in presenting the case studies based on their years of experience and in-depth knowledge in this space.

Data center networking—and application optimization, specifically—are rapidly evolving, and the authors have made sure to provide a good background and fundamentals of the technology and protocols. I would highly recommend this book to anyone who is currently working in this space or wants to learn content switching and its applications in the data center.

Faiz Khan
Director, Data Center Networking Services
Cisco Systems, Inc.

Introduction

Today's data centers are becoming more and more complex, with a number of services such as server load balancing, SSL offloading, and security deployed at the heart of the data center. This book covers several commonly deployed solutions using content switching. The purpose is to inform the reader of the best practices for each solution. The book also covers topics such as scaling server load balancing within a data center, the integrated data center design option, and global server load balancing using DNS or IP. This book is intended for data center architects, network engineers, project managers, and data center managers.

Goals and Methods

The goal of this book is to help readers understand content switching solutions using Cisco content switching products. The sections that describe the various content switching solutions in this book also describe the ideas and theories behind the solutions. These ideas and theories are then examined and understood as part of a case study. The case studies in the book emulate real-world scenarios for solutions covering some of the common features and functionality deployed in real-world production networks. The case study is a key methodology used in this book to help you discover the topics you need to review in more depth and fully understand and remember their details. The chapters in this book try to follow this pattern when discussing a topic:

- Motivation and need for the solution
- How the solution works
- Case study to understand the solution at work in a real world network

The case study also helps network administrators currently deploying or maintaining content switching products to identify gaps and techniques used in their roles in managing their content switching solutions.

Who Should Read This Book?

This book is intended for readers who have an interest in understanding, managing, and maintaining content switching solutions. The material discussed provides an introduction to these content switching solutions; however, the chapter discussion assumes that the reader has basic knowledge of data networking focusing on the TCP/IP, client/server communication, and basic routing and switching technologies.

Content switching solutions such as load balancing, caching, and providing disaster recovery for applications are key technologies needed for network administrators and designers because they allow business applications to run in an efficient and redundant fashion. With the advent of e-commerce and Internet-accessible applications, more and more enterprises and service providers rely on these online services to grow their businesses today. Thus having a content switching solution in order to scale with the demands of business is a must, and these topics are covered in detail in this book.

How This Book Is Organized

This book is organized into four parts. Even though the chapters in the book can be read in any order, it is recommended to read Part I first and in sequential order. Part I covers the basics of content switching, which is applied in Parts II, III, and IV of the book. Following is a description of the fours parts of the book and the chapters within each part:

Part I, "Server Load Balancing (SLB)" (Chapters 1–9), includes introductions to SLB using the Cisco products, as well as discussion of load balancing HTTP, virtual private networks (VPNs), firewalls, and migrations between SLB devices.

- **Chapter 1, "Introduction to Server Load Balancing,"** introduces the world of content switching within data centers. Major topics discussed in this chapter are motivations behind, evolution, history, modes, and designs of SLB, as well as characterization of SLB applications.

- **Chapter 2, "Introduction to the Cisco Content Services Switch,"** introduces the architecture, features, and design details of the Cisco appliance-based load balancer, the Content Services Switch (CSS). The platform discussed is the CSS 11500 series. The Cisco CSS 11500 Series is made up of high-performance, high-availability modular architecture load balancers for web infrastructures.

- **Chapter 3, "Introduction to the Cisco Content Switching Module,"** introduces the architecture, features, and design details of the Cisco module-based load balancer for the Catalyst 6500, the Content Switching Module (CSM). The Cisco CSM is a line card for the Cisco Catalyst 6500 Series Switch. It provides a high-performance, cost-effective load-balancing solution for enterprise and Internet service provider networks, allowing these organizations to provide customers, employees, and business partners with the best possible online experience.

- **Chapter 4, "Layer 7 Load Balancing and Content Customization,"** discusses the methods and protocols involved in accomplishing a Layer 7 load-balancing solution. The reasons for and benefits of deploying persistent and customized load balancing are explored. TCP is the building block for Layer 7 protocols such as HTTP. This chapter examines the interaction between HTTP and TCP, and how client and server communication at the TCP and HTTP layers is accomplished.

- **Chapter 5, "Firewall Load Balancing,"** introduces firewall load-balancing (FWLB) concepts, technology, and designs. We talk about motivations behind firewall load-balanced solutions, different types of firewalls, and how to load balance them. We also discuss design options and configurations.

- **Chapter 6, "Transparent and Proxy Cache Load Balancing,"** introduces transparent and proxy cache load-balancing concepts, technology, and designs. In order to understand the load balancing of caches, we take an in-depth look the HTTP protocol, caching technology, terminology, and various design methodologies.

- **Chapter 7, "Load Balancing Streaming Video Servers,"** introduces streaming video server load-balancing concepts, technology, and designs. In order to understand the load balancing of streaming video servers, we take an in-depth look at the protocols, products, and types of servers used for this purpose. Since Application and Content Networking System (ACNS) software on the Cisco Content Engine (CE) possesses extensive video streaming functionality, we use the CE as a video proxy example within this chapter.

- **Chapter 8, "Virtual Private Network Load Balancing,"** discusses VPN load balancing, which provides the scalability and availability that enterprise and service provider customers are looking for. VPN load balancing allows customers to scale their VPN infrastructures easily and at the same time improve the redundancy level by simply adding new devices.

- **Chapter 9, "Content Switching Device Migrations,"** looks at the evolution of load-balancing devices and discusses how to plan a migration. A case study provides the configuration information for a sample migration from a CSS solution to a CSM solution.

Part II, "Secure Socket Layer (SSL)" (Chapters 10 and 11), includes introductions to SSL using the Cisco products and discusses end-to-end encryption from client to server, as well as using back-end SSL.

- **Chapter 10, "SSL Offloading,"** provides an introduction to the SSL protocol and reviews the SSL Modules (SSLMs) available for the Cisco Catalyst 6500, as well as SSL's integration with the Content Switching Module (CSM). The chapter also reviews the SSLM solution for the Content Services Switch (CSS). A case study looks at a deployment solution using the CSM and SSLM, including design and configuration details.

- **Chapter 11, "Back-End SSL Offloading,"** introduces the Cisco back-end SSL solution implemented on the SSLM for the Cisco Catalyst 6500 Switch and on the SSLM for the Content Services Switch. A case study explains the details of the back-end SSL solution on the SSLM for the Cisco Catalyst 6500 Switch.

Part III, "Distributed Data Centers" (Chapters 12 and 13), includes introductions to providing distributed data center solutions using global server load balancing (GSLB), reviews GSLB solutions using DNS and Route Health Injection (RHI), and discusses techniques within routing protocols for providing GSLB solutions.

- **Chapter 12, "Global Server Load Balancing,"** introduces GSLB and its benefits, provides an overview of the Domain Name System (DNS), and discusses the Global Site Selector (GSS). The chapter also provides a case study that shows how GSLB can be deployed using GSS.

- **Chapter 13, "IP-Based GSLB Using RHI,"** introduces example topologies that use the Interior Gateway Protocol (IGP) and the Border Gateway Protocol (BGP) for achieving site-to-site recovery and load distribution between data centers. Today's enterprises have strict requirements for high availability of services and application uptime that must be met through a business continuance and disaster recovery solution. Multiple data centers provide business continuance, disaster recovery, and load-sharing solutions. Some organizations use DNS for managing business continuance and load sharing between data centers. However, organizations that do not want to make changes to the DNS can use IGP/BGP mechanisms for their business continuance and disaster recovery solutions.

Part IV, "Data Center Designs" (Chapters 14 and 15), reviews how scaling and integration of server load balancing with SSL and GSLB is conducted.

- **Chapter 14, "Scaling Server Load Balancing within a Data Center,"** introduces the concepts and design methodologies of scaling load-balancing services within a single data center. We discuss how load-balanced applications can be scaled using DNS or IP and how they are scaled when server capacity within a load balancer is maximized. In other words, we cover how the same application is load balanced in two different SLB devices and then discuss the approaches to SLB device selection, as well as the methods of scaling when the servers within an SLB device have reached their maximum capacity or have failed health checks.

- **Chapter 15, "Integrated Data Center Designs,"** takes content switching to the next level. Prior chapters discussed key aspects of server load balancing, SSL offloading, and global server load-balancing solutions. They talked about the data center products such as the CSS, CSM, SSLM, and GSS and discussed how they can be designed and deployed. This chapter takes these concepts and presents several integrated design methodologies.

Server Load Balancing (SLB)

CHAPTER 1

Introduction to Server Load Balancing

This chapter introduces you to server load balancing (SLB), which is also known as content switching. Load balancers or content switches are network devices that route user requests or sessions to the appropriate server based on the characterization of the request. We will discuss the reasoning behind SLB and its evolution from the DNS days to current hardware-accelerated content switches. It is important to understand the concepts presented in this chapter, as they will be used extensively in the case studies presented in the rest of the book. These concepts and the case studies will help you to determine the right SLB design for your network.

Why Load Balance?

In the computer networks space, load balancing means to distribute requests or raw data across two systems, devices, routes, or paths. In other words, load balancing provides redundancy and scalability so that no single device is overwhelmed. The idea is to scale any environment comprised of a device that serves or processes requests (such as to distribute IP packets to multiple next-hop devices across multiple paths using Open Shortest Path First, or OSPF, in a router).

This discussion focuses on SLB by content switches within data centers. This load balancing can be performed at any layer of OSI model, from Layer 3 to Layer 7, depending on the application hosted on the server. Other devices that can be load balanced by content switches are firewalls, web/app/db servers, virtual private network (VPN) concentrators, caches, and Secure Socket Layer (SSL) offload devices. A basic SLB device is depicted in Figure 1-1.

When you enable SLB, the content switch becomes the virtual representation of the application. In Figure 1-1, the web application server farm is represented by the load balancer as 10.1.1.10 (virtual IP, or VIP) listening on TCP port 80. The web servers' IP addresses are 10.1.1.11, 10.1.1.12, and 10.1.1.13. As a client makes a connection to the VIP address (after the DNS resolution for the particular domain), the connection gets load balanced by the SLB device to the next available web server. The SLB device makes the server selection decision based on the configured load balancing method.

Figure 1-1 *Server Load Balancing*

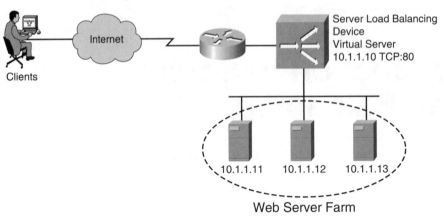

SLB is needed to scale the server farms within the data center and to provide redundancy. This ensures that the application being hosted for clients and partners is available. The following sections explain the advantages of using SLB:

- Scalability
- Availability and redundancy
- Security
- Cost effectiveness

Scalability

Ease of scalability of the server farm is the primary advantage of SLB. After the content switch is configured and load balancing is enabled for a particular application, the capacity of that application in terms of the number of concurrent requests serviced can be seamlessly increased by adding another application server to the server farm. This change can be performed without any application outage at all.

Availability and Redundancy

Server health check and availability of the load-balanced application is another key advantage of SLB. The health check feature, also known as keepalives or probes, is critical in content switching deployment, and the capability to do extensive server health monitoring is always a key product differentiator. SLB devices use the server health checks or probes to monitor not just the server's IP connectivity but the status of the application or daemon running on the server.

In older load balancing methods, such as DNS round robin, server health is undetermined. Thus in a DNS-based solution, a client request could be directed to a server that is unavailable or out of service.

Today's content switches can readily identify whether the server is experiencing problems or is unavailable and take it out of rotation. Health of the server can be checked by a ping to the server, a TCP connect to the application port, or an application layer request with the appropriate response verification. For example, an HTTP daemon on the server can be probed by sending an HTTP request to the server and then verifying the HTTP response content, which can be the HTTP return code or the actual page content.

When you enable SLB on a content switch, the network device becomes the virtual representation of the application. In order to ensure that this virtualized representation of the web or application servers is highly available, the content switches are deployed in a redundant fashion. The content switches have minimal failover times in seconds. Furthermore, this redundancy can be stateful, meaning that the state table or user session information is shared from the active to the backup content switch, ensuring that after a failover the user session stays up.

Security

Content switches provide not only a secure and protected server farm, but also provide security for the application itself. One of the traditional security features is access control lists (ACLs). ACLs can be used on the content switches to allow or deny requests from particular users. This can be accomplished based on client-side information, such as the following:

- Layer 3 source address (source IP address)
- Layer 4 protocol
- Layer 4 protocol and port
- Layer 7 request (e.g., HTTP URL)
- Combination of the above

Another key security feature on the content switch is denial of service (DoS) attack protection. Since the content switch is looking at all the requests coming in for a particular domain, it can determine whether a DoS attack is in progress or not. A corrective action or notification to the site admin can be performed. For example, the Cisco Content Services Switch (CSS) generates SNMP enterprise traps when a DoS attack event occurs. One trap is generated each second when the number of attacks during that second exceeds the threshold for the configured DoS attack type. Load balancers mark a user request as a SYN Attack in the absence of a TCP Client ACK in the three-way handshake within a set time. In this case, a DoS attack is detected, but after the initial TCP SYN makes it to the server. The SYN packets that make it to the server can potentially exhaust the server's TCP socket resources.

You can enhance the security by moving the TCP termination from the server to the SLB device. This feature enables the load balancer to terminate the TCP request from the client and only send the request to the server if the client session is valid. For example, in the case of HTTP, the load balancer only sends the client request to the server if the user establishes the TCP connection properly within a few seconds and sends a proper HTTP GET. Depending on the load balancer in question, this feature is known as Layer 5 or Layer 7 load balancing or as the TCP termination feature.

Cost Effectiveness

Introduction of a SLB device does improve the economics of a data center. With a content switch, the server farm does not need to be comprised of expensive servers with huge hard disks but can be the more economical type with minimal disk space and a shared storage area network backend. Server load balancers help in reducing the server maintenance and licensing cost also.

Thus a content switching device enables server and application redundancy, scalability, security, and reduction in overall data center maintenance and serviceability expenditures.

History of Server Load Balancing

In the early days of the Internet evolution, the applications available on the Internet were research applications, databases, or FTP repositories hosted on a single server. In the early 1990s, as the Internet started being used by businesses and by consumers, additional applications were hosted on the Internet—still on individual servers.

Initial scalability needs of these servers were met by increasing the capacity and capability of the individual server, such as by upgrading the server with a faster CPU, a network interface card, more memory, more disk space, etc. This is usually referred to as *vertical scaling*. Another approach that was taken was to separate the application components into different servers. A web instance would be hosted on one server and a database instance on another server. This is a good approach but does not provide complete scalability as each server is still a single point of failure and a potential bottleneck. Comprehensive scalability and high availability are achieved by combining the heterogeneous farms, where each server performs a certain task, with content switching. The following sections explain the evolution of content switching for the past two decades.

First-Generation Load Balancers

During the days of having a single server for a particular domain, scalability needs appeared as the usage increased. There were two initial thoughts about how to solve this problem. One was to use the DNS control plane and distribute user traffic over multiple servers using BIND (Berkeley Internet Name Domain) Round Robin. The other solution was the use of

IP Anycast across the Internet IP routing infrastructure. This section provides the details of these two mechanisms of first-generation SLB devices, namely:

- DNS-based load balancing
- IP Anycast

DNS-Based Load Balancing

In 1993, BIND 4.9 came out with the DNS Round Robin feature, which was used extensively for distributing load across multiple servers for a particular domain. In Example 1-1, the domain www.testexample.com is distributed across four answers, where an answer is an IP mapping to a domain name. Notice how the order of answer IP addresses changes in the second response, shown in Example 1-2.

Example 1-1 *First Response from the DNS Server*

```
C:\>nslookup www.testexample.com
Server:  test.mylab.com
Address:  10.10.226.120

Non-authoritative answer:
Name:    www.testexample.com
Addresses:  66.94.230.48, 66.94.230.49, 66.94.230.50, 66.94.230.34
```

Example 1-2 *Second Response from the DNS Server*

```
C:\>nslookup www.testexample.com
Server:  test.mylab.com
Address:  10.10.226.120

Non-authoritative answer:
Name:    www.testexample.com
Addresses:  66.94.230.49, 66.94.230.50, 66.94.230.34, 66.94.230.48
```

These DNS responses ensure load distribution. This is also the default behavior in BIND 8 and 9. In most versions of BIND, there is a feature to disable this default behavior by setting the *rrset-order* option to one of the following:

- **Fixed**—Do not change the order of answers.
- **Random**—Change the order in random fashion.
- **Cyclic**—Change the order in cyclic fashion. (This is default behavior, which is the same as Round Robin, defined above.)

In any case, you see that the Round Robin feature in BIND is a quickly and easily administered client request distribution method. This does not give us true load balancing, though. Following are a few caveats against using this approach:

- BIND has no knowledge of server health.
- Weighted Round Robin and other methods of load balancing are not possible.

- DNS caching prevents true load balancing.
- Negative DNS caching can also influence load balancing.
- No measures are available to prevent DoS attacks against servers.

These reasons show that using DNS for SLB is not a desired solution because it can easily result in a client's traffic being sent to a server that is out of service.

IP Anycast

IP Anycast is a simple way to do geographic server load balancing. The idea is to use servers with the same IP address on multiple points of presence (POP) on the Internet. BGP routing in the Internet core, which uses the closest exit, provides routing for the client to the closest server. This has been used in small scale for FTP servers to download content faster across the globe. Of course, this effort needs to be coordinated with the service providers because in BGP routing the same subnet would show up in their routing table from multiple locations. Most service providers will not accept host routes, so the addresses have to be summarized before being sent to them.

As can be seen, this solution never got widely deployed due to the difficulties associated with it. IP Anycast does have its place for data center disaster recovery solutions. (See Chapter 13, "IP-Based GSLB Using RHI," for more details.)

IP Anycast is difficult to implement with IP Version 4, but its application is understood and recognized. This is the reason IP Version 6 has a separate address type of Anycast. The address corresponds to a set of computers that share a common address prefix. IP packets are delivered to exactly one member of the group, that is, the one closest to the client (sender).

Second-Generation Load Balancers

As previously discussed, web-based server utilization was increasing and there was a desperate need for a comprehensive SLB solution. This was recognized by network device providers, such as Cisco Systems, as an emerging market. This section explains initial server load balancer offerings by Cisco Systems, namely:

- Local Director
- Accelerated SLB
- IOS SLB

These solutions mostly performed load balancing in software.

Local Director

In 1996, Cisco Systems, Inc. came out with the Local Director (LD) solution. This was a 2-RU hardware appliance that performed SLB and health checks. LD was one of the first appliance-based solutions seen in the industry and was appreciated for its high performance Layer 4 load balancing.

Accelerated SLB

In 1998, the Accelerated SLB solution was introduced. This was a combo solution of LD and Catalyst 6000 (Cat6000 or Cat6K). In essence, this solution utilized the Multilayer Switching (MLS) feature on the Cat6000 to accelerate the user session. The LD still receives the client request (TCP SYN), the server response (TCP SYN ACK), and other control packets, such as TCP RST and TCP FIN, but the data traffic between the client and the server bypasses the LD. The Data traffic utilizes the MLS flows within the Cat6000.

IOS SLB

In 1999, the IOS Server Load Balancing (ISLB) solution was introduced with hardware acceleration for Layer 2 rewrite, that is, Dispatch mode. This solution is a feature in Cisco IOS and is supported on the Catalyst 6500 (Cat6500). In 2000, the second release of ISLB on Cat6500 came out with stateful redundancy, Dynamic Feedback Protocol (DFP), Firewall Load Balancing (FWLB), and other features. Overall, ISLB was still a software-based solution.

Third-Generation Load Balancers

The third generation of load balancers is comprised of appliances with hardware acceleration. Several network providers came out with these high performance devices, namely Alteon, Foundry, Cisco Systems, Inc., and so on. The following sections discuss the CSS and Content Switching Module (CSM), offered by Cisco Systems.

Content Services Switch

In 2000, Cisco shipped the CSS, which uses an MMC chipset-based hardware technology. CSS 11000 has the capability to install flows for the client to server communication and NAT source or destination IP in hardware. TCP spoofing was also performed in hardware. CSS came out with extensive features for Layer 4 and Layer 5 SLB, including FWLB, cache load balancing (cache LB), access control list (ACL), NAT, and global server or site load balancing (GSLB). In 2002, CSS 11506 was released. It's a high performance, modular CSS with distributed architecture.

Content Switching Module

In 2001, the CSM on the Cat6500 was released. CSM uses a pipeline architecture composed of five Intel IXP processors. CSM changed the way content switches perform its functions, as it could do 200,000 Layer 4 connections per second and 1 million concurrent sessions.

CSM together with SSLM (Secure Socket Layer Module) and FWSM (Firewall Services Module) make for an ideal integrated data center solution. Please see Chapter 15, "Integrated Data Center Designs," for more details. CSM has a comprehensive SLB feature built into hardware along with stateful redundancy and IP any protocol load balancing.

Characterization of the Application

In order to decide which design is the most appropriate for the application environment, you need to analyze the application. This section defines a few aspects of typical software applications that should be understood. Each application is different, and it is critical to characterize each before implementing a content switching solution for it. The following are commonly used servers and applications within a data center:

- Web servers (for example, Apache, Web Logic, MS IIS – TCP/80)
- HR apps (for example, PeopleSoft)
- Database (for example, Oracle)
- DNS servers (for example, BIND)
- RADIUS servers (for example, Cisco CAR)

When you characterize an application, you need to consider the following aspects:

- Protocol and port
- Sessions per second
- Duration of transaction
- Concurrent sessions
- Idle timeout
- Back end sessions
- Session stickiness

NOTE   One point that should be understood before characterizing an application is the difference between a Session and a Connection. A Session is a client/server transaction that could use multiple TCP or UDP connections. A Connection is a single TCP connection.

Protocol and Port

Almost all software applications use TCP/IP for the transfer of information between the client and server. This is where application characterization begins. The protocol is the

Layer 4 protocol, whether TCP or UDP, that is used by the application for the client/server transactions. The port is the listener configured on the server to which the client sends the initial request. In some protocols, such as FTP and Real-Time Streaming Protocol (RTSP), the connections are dual session based, also known as *buddy* connections. In this case, if available, protocol and port information for both buddy connections needs to be characterized. It should also be noted whether fixed ports are used in any of the transactions or whether the application uses embedded IP or port information in its transactions.

Sessions per Second

Sessions per second is the number of hits per second that the application has. This is a critical value that is used to determine the activity of the web site and thus the performance of the SLB device. The aggregate sessions per second value of all the applications hosted on an SLB device must not exceed the device's maximum sessions per second performance value.

Duration of Transaction

The duration of a session is the length of the transaction of a client/server session. For example, this would be around 20 minutes for a Telnet session while less than 1 minute for an HTTP session.

Concurrent Sessions

Concurrent sessions are the active sessions at a given time on an SLB device. The above two data points, sessions per second and duration of transaction, are used to compute the concurrent session. This number is needed to ensure enough memory is available on the SLB device to install and maintain the needed concurrent flows.

Use the following formula to calculate concurrent sessions:

Current session = sessions per second * duration of transaction

Idle Timeout

Idle timeout is the length of time a session or a TCP connection is inactive. This is critical because if the single TCP connection is idle for a long time, you need to ensure proper handling of those flows on the SLB device. SLB devices have garbage collection built in, where idle flows are cleaned up within minutes. This is done to reclaim memory space for new connections. Idle timeout or flow cleanup time can be adjusted on most SLB devices.

Multiple TCP connections typically are used to form a client/server session. In most applications, sessions require persistence, meaning a client should go to the same server for all the TCP connections. This persistence is achieved by sticky configurations on the SLB device. Thus the sticky timeout configuration on the SLB device for a particular application should be the same or more than the session timeout of that application.

Back End Sessions

Back end sessions are connections or requests made by the server to other servers or applications in order to service the client's request. Knowledge of back end sessions can reveal how chatty the application is. This knowledge is used to diagnose how much non-load-balanced traffic would have to go through the SLB device. A one-armed design, where the SLB device is connected by a single physical link to the infrastructure, would be better suited for an application where the back end sessions use a majority of the bandwidth.

Session Stickiness

Session stickiness requires that multiple requests (TCP connections) from the same client go to the same server. It is required when the idle session timeout is high and session state information is kept on the same server. The simplest form of session stickiness is based on the client's source IP address. So a client with a particular source IP address will be load balanced to the same server where that client's initial connection was sent.

SLB and SLB Modes

In this section we will talk about typical load-balanced traffic flows and a critical functionality of the load balancer, which is how the load balancer rewrites the packet it is sending in the direction of the real server.

These steps describe the operation of a typical flow:

1 The client request reaches the virtual server on the SLB device (TCP SYN).

2 The client request is processed and a server farm is selected.

3 Within the server farm, a server is selected based on the balancing method.

4 The SLB device will NAT the VIP to the server IP and send the packet (TCP SYN) toward the server based on the configured SLB mode.

5 The server responds back to the client (TCP SYN ACK).

6 The SLB device performs NAT-back if needed. This means the SLB device will translate the source IP address of the packet from the server's IP address to the VIP.

7 The packet is sent along toward the client (TCP SYN ACK).

8 The client completes the TCP handshake by sending the TCP ACK.

9 The SLB device establishes the flow in hardware and sends the packet (TCP ACK) toward the server based on the configured SLB mode.

10 The TCP is established.

Figure 1-2 illustrates each step of the operation.

Figure 1-2   *Steps for Establishing a Server Load-Balanced TCP Connect*

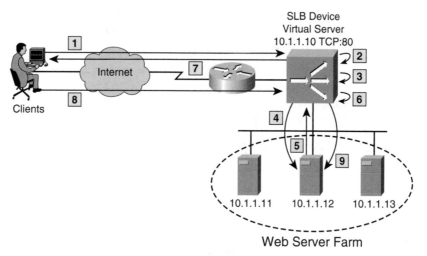

As seen in the previous traffic flow example, SLB server selection and SLB mode are two of the many critical tasks that the load balancer performs. The following sections discuss the two available SLB modes: Dispatch mode and Directed mode.

SLB balancing methods are discussed in detail in Chapter 2 and Chapter 3.

Dispatch Mode

Dispatch mode is when the load balancer rewrites only the destination MAC address before sending the packet toward the server. It is also known as the Layer 2 rewrite feature. Since the packet is sent as it is with the destination IP being the VIP on the load balancer, the server needs to recognize the packet as addressed to self. This is achieved by configuring the VIP address as a loopback or a secondary IP on the server.

This method was commonly used in the past as earlier load balancers would perform faster in Layer 2 rewrite mode. Layer 3 NAT used to be costly in terms of CPU utilization. Today's load balancers have the same performance for Layer 2 or Layer 3 rewrite. Layer 3 NAT is hardware accelerated now.

Figure 1-3 shows how Dispatch mode functions. In this example the client's IP address is 31.12.11.17 and the VIP address of the application represented by the load balancer is 10.1.1.10 (TCP port 80). The selected real server's IP address is 10.1.1.13. Following are the steps for a single packet from client to server and the response from server to client:

Step 1 The client sends the TCP packet on port 80 with its own source IP and the destination IP of the VIP.

Step 2 The SLB device listening on 10.1.1.10 (TCP port 80) receives the packet and then load balances it to the next available real server. Notice the destination IP is not the real server IP (10.1.1.13) but the VIP (10.1.1.10). Also see how the destination MAC used is that of the real server (0003.47d6.922b).

Step 3 Even though the destination IP is not the server's own IP, the real server accepts the packet as destined to self. This is because we have the VIP address configured as a secondary IP on the real server. The source IP for the server response is the VIP address.

Step 4 The response of the server is simply switched by the SLB device to the client.

Figure 1-3 *Dispatch Mode, also Known as Layer 2 Rewrite*

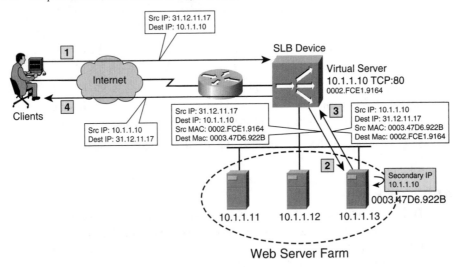

Dispatch mode is commonly used for load balancing of devices where the destination IP is not supposed to be changed. For example:

- FWLB
- Transparent cache load balancing

Directed Mode

Directed mode is when the load balancer rewrites the destination IP from the VIP to the selected server's real IP before sending the packet toward the server. This is the commonly used SLB mode in most web and application load balancing. In most devices, this is the default method of operation also.

Figure 1-4 shows how Directed mode functions. In this example, the client's IP address is 31.12.11.17 and the VIP address of the application represented by the load balancer is 10.1.1.10 (TCP port 80). The real server's IP address is 10.1.1.13. Following are the steps for a single packet from client to server and the response from server to client:

Step 1   The client sends the TCP packet on port 80 with its own source IP and the destination IP of the VIP.

Step 2   The SLB device listening on 10.1.1.10 (TCP port 80) receives the packet and then load balances it to the next available real. Notice that the destination IP is the real server IP (10.1.1.13).

Step 3   The source IP address for the server response is its own IP address.

Step 4   The response of the server is simply switched by the SLB device toward the client. The SLB device performs NAT-back—that is, it rewrites the source IP address from the server's real address to the VIP.

Figure 1-4   *Directed Mode, also Known as Layer 3 Rewrite*

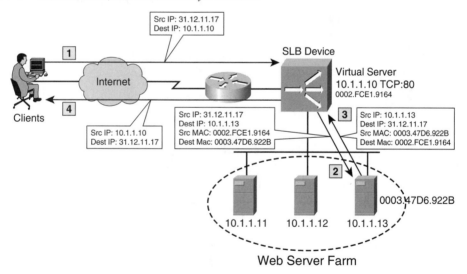

SLB Designs

We have discussed content switching and understood its importance, how it evolved, and how it functions. Now we will review how to design a content switching solution and particularly review the SLB terminology around designs. This is the knowledge that we will use when discussing various case studies and custom solutions in the following chapters.

In the following designs, the client side is referred to as the front end—the interface or VLAN from where the client request reaches the load balancer. Below the server side is referred to as the back end with respect to the SLB device—the interface, or VLAN, from where the real servers connect to the load balancer.

This section covers the following topics:

- Layer 2 design
- Layer 3 design
- One-armed design
- Direct sever return

Layer 2 Design

Layer 2 SLB design basically implies that the SLB device is used in a bridged mode; that is, the device merges two VLANs together, with both the VLANs existing in the same IP subnet. In simplest terms, the SLB acts as a crossover cable, bridging or merging two different VLANs. In a Layer 2 design, the subnet used on the SLB device is the same across the two VLANs—one VLAN is the client side and the other is the server side. Figure 1-5 shows a topology of how a bridged design would be set up.

Figure 1-5 *Layer 2 Design, also Known as Bridged Design*

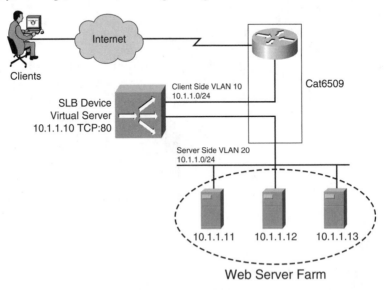

The key point of Figure 1-5 is that the client-side VLAN (VLAN 10) and server-side VLAN (VLAN 20) are in the same subnet, which is 10.1.1.0/24. In this case, the SLB device bridges the two VLANs. This is sometimes also referred to as *merging VLANs*.

This design is easy to implement and is usually the first phase of deployment. It is easier to introduce a load balancer in an existing network using bridged design without changing the IP addresses, netmask and default gateway settings on the servers, or the IP addresses on the routers and firewalls. The load balancer goes in as a bump on the wire without any infrastructure changes. With a bridged design, one has to be careful about introducing loops in the infrastructure. Proper STP analysis needs to be performed on the infrastructure to ensure loop-free robust topology. In this design, all load-balanced and non-load-balanced traffic to and from the server go through the SLB device.

Layer 3 Design

Layer 3 SLB design basically implies that the SLB device is used in a routed mode; that is, the device routes between two (VLANs)—two different IP subnets. One VLAN is the client side and the other is the server side.

Figure 1-6 provides a topology showing how a Layer 3 design would be set up.

Figure 1-6   *Layer 3 Design, also Known as Routed Design*

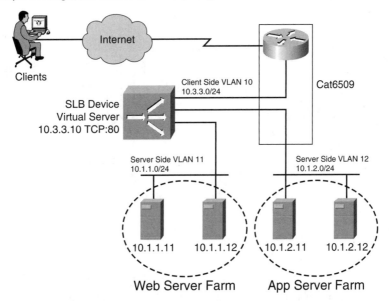

The key point of Figure 1-6 is that the client-side VLAN (VLAN 10) and server-side VLANs (VLANs 11 and 12) are in three unique subnets. VLAN 10 uses IP subnet 10.3.3.0/24, while the server-side VLAN 11 uses IP subnet 10.1.1.0/24 and the server VLAN 12 uses 10.1.2.0/24. In this case, the SLB device routes between the three VLANs.

As Figure 1-6 shows, the Layer 3 design is disruptive to the existing data center network and may require IP address, netmask, or gateway changes on the servers. This design may also require IP addresses and IP routing changes on the routers and firewalls. Even though there are more changes involved in the Layer 3 design, this design will eventually be more flexible, scalable, and manageable. Since the design is Layer 3, there are no spanning tree concerns. In this design, all load-balanced and non-load-balanced traffic to and from the server goes through the SLB device.

One-Armed Design

One-armed design refers to an approach where the SLB device is connected by a single physical link to the infrastructure. Layer 3 design, covered in the previous section, could be one-armed also by using a dot1q trunk on the single link and carrying both the client-side and server-side VLANs. Typically, though, a one-armed design refers to a load balancer using a single link, carrying a single VLAN, to connect to the infrastructure.

Figure 1-7 provides a topology showing how a one-armed design would be set up with policy-based routing (PBR).

Figure 1-7   *One-Armed Design with Policy-Based Routing*

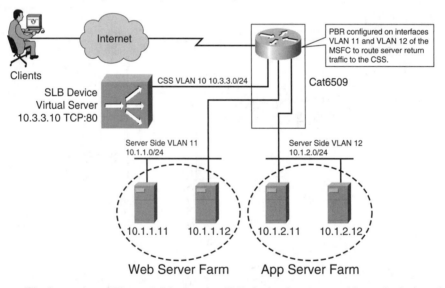

The key point of Figure 1-7 is that the SLB device is connected by a single interface (or VLAN) to the infrastructure. The SLB device resides on its own subnet and has no direct connectivity with the server-side VLANs. Also, the infrastructure (Multilayer Switch Feature Card, or MSFC) is configured with PBR on the server-side VLANs for return load-balanced traffic to be forwarded to the SLB device.

One of the key advantages of one-armed design is that only load-balanced traffic goes through the SLB device. Server-initiated and server management sessions, server backup, and so on, bypass the SLB devices. Just like the two Layer 2 and Layer 3 designs, in this design, you also need to ensure that the load-balanced client-to-server session is seen by the SLB device in both directions. Thus, you need to ensure that the server return traffic goes through the SLB device. This can be achieved by using either PBR or source NAT. The following sections provide details on policy-based routing and source NAT methods.

Policy-Based Routing

Policy-based routing can be configured on the server gateways to punt server responses to load-balanced requests to the SLB devices. The PBR route-maps can use Layer 4 ACLs comprised of protocol and port information. The port in these ACLs would be the same as the listeners on the servers for the load-balanced application. In order to prevent non-load-balanced traffic from being policy-based routed to the SLB device, one should ensure that the load balance listeners (ports) on the servers are different than the ports used for direct access, management traffic, and so on.

The setback of this design is that it requires management of the PBR rules. As SLB device policies are changed, the PBR ACL would need to be updated also.

Source NAT

Source NAT is another method of ensuring that the server return traffic for load-balanced traffic goes through the SLB device. In this approach, the client IP address is NATed to a local IP on the SLB device. This enables the server responses to be seamlessly routed to the load balancer. Management is a lot easier with Source NAT, but this design prevents the servers from logging or tracking the client requests based on the client IP. All requests reaching the server have the NAT-translated IP of the SLB device.

Direct Server Return

Direct server return (DSR) refers to designs where the SLB design uses Dispatch mode toward the server and the server responds directly to the client, bypassing the load balancer. Figure 1-8 provides a topology showing how a DSR design would be set up.

The key point of Figure 1-8 is that the SLB device is directly adjacent to the server VLANs (VLANs 11 and 12) and the servers all have respective VIP addresses (10.1.1.10 for web servers and 10.1.2.10 for SSL traffic) configured as their secondary IP addresses. This is to show that Dispatch mode is used when sending traffic from the SLB device to the real server. The servers in subnets 10.1.1.0/24 and 10.1.2.0/24 send responses directly to the client bypassing the SLB device.

Figure 1-8   *Direct Server Return*

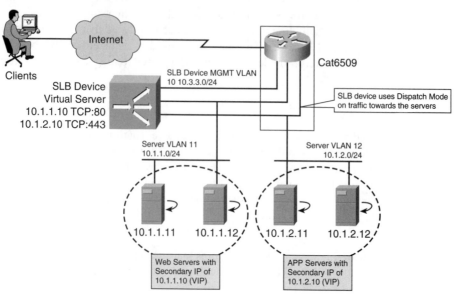

This design ensures that all load-balanced and non-load-balanced traffic from the server bypasses the SLB device. Only load-balanced requests from client to server go through the SLB device. This design is extremely useful for applications that require high bandwidth for server response. A good example is the RTSP. In RSTP, the initial client TCP connect goes through the load balancer; the UDP stream from the server, however, bypasses the SLB device all together.

One of the major disadvantages of this design is the fact that the SLB device has to reside in the same VLAN as the server; that is, the load balancer has to be *Layer 2 adjacent* to the server. Layer 2 adjacent means the servers and the SLB exist in the same broadcast domain or VLAN. Another caveat is that since the server response bypasses the SLB devices, the load balancer cannot make Layer 7 load-balancing decisions.

Deciding on a Load Balancer

After you have characterized the application, you are in a good position to decide which optimal design to use as well as which load balancer to consider that would service your data center. With the data in hand, you can compare notes with the specification or data sheets of various load balancers, including the following:

- **Performance**—Defined in terms of Layer 4 and Layer 7 connections per second and the bandwidth available on the SLB device.

- **Capacity**—Defined in terms of the memory available for flows in hardware. Capacity also includes the number of servers, health checks, ACLs, policies, VIPs, and virtual servers supported by the SLB device.

- **Throughput**—Defined in terms of packets per second switching performance of the device.
- **Interfaces**—Defined in terms of number and types of interfaces and ports available on the SLB device.
- **Features**—Defined in terms of Layer 4 and Layer 7 load-balancing options, health check capabilities, and sticky options on the SLB device.

Review of Infrastructure Design Concepts

This section briefly reviews the infrastructure design concepts and terminology, including:

- VLANs
- STP
- Dot1Q trunking
- Dual homed servers

VLANs

A VLAN is a group of end stations with a common set of requirements, independent of physical location. VLANs have the same attributes as a physical LAN, but they allow you to group end stations even if they are not located physically on the same LAN segment.

VLANs are usually associated with IP subnetworks. For example, all the end stations in a particular IP subnet belong to the same VLAN. Traffic between VLANs must be routed. VLAN membership is assigned manually on a port-by-port basis.

STP

STP is a Layer 2 link management protocol that provides path redundancy while preventing undesirable loops in the network. For a Layer 2 Ethernet network to function properly, only one active path can exist between any two stations. STP operation is transparent to end stations, which cannot detect whether they are connected to a single LAN segment or a switched LAN of multiple segments.

Catalyst 6500 series switches use STP (the IEEE 802.1D bridge protocol) on all VLANs. By default, a single instance of STP runs on each configured VLAN (provided you do not manually disable STP). You can enable and disable STP on a per-VLAN basis.

When you create fault-tolerant networks, you must have a loop-free path between all nodes in a network. The STP algorithm calculates the best loop-free path throughout a switched Layer 2 network. Layer 2 LAN ports send and receive STP frames at regular intervals. Network devices do not forward these frames, but use the frames to construct a loop-free path.

Multiple active paths between end stations cause loops in the network. If a loop exists in the network, end stations might receive duplicate messages and network devices might learn end station MAC addresses on multiple Layer 2 LAN ports. These conditions result in an unstable network.

STP defines a tree with a root bridge and a loop-free path from the root to all network devices in the Layer 2 network. STP forces redundant data paths into a standby (blocked) state. If a network segment in the spanning tree fails and a redundant path exists, the STP algorithm recalculates the spanning tree topology and activates the standby path.

When two Layer 2 LAN ports on a network device are part of a loop, the STP port priority and port path cost setting determine which port is put in the forwarding state and which port is put in the blocking state. The STP port priority value represents the location of a port in the network topology and how well it is located to pass traffic. The STP port path cost value represents media speed.

Dot1Q Trunking

A trunk is a point-to-point link between the switch and another networking device. Trunks carry the traffic of multiple VLANs over a single link and allow you to extend VLANs across an entire network. 802.1Q is an industry standard trunking encapsulation. You can configure a trunk on a single Ethernet port or on an EtherChannel.

Dual Homed Servers

Dual homed servers are referred to a server having two network interface cards. Usually this configuration is used to provide high availability. When set up in the same VLAN (same IP subnet), the NICs can be configured in load-balanced active/active mode or in active/backup mode. It is recommended to set up the servers in an active/backup mode when multiple NICs are available and the servers are used in conjunction with content switching.

Summary

This chapter discussed key motivations for SLB, which include scalability, availability, security, and cost. You learned about the evolution of SLB and the advancements in content switching solutions.

You learned about SLB functionality and packet flow of a typical load-balanced session, as well as how to characterize an application to determine your best choice for a load-balanced platform. Options, such as SLB modes and SLB designs, have been discussed at a high level. This information will help you make an educated decision on a particular SLB design approach. The last section of the chapter reviewed some of the essential underlying infrastructure protocols and technologies that are the building blocks of a data center. Refer to *Cisco LAN Switching,* by Clark and Hamilton (Cisco Press, ISBN: 1-57870-094-9), for a detailed review of the infrastructure technology.

Chapter 2, "Introduction to the Cisco Content Services Switch," introduces the Cisco Content Services Switch and how it is deployed in the data center.

Introduction to the Cisco Content Services Switch

This chapter introduces you to the architecture, features, and design details of Cisco's appliance-based load balancer, the Content Services Switch (CSS). We will discuss the CSS 11500 series platform. The Cisco CSS 11500 Series is made up of high-performance, high-availability modular architecture load balancers for web infrastructures. There are three models of the CSS 11500 series platform: CSS 11501, CSS 11503, and CSS 11506. The differences between the three models of the CSS 11500 architecture will be covered along with their software features and functionality.

Successfully designing and deploying the CSS 11500 switches in the network infrastructure requires an understanding of the applications being deployed, the security policies for load balancing the applications, and the design of the existing network infrastructure. These factors will be discussed in relation to the WebNS software.

Real-world implementations of the CSS 11500 series switches will be covered as part of the case study. The details of the design, caveats during the implementation, traffic flow analysis through the CSS 11500, testing of the implementation, and post deployment scenarios will also be addressed.

CSS 11500 Platforms Overview

The CSS 11500 switches are offered to customers in three flavors: CSS 11501, CSS 11503, and CSS 11506. The choice for a particular platform is dependent on the requirements that each particular platform can fulfill.

CSS 11501

The Cisco CSS 11501 Content Services Switch is a compact, fixed-configuration platform that delivers rich Layer 4–7 traffic management services for e-business applications. The Cisco CSS 11501 is a one-rack unit and is appropriate for load balancing small web server clusters. It supports:

- 8 10/100 Ethernet ports
- 1 Gigabit Ethernet port through an optional small form-factor pluggable (SFP) gigabit interface converter (SFP GBIC).

- 6 Gbps aggregate throughput
- Session processor and forwarding engine
- 8 Fast Ethernet ports and optional GE port (SFP—1000BASE-SX or 1000BASE-LX)
- Full content switch functions
- SSL termination (CSS 11501S model)
- WebNS software
- Dual disks (hard or flash)
- 1 AC supply

Figure 2-1 shows a front view of the CSS 11501. Notice that interfaces e1 to e8 are copper-based 10/100 Fast Ethernet, while interface e9 is a gigabit fiber interface (SFP GBIC).

Figure 2-1   *CSS 11501*

CSS 11503

The CSS 11503 is a three-slot modular mini-chassis that is two rack units high. It supports:

- A total of 20 Gbps aggregate throughput
- Up to three modules, each with session processor and forwarding engine
- A single Switch Control Module (SCM) with 2 GE ports, capable of accepting I/O modules with 2 GE, 8 FE, or 16 FE or service modules (session, SSL)
- Ethernet port configurations that can have up to 6 GE or up to 32 FE plus 2 GE

Figure 2-2 shows a front view of the CSS 11503.

Figure 2-2   *CSS 11503*

CSS 11506

The CSS 11506 is a six-slot modular chassis that is five rack units high. It supports:

- A total of 40 Gbps aggregate throughput
- Up to six modules, each with session processor and forwarding engine
- A SCM with 2 GE ports (and a redundant SCM in standby mode) with I/O modules (2 GE, 8 FE, 16 FE) or service modules (session, SSL)
- A redundant switch fabric with up to 12 GE or up to 80 FE plus 2 GE
- Dual disks (hard or flash)
- Redundant AC or DC power supplies

Figure 2-3 shows a front view of the CSS 11506.

Figure 2-3   *CSS 11506*

Table 2-1 explains the differences between the CSS 11503 and CSS 11506. CSS 11501 is not included here because it is a fixed-configuration appliance with 8 10/100 RJ-45 Ethernet and a fiber Gigabit Ethernet interface. CSS 11501 supports aggregate 6 Gbps bandwidth.

Table 2-1   *Comparison of Cisco CSS 11500 Models*

Feature	Cisco CSS 11503	Cisco CSS 11506
Number of modular slots	3	6
Included in base configuration	SCM 2 Gigabit Ethernet (GBIC) ports	SCM 2 Gigabit Ethernet (GBIC) Ports
Maximum Gigabit Ethernet ports	6	12
Maximum 10/100 Ethernet ports	32	80

continues

Table 2-1   *Comparison of Cisco CSS 11500 Models (Continued)*

Feature	Cisco CSS 11503	Cisco CSS 11506
2-port Gigabit Ethernet I/O Module	Maximum of 2	Maximum of 5
16-port 10/100 Ethernet I/O Module	Maximum of 2	Maximum of 5
8-port 10/100 Ethernet I/O Module	Maximum of 2	Maximum of 5
SSL modules	Maximum of 2	Maximum of 5
Session accelerator modules	Maximum of 2	Maximum of 5
Redundancy features	Active-active Layer 5 adaptive session redundancy VIP[1] redundancy	Active-active Layer 5 adaptive session redundancy VIP redundancy Active-standby SCM Redundant switch fabric module Redundant power supplies
Height	3.5 (2 rack units)	8.75 (5 rack units)
Bandwidth	Aggregate 20 Gbps	Aggregate 40 Gbps
Storage	512 MB hard disk or 256 MB flash memory disk	512 MB hard disk or 256 MB flash memory disk
Power	Integrated AC or DC	Up to 3 AC or 3 DC

CSS 11500 Architecture

CSS 11500 is an SLB appliance that uses distributed and modular hardware architecture. In the following sections, we will be discussing the hardware architecture details of the appliance and its modules.

Distributed Architecture

In a typical deployment, the Cisco CSS 11500 intercepts a request from a client's browser, characterizes the flow by reading HTTP headers, selects a destination server based on resource availability, and forwards the flow. Because it processes the entire HTTP header (full URL, cookie, and extensive resource verification information), the Cisco CSS 11500 knows who the client is, what the client wants to do, and how best to service the client's request quickly within a global web infrastructure.

The Cisco CSS 11500 provides a fully distributed architecture. All modules in the system contribute to the overall processing and memory needs for policy-based flow setup and flow forwarding. In this way, performance scales linearly as modules are added, and heavy traffic that hits one module can be balanced to other modules within a single system. So the Cisco CSS 11500 balances traffic not only within a data center but also across its own internal modules.

This innovative architecture addresses the primary limitations of PC- and ASIC–based solutions. Unlike PC-based systems, the network processors of the Cisco CSS 11500 provide ample packet processing power and bandwidth, avoiding the bottlenecks of the PC bus and a single central processor. And unlike ASIC-based platforms, the powerful, yet adaptable processors of the Cisco CSS 11500 enable easy integration of new software features.

The Cisco CSS 11500 can apply all its processing power to any port at any time, and it can grow with changing feature and scalability requirements. The system is designed to readily adapt to changing e-business needs—without complex and costly hardware upgrades. Figure 2-4 shows the CSS 11500 distributed architecture.

Figure 2-4   *CSS 11500 Distributed Architecture*

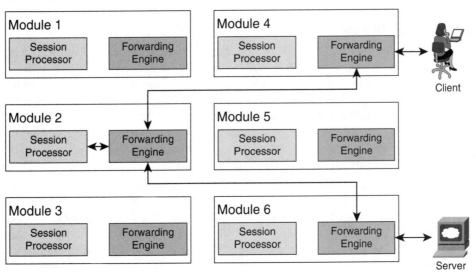

The following steps show how a potential connection is processed within a CSS 11500.

1 The SYN arrives on the uplink port on Slot4. Bridge lookups are performed. The TCP port hash selects a different slot number. The packet is transmitted across the switch to the proper slot (Slot2).

2 Lookup in the flow database is performed—no match. An ACL check is done—OK. The destination IP and TCP port match "spoof" the result in the content database. The SYN/ACK is sent back to the client.

3 The ACK arrives on the uplink port on Slot4. Bridge lookups are performed. TCP port hash selects a different slot. The packet is transmitted across the switch to the proper slot (Slot2). That module does a flow lookup, finds an entry for the spoofed flow, and discards the ACK.

4 The content request frame arrives on the uplink port on Slot4. Bridge lookups are performed. The TCP port hash selects a different slot (Slot2). The packet is transmitted across the switch to the proper module.

5 On the module (Slot2), a flow lookup is performed. Spoofed flow is found. Since this is a content frame, a content database lookup is performed. An L5 match is found, and a server is selected. A frame is forwarded to the module connected to the server.

6 On Slot6, the flow manager saves the content packet and a SYN is sent to the selected server.

7 The flow manager calculates the NAT transformations. It creates the fast path state for both directions in the local flow database. The translated content request is sent to the server.

CSS 11500 Modules

All modules of the CSS 11500 participate in flow setup, but they differ primarily in control functions, performance, SSL capabilities, and I/O. Each Cisco CSS 11500 Module consists of one high-speed MIPS RISC processor for flow setup, one network processor for flow forwarding, one classification engine for accelerated lookups in bridge/access control list (ACL) tables, and up to 288 MB of Rambus Dram (RDRAM).

Switch Control Module for the Cisco 11500

The Cisco CSS 11500 SCM not only governs the whole system but also contributes to I/O density and flow performance. The SCM comes standard with 2 Gigabit Ethernet ports supporting SFP gigabit interface converters (SFP GBICs) and has a console port and an Ethernet port for management. The SCM also features two PCMCIA slots that can hold up to two 256 MB flash memory disks, up to two 512 MB hard disks, or one of each.

SSL Module for the Cisco 11500

The Cisco CSS 11500 SSL Module is the ideal solution for handling high-volume SSL transactions that occupy today's e-business data centers. The module integrates state-of-the-art SSL processors into the leading content switching technology of Cisco WebNS. In addition to superior price performance, the SSL module simplifies the management of digital certificates and offers new possibilities for optimizing the switch-to-server architecture for security and performance.

I/O Modules for the Cisco 11500

The Cisco CSS 11500 I/O Modules deliver port density and flow performance. The product line supports three types of I/O modules:

- 2-port Gigabit Ethernet
- 16-port Fast Ethernet
- 8-port Fast Ethernet

The Fast Ethernet ports are 10/100BASE-TX with standard RJ-45 connectors, whereas the Gigabit Ethernet ports require SFP GBICs (1000BASE-SX or 1000BASE-LX).

Session Accelerator Module for the Cisco 11500

The Session Accelerator Module is a cost-effective way to add flow performance when additional connectivity is not required. Using the same flow setup and forwarding processors as the I/O modules, it provides the flexibility to optimize the system for port density and performance.

Load Balancing with CSS 11500

Content load balancing is the process used to define how the connections (from client to server and from server to client) destined for applications are serviced by the CSS 11500. In order to better understand the process of load balancing from the CSS 11500's perspective, certain entities of the CSS 11500 configuration and their relationship to each other need to be defined. We will cover the following basic entities and their relationship:

- Service
- Owner
- Content rule

Once these entities are defined, the details of the connection handling for TCP and UDP flows will be described.

Services, Owners, and Content Rules

The CSS enables you to configure services, owners, and content rules in order to direct requests for content to a specific destination service (for example, a server or a port on a server). By configuring services, owners, and content rules, you optimize and control how the CSS handles each request for specific content. Services, owners, and content rules are described as follows:

- A *service* is a destination location where a piece of content resides physically (a local or remote server and port). You add services to content rules. Adding a service to a content rule includes it in the resource pool that the CSS uses for load-balancing requests for content. A service may belong to multiple content rules.

- An *owner* is a hierarchical representation of where the content for a service is stored. It is a high-level entity used to group multiple content rules under a logical name. The owner is a name that can be used for multiple content rules, which in our case is the name of an organization called Cisco-HR; the content rules underneath load balance the applications that Cisco-HR uses.

- A *content rule* is a hierarchical rule set containing individual rules that describe which content (for example, an .html file) is accessible by visitors to the web site, how the content is mirrored, on which server the content resides, and how the CSS should process requests for the content. Each rule set must have an owner.

The CSS uses content rules to determine:

- Where the content physically resides, whether local or remote

- Where to direct the request for content (which service or services)

- Which load-balancing method to use

When a request for content is made, the CSS:

1 Uses the owner content rule to translate the owner's virtual IP (VIP) address or domain name using NAT to the corresponding service IP address and port.

2 Checks for available services that match the request.

3 Uses content rules to choose which service can best process the request for content.

4 Applies all content rules to service the request (for example, load-balancing method, redirects, failover, stickiness).

Figure 2-5 illustrates the CSS service, owner, and content rule concepts.

Figure 2-5 *Relationship of Service, Owner, and Content Rule in CSS*

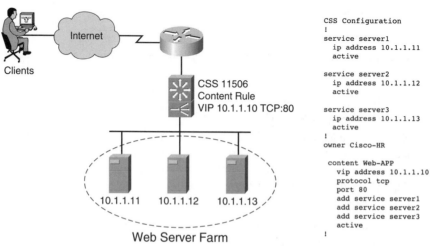

In Figure 2-5, the client is making an HTTP connection to the VIP address of 10.1.1.10 on TCP port 80. This request is intercepted by the CSS 11500 and is matched to the content rule of *Web-APP*; the request is then directed to one of the available services: server1, server2, or server3. The owner Cisco-HR is the name used to hold the content rule Web-APP.

CSS 11500 Flow Overview

A flow is the transfer of a sequence of related packets over a TCP or UDP connection between a source (client) and a destination (server) through the CSS. All packets in an ingress flow (traffic entering the CSS) share a common TCP and UDP connection, consisting of:

- Source address
- Destination address
- Protocol
- Source port
- Destination port

TCP flows are bidirectional, as shown in Figure 2-6. Packets traverse from the client to the server and from the server to the client through the CSS. Strictly speaking, a TCP connection consists of two flows, one in each direction. A TCP flow begins with a SYN and ends with an ACK to a FIN/ACK, or an RST.

Figure 2-6   *Example of TCP Flow in CSS*

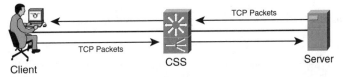

UDP flows, as shown in Figure 2-7, are typically unidirectional (for example, streaming audio transmitted by a server to a client). A UDP flow has no definitive beginning or end and is considered completed only after a period of time has elapsed during which the destination device receives no packets that share the same addresses, protocol, and ports that defined the original flow.

Figure 2-7   *Example of UDP Flow in CSS*

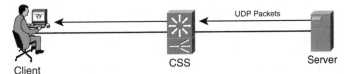

Flow Control Block

A CSS uses data structures called flow control blocks (FCBs) to set up and keep track of ingress flows. FCBs contain all the information the CSS needs to process and manage flows. The creation of an FCB from flow information is called *flow mapping*. The flow manager in the session processor of each module is responsible for FCB creation and flow mapping.

Each unidirectional flow uses one FCB. Therefore, a TCP flow uses two FCBs and a UDP flow typically uses one.

Each client-CSS-server connection consists of two parts, shown in Figure 2-8:

- **Front end**—Connection between a client and the CSS
- **Back end**—Connection between the CSS and a server

Figure 2-8   *Example of a TCP Flow with Front-End and Back-End Connections*

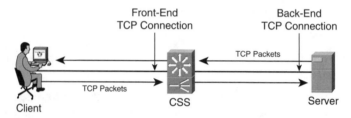

A Layer 5 connection is a flow where the OSI session, presentation, or application layer headers need to be inspected before a load-balancing decision is made by the CSS. The typical case is when HTTP URL load balancing is configured on the CSS. The CSS establishes the front-end TCP connection with the client using the TCP three-way handshake (Figure 2-9).

Figure 2-9   *Setting Up the Front-End TCP Connection—Delayed Binding*

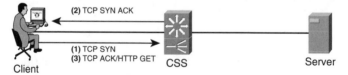

When it establishes a Layer 5 flow, the CSS "spoofs" the back-end TCP connection by acting as a proxy for the destination device (server) for the client's SYN. In other words, the CSS responds to the client's SYN with a SYN/ACK before the CSS sets up the back-end TCP connection with the server.

This process is referred to as *delayed binding*. Delayed binding causes the client to respond with an ACK and an HTTP GET request. This process allows the CSS to gather the information it needs to select the best service (a server port where content resides or an application running on a server, such as FTP) for the content request.

The CSS examines the HTTP header and URL in the HTTP request method, such as GET, HEAD, or POST. Based on the information in the HTTP header, the URL, and the content rules configured on the CSS, the CSS selects the best service to satisfy the request. A CSS bases service selection (server load balancing) on factors such as:

- Content rule match
- Service availability
- Service load
- Cookies
- Source IP address

After the CSS selects the best service to provide the requested content to the client, the CSS establishes the back-end connection with the service using the TCP three-way handshake and splices the front-end and back-end connections together. The CSS forwards the content request from the client to the service (Figure 2-10). The service responds to the client through the CSS. For the remaining life of the flow, the CSS switches the packets between the client and the service and performs NAT and other packet transformations as required.

Figure 2-10 *Setting Up the Back-End TCP Connection—Delayed Binding*

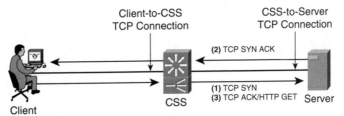

For subsequent content requests from the same client over the same TCP connection (HTTP 1.1 and higher), the CSS attempts to maintain the back-end connection with the service that provided the content for the first HTTP request by default. This condition is called *persistence*.

During the life of a persistent connection, a CSS must determine if it needs to move a client connection to a new service based on content rules, load balancing method, and service availability. In some situations, moving the client connection is not necessary; in other situations, it is mandatory.

You can configure the CSS to perform a redirect or remap when it becomes necessary to move the client to a new service.

Persistent Reset Redirect

Using the **persistence reset redirect** command, a CSS closes the back-end connection by sending an RST to the service (Figure 2-11). The CSS sends a 302 redirect to the client's browser to tell the browser to reconnect using the same DNS name, but this time the HTTP request matches on a different content rule. The CSS then establishes a new flow between the client and the best service.

Figure 2-11 *Example of HTTP Redirection*

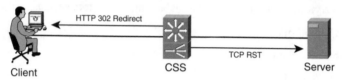

Persistent Reset Remap

Using the **persistence reset remap** command, a CSS closes only the back-end connection by sending an RST to the service (server1 in Figure 2-12). The CSS then establishes a new back-end connection with service server2 and splices the back-end and front-end connections together. The CSS forwards the content request from the client to server2. Packets now flow between the client and server2.

Figure 2-12 *Example of Remapping the Back-End Connection*

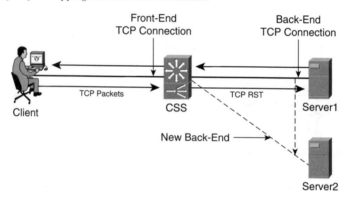

Flow Cleanup

Periodically, the CSS flow manager tears down old, idle flows and reclaims the system resources (FCBs). This process is called *flow resource reclamation*. It is also referred to as *flow cleanup* or *garbage collection*. Flow resource reclamation involves removing FCBs from the TCP and UDP lists. For optimal performance, the CSS reuses FCBs that are no longer needed for flows.

Normally, flow cleanup occurs at a rate that is directly related to the total number of flows currently active on a CSS. A CSS always cleans up UDP flows. For TCP flows, a CSS reclaims resources when the number of used FCBs reaches a certain percentage of the total FCBs. A CSS also cleans up long-lived TCP flows that have received a FIN or an RST or whose timeout values have been met. You can configure various commands to change the default flow-cleanup behavior of the CSS. In some instances it may not be desirable for the CSS to clean up idle TCP flows, such as during a connection to a database server that must permanently remain active even when no data passes through the connection. If you observe the CSS dropping long-lived idle connections that need to be maintained, you can configure the following TCP flow commands:

- **flow permanent** command—Creates permanent TCP or UDP ports that are not reclaimed.

- **flow-timeout-multiplier** command—Configures flow inactivity timeout values for TCP and UDP flows on a per–content rule and per-source group basis.

WebNS Software Features

The CSS software contains the files needed to run the CSS, including boot files, directories for archiving and logging files, and Management Information Base (MIB) files. This software is pre-installed on the CSS conventional hard disk or on an optional flash disk, which is a flash memory-based storage device. The CSS software is approximately 50 MB, and you can install a maximum of two software versions.

The CSS software image is available from Cisco.com as an ArrowPoint Distribution Image (ADI), network boot ZIP (.zip) image, or GZIP-compressed (adi-gz) image.

You can install the CSS software on an FTP server, which the CSS accesses through the FTP. The CSS accesses the ADI or GZIP file containing the CSS software from an FTP server, copies the file to the CSS disk, and unpacks it. The CSS then boots from the disk.

The following sections highlight some of the features of the CSS 11500 platform, including:

- Infrastructure-level features
- Load-balancing algorithms
- High availability
- SSL integration for security and performance
- Local and global load balancing
- Site and system security

Infrastructure-Level Features

Some of the features used in integrating the CSS 11500 at the infrastructure or the routing or bridging layers are:

- Spanning-tree bridging

The CSS supports configuration of Spanning-Tree Protocol (STP) bridging. Spanning-tree bridging detects and then prevents loops in the network. CSS allows for configuration of global spanning-tree bridging options, such as bridge aging time, forward delay time, hello time interval, and maximum age.

- Open Shortest Path First

  The CSS, operating as an Open Shortest Path First (OSPF) router, provides:

  — Intra-area route support for routing in a single area between other OSPF routers

  — Inter-area route support for routing between multiple OSPF areas

  — Route summarization between areas as an Area Border Router (ABR)

  — Stub area and AS boundary router support

  — Redistribution of local, Routing Information Protocol (RIP), static, and firewall routes into an OSPF domain

  — Advertisement of VIP addresses for content as AS external routes

  — Simple authentication

- Address Resolution Protocol

  Configure Address Resolution Protocol (ARP) to statically map IP to MAC translations, necessary for the CSS to send data to network nodes.

- Routing Information Protocol

  The CSS enables you to configure global RIP attributes used to advertise routes on the CSS. By default, RIP advertises RIP routes and local routes for interfaces running RIP. The **rip** command advertises other routes.

  The timers used by RIP in the CSS include the following default values. These RIP timer values are not user-configurable in the CSS.

  — Transmit (Tx) time, a random value between 15 and 45 seconds, used to avoid router synchronization problems.

  — Route expiration time of 180 seconds. (If the CSS loses the link to the next-hop router, the route is immediately removed.)

  — Hold-down time (the amount of time the CSS transmits with an infinite metric) of 120 seconds.

- Cisco Discovery Protocol

  The Cisco Discovery Protocol (CDP) is a medium-independent protocol that runs over Layer 2 (the data link layer) on the CSS and other Cisco-manufactured equipment, such as routers, switches, bridges, and access servers. The CSS advertises itself to all other neighboring Cisco

CDP-compatible devices on a network. The CSS only transmits CDP advertisements to other CDP-compatible devices on the network; the CSS does not listen for CDP messages from the other CDP-compatible devices and does not maintain a CDP table.

Load-Balancing Algorithms

The following are the load-balancing algorithms available on the CSS 11500:

- balance aca—ArrowPoint Content Awareness (ACA). The load-balancing algorithm ACA balances the traffic over the services based on load or on server weight and load.

- balance destip—Destination IP address division algorithm. The CSS directs all client requests with the same destination IP address to the same service. This option is typically used in a caching environment.

- balance domain—Domain name division algorithm. The CSS divides the alphabet evenly across the number of caches. It parses the host tag for the first four letters following the first dot and then uses these characters of the domain name to determine to which server it should forward the request. This option is typically used in a caching environment.

- balance domainhash—Internal CSS hash algorithm based on the domain string. The CSS parses the host tag and does an exclusive OR (XOR) hash across the entire host name. It then uses the XOR hash value to determine to which server to forward the request.

- balance srcip—Source IP address division algorithm. The CSS directs all client requests coming from the same source IP address to the same service. This option is generally used in a caching configuration.

- balance url—URL division algorithm. The CSS divides the alphabet evenly across the number of caches. It then parses the URL for the first four characters located after the portion of the URL matched by the rule. For example, if the URL in a content rule is configured for "/news/*", the CSS will balance on the first four characters following "/news/". This option is typically used in a caching environment.

- balance weightedrr—Weighted roundrobin algorithm. The CSS uses round robin but weighs some services more heavily than others depending on the server's configured weight. All servers have a default weight of 1.

- balance urlhash—Internal CSS hash algorithm based on the URL string. The CSS parses the URL and performs an XOR hash across the URL. It then uses the XOR hash value to determine to which server to forward the request. This method guarantees that all requests for the same URL will be sent to the same server in order to increase the probability of a cache hit. This option is typically used in a caching environment.

- balance leastconn—Least connection algorithm. This balance method chooses a running service that has the fewest number of connections.

- balance roundrobin—Roundrobin algorithm (default). The CSS resolves the request by evenly distributing the load to resolve domain names among local and remote content domain sites.

Typically, for a SLB environment, the default load-balancing method, *round robin*, is ideal. This method requires minimum processing by the SLB devices and is best suited for applications, such as HTTP, which are extremely short lived (in msecs). Long-lived applications, such as FTP, which have active sessions (continuous transmission of packets), may benefit from the leastconn balancing method. For transparent cache load balancing, the destination IP hash is a good choice, as it operates in Layer 4. For proxy cache load balancing, urlhash or domainhash are ideal.

High Availability

The Cisco CSS 11500 supports a stateful Layer 5 session redundancy feature that enables failover of important flows while maximizing performance.

Some flows—such as a long-lived FTP or a database session—may be mission critical, but many are not. Most solutions on the market today require all traffic—important or not—to be replicated from one box to another. If the majority of flows are not critical, then most of the system performance is wasted on unnecessary replications.

With Adaptive Session Redundancy (ASR), the Cisco CSS 11500 may be configured so that critical flows are marked as replication worthy, whereas others do not need to be so marked. ASR focuses traffic management resources precisely where needed.

SSL Integration for Security and Performance

Cisco offers the most scalable integrated SSL solutions of any Layer 4–7 switches. Secure Socket Layer (SSL), the industry standard for secure transport of traffic from client browsers to web servers, presents two key challenges for today's e-business infrastructure. First, because SSL encrypts data and headers, it obscures the request-specific information that Layer 4–7 switching decisions are made on. Second, SSL authentication places a high processing load for each SSL flow setup.

The Cisco CSS 11500 with integrated SSL modules meets both of these challenges by combining leading SSL acceleration technology with the Cisco WebNS technology. The SSL module simplifies the management of digital certificates and offers new possibilities in optimizing the switch-to-server architecture for security and performance. And SSL transaction performance may be scaled by adding multiple SSL modules to a chassis.

Local and Global Load Balancing

The Cisco CSS 11500 learns where specific content resides, either locally or remotely, and dynamically selects the best web server or cache for specific content requests.

Local server selection is based on server load and application response time, as well as traditional least-connection and round-robin algorithms. Any application that uses standard TCP or UDP protocols can also be load balanced, including firewalls, mail, news, chat, and Lightweight Directory Access Protocol (LDAP).

The Cisco CSS 11500 also provides a complete solution for building and provisioning Internet-scale global content distribution and delivery. Whereas local load-balancing features determine the best device within a data center, global load-balancing functions choose the best data center in the Internet to service requests.

The Cisco CSS 11500 performs resource verification before routing users' requests, ensuring that they are directed to the location that has the best response time and the least load for the requested content. Cisco supports global load balancing through redirection based on both Domain Name System (DNS) and HTTP. The DNS mechanism is fast and scalable; the HTTP method provides the highest degree of control.

Site and System Security

The Cisco CSS 11500 provides stateful, content-based access control and supports security policies based on any combination of source address, destination address, protocol, TCP port, or URL. The Cisco CSS 11500 monitors start-to-finish web transaction activity and guards against denial-of-service (DoS) attacks, such as SYN floods, ping floods, "smurfs," and any other undesirable connection attempts. Wire-speed NAT protects real server IP addresses.

For additional security, the Cisco CSS 11500 intelligently directs traffic across multiple firewalls. By load balancing firewalls, the Cisco CSS 11500 eliminates performance bottlenecks and single points of failure that result in system downtime.

Summary of WebNS Features

WebNS is the software that runs on the Cisco CSS 11000 line of products. The Cisco CSS 11500 supports all WebNS 7.50 features, including these key features:

- Full URL parsing
- HTTP Session Sticky using cookie insertion, a.k.a. ArrowPoint cookies
- Integrated global load balancing with HTTP and DNS-based redirection
- Content policy ACLs on all HTTP headers
- DoS protection against SYN floods and other Layer 4 attacks

- HTTP (1.0, 1.1)
- All TCP services, UDP, and SSL
- RIP versions 1 and 2; OSPF
- VLAN 802.1Q
- Server/node operating system compatibility: Any TCP/IP OS, including Windows XP, Windows 2000, Windows NT, Windows 98, Windows 95, all UNIX platforms, Linux, and Mac OS
- Dynamic content support: Active Server Pages (ASP), Visual Basic Script, ActiveX, Java, Virtual Reality Markup Language (VRML), Common Gateway Interface (CGI), CoolTalk, NetMeeting, RealAudio, RealVideo, NetShow, QuickTime, PointCast, any HTTP-encapsulated data
- Management: Secure Shell (SSH) protocol, SNMP, SSL browser-based interface, embedded GUI

Case Study: CSS-Based Solution

Now that you understand the software and hardware architecture of the CSS 11500 platform, we will start our discussion of how this product should be deployed. Placement of the CSS 11500 in the existing or new network requires planning and understanding of the application, security, and underlying infrastructure requirements. As there are many applications with different security policies, we shall examine some specific ones deployed in the following case study.

This case study examines a specific customer deployment where CSS is used to load balance the web and SSL application. The idea behind the following case study and others in chapters in the rest of the book is to understand not only the concepts but also the implementation details. In this case study, we will discuss the following topics:

- Server and application requirements
- Management and security requirements
- Infrastructure requirements
- Design options

Server and Application Requirements

Server and application requirements for this case study are defined as follows:

- Directly manage the servers from the front end (client-side network)
- Number of servers: 20–100 per site

- Web server
    - TCP/80.
    - A client-specific cookie is sent to the client.
    - Currently, the web server farm consists of two servers, represented by a VIP.
    - Web servers do not need to record the client IP address.
    - Web servers on different ports than 80; e.g., 8081–8084.
- HTTPS application server
    - TCP/443
    - The application uses a keepalive mechanism to maintain the session. The timeout is important because you want to make sure the flow is maintained and not aged out by CSS.
    - Stickiness between client and Citrix servers is not necessary.
    - Currently, the application server farm consists of two SSL servers, represented by a VIP.
    - Application servers do not need to record the client IP address.
- TCP-based keepalive is required both for web and application servers.
- Potentially, server persistence is needed when the user transitions from HTTP to HTTPS.

Management and Security Requirements

Following are the security requirements for this case study:

- Sys logging and SNMP traps from the CSS
- Commonly configured management services: http, https, SSH
- User and password management
- Access list support to control content requests

Infrastructure Requirements

Following are Layer 2 and Layer 3 infrastructure requirements for this case study:

- OSPF stubbiness on the front-end routers must be maintained, thus static routes pointing to server-side networks cannot be used.
- In the current environment, server IPs, VIPs, and the front-end router exist in the same IP subnet. Currently, Local Director (LD) merges the server-side VLAN with the front-end VLAN. The default gateways of the servers are the HSRP group IP on the Multilayer Switch Feature Card (MSFC).
- Seamless integration of the CSS in the current Layer 2 and Layer 3 infrastructure.

Design Options

In this SLB design, the CSS is used as an Layer 3 appliance on a stick with a single GE link to the Catalyst 6500. This link exists in the same VLAN as the servers. The server's default gateway is the MSFC on the Cat6500. The same IP address is the default gateway of the CSS:

ip route 0.0.0.0 0.0.0.0 172.21.51.226 1

Figure 2-13 shows the recommended infrastructure design.

Figure 2-13 *CSS 11506 Case Study Topology*

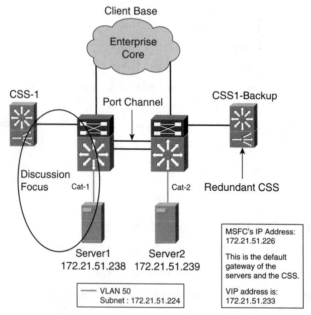

The focus of our discussion is the circle in the diagram. In this example, the CSS exists in the same VLAN as the servers.

NOTE The CSS Layer 2 adjacency to the servers is not a must requirement. The CSS could be connected to a separate Layer 3 VLAN connecting the CSS with the MSFC.

Figure 2-13 shows a server environment that uses CSS 11501 for SLB. Following are the details of this design:

- The CSS's interface e3 connects to the Cat6500 and is part of VLAN 50. The circuit IP address of the CSS is 172.21.51.232. The VIP also exists in the same subnet.

- Servers are also present in VLAN 50 with their default gateway being the MSFC.

- Management traffic can directly access the servers bypassing the CSS.

- Server data backup traffic and server back-end sessions to application or database servers also bypass the CSS.

Figure 2-14 shows a capture of CSS flows while a Telnet connection to the server is initiated from the front end. The server being accessed is 172.21.51.235. As can be viewed in the figure, this session is not seen by the CSS. In the way we have configured the CSS, non-load-balanced traffic bypasses the CSS. So if a server is directly accessed, that flow is not going to traverse the CSS.

Figure 2-14 *CSS 11506 Console Capture*

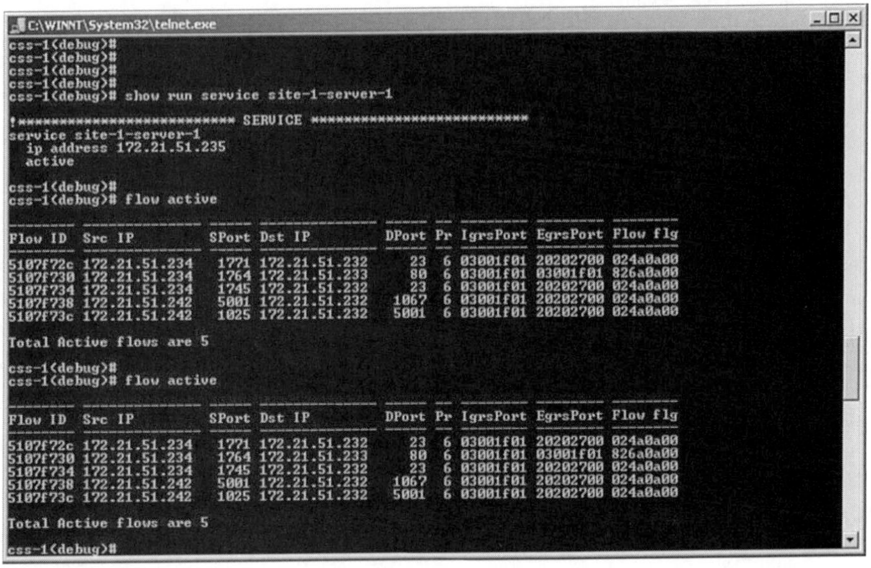

HTTP and HTTPS Server Stickiness

It may become a future requirement for our sample application load balancing to maintain web server persistence between HTTP and HTTPS sessions. The client establishes an HTTP session with the web server and logs in. After login, the HTTPS session from the client should land on the same web server to which the client first logged in using HTTP. Next, we will discuss two options for how to meet this requirement:

- Server-specific VIPs for HTTPS

- Source IP–based hash for HTTP and HTTPS rules

Option A: Server-Specific VIPs for HTTPS

In the following configuration, stickiness between the client and the server is maintained using ArrowPoint cookies. The cookies are defined using a "*string*" command within the service definition. Assuming we have two servers, configuration would be as follows:

```
!*****************SERVICE*********************
service www1.customerx.com
  ip address 172.21.51.238
  keepalive frequency 20
  keepalive type http
  keepalive uri "/index.html"
  string www1.customerx.com
  active
service www2.customerx.com
  ip address 172.21.51.239
  keepalive frequency 20
  keepalive type http
  keepalive uri "/index.html"
  string www2.customerx.com
  active
!*****************OWNER***********************
owner customerx.com
content L5_cookie_rule
    add service www1.customerx.com
    add service www2.customerx.com
    vip address 172.21.51.233
    protocol tcp
    port 80
    url "/*"
    advanced-balance arrowpoint-cookie
    active
! HREF Configuration information
!
! https://www1.customerx.com
content L5_ssl_www1
    vip address 172.21.51.234
    add service www1.customerx.com
    protocol tcp
    port 443
    advanced-balance ssl
    application ssl
    active
! https://www2.customerx.com
content L5_ssl_www2
    vip address 172.21.51.235
    add service www2.customerx.com
    protocol tcp
    port 443
    advanced-balance ssl
    application ssl
    active
```

This approach works nicely because there is one-to-one matching. In the preceding configuration, domain name www1.customerx.com maps to 172.21.51.234 and domain name www2.customerx.com maps to 172.21.51.235. HTML code modification would be needed on the web server side; that is, Server1's (www1.customerx.com: 172.21.51.238) code would say:

```
<A HREF="https://www1.customerx.com/login">Login</A>
```

and Server2's (www2.customerx.com: 172.21.51.239) code would say:

```
<A HREF="https://www2.customerx.com/login">Login</A>
```

NOTE   In SSL environments, stickiness improves performance dramatically. If a user does not stick to the same server, they will be forced to restart the key exchange with the new server. This can typically take 75–100 ms. SSL version 3.0 introduced an optional caching scheme, which allows the servers to reuse previous SSL sessions, thus eliminating the need to exchange keys. In order for the SSL stickiness to work on the CSS, the SSL version must be 3.0 because previous versions of SSL encrypted the session IDs, making them unavailable to the CSS for sticky decisions.

Option B: Source IP–Based Hash for HTTP and HTTPS Rules

Another option would be to use the source IP hash algorithm for load balancing for both the HTTP and HTTPS content rules.

Thus, the source IP of the client would be used to balance the appropriate server. Combining this with ArrowPoint cookies would result in stickiness even when the client source IP changes (such as with proxy hopping).

```
!*****************OWNER*******************
owner customerx.com
content L5_cookie_rule
    add service www1.customerx.com
    add service www2.customerx.com
    vip address 172.21.51.233
    protocol tcp
    port 80
    balance srcip
    url "/*"
    advanced-balance arrowpoint-cookie
    active
!
content L5_ssl_www1
    vip address 172.21.51.233
    add service www1.customerx.com
    add service www2.customerx.com
    protocol tcp
    port 443
    balance srcip
    advanced-balance ssl
    application ssl
    active
```

Traffic Flow

Now that you understand how to design CSS to accommodate all the application, security, and infrastructure requirements, this section covers a simple load-balanced user session going through the CSS:

1 The client's request to the VIP (172.21.51.233) is forwarded to the CSS by the MSFC.

2 CSS makes the load-balancing decision and forwards the request to the server. Before exiting the CSS, this packet hits the source-group *nat-2-vip*.

```
group nat-2-vip
  add destination service www1.customerx.com
  add destination service www2.customerx.com
  vip address 172.21.51.233
  active
```

3 This source group is configured with the destination service of the web server1 (multiple services can be added here). Thus, any packet forwarded to the real server by the CSS would have its source IP address NATed to that of the VIP defined in the source group. Notice that the VIP in the source group is the same as the VIP in the content rule.

4 The server responds to the request and sends the packet to the CSS. Thus, you maintain symmetric flows through the CSS for all load-balanced traffic.

Test and Verification

The behavior of a load balancer is not the same from data center to data center. This is because each data center or content-switching environment can have a different application. Each application is unique with respect to the number of sockets used, the duration of TCP connections, the activities in each session in terms of packets per second, idle timeouts, and so on. Thus it is critical to test and verify the SLB environment with the particular applications.

Following are a few critical test cases that should be verified after a new deployment or a major or minor infrastructure change—including a CSS WebNS code upgrade:

- An exact production client load-balanced session. A complete transaction with authentication and authorization. User behavior should match production clients with appropriate idle times and delays.
- Content retrieval from the server.
- A server-initiated session to the back-end database or internal application server.
- A server-initiated backup or data replication session.
- Application daemon failure and detection by the CSS.
- Primary CSS failure, measurement of the recovery time.
- Primary Cat6500 failure, measurement of the recovery time.

Summary

This chapter introduced you to the CSS 11500 platform. This chapter also covered the software and hardware architecture, flow management, device management, and introduction to basic entities used in SLB. Additionally, highlights of the WebNS software features were discussed.

In order to combine all concepts of SLB from the perspective of the CSS 11500 platform, this chapter also presented a case study. This case study focused on the deployment scenario of a real-world enterprise solution using the CSS 11500. CSS configurations have been provided to introduce the reader to the WebNS CLI.

Chapter 3, "Introduction to the Cisco Content Switching Module," introduces the Cisco Content Switching Module in the Cat6500 and discusses how it is deployed in the data center.

Introduction to the Cisco Content Switching Module

This chapter introduces the reader to the architecture, features, and design details of Cisco's module-based load balancer for the Catalyst 6500 (Cat6500), the Content Switching Module (CSM). The Cisco CSM is a line card for the Cisco Cat6500 Series Switch. The Cisco CSM provides a high-performance, cost-effective load-balancing solution for enterprise and Internet service provider networks, allowing these organizations to provide customers, employees, and business partners with the best possible online experience.

In this chapter, we will cover the details of the major software features and functionality of the CSM, including traffic flow and routing. We will also discuss several network integration options using the CSM.

Real-world implementations of the CSM will be covered as part of the case study. The details of the design, caveats during the implementation, traffic flow analysis through the CSM, testing of the implementation, and post-deployment scenarios will also be addressed.

Benefits of the Content Switch Module

Following are some of the key benefits of the Cisco CSM:

- The Cisco CSM establishes up to 165,000 connections per second and provides high-speed content switching while maintaining one million concurrent connections.

- The Cisco CSM features a low connection cost and occupies a small footprint sliding into a slot in a new or existing Cisco Catalyst 6500 Series chassis.

- The Cisco CSM allows organizations to increase the scalability and performance of server farms, cache clusters, and groups of VPNs, SSLs, and firewall devices. In addition, the Cisco CSM also provides organizations with the highest level of device redundancy for business-critical applications and services.

- Cisco CSMs can be installed in the same Cisco Catalyst 6500 Series chassis to provide scalable performance as well as redundancy.

- The Cisco CSM uses the same IOS command-line interface (CLI) that is used to configure the Cisco Catalyst 6500 Series Switch.

- By adding a Cisco CSM to a new or existing Cisco Catalyst 6500 Series Switch, customers can enable every port in the Cisco Catalyst switch to perform Layer 2 to Layer 7 services, providing the capability to intelligently switch traffic.

CSM Architecture

The CSM is a bus-based line card on the Catalyst 6500, which is supported with Catalyst 6500 Supervisor module type 1a (Sup1a), Catalyst 6500 Supervisor module type 2 (Sup2), and Catalyst 6500 Supervisor module type 720 (Sup720). CSM requires the Multilayer Switch Feature Card (MSFC, the routing daughter card on the Catalyst 6500 Supervisor module) to be present on the supervisor for configuration management and functions both with Native IOS and CatOS. The CSM does not have any ports or interfaces on it. The CSM has a 4 gigabit, dot1q trunk that is carried via a port-channel to the Catalyst 6500 backplane. The Catalyst 6500 Supervisor Layer 2 forwards the relevant packets to the CSM or the trunk. CSM can access all servers within the data center using the dot1q trunk.

The hardware architecture of the CSM is optimized with custom network processors, each performing a particular task. This robust architecture enables CSM to support 165,000 connections per second and 1 million concurrent connections. Figure 3-1 shows a CSM module with the processors highlighted.

Figure 3-1 *CSM on Catalyst 6500*

CSM Hardware

The Cisco CSM hardware processes packets from clients and servers using packet processors that are arranged in a pipeline configuration, as shown in Figure 3-2. Packets from clients and servers enter the CSM, move through the packet-processing units sequentially, and exit the system.

The five packet-processing units include the following:

- Session Module—Establishes sessions, classifies packets, sends packets to appropriate path
- TCP Module—Establishes connections between clients and servers, terminates TCP sessions, sends packet header to Layer 7 module
- Layer 7 Module—Buffers all packets it receives, examines HTTP header information, determines match information, forwards match information to the load balancer
- Load Balancer Module—Selects a server using match information received from Layer 7
- NAT Module—Translates network addresses for all packets it receives and sends them to selected servers

Figure 3-2   *CSM on Catalyst 6500, Pipeline Architecture*

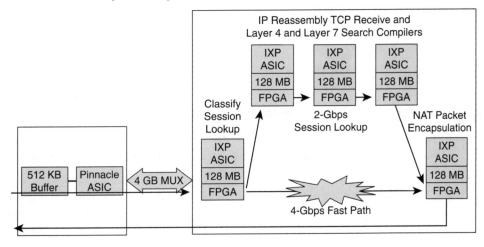

CSM Configuration Limits

Following are some important configuration limits on the CSM:

- Total VLANs (client and server): 512
- Virtual servers: 4000
- Server farms: 4000
- Real servers: 16,000
- Probes: 4000
- Access control list (ACL) items: 16,000

Load Balancing with Content Switching Module

Content switching is the mechanism that provides load balancing and redundancy for the application. CSM is a load balancer that provides a powerful set of features that can be used to enable a secure, scalable load-balanced application environment.

In order to better understand the process of load balancing from the perspective of the CSM, certain definitions of the entities used to make up the load-balancing policy on the CSM will be defined. These policies include:

- Real, virtual server, and SLB policy
- Load-balancing methods
- VLAN tag
- Client group (ACL)
- IP protocol support
- High availability
- Connection redundancy
- User session persistence

Real Server, Virtual Server, SLB Policy, and More

The CSM enables you to configure real servers, server farms, virtual servers, and SLB policies to perform optimal content switching. Following is the definition of some of the key terminology that is used in the CSM world:

- A *real* server is a destination location where a piece of content resides physically (a local or remote server). A real server is defined by an IP address and an optional port. Typically, a port is configured with a real IP address to perform port address translation; for example, the TCP destination port 80 could be mapped to 8080. Typically, real servers are configured as IP addresses within a server farm, but they can also be configured individually as *named real* servers. In the following example, a real server with the IP address 10.10.1.11 is a *named real* server with the name SERVER1.

- A *server farm* is a cluster or grouping of real servers. Apart from real servers (named or IP-based), server NAT, and client NAT, the predictor options also go within the server farm configurations. Following is an example of server farm configuration:

```
real SERVER1
  address 10.10.1.11
  location data_center1_phase2
  inservice
!
serverfarm SFARM_HTTP
  nat server
```

```
   no nat client
   predictor hash address source
   real name SERVER1 8080
    inservice
   real 10.10.1.12
    inservice
   real 10.10.1.13 8080
    inservice
  !
```

- A *map* is a definition of match criteria based on a client request, used for server farm selection. Mostly, maps are used for Layer 7 SLB where HTTP URL and cookie information could be used in the optimal server selection for the client. The following example shows MAP configuration options. The DNS map type is used for global SLB functionality provided by the CSM.

```
CAT-Native-1#conf t
Enter configuration commands, one per line.  End with CNTL/Z.
CAT-Native-1(config)#
CAT-Native-1(config)#module ContentSwitchingModule 6
CAT-Native(config-module-csm)#map EXAMPLE_MAP ?
  cookie   cookie map type
  dns      domain name service map type
  header   generic header map type
  retcode  return code map type
  url      URL map type
CAT-Native(config-module-csm)#map EXAMPLE_MAP
```

- An *SLB policy* is the criterion that is used to select a particular server farm. It's a binding that combines maps and access lists with server farms. In other words, the server farm defined in the policy is selected for the client request if other conditions of the policy are met.

```
 !
  policy POLICY_1
   url-map EXAMPLE_MAP
   serverfarm SFARM_HTTP
!
```

- A *virtual server* is the virtual representation of the application. It binds the server farm with the virtual IP (VIP), protocol, and port. SFARM_DEF, as follows, is the default server farm. It is used if there is no policy match.

```
 !
  vserver HTTP
   virtual 10.10.1.101 tcp www
   serverfarm SFARM_DEF
   persistent rebalance
   slb-policy POLICY_1
   inservice
  !
```

Load Balancing Methods

Load-balancing methods are a key functionality of a content switching device. The Cisco CSM supports the following load-balancing algorithms:

- Round robin
- Weighted round robin

- Least connections

- Weighted least connections

- Source and/or destination IP hash

- URL hashing

The following example shows the load-balancing or predictor configuration options within server farm configurations:

```
CAT-Native(config-module-csm)#
CAT-Native-(config-slb-sfarm)#serverfarm SFARM_HTTP
CAT-Native-(config-slb-sfarm)#
CAT-Native-(config-slb-sfarm)#predictor ?
  forward     forwarding based on destination lookup
  hash        hashing algorithms
  leastconns  least connections algorithm
  roundrobin  roundrobin algorithm (default)
CAT-Native-(config-slb-sfarm)#
CAT-Native-(config-slb-sfarm)#predictor hash ?
  address  IP source/dest address hash algorithm
  url      URL hash algorithm
CAT-Native-(config-slb-sfarm)#
CAT-Native-(config-slb-sfarm)#predictor hash address ?
  /nn or A.B.C.D  IP address hash network mask
  destination     Destination IP address hash algorithm
  source          Source IP address hash algorithm
  <cr>
CAT-Native-(config-slb-sfarm)#
```

VLAN Tag

As discussed previously, Cisco CSM does not have any interfaces. The module has a dot1q trunk to the supervisor over a 4 gigabit port-channel. CSM, in other words, receives client requests and server responses over VLANs. A VLAN tag refers to the CSM functionality where a VLAN ID can be configured in a virtual server. This forces the CSM to only accept client requests from the configured VLAN ID to that particular virtual server and not from any other VLAN.

Thus this feature becomes a powerful and yet simple tool to implement security and to prevent routing loops. A VLAN tag is a critical functionality used with firewall load balancing (FWLB), Secure Socket Layer (SSL) offload load balancing, transparent cache load balancing, secure demilitarized zone (DMZ) implementations, and so on. You will see several implementation examples of this feature in the following chapters.

In the following example, virtual server HTTP only accepts connections coming in from VLAN 51. Connections sourced from VLANs other then 51 and destined for 10.10.1.101:80 are dropped.

```
!
 vserver HTTP
  virtual 10.10.1.101 tcp www
  vlan 51
  serverfarm SFARM_HTTP
```

```
    persistent rebalance
    slb-policy POLICY_1
    inservice
!
```

Client Group (Access Control List)

A client group is another feature of CSM that can be used to provide security and content customization. This is a further enhancement over VLAN tags, as the user access to virtual servers can be controlled based on their IP address, whether the users come from the same or different VLAN. An IOS-based standard access list is used to permit or deny access to a particular application. In the following example, users in 171.68.0.0 and 171.69.0.0 subnets are the only ones that are allowed access to server farm SFARM_HTTP. The access lists are configured in global configuration mode and not in CSM module configuration mode.

```
access-list 10 permit 171.68.0.0 0.0.255.255
access-list 10 permit 171.69.0.0 0.0.255.255
access-list 10 deny    any
!
 policy POLICY_2
  client-group 10
  serverfarm SFARM_HTTP
!
```

IP Protocol Support

The Cisco CSM accommodates a wide range of common IP protocols, including TCP and User Datagram Protocol (UDP). Additionally, the Cisco CSM supports higher-level protocols, including HTTP, FTP, Telnet, Real Time Streaming Protocol (RTSP), Domain Name System (DNS), and Simple Mail Transfer Protocol (SMTP).

High Availability

The Cisco CSM continually monitors server and application availability using a variety of probes, in-band health monitoring, return code checking, and the Dynamic Feedback Protocol (DFP). When a real server or gateway failure occurs, the Cisco CSM redirects traffic to a different real server. Real servers can be added and removed without disrupting service, so systems can be easily scaled up or down.

Connection Redundancy

Two Cisco CSMs can be setup in a fault-tolerant (redundant) configuration to share state information about user sessions and provide hitless connection redundancy — an important requirement for e-commerce sites and sites where encryption is used. If an active Cisco CSM fails, open connections quickly are switched to a standby Cisco CSM without interruption, providing failover that is transparent to the user.

User Session Persistence

In many cases it is important that an end user consistently is directed to the same end device for the duration of a session. This is particularly important where SSL is employed for data encryption or where shopping carts are used, as in e-commerce environments. The Cisco CSM offers the following solutions to provide session persistence to ensure that a client request goes to the proper end device:

- Stickiness based on SSL session ID, source IP address, cookie, or HTTP redirection

- Cookie insert enabling the ability to use cookies for stickiness even if the back-end application is not able to set a cookie

- Cookie offset and length, allowing an administrator to define the static portion of a dynamic cookie to use for persistence

The Cisco CSM synchronizes persistence information from an active Cisco CSM to a backup Cisco CSM to provide a failover that is transparent to a user.

A Typical CSM Traffic Flow

This section describes how a typical session flows between the client and server in a load-balanced environment where CSM is the SLB device. As you can see, this flow is similar to a client server flow in any other load-balanced environment. Figure 3-3 helps visualize the simple environment.

1 A URL is entered in a web browser; such as www.test.example.com.

2 The client contacts a DNS server to locate the IP address associated with the domain; lets say www.test.example.com maps to 10.12.1.101.

3 The DNS server sends the IP address of the virtual IP (VIP) to the client.

4 The client sends the HTTP request to the IP address that resides on the CSM as a VIP.

5 The CSM receives the request with the URL, makes a load-balancing decision, and selects a server from the server farm associated with the www.test.exmaple.com application.

6 The CSM NATs the destination IP (which was the VIP) to the real IP of the server; that is, 10.12.1.101 gets changed to 10.12.1.31 (directed mode) and forwards the traffic to the server. If the NAT server option is disabled, the destination IP (VIP address) remains unchanged (dispatch mode).

7 CSM maps the flow in the fast path.

Figure 3-3 *CSM Traffic Flow*

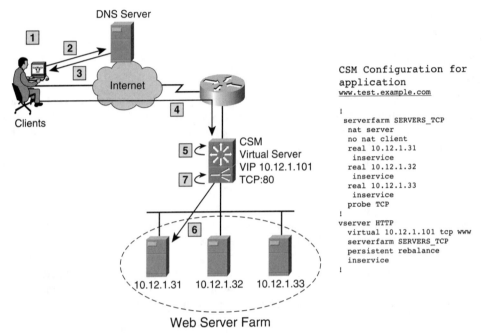

```
CSM Configuration for
application
www.test.example.com

!
 serverfarm SERVERS_TCP
  nat server
  no nat client
  real 10.12.1.31
   inservice
  real 10.12.1.32
   inservice
  real 10.12.1.33
   inservice
  probe TCP
!
vserver HTTP
  virtual 10.12.1.101 tcp www
  serverfarm SERVERS_TCP
  persistent rebalance
  inservice
!
```

Routing with CSM

When forwarding and maintaining load-balancing connections, the CSM must make IP routing decisions. However, the CSM does not run any routing protocols and does not have access to the MSFC routing tables. The CSM builds its own routing table with three types of entries:

- **Directly attached IP subnets**—These subnets are configured on the CSM client or the server VLANs.

- **Default gateways**—Default gateways are configured with the **gateway** keyword from within a client or server VLAN configuration mode.

- **Configured static routes**—Static routes are configured with the **route** keyword from within a client or server VLAN. Static routes are very useful when some servers are not Layer 2 adjacent.

The following configuration example shows how gateway and routes are used:

```
!
module ContentSwitchingModule 6
!
 vlan 51 client
  ip address 172.21.55.179 255.255.255.224
```

```
   gateway 172.21.55.162
 !
 vlan 5 client
  ip address 162.5.5.199 255.255.255.0
  route 33.1.2.0 255.255.255.0 gateway 162.5.5.51
 !
 vlan 55 server
  ip address 162.5.5.199 255.255.255.0
 !
```

The CSM supports multiple gateways on multiple VLANs; however, if the CSM needs to
make a routing decision to an unknown destination, the CSM will randomly select one of
the gateways without your intervention or control. A predictor *forward* option can be used
to control this behavior. This predictor instructs the CSM to route the connection instead
of load balancing it. There are four situations in which the CSM must make a routing
decision:

- Upon receiving a new connection

  At this time, the CSM needs to decide where to send the return traffic for that
  connection. Unlike other devices, the CSM will not perform a route lookup,
  but it memorizes the source MAC address from where the first packet of the
  connection was received. Return traffic for that connection is sent back to the
  source MAC address. This behavior also works with redundancy protocols
  between upstream routers, such as Hot Standby Router Protocol (HSRP).

- For server-originated sessions when the CSM is configured in router mode

  The servers are pointing to the CSM as their default gateway, and the servers
  are originating connections.

- For direct access to servers when the CSM is configured in router mode

- When a server farm is configured with the predictor forward option

By default, in a nonbridged mode, the CSM drops packets that do not match a virtual server.
In other words, CSM needs to be configured for how to handle those packets by using
masked virtual servers. This applies to sessions from CSM-connected VLANs. As indicated
earlier, you can use the predictor forward method to route the packets across CSM.
Predictor forward enables the CSM to use its routing table and make a forwarding decision.

In the following example, we have configured a catch-all virtual server to route packets that
do not match a load-balanced virtual server using its own routing table:

```
 !
 serverfarm ROUTE
  no nat server
  no nat client
  predictor forward
 !
 vserver ROUTE
  virtual 0.0.0.0 0.0.0.0 any
  serverfarm ROUTE
  persistent rebalance
  inservice
```

CSM Network Integration Options

There are several different configuration options that can be used to integrate the CSM with the Layer 2/Layer 3 infrastructure of the data center. The primary design options are:

- Bridged mode
- Routed mode
- One-armed mode
- Direct server return

A combination of the above could also be used to have an optimal design for your data center. In our design discussions, we would commonly use the terms client side and server side. Here are some explanations of the CSM terminology:

- The *client side* is where the client request is coming from. In typical designs topologies, this is the top portion of the design where the ISP links and core routers reside. In some documentation, this is also referred to as the front end. In the CSM configurations, the client side is clearly identified as the VLAN of type client.

- The *server side* is where the web or application servers reside. This is typically the VLANs in the data center where all the servers are present. This is sometimes referred to as the back end. However, nowadays, the term *back end* is mostly used to refer to the storage back end. In the CSM configurations, the server side is clearly identified as the VLAN of type server.

CSM Layer 2 Design—Bridged Mode

Bridged mode is a simple design strategy where the client side is bridged with the server side across the CSM. In other words, the CSM merges the client- and server-side VLANs. Both VLANs have the same IP subnet.

For example, in the following configuration, VLAN 10 and 20 are in bridged mode.

```
!
module ContentSwitchingModule 6
!
 vlan 10 client
   ip address 10.10.1.199 255.255.255.0
   gateway 10.10.1.1
!
 vlan 20 server
   ip address 10.10.1.199 255.255.255.0
!
```

Figure 3-4 shows a CSM topology in bridged mode. Notice that the client-side VLAN on the CSM is VLAN 10. This is the VLAN where the CSM will have a default gateway pointing to the HSRP group IP on the MSFC on the same VLAN. The servers in VLAN 20 will have their default gateways pointing to the same HSRP group IP on the MSFC on VLAN 10.

Figure 3-4 *CSM Bridge Mode Design*

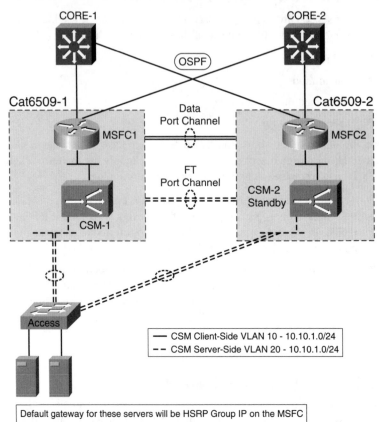

This is a useful design approach in secure DMZ implementations using Firewall Services Modules. This design is also used in Local Director (LD), which is deployed only in bridged mode to CSM migrations.

CSM Layer 3 Design I—Routed Mode with MSFC on the Client Side

In this design, we have two Catalyst 6509s with one CSM module each. CSM's Alias IP on the server-side VLANs (20 and 30) acts as the default gateway of the servers. The HSRP group active on VLAN 10 (configured on the MSFC) is the default gateway of the CSM. MSFC can either have static routes for server-side subnets (10.20.1.0, 10.30.1.0) pointing to the CSM or the Route Health Injection (RHI) feature on the CSM can be used to dynamically inject routes into the MSFC's routing table. MSFC exchanges routes with the core routers dynamically using OSPF.

Figure 3-5 shows an example CSM routed mode design with MSFC on the client side. The topology shows how the logical connectivity would be for VLAN 10, 20, and 30.

Figure 3-5   *CSM Layer 3 Design I—MSFC on Client Side*

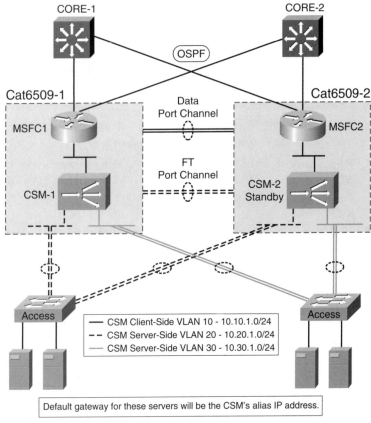

Default gateway for these servers will be the CSM's alias IP address.

Following is a configuration example of CSM routed mode design with MSFC on the client side.

```
!
interface Vlan10
 ip address 10.10.1.2 255.255.255.0
 standby 10 10.10.1.1
 standby 10 priority 150
 standby 10 preempt
 !
!
module ContentSwitchingModule 3
 !
 vlan 10 client
  ip address 10.10.1.5 255.255.255.0
  gateway 10.10.1.1
  alias 10.10.1.4 255.255.255.0
 !
 vlan 20 server
  ip address 10.20.1.2 255.255.255.0
  alias 10.20.1.1 255.255.255.0
 !
 vlan 30 server
```

```
ip address 10.30.1.2 255.255.255.0
alias 10.30.1.1 255.255.255.0
!
```

There are a few key points in this design:

- The data trunk used between the Catalyst 6509s (with the CSMs) would carry the client-side CSM and MSFC VLANs. Server-side VLANs are not carried over this trunk.

- A separate port-channel is used for the control traffic (CSM fault-tolerant traffic, a.k.a. CSRP communication).

- Each catalyst with the CSM would have a link to each access switch. For high availability, this link would be a Layer 2 port-channel.

- Redundancy could be further enhanced by making sure each server farm within each VIP uses servers from at least two VLANs (VLANs going to two different access switches)—this ensures that the web site stays up even if one of the access switches goes down.

- IGMP snooping needs to be disabled on the Catalyst 6509s carrying the CSMs. This could be done globally or on a per-FT VLAN basis.

Advantages of this design approach:

- No client NAT would be needed for server-to-VIP sessions. The only time you would need client NAT is when a session is initiated from a server in VLAN x to a VIP that balances sessions to a server in the same VLAN x.

- MSFC exists on the client side of the CSM, thus RHI can be used. There would be no need for static routing. The key requirement of the RHI feature is that CSM should be directly connected to the MSFC over a Layer 3 VLAN. In the previous design, this requirement is met by VLAN 10; thus RHI is possible.

Disadvantages of this design over approach:

- Traffic between all load-balanced servers (for which CSM acts as the default gateway) would go through the CSM. Appropriate predictor forward virtual servers would have to be configured on the CSM to make these flows work.

- Server management and backup traffic (non-load-balanced sessions) would go through the CSM.

CSM Layer 3 Design II—Routed Mode with MSFC on the Server Side

In this design, we have two Catalyst 6509s with one CSM module each. The HSRP group active on VLAN 20 and 30 (configured on the MSFC) would be the default gateway of the servers. MSFC would default route all traffic to the CSM Alias IP on VLAN 10. CSMs would have static routes for server-side subnets (10.20.1.0, 10.30.1.0) down to the MSFC on VLAN 10 and a default route up to the HSRP active on VLAN 5 on the core routers. Similarly, static routes would need to be configured on core routers to point down to the CSM Alias IP. These static routes are to reach the VIPs on the CSMs and the server-side VLANs.

Figure 3-6 shows an example CSM routed mode design with MSFC on the server side. The topology shows how the logical connectivity would be for VLAN 5, 10, 20, and 30. Notice how the MSFC has moved from the top of the CSM to the bottom.

Figure 3-6   *CSM Layer 3 Design II—MSFC on Server Side*

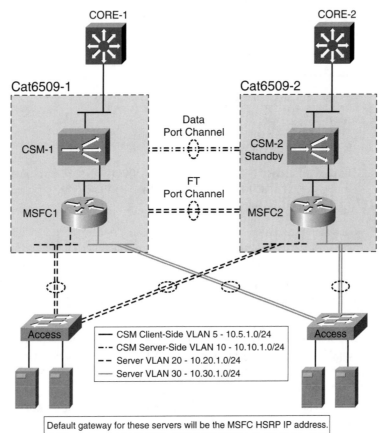

Following is a configuration example of CSM routed mode design with MSFC on the server side.

```
!
interface Vlan10
 ip address 10.10.1.2 255.255.255.0
 standby 10 10.10.1.1
 standby 10 priority 150
 standby 10 preempt
!
interface Vlan20
 ip address 10.20.1.2 255.255.255.0
 standby 20 10.20.1.1
 standby 20 priority 150
 standby 20 preempt
!
```

```
interface Vlan30
 ip address 10.30.1.2 255.255.255.0
 standby 30 10.30.1.1
 standby 30 priority 150
 standby 30 preempt
!
module ContentSwitchingModule 3
!
vlan 5 client
  ip address 10.5.1.5 255.255.255.0
  gateway 10.5.1.1
  alias 10.5.1.4 255.255.255.0
!
vlan 10 client
  ip address 10.10.1.5 255.255.255.0
  route 10.20.1.0 255.255.255.0 gateway 10.10.1.1
  route 10.30.1.0 255.255.255.0 gateway 10.10.1.1
  alias 10.10.1.4 255.255.255.0
!
```

A few key points in this design:

- The data trunk used between the Catalyst 6509s (with the CSMs) would carry the server-side CSM and MSFC VLANs. Client-side VLANs are not carried over this trunk.

- A separate port-channel is used for the control traffic (CSM fault-tolerant traffic).

- Each catalyst with the CSM would have a link to each access switch. For high availability, this link would be a Layer 2 port-channel.

- Redundancy could be further enhanced by making sure each server farm within each VIP uses servers from at least two VLANs (VLANs going to two different access switches). This ensures that the web site stays up even if one of the access switches goes down.

- IGMP snooping needs to be disabled on the Catalyst 6509s carrying the CSMs. This could be done globally or on a per-FT VLAN basis. This is done to ensure that FT control packets are not confused by the switch as IGMP requests—FT control packets use multicast Layer 2 (MAC) destination addresses.

- Higher-layer probes are a must, as the default probe of the CSM (ARP) will not work when servers are not Layer 2 adjacent.

Advantages of this design approach:

- Traffic between all servers (for which MSFC acts as the default gateway) would go through the MSFC and bypass the CSM.

Disadvantages of this design approach:

- Sessions from server to VIP would need to be client NATed; otherwise, server return traffic would bypass the CSM. Appropriate client groups (ACLs) can be used to make sure NATing is only performed when requests originate from the server subnets and not when the requests come from the intranet.

- Since MSFC is not used on the client side of the CSM, RHI cannot be used.

CSM Layer 3 Design III—One-Armed CSM Design

In this design, we have two Catalyst 6509s with one CSM module each. The HSRP group active on VLAN 20 and 30 (configured on the MSFC) would be the default gateway of the servers. We can fully deploy a dynamic routing protocol in the data center. CSM would connect with the MSFC using VLAN 10. CSM would default route all traffic to the active HSRP on VLAN 10.

This design implies using a single logical link (VLAN) on the CSM and directing appropriate traffic to the CSM using policy-based routing (PBR) on the MSFC. Traffic from clients to VIPs is routed to the CSM while PBR is used on return traffic from the server to make sure it does not bypass the CSM.

However, PBR is not the only option for the one-armed design approach. One can easily achieve this by using client NAT (also known as source NAT) on the CSM. This means that CSM would translate the source IP address to a local IP, as it forwards traffic to the real server, which would ensure that the server return traffic would go through the CSM.

Figure 3-7 shows an example CSM one-armed design with the CSM connected to the MSFC using VLAN 10.

Figure 3-7 *CSM Layer 3 Design III—One-Armed CSM Design*

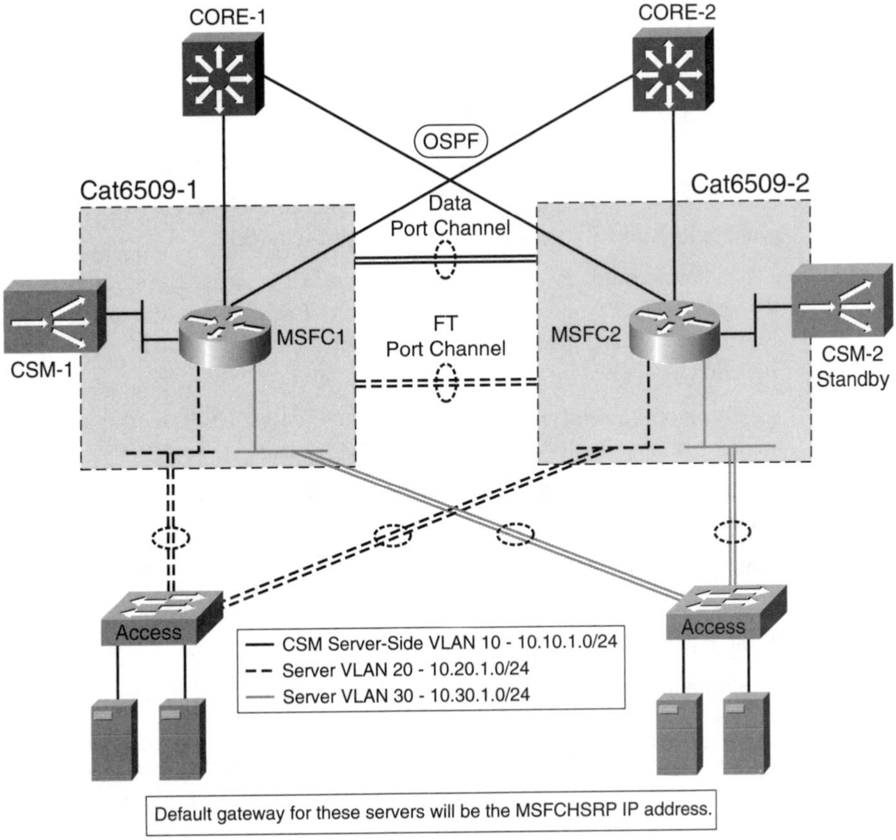

Following is a configuration example of CSM one-armed design.

```
!
interface Vlan10
 ip address 10.10.1.2 255.255.255.0
 standby 10 10.10.1.1
 standby 10 priority 150
 standby 10 preempt
!
interface Vlan20
 ip address 10.20.1.2 255.255.255.0
 standby 20 10.20.1.1
 standby 20 priority 150
 standby 20 preempt
!
interface Vlan30
 ip address 10.30.1.2 255.255.255.0
 standby 30 10.30.1.1
 standby 30 priority 150
 standby 30 preempt
!
module ContentSwitchingModule 3
 !
 vlan 10 server
  ip address 10.10.1.5 255.255.255.0
  gateway 10.10.1.1
  alias 10.10.1.4 255.255.255.0
 !
```

There are a few key points in this design:

- The data trunk used between the Catalyst 6509s (with the CSMs) would carry the server-side CSM and MSFC VLANs.

- A separate port-channel is used for the control traffic (CSM fault-tolerant traffic).

- Each catalyst with the CSM would have a link to each access switch. For high availability, this link would be a Layer 2 port-channel.

- Redundancy could be further enhanced by making sure each server farm within each VIP uses servers from at least two VLANs (VLANs going to two different access switches). This ensures that the web site stays up even if one of the access switches goes down.

- IGMP snooping needs to be disabled on the Catalyst 6509s carrying the CSMs. This could be done globally or on a per-FT VLAN basis.

- Higher-layer probes is a must, as the default probe of the CSM (ARP) would not work when servers are not Layer 2 adjacent.

Advantages of this design approach:

- Traffic between all servers (for which MSFC acts as the default gateway) would go through the MSFC and bypass the CSM.

- Server management and backup traffic (non-load-balanced sessions) would also bypass the CSM.

- Only relevant, load-balanced traffic would be sent to the CSM.

Disadvantages of this design approach:

- Configuration management may become an issue as the number of sites increases.
- ACL mishaps on the MSFC can bring down web sites.
- Load-balanced protocol/ports for virtual (client to VIP) needs to be different than client to direct server traffic.
- Server management traffic should also use different ports than load-balanced traffic.
- Server-to-server load balancing would be possible again only with distinct ports.
- Higher-layer probes are a must, as the default probe of the CSM (ARP) will not work when servers are not Layer 2 adjacent.

There is a default next-hop option within PBR that can make policy-based routing configuration management easier. This option enables redirecting of traffic to the CSM when a better route is not found on the routing table. So all traffic that matches the default route in the routing table would be forwarded to the next-hop defined in the route-map, which in our case would be the CSM IP address.

This option would work for load-balanced environments where the client base is coming from the Internet such that the server return traffic has to go through the default route on the MSFC. This option will not work when internal clients also use the same VIP nor will it work for server-to-server load-balanced sessions. Again, before selecting any option, you should consider how complicated the configurations would get in the customer's environment. Here is a configuration example of a simple scenario using the default option within PBR. In this example, it is assumed that all clients are coming from the Internet:

```
On the CSM:
!
module ContentSwitchingModule 6
 vlan 10 server
  ip address 10.10.1.8 255.255.255.0
  gateway 10.10.1.1
  alias 10.10.1.10 255.255.255.0
!
On the MSFC:
!
interface Vlan10
 ip address 10.10.1.2 255.255.255.0
 standby 10 ip 10.10.1.1
 standby 10 priority 110
 standby 10 preempt
!
interface Vlan20
 description Server Side Vlan
 ip address 10.20.1.2 255.255.255.0
 ip policy route-map pbr-server-return
 standby 20 ip 10.20.1.1
 standby 20 priority 110
 standby 20 preempt
!
route-map pbr-server-return permit 10
 set ip default next-hop 10.10.1.10
!
```

CSM Layer 3 Design IV—Direct Server Return

In this design, we have two Catalyst 6509s with one CSM module each. This implementation is similar to the one-armed design approach previously described. Following are two key differences between this design and the previous one:

- Dispatch mode is used when sending requests to the servers.

- No PBR or source NAT is used. Servers respond directly to the client.

Figure 3-8 shows an example of direct server return (DSR)-based CSM routed design. Notice that in this design approach CSM has to have Layer 2 adjacency to all of the server VLANs.

Figure 3-8 *CSM Layer 3 Design IV—DSR*

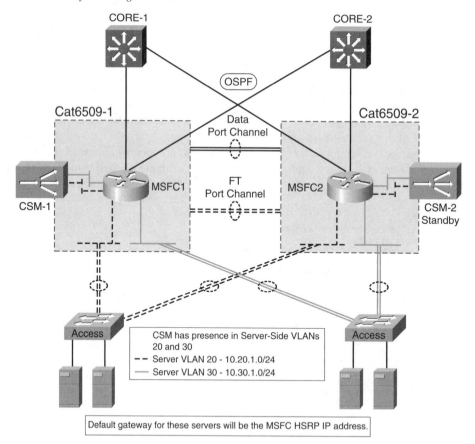

Advantages of this design approach:

- Traffic between all servers (for which MSFC acts as the default gateway) would go through the MSFC and bypass the CSM:

- Server management and backup traffic (non-load-balanced sessions) would also bypass the CSM.
- Only relevant, load-balanced client requests are sent to the CSM.
- Server responses to clients would bypass the CSM.

Disadvantages of this design approach:

- Servers have to be Layer 2 adjacent to the CSM.
- Loopback or secondary IP addresses have to be configured on the servers.
- TCP flows always have to be timed out.
- TCP termination is not possible (only Layer 4 load balancing is possible).
- In-band health monitoring is not possible.

Case Study: CSM-Based Solution

Now that we understand the software and hardware architecture of the CSM platform, we will start our discussion of how this product should be deployed. Placement of the CSM in the existing or new network requires planning and understanding of the application, security, and underlying infrastructure requirements. As there are many applications with different security policies, we shall examine some specific ones deployed in the following case study.

In this case study, we will examine a specific customer deployment where CSM is used to load balance DNS and RADIUS applications. The idea behind the following case study is to understand not only the concepts but also the implementation details.

Topics covered in this section include:

- Server and application requirements
- Management and security requirements
- Infrastructure requirements
- Design options

Server and Application Requirements

Server and application requirements for this case study are defined as follows:

- Directly manage the servers from the front end (client-side network).
- Servers should be able to initiate sessions for application software and driver upgrades.
- Number of servers: 15–80 per site

- DNS server
  - UDP/TCP/53
  - Flows are short lived. There is one client request packet and a single server response packet.
  - 500,000 clients use this DNS service with a session rate as high as 30,000 requests per second.
  - DNS servers should be able to initiate sessions to the Internet for zone transfers.
- RADIUS server
  - UDP/1645/1646
  - Flows are short lived. There is one client request packet and a single server response packet.
  - 500,000 clients uses this RADIUS service for authentication with many requests per second.
- Both DNS and RADIUS applications need to be monitored with extended keepalives.
- No server persistence is needed.

Management and Security Requirements

Following are the security requirements for this case study:

- Sys logging and SNMP traps from the Catalyst 6509 for the CSM real and virtual server state changes and fault-tolerant events
- Commonly configured management services, such as telnet and SSH, for access to CLI on Catalyst 6509

Infrastructure Requirements

Following are Layer 2 and Layer 3 infrastructure requirements for this case study:

- Minimal disruption to the IGP domain.
- No static routes permitted in the infrastructure.
- Seamless integration of the CSM in the current Layer 2 and Layer 3 infrastructure.
- Robust failover is needed for servers with dual network interface cards (NICs). Server NICs would be in Active/Passive mode, residing in the same VLAN but connected to different Catalyst 6509s.

Design Options

To meet the previously mentioned requirements in this data center design, CSM is configured in a Layer 3 fashion with the MSFC being on the client side. The CSM is Layer 2 adjacent to the servers. The server's default gateway is the alias IP of the CSM in VLAN 201 (10.4.1.4). The CSM points to the HSRP group IP on the MSFC on VLAN 200 as its default gateway.

Figure 3-9 shows the topology of a CSM routed mode design with MSFC on the client side. Notice that the CSM has two VLANs—200 is the client-side VLAN, and 201 is the server-side VLAN.

Figure 3-9   *CSM Case Study Topology for DNS and RADIUS Load Balancing*

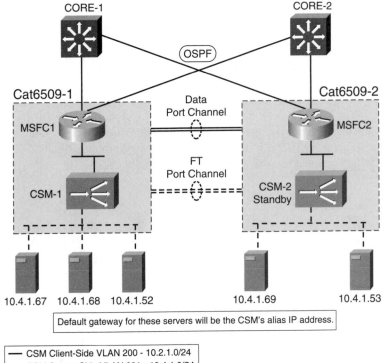

This section goes over the configuration details that would be used to implement this solution.

CSM Configurations

Following is the CSM configuration with comments on the features being used. As can be seen in the configuration example, the fault-tolerant VLAN is VLAN 32, and CSM in CAT1 would be the active CSM. The service module is configured in routed mode with VLAN 200 being the client-side VLAN and VLAN 201 being the server-side VLAN. The client VLAN uses a routable IP subnet, while the server-side VLAN uses a private subnet. In our example, we are using a 10.0.0.0 subnet for both.

```
!
module ContentSwitchingModule 3
 ft group 2 vlan 32
  priority 30
  preempt
!
 vlan 200 client
  ip address 10.2.1.5 255.255.255.0
  gateway 10.2.1.1
  alias 10.2.1.4 255.255.255.0
!
 vlan 201 server
  ip address 10.4.1.5 255.255.255.0
  alias 10.4.1.4 255.255.255.0
!
```

The NAT pool is used to NAT the DNS server's initiated sessions. The NAT-overloaded IP is part of the VLAN 200 subnet.

```
!
 natpool POOL 10.2.1.100 10.2.1.100 netmask 255.255.255.0
!
```

Following are probe configurations with www.cisco.com being the domain checked. Notice that we are using ICMP as the keepalive method for probing RADIUS servers. We can use RADIUS-scripted keepalive to optimize this health check.

```
!
 probe PROBE_DNS dns
  name www.cisco.com
  address 198.133.219.25
  interval 10
  failed 20
!
 probe PROBE_ICMP icmp
  interval 5
  failed 10
!
```

As discussed earlier, CSM in routed mode (also known as secure mode) does not forward packets unless it hits a virtual server. To route non-load-balanced packets across the CSM, we will use **serverfarms** configuration command on the CSM along with the **predictor forward** load-balancing algorithm. The **serverfarm ROUTE_OUT_DNS** is unique configuration, as it is used to source-NAT the DNS servers initiated requests.

```
!
 serverfarm ROUTE_IN
  no nat server
  no nat client
  predictor forward
!
 serverfarm ROUTE_OUT
  no nat server
  no nat client
  predictor forward
!
```

```
serverfarm ROUTE_OUT_DNS
  no nat server
  nat client POOL
  predictor forward
!
```

Following are the load-balanced **serverfarm** configurations with appropriate probes applied.

```
!
serverfarm SERVERS_DNS
  nat server
  no nat client
  real 10.4.1.67
   inservice
  real 10.4.1.68
   inservice
  real 10.4.1.69
   inservice
  probe PROBE_DNS
!
serverfarm SERVERS_RADIUS
  nat server
  no nat client
  real 10.4.1.52
   inservice
  real 10.4.1.53
   inservice
  probe PROBE_ICMP
!
```

The following policies are used to distinguish between the DNS server's initiated sessions and the RADIUS server's initiated requests. For DNS servers, we will perform NAT using the configured NAT pool.

```
!
policy DNS_NAT
  client-group 11
  serverfarm ROUTE_OUT_DNS
!
policy ROUTE_OUT
  serverfarm ROUTE_OUT
!
```

Following are virtual servers for DNS. Notice that we have deployed them for both UDP and TCP requests.

```
!
vserver DNS_TCP
  virtual 10.2.1.10 tcp 53
  serverfarm SERVERS_DNS
  idle 10
  replicate csrp connection
  persistent rebalance
  inservice
!
vserver DNS_UDP
  virtual 10.2.1.10 udp dns
  serverfarm SERVERS_DNS
  idle 10
  replicate csrp connection
  persistent rebalance
  inservice
!
```

Below are virtual servers for RADIUS servers. Notice that we have deployed them for both RADIUS Authentication (port 1645) and RADIUS Accounting requests (port 1646).

```
!
 vserver RADIUS_1645
  virtual 10.2.1.66 udp 1645
  serverfarm SERVERS_RADIUS
  idle 10
  replicate csrp connection
  persistent rebalance
  inservice
!
 vserver RADIUS_1646
  virtual 10.2.1.66 udp 1646
  serverfarm SERVERS_RADIUS
  idle 10
  replicate csrp connection
  persistent rebalance
  inservice
!
```

Following is the predictor forward routing virtual server that is used to direct access to the servers for management purposes. We are using the **advertise** command in this case to enable the dynamic injection of this route into the MSFC routing table. The VLAN tag in this virtual server protects against routing loops and is also necessary for proper functionality of the **advertise** command.

```
!
 vserver ROUTE_IN
  virtual 10.4.1.0 255.255.255.0 any
  vlan 200
  serverfarm ROUTE_IN
  advertise
  replicate csrp connection
  persistent rebalance
  inservice
!
CAT-Native-2#sh ip route 10.4.1.0
Routing entry for 10.4.1.0/24
  Known via "static", distance 1, metric 0
  Redistributing via ospf 1
  Advertised by ospf 1 metric-type 1 subnets
  Routing Descriptor Blocks:
  * 10.2.1.4, via Vlan200
      Route metric is 0, traffic share count is 1
CAT-Native-2#
!
```

The following virtual server is used for routing all server-initiated traffic to the default gateway of the CSM. Notice that we are using different policies to distinguish between the DNS servers and the rest.

```
!
 vserver ROUTE_OUT
  virtual 0.0.0.0 0.0.0.0 any
  vlan 201
  idle 20
  replicate csrp connection
  persistent rebalance
  slb-policy DNS_NAT
  slb-policy ROUTE_OUT
  inservice
!
```

Catalyst 6509 Layer 2 Configurations

Following are the Layer 2 interface configurations on the Catalyst 6509s. We have separate port-channels for data and control traffic. Notice that VLAN 32, the fault-tolerant VLAN, is removed from the Data port-channel. For high availability, it is important to keep the port-channel links on different modules.

```
!
interface Port-channel32
 description FT Link CAT1---CAT2
 no ip address
 switchport
 switchport access vlan 32
 switchport mode access
!
interface GigabitEthernet6/47
 no ip address
 switchport
 switchport access vlan 32
 switchport mode access
 channel-group 32 mode desirable
!
interface GigabitEthernet7/47
 no ip address
 switchport
 switchport access vlan 32
 switchport mode access
 channel-group 32 mode desirable
!
!
interface Port-channel30
 description Data Trunk CAT1---CAT2
 no ip address
 switchport
 switchport trunk encapsulation dot1q
 switchport trunk allowed vlan 1-31,33-1005
 switchport mode trunk
!
interface GigabitEthernet6/48
 no ip address
 switchport
 switchport trunk encapsulation dot1q
 switchport trunk allowed vlan 1-31,33-1005
 switchport mode trunk
 channel-group 30 mode desirable
!
interface GigabitEthernet7/48
 no ip address
 switchport
 switchport trunk encapsulation dot1q
 switchport trunk allowed vlan 1-31,33-1005
 switchport mode trunk
 channel-group 30 mode desirable
!
```

Catalyst 6509 Layer 3 Configurations

Following are the Layer 3 configurations on the Catalyst 6509. Interface VLAN 200 is the one that links the CSM with the MSFC. OSPF VLAN 200 is added to area 4, and static routes (which are installed from CSM) are redistributed with metric type 1.

```
!
interface Vlan200
 ip address 10.2.1.2 255.255.255.0
 no ip redirects
 standby 2 ip 10.2.1.1
 standby 2 priority 150
 standby 2 preempt
!
access-list 11 permit 10.4.1.69
access-list 11 permit 10.4.1.68
access-list 11 permit 10.4.1.67
!
router ospf 1
 log-adjacency-changes
 redistribute static metric-type 1 subnets
 network 10.2.1.0 0.0.0.255 area 4
 network 10.201.1.0 0.0.0.255 area 0
 network 10.202.1.0 0.0.0.255 area 4
!
```

Traffic Flow

Now that you understand how to design CSM to accommodate all the application, security, and infrastructure requirements, this section presents a simple load-balanced user session going through the CSM:

1 The client's request to the VIP (10.2.1.10) is forwarded to the CSM by the MSFC. Since 10.2.1.0 is directly connected, MSFC issues an ARP request for the VIP and forwards the DNS query to the CSM.

2 CSM makes the load-balancing decision and forwards the request to an available server. CSM translates the packets from the VIP to the real IP of the server and forwards the packet to the server.

3 The server responds to the request and sends the packet to the CSM.

4 The CSM forwards the response toward the MSFC based on the installed flow entry.

Test and Verification

Each application is unique with respect to the number of sockets used, the duration of TCP or UDP connections, the activity in each session in terms of packets per second, idle timeouts, and so on. Thus it is critical to test and verify the SLB environment with the particular applications.

Following are a few critical test cases that should be verified after a new deployment or a major or minor infrastructure change—including a CSM code upgrade:

• An exact production client load-balanced session for DNS and RADIUS services. The test clients' behavior should match the production clients' behavior, with appropriate idle times and delays.

• Content retrieval from the server.

- A server-initiated session to a back-end database or internal server; this can be a DNS zone transfer.
- A server-initiated backup or data replication session.
- Application daemon failure and detection by the CSM.
- Primary CSM failure and measurement of the recovery time.
- Primary Catalyst 6500 failure and measurement of the recovery time.

Summary

This chapter introduced you to the Cisco CSM on the Catalyst 6500. The chapter covered the software and hardware architecture, flow management, device management, and introduction to basic entities used in SLB. Additionally, highlights of the CSM software features were discussed.

In order to combine all concepts of SLB from the perspective of the CSM platform, this chapter presented a case study. This case study focused on the deployment scenario of a real-world service provider solution using the CSM. The CSM configurations were provided and explained to introduce the reader to the CLI.

Chapter 4, "Layer 7 Load Balancing and Content Customization," introduces the Layer 7 protocol, mainly HTTP. The HTTP protocol's interaction with TCP will also be examined.

Layer 7 Load Balancing and Content Customization

This chapter will discuss the methods and protocols involved in accomplishing a Layer 7 load-balancing solution. The reasons for and benefits of deploying persistent and customized load balancing will be explored.

TCP is the building block for Layer 7 protocols, such as the HTTP. This chapter will examine the interaction between HTTP and TCP and how client and server communication at the TCP and HTTP layers are accomplished.

Following the discussion of the TCP and HTTP, we will present a case study involving the requirement for Layer 7 load balancing from the application, security, and infrastructure perspective.

Benefits of Layer 7 Load Balancing

Load balancing for most applications can be accomplished using the basic information about the clients and the services that they are trying to reach, be that web-based content or VPN concentrators. Usually these decisions are made at the IP and TCP layers, which include looking at either the source or destination IP address or the destination TCP or UDP port number. However, as the applications and services offered become more complex, there is an increasing need to provide load-balancing decisions at layers above the transport layer (the TCP layer). This is where Layer 7 load balancing comes into the picture. Layer 7 load balancing provides inspection into the packet payload and identification of headers and fields to allow for more intelligent load balancing of user requests. The decision could be based on various HTTP method URLs or HTTP protocol headers, which we will discuss in detail in the section "Introduction to HTTP."

The three major reasons for Layer 7 load balancing are:

- Scalability and acceleration of the application
- Persistent user sessions on a server
- Content customization based on user profile

The following sections describe these advantages.

Scalability and Application Acceleration

As the number of clients of popular web-based applications increase multifold over a year, scaling internal and external applications is one of the key worries of data center application teams. Typically, the applications are scaled by adding more servers with replicated content and adding real servers to the Layer 4 load balancer. This works well for the networking team but is a cumbersome activity for the application team. This is because any change in the application or server content needs to be updated on more servers.

Layer 7 load balancing provides a solution which is desirable by both the network and application teams. The load balancer with its hardware-based Layer 7 packet inspection capabilities can be used to direct clients to different groups of servers. The server load balancing (SLB) devices can look into the URL and distinguish between various content requests. For example, content distribution can be performed as users make request for an URL, such as http://www.cisco.com/**partner**/index.html, which can be distinguished from an URL http://www.cisco.com/**cust**/index.html for the same domain. An SLB device can direct users for partner and cust to separate server farms respectively. Thus any change to partner-related content would only need to be updated on the partner server farm. Application distribution can also be performed by distinguishing */*.cgi from */*.html.

This is not just a method but also a great tool for improving server and application management, as it makes a substantial difference in the end user's experience. Because of dedicated content and application servers that will function faster, users will notice faster page download times.

Session Persistence

User session persistence to applications is another key benefit of Layer 7 load balancing. As the user's request is load balanced to a particular server, it needs to be persisted to that server. This is critical, as a client's authentication or shopping cart (browsing history) may exist in one server and not in the others. If the client's next TCP connection is load balanced to another server that does not have the client's history or session information, then the client would have to start from scratch.

In typical load-balanced environments, session persistence is provided by using the source IP sticky method. The source IP sticky method is used by the load balancer to track client connections to the application based on the client's source IP address. Any time the client with the same source IP address makes a connection via the load balancer, the load balancer will stick or forward that client's connection to the same application to which the client initially connected. This works well, but it can result in uneven load balancing when a large number of clients visit the site from behind mega proxies. Since mega proxies NAT multiple client source addresses to a single IP address, multiple clients can be using the same IP address; and if the source IP sticky method is enabled on the load balancer, multiple client connections will be forwarded to the same application, resulting in uneven load balancing.

Layer 7 load balancing session persistence can be based on an HTTP cookie, a URL, or a SSL session ID. This enables the load balancers to distinguish between users and also provide persistence for connections to servers even when they have the same source IP address.

Content Customization

As the global world is adapting to the Internet rapidly, providing customized content based on language or geographic region is becoming increasingly important. By inspecting the HTTP header requests, content can be inspected at the Layer 7 level (the HTTP protocol level) and connection can be redirected to a geographically or linguistically appropriate server or site. For example, if a client is making connections in Chinese, its requests should be catered to the servers that serve content in Chinese.

Introduction to TCP

The TCP was designed to provide reliable mechanisms for communications between a client and a server. Since TCP ensures the integrity of the data being transferred, not only in the proper sequence but also in utilizing the network bandwidth optimally, it is applied as a reliable connection-oriented protocol. A good understanding of TCP is essential for Layer 7 load balancing. This is the protocol used by HTTP and SSL. In the following sections, we will cover the details of the TCP protocol, which is a standard-based protocol defined in RFC 793, including:

* Data segments
* TCP headers
* TCP connection establishment and termination
* TCP flow control

Data Segments

In order to provide reliability for data communication, TCP provides retransmission and sequencing of the data segments being carried between the client and the server. A message sent from the client to the server or vice versa is called a *segment* in the TCP world. In order to ensure that a segment has reached the destination, the receiver sends an *acknowledgement* to the sender.

The postal service is a great analogy that can be used to understand TCP/IP. For example, when one sends a certified package in the mail, a message for the receipt of the package is sent to the sender as soon as the package arrives at the destination. Similarly, once the data has been successfully received in its original form, the receiver sends an acknowledgement back to the sender that it has received the data properly and the data is in its original and undamaged state. If the sent data is damaged or changed, the receiver simply ignores it. After a certain specified time, if an acknowledgement from the receiver has not been received, the sender checks to see the status of the sent data. Using TCP as the Layer 4 transport protocol ensures reliable communication and data integrity between the client and the server.

TCP Headers

In this section, we will cover some of the important TCP header fields, such as source and destination port, sequence number, acknowledgement number, header length, and more.

Figure 4-1 illustrates the structure of the TCP header. The size of the TCP header is 20 bytes when the Options fields are not set.

Figure 4-1   *TCP Protocol Header*

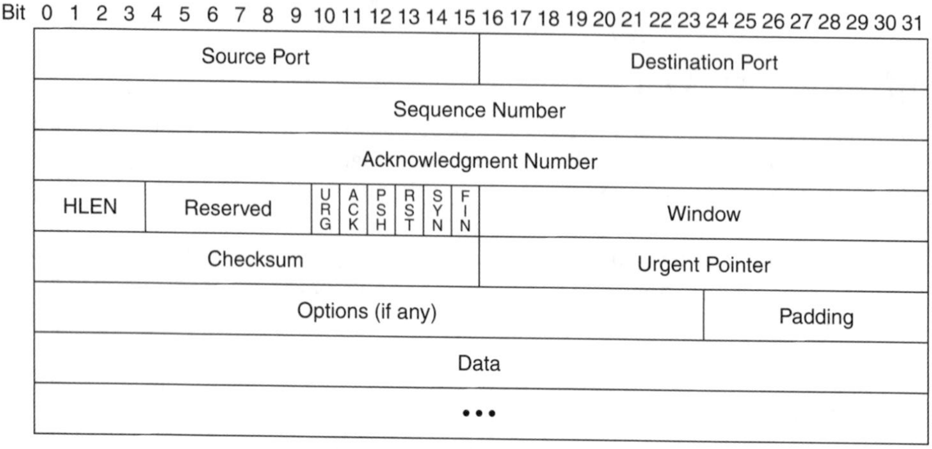

Bit	0 1 2 3 4 5 6 7 8 9 10 11 12 13 14 15	16 17 18 19 20 21 22 23 24 25 26 27 28 29 30 31

Source Port	Destination Port
Sequence Number	
Acknowledgment Number	

HLEN	Reserved	URG	ACK	PSH	RST	SYN	FIN	Window

Checksum	Urgent Pointer
Options (if any)	Padding
Data	
•••	

The following subsections provide descriptions of the TCP header fields.

Source and Destination Port

A TCP segment is carried within an IP packet; thus the source and destination IP addresses of the client and server are present within the IP header. The TCP header starts with a 16-bit Source Port field and a 16-bit Destination Port field. This port is the communication channel that the client and server use to transmit TCP segments to and receive TCP segments from each other. A very common example for identifying these values is when a client makes a connection to a web server on TCP port 80 (the TCP Destination Port), while the source port for a client is usually a random port above the well-known reserved ports of 1024. As many clients with random source ports make connections to a server on port 80, the way for the server to distinguish between the connections as being separate from client to client is to identify the connection based on the source IP, destination IP, source port, and destination port. Since the destination IP and port stay the same, the IP address and source port combination has to be unique in order for a connection to be unique.

Sequence Number

The 32-bit Sequence Number field in the TCP header indicates the first byte of data (the start of the data byte) in this particular segment. This is important in order to track and accomplish the reassembly of the TCP segments on the receiving end.

Acknowledgement Number

The 32-bit Acknowledgement Number field is used to identify the sequence number that the sender of the acknowledgement is expecting to receive.

Header Length

The 4-bit Header Length field is the total length of the header. It is needed because some of the OPTIONS bit fields can be of variable length. The maximum size for the Header Length fields when all the possible OPTIONS are selected is 60 bytes; otherwise, it is a 20-byte header.

Reserved

This 6-bit field is reserved and will be used for future enhancements to the TCP header.

Control Bits

The control bits are six flag bits, used in identifying and handling the TCP segment. The following are the control bits used:

- *URG*—The Urgent Pointer (URG) flag indicates to the receiver to accept data as it is deemed urgent.
- *ACK*—The Acknowledgment (ACK) flag identifies the successful reception of the segment and the next data byte, as specified in the Acknowledgment Number field, to be expected by the sender from the receiver.
- *PSH*—The Push (PSH) flag, when set, tells the receiver to immediately forward or push the data to the application.
- *RST*—The Reset (RST) flag is used to abort an existing connection and reset it so that the buffers holding the data can be cleared.
- *SYN*—The Synchronization (SYN) flag is used to signal that the sequence number between the receiver and the client need to be synchronized. The SYN bit is used during the initial connection setup between the client and the server.
- *FIN*—The Finished (FIN) flag is used to tell the receiver that the sender is finished sending the data and the receiver can close its half of the connection.

Window

The 16-bit Window field is for flow control using an advertised window size, which is the amount of bytes the sender and receiver are willing to accept during the exchange of TCP segments. The maximum size for the window is 65,535 bytes.

Checksum

The 16-bit *checksum* value is used to verify the integrity of the TCP headers and the data. If a segment contains an odd number of header and text octets to be checked, the last octet is padded on the right with zeros to form a 16-bit word for checksum purposes. The pad is not transmitted as part of the segment. While computing the checksum, the checksum field itself is replaced with zeros.

The checksum also covers a 96-bit pseudo header conceptually prefixed to the TCP header. This pseudo header contains the source address, the destination address, the protocol, and TCP length. This gives the TCP protection against misrouted segments. This information is carried in the IP and is transferred across the TCP/IP interface in the arguments or results of calls by the TCP on the IP.

The checksum value is stored in the Checksum field, and the pseudo header is discarded. On the receiving end, a similar operation is performed and the values are checked. If the checksum does not match, the segment is discarded.

Urgent Pointer

The 16-bit Urgent Pointer field indicates to the receiver that this value must be added to the Sequence Number field to produce the last byte of the urgent data (primarily when the urgent data ends). This field is used in conjunction with the URG flag.

Options

For added features and functionality, TCP has reserved the OPTIONS field. Depending on the option(s) used, the length of this field will vary in size, but it cannot be larger than 40 bytes due to the size of the header length field (4 bits). The Maximum Segment Size (MSS) option is the most common one used. The MSS is used to negotiate between the sender and the receiver the maximum size of the segment they will transfer. Other options for flow and congestion control such as time stamp for TCP segments can also be set using the OPTIONS field. The following are option codes that can be used in the OPTIONS field:

- No-Operation

  This option code may be used between options, such as to align the beginning of a subsequent option on a word boundary. There is no guarantee that senders will use this option, so receivers must be prepared to process options even if they do not begin on a word boundary.

- MSS

  If this option is present, then it communicates the maximum receive segment size at the TCP that sends this segment. This field must only be sent in the initial connection request (that is, in segments with the SYN control bit set). If this option is not used, any segment size is allowed.

Padding

The TCP header padding is used to ensure that the TCP header ends and data begins on a 32-bit boundary. The padding is composed of zeros.

In the next section, we will discuss the TCP header fields in a lot more detail.

TCP Connection Establishment and Termination

There are various steps that need to be completed before data is transferred to and from a client and server. The steps include the negotiations between the client and the server, which are part of the TCP connection establishment phase. Similarly, when the data transfer is complete, the client and server go through the steps of tearing down the connection so that other processes on the client and server can use them. These steps are part of TCP connection termination phase.

TCP Connection Establishment

TCP relies on the connection initiation and setup based on control information called a handshake. This handshake is an exchange of control information between the client and the server before data can be transferred. The handshake or the connection setup uses a three-step process called the three-way handshake. If we follow the communication between host A and host B, the TCP three-way handshake can be illustrated as shown in Figure 4-2.

Figure 4-2   *TCP Connection Establishment*

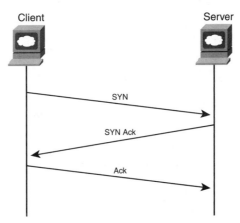

As shown in the figure, the following are steps that specify the details of the TCP connection establishment phase:

1   A client initiates the connection by sending a TCP segment with the SYN flag set. This segment tells the server that the client wants to establish a connection. The segment also contains the sequence number that the client will use as a starting number for its

segments. The segments are used to synchronize the data, as they might arrive out of order on the client or server receiving the data.

2 In response to the SYN segment received from the client, the server responds to the client with its own segment, which has the SYN bit and the ACK bit set (basically acknowledging the segment sent from client to server). The server will also set the sequence number that it will use for the communication.

3 Finally, the client sends a segment that acknowledges receipt of the server's segment, and this is the start of the transferring of data.

TCP Connection Termination

When the server and the client finish with the data transfers, they will conduct another exchange of segments containing the FIN bit set to close the connection. As opposed to the connection establishment phase, the connection termination phase includes the exchange of four segments. Because in TCP, the segments are arriving independently of each other in each direction, each connection end must shut down independently of the other. The connection termination phase can be illustrated as in Figure 4-3.

Figure 4-3 *TCP Connection Teardown*

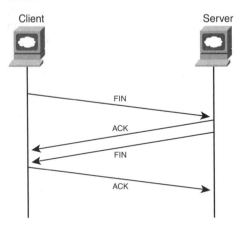

As shown in the figure, the following are steps that specify the details of the TCP connection termination phase:

1 The client generates a FIN segment because the application running on the client is closing the connection.

2 The server receives the FIN and signals its application that the client has requested to close the connection. The server immediately acknowledges (ACK) the FIN from the client.

3 As the application on the server decides to shut down, it initiates a FIN segment to the client to close the connection.

4 Upon receipt of the FIN segment from the server, the client acknowledges it with an ACK.

TCP Flow Control

The TCP flow control techniques are implemented to optimize the transfer of data between the client and the server along with the network parameters. The following sections discuss these flow control techniques:

- TCP acknowledgements, retransmission, and timeout
- Sliding window

TCP Acknowledgements, Retransmission, and Timeout

TCP manages the data it sends as a continuous byte stream, and it has to maintain the sequence in which bytes are sent and received. The Sequence Number and Acknowledgement Number fields in the TCP header keep track of the bytes.

To ensure that the segments of the data stream are properly received, both the client and the server need to know the segment's initial sequence number. The two ends of the connection synchronize byte-numbering systems exchanging SYN segments during the handshake. The Sequence Number field in the SYN segment contains the initial sequence number (ISN), which is the starting point for the byte-numbering system.

Each byte of data is numbered sequentially from the ISN, so the first real byte of data sent has a sequence number of ISN + 1. The sequence number in the header of a data segment identifies the sequential position in the data stream of the first data byte in the segment.

Since TCP's underlying network protocol is IP, one of the challenges that TCP faces is to manage segments that are received out of order or are lost. TCP has to manage all flow control and retransmissions because IP does not have any mechanisms to do so. During the TCP data transfer phase, the receiver acknowledges the longest contiguous prefix of stream that was received in order. Each segment is acknowledged, providing continuous feedback to the sender as the data transfer progresses. The TCP acknowledgement specifies the sequence number of the next octet that the receiver expects to receive. For example, if the first byte sent was numbered 1 and 5200 bytes have been successfully received, the acknowledgement number will be 5201.

For identifying the successful receipt of a segment, each time a TCP segment is delivered, there is a timer that starts and waits for an acknowledgement. If the timer expires before the segment has been acknowledged by the receiver, the TCP sender assumes that the segment was lost or corrupted and needs to be retransmitted. This timer is referred to as the retransmission timeout (RTO). This mechanism adapts to the changes in the networks and delays in acknowledgments and adjusts the RTO.

Sliding Window

TCP uses the Window field to manage the number of bytes the remote end is able to accept. If the receiver is capable of accepting 1000 more bytes, the window would be 1000. The window indicates to the sender that it can continue sending segments as long as the total number of bytes that it sends is smaller than the window of bytes the receiver can accept. The receiver controls the flow of bytes from the sender by changing the size of the window. A zero window tells the sender to cease transmission until it receives a non-zero window value. Both the sender and the receiver advertise the number of bytes each is willing to receive from the other. The window size reflects how much buffer size the receiving end is capable of handling. The sender has to obey the size of the window before delivering the segment.

Now that we have reviewed TCP and understood the session establishment and teardown, we will discuss our core Layer 7 protocol, HTTP, which rides on TCP.

Introduction to HTTP

When the Internet was first designed, the designers had to come up with the solution of clients being able to retrieve resources from servers. One of the most common features of a web page is a hyperlink. This is the clickable link on the web page that points to other resources.

For this concept to work, the uniqueness of the documents and names had to be globally maintained. The naming convention on the Web that is used to maintain the uniqueness of resources (web pages) is accomplished by the URL. The other issue that web designers had to address was how these resources would be represented and formatted in a uniform and readable format. This problem was solved by HTML. Web designers defined HTTP to determine how the various formats, such as text, graphics that make up the web content (HTML), and web page names (URLs), are transported from the client to the server and back.

The HTTP is the most common protocol for transferring resources on the Web. HTTP defines the format and meaning of messages exchanged between web components, such as clients and servers. A protocol is simply a language, similar to natural languages used by humans, except that it is used by machines or software components. In the next sections, we will look at the following:

- Protocol details
- HTTP header field
- Differences between versions

The protocol definitions can be found in RFC 2068, which defines HTTP version 1.1.

Protocol Details

HTTP is a stateless protocol. Statelessness implies the absence of a state maintenance, during the client and server communication. The HTTP protocol does not have any awareness of the previous client or server request or response. The decision not to maintain state in the HTTP protocol was to provide scalability on the Internet, where a large number of clients could be making connections to the server. If the server started to maintain state for each connection, the resources and the time for connections would increase drastically, hampering end user experience. However, for applications that did require state across the multiple HTTP requests, other enhancements and headers were included (such as cookies) to satisfy the requirements. Figure 4-4 shows a client browser accessing www.example.com.

Figure 4-4   *A Client Browser Accessing www.example.com*

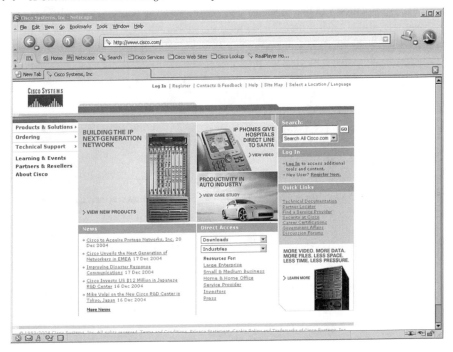

Following are some of the key details of the HTTP header.

HTTP Methods

A request method notifies the HTTP server of what action should be performed on the resource identified by the requested Uniform Resource Identifier (URI). The request method is included in a client's request along with several headers and a URI. The method is applied to the resource by the origin server, and a response is generated. The response consists of a response code, metadata information about the resource, and the other response headers. Following are some of the key HTTP request methods.

GET Method

The GET method requests a document from a specific location on the server. This is the main method used for document retrieval. The response to a GET request is returned to the requesting client. If the URI refers to a static file, a GET request will read the file and return it to the client. If the URI refers to an executable program or a script, the result of the program or script is returned as part of the body within the entity body portion of the request.

The GET method can be constructed to add modifier headers to yield different results; for example, if the If-Modified-Since modifier is used with the GET request along with a specified date, the server sends the appropriate response code based on the changes made to the resource according to the date specified.

Figure 4-5 shows a Sniffer capture of an HTTP GET request.

Figure 4-5   *Sniffer Capture of an HTTP Get Request*

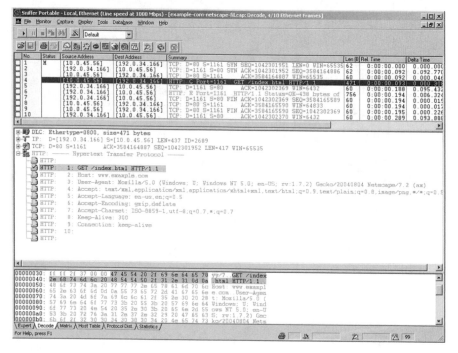

HEAD Method

The HEAD method is used to obtain the metadata information for the resource. There is no response body returned as a result of a HEAD request. However, the metadata that a server returns should be the same metadata that would be returned if the request method had been GET. One of the biggest advantages of using the HEAD method is to check the status of the resource without the overhead of the resource being returned. This method is widely used in SLBs to provide probes to check the resource availability of a server before being brought into rotation for load balancing client requests. Another advantage is that the HEAD method uses the modification time of a document.

POST Method

The POST method allows clients to provide data input to a data handling program, such as an executable script running on the server. The server on which this data handling program is being executed allows only for specific actions to be performed. Since the POST method can potentially change the contents of the resource, the clients need to have access rights to execute the process on the server. The POST method can be used for Common Gateway Interface (CGI) programs, gateway-to-network services, CLI programs, and database operations. In a POST request, the data sent to the server is in the entity body of the client's request. After the server processes the POST request and headers, it may pass the entity body to another program for processing. In some cases, a server's custom application programming interface (API) may handle the data, instead of a program external to the server. POST requests should be accompanied by a content-type header, describing the format of the client's entity body. The most commonly used format with POST is the URL-encoding scheme used for CGI applications. It allows form data to be translated into a list of variables and values.

PUT Method

The PUT method is similar to the POST in that processing in the method would typically result in a different version of the resource identified by the URI in the request. If the request URI does not exist, it is created, and if it already exists, it is modified. However, the resource identified in the PUT method alone would change as a result of the request. When using the PUT method, the data is sent as part of the request and not as part of the URI. When the client uses the PUT method, it requests that the included entity body should be stored on the server at the requested URL.

DELETE Method

The DELETE method is used to delete the resource identified by the request URI. This method is used to delete resources remotely; however, authorization with processing of the DELETE method is required.

TRACE Method

The TRACE method allows programmers to see how a client's message is modified as it passes through a series of proxy servers. The recipient of the TRACE method echoes the HTTP request headers back to the client. When the TRACE method is used with the Max-Forwards and Via headers, a client can determine the chain of intermediate proxy servers between the original client and the server.

URL

An URL is a means of identifying a resource that is accessible through the Internet. The URL is a special case of a URI that is understood by web servers. A URL is any string that uniquely identifies an Internet resource.

Each URL is composed of three parts, a mechanism (or protocol) for retrieving the resource, the hostname of the server that can provide the resource, and a name for the resource. The resource name is usually a filename preceded by a partial path, which is relative to the path defined for the root of the web server. Here is an example:

    http://www.cisco.com/en/US/support/index.html

In this example:

- The protocol is http; if no protocol is present, then most browsers default to http.
- The hostname or resource is www.cisco.com; this can be an IP address or a fully qualified domain name.
- The resource has a file called index.html; the path to the resource is en/US/support/.

HTTP Cookie

As the Internet has taken over the task of providing e-commerce applications to users, new requirements, such as maintaining a user to a specific server for a persistent connection, have become important. As mentioned earlier, HTTP is a stateless protocol where each HTTP request is independent of the other. For many applications, a server needs to track the user's request to send appropriate customized content to the user. This user tracking is extremely important for dynamic content, which provides user-specific information, such as the contents of a shopping cart. Earlier web servers tracked users by their IP addresses, but this became difficult as users starting connecting to servers from behind mega proxy links, such as AOL. In other words, an application cannot present the same shopping cart information for everyone using AOL.

Netscape resolved this issue by proposing the use of strings called cookies within HTTP headers. When the client sends the initial request to the server, the server returns a "Set-Cookie" header that gives a cookie name, expiry time, and other info. When the user returns to the same URL, the user's browser returns the cookie if it has not expired. Cookies can be long lived or per-session based.

Cookies are simply text-based strings. When a client makes a connection to a web server, a cookie is inserted in the HTTP response from the server back to the client. An additional line with the Set-Cookie field is added. For example, Figure 4-6 shows a response from a server with an HTTP Set-Cookie header.

Figure 4-6   *Sniffer Capture of an HTTP Response with a Set-Cookie*

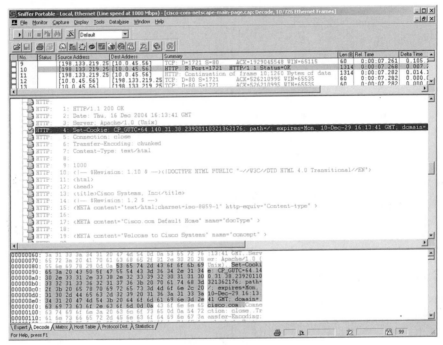

As the figure illustrates, the name of the cookie is the string "CP_GUTC," and the value for the cookie "CP_GUTC" is the numeric string that starts with "64.140." The path field indicates the particular directory within the site for which this cookie is valid. The path "/" indicates that the cookie is valid for all subdirectories and URL paths. The "expires" field specifies the validity time of the cookie. The client receives this cookie and stores it with the path and domain information for the period of time specified by the "expires" value. When the same client makes subsequent requests to the same URL, it uses the stored cookie in the HTTP GET. The Sniffer capture in Figure 4-7 shows how the client's second request has the cookie in the HTTP header.

Figure 4-7 *Sniffer Capture of the Second HTTP Request from the Client with the Cookie*

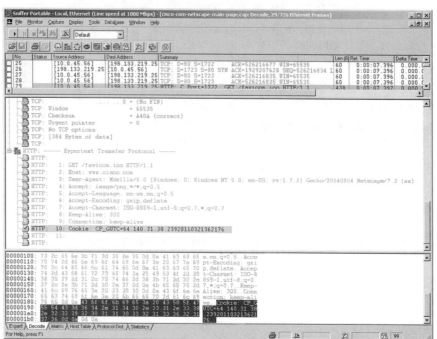

HTTP Cookie Parameters

As seen in the previous section, an HTTP cookie has six key parameters associated with it:

- The *name* and *value* of the cookie, a pair of strings used to identify the cookie and the value set for it. This is a mandatory header required by the Set-Cookie field.

- The *expiration date* of the cookie attribute specifies a date string that defines the validity of the cookie. The cookie is expired from the client browser and is no longer sent once the date has been reached. This is an optional header and is not required by the Set-Cookie field. If there is no expiration date sent from the server to the client, the cookie is considered a session cookie and is only valid for the length of the session to the URL. Once the client browser is closed, the cookie is not saved.

- The *path* the cookie sets is for the URL within which the cookie is valid. Pages outside of that path cannot read or use the cookie. If the path parameter is not set explicitly, then it defaults to the URL path of the document that the server is creating. If the path for the cookie is /test and the cookie value pair is test=ing123, the cookie will be sent along with the HTTP requests if those paths include /test/cgi-bin or /test/Cisco. As long as the /test is in the path, the cookie will be sent. The path "/" is the most general path and will send cookies to the sites associated with any HTTP requests the client issues.

- The *domain* value for the cookie is used when the server is doing a cookie match, and a comparison of the domain attributes of the cookie is made with the Internet domain name of the host from which the HTTP URL request is being requested. If a domain is matched, the request will be matched to the path of the request. The default value of the domain attribute is the domain of the server that generates the cookie response.

- The *secure* field specifies to transmit the cookie only if the connection is HTTPS, an SSL-encrypted connection. If secure is not specified, a cookie is considered safe to be sent in the clear text.

HTTP Header Fields

Headers are crucial to HTTP, as they determine the handling of a request. If a header is not recognized by the recipient, it should be ignored; if it is received by a proxy, it should be forwarded. HTTP (1.0) defines the following headers:

- General headers
- Request headers
- Response headers
- Entity headers

General Headers

General headers indicate general information, such as the date or whether the connection should be maintained. They are used by both clients and servers. The following are some of the general header fields:

- *The Date Header* in the corresponding response message indicates that the message was generated at the indicated time and has no bearing on when the associated entity may have been created or modified.

- *The Pragma* header permits directives to be sent to the recipient of the message. A directive is a way to request that components behave in a particular way while handling a request or a response.

- The *Connection* general header field allows the sender to specify options that are desired for that particular connection but that are not to be communicated by proxies over further connections.

- The *Trailer* general field value indicates that the given set of header fields is present in the trailer of a message encoded with chunked transfer coding.

- The *Transfer-Encoding* general header field indicates what (if any) type of transformation has been applied to the message body in order to safely transfer it between the sender and the recipient.

- The *Upgrade* general header allows the client to specify what additional communication protocols it supports and would like to use if the server finds it appropriate to switch protocols. The server must use the Upgrade header field within a 101 (Switching Protocols) response status code to indicate which protocol(s) are being switched.

- The *Upgrade* header field only applies to switching application-layer protocols upon the existing transport-layer connection. Upgrade cannot be used to insist on a protocol change; its acceptance and use by the server is optional. The capabilities and nature of the application-layer communication after the protocol change is entirely dependent upon the new protocol chosen, although the first action after changing the protocol must be a response to the initial HTTP request containing the Upgrade header field.

- The *Via* general header field must be used by gateways and proxies to indicate the intermediate protocols and recipients between the user agent and the server on requests, and between the origin server and the client on responses.

- The *Warning* general header field is used to carry additional information about the status or transformation of a message that might not be reflected in the message. This information is typically used to warn about a possible lack of semantic transparency from caching operations or transformations applied to the entity body of the message.

Request Headers

Request headers are used only for client's requests. They convey the client's configuration and desired format to the servers. Following are some of the request header fields:

- The *Authorization* header is used by the client to include the appropriate credentials required to access a resource. Certain resources cannot be accessed by the servers without proper authorization.

- The *From* header allows users to include their e-mail address as an identification. General use of the From header is discouraged, as it violates the privacy of the user.

- The *If-Modified-Since* header is a conditional header, indicating that the request may be handled in a different way based on the value specified in the header field.

- The *Referer* header lets the clients include the URI of the resource from which the request URI was obtained.

- The *Accept-Charset* request header field can be used to indicate what character sets are acceptable for the response. This field allows clients capable of understanding more comprehensive or special-purpose character sets to signal that capability to a server capable of representing documents in those character sets.

- The *Accept-Encoding* request header field is similar to Accept-Charset but restricts the content codings that are acceptable in the response. If an Accept-Encoding field is present in a request, and if the server cannot send a response that is acceptable according to the Accept-Encoding header, then the server should send an error response with the 406 (Not Acceptable) status code.

- The *Accept-Language* request header field is similar to Accept-Charset, but restricts the set of natural languages that are preferred as a response to the request.
- The *Authorization* field value consists of credentials containing the authentication information of the user agent for the realm of the resource being requested.
- The *Expect* request header field is used to indicate that particular server behaviors are required by the client.
- The *From* request header field, if given, should contain an Internet e-mail address for the human user who controls the requesting user agent.
- The *Host* request header field specifies the Internet host and port number of the resource being requested, as obtained from the original URI given by the client.
- The *If-Match* request header field is used with a method to make it conditional. A client that has one or more entities previously obtained from the resource can verify that one of those entities is current by including a list of their associated entity tags in the If-Match header field.
- The *If-Unmodified-Since* request header field is used with a method to make it conditional. If the requested resource has not been modified since the time specified in this field, the server should perform the requested operation as if the If-Unmodified-Since header were not present.
- The *Location* response header field is used to redirect the recipient to a location other than the Request-URI for completion of the request or identification of a new resource.
- The *Max-Forwards* request header field provides a mechanism with the TRACE and OPTIONS methods to limit the number of proxies or gateways that can forward the request to the next inbound server. This can be useful when the client is attempting to trace a request chain that appears to be failing or looping in mid-chain.
- The *Proxy-Authorization* request header field allows the client to identify itself (or its user) to a proxy that requires authentication. The Proxy-Authorization field value consists of credentials containing the authentication information of the user agent for the proxy and/or realm of the resource being requested.
- The *Referer* request header field allows the client to specify, for the server's benefit, the address (URI) of the resource from which the Request-URI was obtained (the "referrer," although the header field is misspelled.) The Referer request header allows a server to generate lists of back-links to resources for interest, logging, optimized caching, and so on. It also allows obsolete or mistyped links to be traced for maintenance.
- The *TE* request header field indicates what extension transfer-codings it is willing to accept in the response and whether it is willing to accept trailer fields in a chunked transfer coding.
- The *User-Agent* request header field contains information about the user agent originating the request. This is for statistical purposes, the tracing of protocol violations, and the automated recognition of user agents for the sake of tailoring responses to avoid particular user agent limitations.

Response Headers

Response headers are used only in server responses. They describe the server's configuration and information about the requested URL. The response headers start with the status line followed by the other request-initiated headers. The status line of the server's response includes the HTTP version number, a three-digit status code, and a textual description of the result.

HTTP defines a few specific codes in each range, although these ranges will become more populated as HTTP evolves. If a client cannot decipher a status code, it should be able to understand its basic meaning from its numerical range.

Following are some of the response header fields:

- *Status-Line* is the first line of a response message and consists of the protocol version followed by a numeric status code and its associated textual phrase. HTTP status codes are extensible. Following are key status code definitions from RFC 2616:
  - 1xx Informational
  - 100 Continue
  - 101 Switching Protocols
  - 2xx Successful
  - 200 OK
  - 201 Created
  - 202 Accepted
  - 203 Non-Authoritative Information
  - 204 No Content
  - 205 Reset Content
  - 206 Partial Content
  - 3xx Redirection
  - 300 Multiple Choices
  - 301 Resource Moved Permanently
  - 301 Resource Moved Temporarily
  - 303 See Other
  - 304 Not Modified
  - 305 Use Proxy
  - 306 (Unused)
  - 307 Temporary Redirect

- — 4xx Client Error
- — 400 Bad Request
- — 401 Unauthorized
- — 402 Payment Required
- — 403 Forbidden
- — 404 Not Found
- — 405 Method Not Allowed
- — 406 Not Acceptable
- — 407 Proxy Authentication Required
- — 408 Request Timeout
- — 409 Conflict
- — 410 Gone
- — 411 Length Required
- — 412 Precondition Failed
- — 413 Request Entity Too Large
- — 414 Request-URI Too Long
- — 415 Unsupported Media Type
- — 416 Requested Range Not Satisfiable
- — 417 Expectation Failed
- — 5xx Server Error
- — 500 Internal Server Error
- — 501 Not Implemented
- — 502 Bad Gateway
- — 503 Service Unavailable
- — 504 Gateway Timeout
- — 505 HTTP Version Not Supported

- The *Age* response header field conveys the sender's estimate of the amount of time since the response (or its revalidation) was generated at the origin server. A cached response is "fresh" if its age does not exceed its freshness lifetime.

- The *ETag* response header field provides the current value of the entity tag for the requested variant.

- The *Location* response header field is used to redirect the recipient to a location other than the Request-URI for completion of the request or identification of a new resource.

- The *Proxy-Authenticate* response header field must be included as part of a 407 (Proxy Authentication Required) status code response. The field value consists of a challenge that indicates the authentication scheme and parameters applicable to the proxy for this Request-URI.

- The *Server* response header field contains information about the software used by the origin server to handle the request.

- The *Vary* field value indicates the set of request header fields that fully determines, while the response is fresh, whether a cache is permitted to use the response to reply to a subsequent request without revalidation.

- The *WWW-Authenticate* response header field must be included in 401 (Unauthorized) response messages. The field value consists of at least one challenge that indicates the authentication scheme(s) and parameters applicable to the Request-URI.

Entity Headers

Entity headers describe the document format of the data being sent between the client and the server. Although entity headers are most commonly used by the server when returning a requested document, they are also used by clients when using the POST and PUT methods. Following are some of the entity header fields:

- The *Content-Encoding* entity header field is used as a modifier to the media-type. When present, its value indicates what additional content codings have been applied to the entity body, and thus what decoding mechanisms must be applied in order to obtain the media type referenced by the Content-Type header field.

- The *Content-Language* entity header field describes the natural language(s) of the intended audience for the enclosed entity. Note that this might not be equivalent to all the languages used within the entity body.

- The *Content-Length* entity header field indicates the size of the entity body, in decimal number of OCTETs, sent to the recipient—or, in the case of the HEAD method, the size of the entity body that would have been sent had the request been a GET.

- The *Content-Location* entity header field may be used to supply the resource location for the entity enclosed in the message when that entity is accessible from a location separate from the requested resource's URI. A server should provide a Content-Location for the variant corresponding to the response entity. Especially in the case where a resource has multiple entities associated with it and those entities actually have separate locations by which they might be individually accessed, the server should provide a Content-Location for the particular variant returned.

- The *Content-MD5* entity header field, as defined in RFC 1864, is an MD5 digest of the entity body for the purpose of providing an end-to-end message integrity check (MIC) of the entity body. (Note that a MIC is good for detecting accidental modification of the entity body in transit, but it is not proof against malicious attacks.)

- The *Content-Range* entity header is sent with a partial entity body to specify where in the full entity body the partial body should be applied. The Content-Type entity header field indicates the media type of the entity body sent to the recipient or, in the case of the HEAD method, the media type that would have been sent had the request been a GET.

- The *Expires* entity header field gives the date and time after which the response is considered stale. A stale cache entry cannot normally be returned by a cache (either a proxy cache or a user agent cache) unless it is first validated with the origin server (or with an intermediate cache that has a fresh copy of the entity).

- The *Last-Modified* entity header field indicates the date and time at which the origin server believes the variant was last modified.

Differences Between HTTP Versions 1.0 and 1.1

The following sections discuss some of the key differences between HTTP 1.0 and 1.1:

- Persistent connections
- Chunked messages
- Hostname
- Pipelining requests

Persistent Connections

Persistent connection is the main difference between version 1.0 and 1.1. HTTP 1.0, in its documented form, made no provision for persistent connections. Some HTTP 1.0 implementations use a Keep-Alive header to request that a connection persist.

HTTP 1.1 makes persistent connections by default. HTTP 1.1 clients, servers, and proxies assume that a connection will be kept open after the transmission of a request and its response. The protocol does allow an implementation to close a connection at any time, in order to manage its resources, although it is best to do so only after the end of a response.

Chunked Messages

HTTP 1.1 resolves the problem of delimiting message bodies by introducing the chunked transfer coding. The sender breaks the message body into chunks of arbitrary length, and each chunk is sent with its length prepended; it marks the end of the message with a zero-length chunk. The sender uses the transfer encoding chunked header to signal the use of chunking.

This mechanism allows the sender to buffer small pieces of the message, instead of the entire message, without adding much complexity or overhead. All HTTP 1.1 implementations must be able to receive chunked messages.

Hostname

HTTP 1.0 requests do not pass the hostname as part of the request URL. For example, if a user makes a request for the resource at URL http://www.cisco.com/index.html, the browser sends a message with the following request line to the server at www.cisco.com:

    GET /index.html HTTP/1.0

This prevents the binding of another HTTP server hostname, such as exampleB.org to the same IP address, because the server receiving such a message cannot tell which server the message is meant for.

HTTP 1.1 requires that requests include a Host header that carries the hostname. This converts the preceding example to:

    GET /index.html HTTP/1.1
    Host: www.cisco.com

If the URL references a port other than the default (TCP port 80), this is also given in the Host header.

Pipelining Requests

Although HTTP 1.1 encourages the transmission of multiple requests over a single TCP connection, each request must still be sent in one contiguous message, and a server must send responses in the order that it received the corresponding requests. However, a client need not wait to receive the response for one request before sending another request on the same connection. In fact, a client could send an arbitrarily large number of requests over a TCP connection before receiving any of the responses. This practice, known as pipelining, can greatly improve performance. It avoids the need to wait for network round-trips, and it makes the best possible use of the TCP protocol.

Layer 7 Load Balancing Mechanisms

In the previous section, we covered the HTTP protocol in detail. You now understand the URLs, methods, and cookies. In Layer 7 load balancing, the SLB device proxies the client's TCP connection and receives the HTTP request. The SLB device buffers the client request and parses through it. The load balancer can perform many functions while inspecting the HTTP header. Following are some of the key mechanisms that can be used in Layer 7 load balancing:

- HTTP methods-based load balancing
- HTTP URL-based load balancing
- HTTP cookie-based load balancing
- HTTP cookie passive-based load balancing
- HTTP cookie learn-based load balancing

HTTP Methods-Based Load Balancing

The SLB device can definitely inspect the HTTP method used by the client and make appropriate load-balancing decisions. For instance, the SLB device can be configured to distribute GET and POST methods to separate server farms. The SLB device can easily drop DELETE method calls to prevent hackers from deleting web content.

HTTP URL-Based Load Balancing

The SLB device can inspect the HTTP URL and make appropriate load-balancing decisions. The device can distribute requests based on access content or application to different server farms. For example, all .cgi requests can be sent to servers optimized for request processing and computation, while all static content requests (.htm, .gif, and so on) can be sent to servers with a lot of disk space. Similarly, server management can be eased up by keeping separate server farms for /sports/* and /news/*. Figure 4-8 shows how a Layer 7 load-balancing device can be used to inspect HTTP requests and distribute client requests based on content type.

Figure 4-8   *Layer 7 SLB Used for Distributed Content*

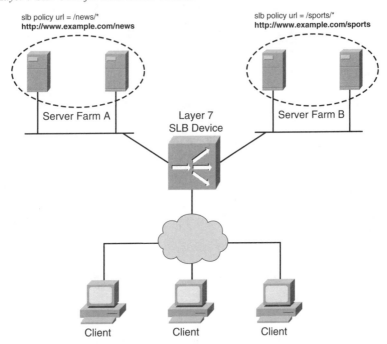

Figure 4-9 shows how a Layer 7 load-balancing device can be used to inspect HTTP requests and distribute client requests based on the applications being accessed.

Figure 4-9   *Layer 7 SLB Used for Distributed Applications*

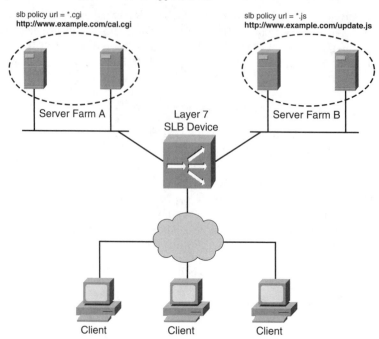

HTTP Cookie-Based Load Balancing

The SLB device can make a load-balancing decision based on the clients' cookies. This is vital for applications, such as Web Logic, which uses multiple cookies to provide client session redundancy.

The Content Switching Module (CSM) has the "Cookie" expression matching feature that can filter for a specific cookie name and value. In this configuration, the CSM is not looking at the "cookie" inserted by the server; it is only matching the cookie in the client HTTP request. For example:

```
 !
 map COOKIE_SERVER1 cookie
  match protocol http cookie CookieName cookie-value 101617
 !
 map COOKIE_SERVER2 cookie
  match protocol http cookie CookieName cookie-value 101327
 !
```

Each cookie map maps to a policy that has a single server farm. All the policies are added to the virtual. A default policy needs to be configured to make sure the user request is load balanced across the servers in case a cookie match is not found in the user HTTP GET. In cookie matching, the cookie name needs to be a specific name, while the value of the cookie can be a regular expression.

The functional steps of the cookie matching feature are as follows:

1 The user connects to the virtual server. The CSM proxies the TCP connect and waits for the HTTP GET.

2 The HTTP GET is received from the user, and then the CSM parses the GET and searches for the configured cookie names. If a match is found, the policy action is taken.

3 If a cookie match is not found, the default policy is used to load balance the user among the servers.

HTTP Cookie Passive-Based Persistence

When making persistent session decisions on cookies, the SLB device can read the cookie value for the specified named cookie that the server has installed and send the next request to the first server. This basically means that the load balancer reads the cookies set by the server. The HTTP cookie values from each server would need to be different and also to be configured on the SLB device.

HTTP Cookie Learn-Based Persistence

Cookie learn-based persistence (also known as cookie sticky) is similar to passive-based persistence except that in this mode the SLB device dynamically learns the cookie values set by the server for each client and stores them in the cookie sticky table.

The CSM supports the cookie sticky feature. It requires the real server to insert the cookie into the HTTP reply. Assume that you configure the real server to insert cookie *"USERID=<xyz>";* where "USERID" is the name of the cookie and "xyz" is a unique per-user value. The CSM can stick the user to a real server based on the value of cookie "USERID".

The cookie name is case sensitive. Configuration is fairly simple; for example:

```
module ContentSwitchingModule 9
 !
 serverfarm REALS
  nat server
  no nat client
  real 10.2.6.17
   inservice
  real 10.2.6.27
   inservice
 !
 sticky 10 cookie USERID timeout 60
 !
 vserver WWW
  virtual 10.2.44.56 tcp www
  serverfarm REALS
  sticky 60 group 10
  inservice
 !
```

Functional steps of the cookie sticky feature are as follows:

1   The user connects to the virtual server. The CSM proxies the TCP connect and waits for the HTTP GET.

2   The HTTP GET is received from the user, and then the CSM parses the GET and searches for the configured cookie name (USERID). If the cookie is found with a non-null value, that value is searched in the sticky table and the user is sent to the server that first issued the cookie.

3   If the cookie "USERID" is not found, the configured load-balancing method is used to select an available server—let's say real 10.2.6.17 is selected.

4   Real server 10.2.6.17 sends an HTTP response. The CSM parses through the response and searches for the "USERID" cookie. If there is a set cookie (let's say USERID=znaseh), then the CSM adds that to the sticky table. Thus the sticky table looks like this:

```
znaseh ---- 10.2.6.17
```

5   Next time the client comes in with USERID=znaseh, the request would be sent to server 10.2.6.17.

HTTP Cookie Insert-Based Persistence

The current load balancer can even insert cookies in the HTTP headers to provide persistence. This is a unique feature where the SLB device adds a cookie (name and value) into the HTTP response from the server. The client accepts the cookie as being sent by the server when in fact it comes from the SLB device.

The CSM supports the cookie insert feature. This feature is used when you want to use a session cookie for persistence if the server is not currently setting the appropriate cookie. With this feature enabled, the CSM inserts the cookie in the response from the server to the client.

The following example shows how to specify a cookie insert feature for session persistence:

```
module ContentSwitchingModule 9
!
sticky 25 cookie USERID insert timeout 30
!
 vserver WWW
  virtual 10.2.44.56 tcp www
  serverfarm REALS
  sticky 30 group 25
  inservice
 !
```

Case Study: Layer 7–Based Solution

Now that we understand TCP and HTTP protocol definitions and Layer 7 load-balancing functionality, we will start our discussion of how this solution should be deployed to solve various application scalability and security needs. Deploying a Layer 7–based load-balancing solution requires extensive planning and research on how the application functions.

In this case study, we will examine a specific customer deployment where three different applications are being deployed: an online download application, an online shop application, and an online user profile application. We will show how each application's requirements are achieved by our Layer 7 load-balancing solution. The product of choice used in this solution is the CSM on the Cisco Catalyst 6500 Series Switch. The idea behind the following case study and others in chapters in the rest of the book is to understand not only the concepts but the implementation details.

In this case study, we will focus on server and application requirements. The management and security requirements as well as the infrastructure requirements stay the same as those defined in the Chapter 3 case study.

Server and Application Requirements

Server and application requirements for this case study are defined as follows:

- Directly manage the servers from the front end (client-side network)
- Number of servers 20—100 per site
- Following three different applications with their own distinct requirements
- Online Download Services Application
  - This custom application provides web-based software download capabilities to the clients.
  - Use TCP server port 80 for the client connections initiated to the server.
  - Clients can be distinguished by the URLs they use. Partner and premium clients should be sent to the high-end server farm. This ensures that the premium customers and partners get expedited services.
  - Source IP—based stickiness is needed for this application for up to 20 minutes.
- Online Shop Application
  - This custom application provides web-based software purchase capabilities to the client.
  - TCP/80, TCP/443
  - This is a secure application and only allowed on TCP port 443. A client that sends requests on HTTP (TCP:80) should be redirected to come back on the HTTPS site.
  - Source IP—based stickiness is needed for this application for up to 30 minutes.

- Online User Profile Application

  — This custom application provides web-based user profile update capabilities to the client.

  — TCP/80.

  — This application provides different features to internal and external users. The internal and external users should be sent to different servers. The internal and external users will use different domain names to reach the application.

  — No stickiness is required for this application.

- TCP-based keep alive required for all the application servers

- Potentially, server persistence needed when user transitions from HTTP to HTTPS

Infrastructure Configuration

In the Layer 7 SLB design, the CSM is used in routed mode with one client-side VLAN (12) and one server-side VLAN (112). The CSM's default gateway is the HSRP group IP on the MSFC, and the server's default gateway is the alias IP address on the CSM.

Following is the infrastructure configuration of the CSM, showing the client- and server-side VLANs. Notice that there are two VLANs defined. The client VLAN 12 is the client-facing VLAN, which also has a gateway defined (acting as the default gateway for the CSM) and the server VLAN 112, which is the server-facing VLAN. These VLANs are part of the port-channel from the CSM to the Supervisor (the Layer 2 Switch on the Cisco Catalyst 6500 Series Switch). Traffic will be forwarded from the Client VLAN 12 and will hit a vserver; from there it will be forwarded to the server VLAN 112 to be forwarded to the server. The alias address is the virtual address that is shared between the active and the standby CSM. The alias IP address shares a virtual MAC (Layer 2) address between the active and standby, and only the active CSM responds to requests for the virtual MAC address.

```
module ContentSwitchingModule 9
 vlan 12 client
  ip address 10.2.10.5 255.255.255.0
  gateway 10.2.10.1
  alias 10.2.10.4 255.255.255.0
 !
 vlan 112 server
  ip address 10.2.12.2 255.255.255.0
  alias 10.2.12.1 255.255.255.0
 !
```

Probe Configuration

Following are the probes that would be used to provide the health check of the applications. Notice the two kinds of probes that are defined (HTTP and TCP). The HTTP probe issues an HTTP GET request to the server under the server farm HTTP (under the server farm configuration for the real servers 10.2.12.27 and 10.2.12.28), and it expects to get a 200 OK status back for it to keep the real server operational and for it to be forwarded connections from the client. Similarly, for the server farm TCP, the probe TCP will issue a TCP SYN to the real servers, and expects to receive a SYN-ACK back for the real servers to be operational and for it to be forwarded connections from the client. The frequencies for the probes to check the status of the real servers are defined by keyword interval (under the probe configuration) in seconds. The interval is the time in between probes when the real server is operational. The keyword **retries** is an integer used to set the number of failed probes that are allowed before marking the server as nonoperational. The **failed** keyword is used to set the time in seconds, in between probes when the real servers have been marked as nonoperational. The port numbers for these probes, if not defined under the probe configurations, are inherited from the server farm; if not defined under the server farm, the port numbers are inherited from the vserver. For the probe to be activated, the vserver (which has the server farm configuration) needs to be activated.

```
!
 probe HTTP http
   request method get url /keepalive.html
   expect status 200
   interval 5
   failed 5
!
 probe TCP tcp
   interval 5
   retries 2
   failed 5
!
serverfarm HTTP
   nat server
   no nat client
   real 10.2.12.27
    inservice
   real 10.2.12.28
    inservice
   probe HTTP
!
serverfarm TCP
   nat server
   no nat client
   real 10.2.12.27
    inservice
   real 10.2.12.28
    inservice
   probe TCP
!
```

Online Download Application

Following is the solution that meets the custom Online Download Application requirements. Notice how the URL maps capture partner and premium client requests. Clients without the partner and premium in their URLs are sent to the default server farm.

```
!
 map ONL_URLS url
   match protocol http url /partner/*
   match protocol http url /premium/*
```

```
!
sticky 11 netmask 255.255.255.255 timeout 20
sticky 12 netmask 255.255.255.255 timeout 20
!
 serverfarm ONL_80_DEF
  nat server
  no nat client
  real 10.2.12.27
   inservice
  real 10.2.12.28
   inservice
  probe TCP
!
 serverfarm ONL_80_URL
  nat server
  no nat client
  real 10.2.12.17
   inservice
  real 10.2.12.18
   inservice
  probe TCP
!
!
 policy ONL_80_URL
  url-map ONL_URLS
  sticky-group 11
  serverfarm ONL_80_URL
!
 policy ONL_80_DEF
  sticky-group 12
  serverfarm ONL_80_DEF
!
 vserver V_ONL_80
  virtual 10.2.10.101 tcp www
  vlan 12
  replicate csrp connection
  persistent rebalance
  slb-policy ONL_80_URL
  slb-policy ONL_80_DEF
  inservice
!
!
```

Online Shop Application

The Online Shop Application solution is shown here. Notice how the *webhost relocation* feature is used to send an HTTP 302 to the client when it arrives on clear text TCP port 80.

```
!
 serverfarm SHOP_443
  nat server
  no nat client
  real 10.2.12.57
   inservice
  real 10.2.12.58
   inservice
!
 serverfarm SHOP_80
  nat server
  no nat client
```

```
  redirect-vserver REDIRECT
  webhost relocation https://shop.example.com/
   inservice
!
!
sticky 13 netmask 255.255.255.255 timeout 30
!
 policy SHOP_80
  serverfarm SHOP_80
!
 policy SHOP_443
  sticky-group 13
  serverfarm SHOP_443
!
 vserver SHOP_443
  virtual 10.2.10.105 tcp https
  vlan 12
  replicate csrp sticky
  replicate csrp connection
  persistent rebalance
  slb-policy SHOP_443
  inservice
!
 vserver REDIRECT
  virtual 10.2.10.105 tcp www
  vlan 12
  persistent rebalance
  slb-policy SHOP_80
  inservice
!
```

Online User Profile Application

The Online User Profile Application requirements are met by the following solution. Notice how the http field and header information is specified by the USER_EXT map for the profile.example.com domain and the USER_INT header for the inprofile.example.com domain. Under the vserver, both the policies are applied and will be checked in linear order (that is, the USER_INT policy will be checked first and then the USER_EXT policy). Once a match is found based on the HTTP HOST header value, the real servers for the server farms defined under the policy will be forwarded the client request.

```
!
!
 map USER_EXT header
  match protocol http header Host header-value profile.example.com
!
 map USER_INT header
  match protocol http header Host header-value inprofile.example.com
!
 serverfarm USER_EXT
  nat server
  no nat client
  real 10.2.12.47
   inservice
  real 10.2.12.48
   inservice
  probe TCP
!
 serverfarm USER_INT
  nat server
```

```
   no nat client
   real 10.2.12.57
    inservice
   real 10.2.12.58
    inservice
   probe TCP
 !
 !
 policy USER_EXT
  header-map USER_EXT
  serverfarm USER_EXT
 !
 policy USER_INT
  header-map USER_INT
  serverfarm USER_INT
 !
 vserver V_ONL_80
  virtual 10.2.10.107 tcp www
  vlan 12
  replicate csrp connection
  persistent rebalance
  slb-policy USER_INT
  slb-policy USER_EXT
  inservice
 !
```

Maximum HTTP Request Parse Length

The key to note in the following captures is the maximum parse length. The parse length is
the number of bytes the CSM will look through in an HTTP request in search of the
configured URLs or cookies. If the configured data is not found within the parse length, the
client request is discarded.

```
CAT-Native-4#show module contentSwitching 9 vservers name V_ONL_80 detail
V_ONL_80, type = SLB, state = OUTOFSERVICE, v_index = 14
  virtual = 10.2.10.101/32:80 bidir, TCP, service = NONE, advertise = FALSE
  idle = 3600, replicate csrp = connection, vlan = 12, pending = 30, layer 7
  max parse len = 2000, persist rebalance = TRUE
  ssl sticky offset = 0, length = 32
  conns = 0, total conns = 0
  Policy          Tot matches  Client pkts  Server pkts
  -------------------------------------------------------
  ONL_80_URL      0            0            0
  ONL_80_DEF      0            0            0
  (default)       0            0            0
CAT-Native-4#
```

Notice next how the parse length can be increased up to 4000 bytes from within the virtual
server configuration mode.

```
CAT-Native-4#conf t
Enter configuration commands, one per line.  End with CNTL/Z.
CAT-Native-4(config)#
CAT-Native-4(config)#module contentSwitchingModule 9
CAT-Native(config-module-csm)# vserver V_ONL_80
CAT-Nativ(config-slb-vserver)#
CAT-Nativ(config-slb-vserver)#parse-length ?
  <1-4000>  maximum number of bytes to parse
CAT-Nativ(config-slb-vserver)#parse-length 4000
CAT-Nativ(config-slb-vserver)#exit
```

```
CAT-Native(config-module-csm)#exit
CAT-Native-4(config)#exit
CAT-Native-4#
CAT-Native-4#show module contentSwi 9 vservers name V_ONL_80 detail
V_ONL_80, type = SLB, state = OUTOFSERVICE, v_index = 14
  virtual = 10.2.10.101/32:80 bidir, TCP, service = NONE, advertise = FALSE
  idle = 3600, replicate csrp = connection, vlan = 12, pending = 30, layer 7
  max parse len = 4000, persist rebalance = TRUE
  ssl sticky offset = 0, length = 32
  conns = 0, total conns = 0
  Policy            Tot matches  Client pkts  Server pkts
  -----------------------------------------------------------
  ONL_80_URL        0            0            0
  ONL_80_DEF        0            0            0
  (default)         0            0            0
CAT-Native-4#
```

Parse length can also be increased globally by adjusting the MAX_PARSE_LEN_
MULTIPLIER global variable.

```
CAT-Native-4#conf t
Enter configuration commands, one per line.  End with CNTL/Z.
CAT-Native-4(config)#
CAT-Native-4(config)#
CAT-Native-4(config)#module contentSwitchingModule 9
CAT-Native(config-module-csm)#
CAT-Native(config-module-csm)#vserver V_ONL_80
CAT-Nativ(config-slb-vserver)#parse-length 1500
CAT-Nativ(config-slb-vserver)#exit
CAT-Native(config-module-csm)#variable MAX_PARSE_LEN_MULTIPLIER 3
CAT-Native(config-module-csm)#exit
CAT-Native-4(config)#exit
CAT-Native-4#
CAT-Native-4#show module contentSwitching 9 vservers name V_ONL_80 detail
V_ONL_80, type = SLB, state = OUTOFSERVICE, v_index = 14
  virtual = 10.2.10.101/32:80 bidir, TCP, service = NONE, advertise = FALSE
  idle = 3600, replicate csrp = connection, vlan = 12, pending = 30, layer 7
  max parse len = 4500, persist rebalance = TRUE
  ssl sticky offset = 0, length = 32
  conns = 0, total conns = 0
  Policy            Tot matches  Client pkts  Server pkts
  -----------------------------------------------------------
  ONL_80_URL        0            0            0
  ONL_80_DEF        0            0            0
  (default)         0            0            0
CAT-Native-4#
CAT-Native-4#
```

CSM Configuration

The following is the completed CSM configuration:

```
module ContentSwitchingModule 9
 vlan 12 client
  ip address 10.2.10.5 255.255.255.0
  gateway 10.2.10.1
  alias 10.2.10.4 255.255.255.0
 !
 vlan 112 server
  ip address 10.2.12.2 255.255.255.0
  alias 10.2.12.1 255.255.255.0
```

```
!
variable MAX_PARSE_LEN_MULTIPLIER 3
!
 map ONL_URLS url
   match protocol http url /partner/*
   match protocol http url /premium/*
!
 map USER_EXT header
   match protocol http header Host header-value profile.example.com
!
 map USER_INT header
   match protocol http header Host header-value inprofile.example.com
!
 probe HTTP http
   request method get url /keepalive.html
   expect status 200
   interval 5
   failed 5
!
 probe TCP tcp
   interval 5
   retries 2
   failed 5
!
sticky 11 netmask 255.255.255.255 timeout 20
sticky 12 netmask 255.255.255.255 timeout 20
sticky 13 netmask 255.255.255.255 timeout 30
!
 serverfarm ONL_80_DEF
   nat server
   no nat client
   real 10.2.12.27
    inservice
   real 10.2.12.28
    inservice
   probe TCP
!
 serverfarm ONL_80_URL
   nat server
   no nat client
   real 10.2.12.17
    inservice
   real 10.2.12.18
    inservice
   probe TCP
!
 serverfarm SHOP_443
   nat server
   no nat client
   real 10.2.12.57
    inservice
   real 10.2.12.58
    inservice
!
 serverfarm SHOP_80
   nat server
   no nat client
   redirect-vserver REDIRECT
    webhost relocation https://shop.example.com/
    inservice
!
 serverfarm USER_EXT
   nat server
   no nat client
```

```
     real 10.2.12.47
      inservice
     real 10.2.12.48
      inservice
     probe TCP
 !
  serverfarm USER_INT
  nat server
  no nat client
  real 10.2.12.57
   inservice
  real 10.2.12.58
   inservice
  probe TCP
 !
  policy ONL_80_URL
   url-map ONL_URLS
   sticky-group 11
   serverfarm ONL_80_URL
 !
  policy ONL_80_DEF
   sticky-group 12
   serverfarm ONL_80_DEF
 !
 policy SHOP_80
   serverfarm SHOP_80
 !
  policy SHOP_443
   sticky-group 13
   serverfarm SHOP_443
 !
 policy USER_EXT
   header-map USER_EXT
   serverfarm USER_EXT
 !
  policy USER_INT
   header-map USER_INT
   serverfarm USER_INT
 !
  vserver V_ONL_80
   virtual 10.2.10.101 tcp www
   vlan 12
   replicate csrp connection
   persistent rebalance
   slb-policy ONL_80_URL
   slb-policy ONL_80_DEF
   inservice
 !
 vserver SHOP_443
   virtual 10.2.10.105 tcp https
   vlan 12
   replicate csrp sticky
   replicate csrp connection
   persistent rebalance
   slb-policy SHOP_443
   inservice
 !
  vserver REDIRECT
   virtual 10.2.10.105 tcp www
   vlan 12
   persistent rebalance
   slb-policy SHOP_80
   inservice
 !
```

```
vserver V_ONL_80
  virtual 10.2.10.107 tcp www
  vlan 12
  replicate csrp connection
  persistent rebalance
  slb-policy USER_INT
  slb-policy USER_EXT
  inservice
!
```

Test and Verification

Test and verification of the Layer 7 application load-balanced environment is a lot more critical than for Layer 4 SLB solutions. This is because in the case of the Layer 7 load-balancing solution the SLB device has to proxy the client TCP connect and to buffer and search through the HTTP request. Each application is unique with respective to the number of sockets used, duration of TCP connections, activity in each session in terms of packets per second, idle timeouts, the size and number of the HTTP cookie, the TCP MSS value used, and so on. Thus, it is critical to test and verify the Layer 7 SLB environment with the particular applications.

Following are a few critical test cases that should be verified after a new deployment or a major or minor infrastructure change.

- Verifying and testing an exact trace of a production client load-balanced session.
- Verifying and testing a completed transaction with authentication and authorization from the client to the server.
- Verifying and testing a server-initiated session to a back-end database or internal application server.
- Verifying and testing a server-initiated backup or data replication session.
- Verifying and testing an application daemon failure and detection by the load balancer.
- Testing with clients using different browser types, such as Netscape, MS IE, Opera, Mozilla Firefox, and so on.
- Testing with clients coming in from behind different service providers and different service types, such as DSL, Cable broadband, wireless, dial-up, AOL, and so on.

Summary

This chapter introduced the Layer 7 load-balancing technology. The chapter covered the TCP and HTTP protocols and defined the protocol header fields and how they can be used in scaling applications. The TCP connection establishment and connection termination via the TCP SYN and SYN-ACK acknowledgements was discussed in detail. Similarly, based on the TCP handshakes between the client and the server, the HTTP Request and Response headers were analyzed. The HTTP Cookie solution and how the URLs are handled by the HTTP protocol brought to light how load balancers handle the implementation of these HTTP features. The enhancements of persistent connections and having hostnames in HTTP 1.1 were reviewed. Several Layer 7 solutions, such as URL or HTTP header-based load balancing were also presented. In order to combine all the concepts of Layer 7 SLB from the perspective of the CSM platform, this chapter also presented a case study. This case study focused on the deployment scenario of a real-world enterprise solution where three distinct applications were being deployed. The applications illustrated the CSM Layer 7 load-balancing functionality via the use of HTTP URLs and HEADERS to match specific client connections to specific servers. The infrastructure setup for the CSM client and server VLANs and how the CSM operates probes to the server farms were reviewed. CSM configurations were provided to introduce the reader to the Layer 7 configuration CLI.

With the increased demand for security and for security devices to perform at greater speeds, Chapter 5 discusses firewall load balancing.

Firewall Load Balancing

This chapter introduces the reader to firewall load-balancing (FWLB) concepts, technology, and designs. We will talk about motivations behind FWLB solutions, different types of firewalls, and how to load balance them. Reference design options and configurations will be discussed.

At the end of the chapter, we discuss a case study that implements FWLB in a network with multiple secure segments using Cisco's module-based load balancer for the Catalyst 6500 (Cat6500), the Content Switching Module (CSM). Details of the CSM and Catalyst 6500 configurations are included together with an explanation of various key commands.

Reasons for and Benefits of FWLB

In today's data centers, the security of the network, servers and application is a key concern. Together with VPN concentrators, Secure Socket Layer (SSL) offload devices, and intrusion detection devices, firewalls are a vital component of secure data center infrastructures. Firewalls are used not just to protect against malicious or unauthorized access from the public segment but also across multiple demilitarized zones (DMZ) and server segments. When a firewall accepts a packet from one segment, it sends the packet through to the other segment. A firewall can modify a packet before passing it through or can send it through unaltered. When a firewall rejects a packet, it usually drops the packet and logs the dropped packet as an event. After a session is established and a flow of packets begins, a firewall can monitor each packet in the flow or allow the flow to continue unmonitored, depending on the policies configured on that firewall.

There are several motivations behind load-balancing firewalls, the key ones being scalability, redundancy, and manageability.

Scalability

Firewalls are physical devices that exist between network segments, typically in a routed design. They perform stateful inspection of sessions going through them from one segment to the other. Firewalls block or permit sessions based on configured security policies and rules. A firewall has limited resources in terms of link speed, memory, and processor power. These factors determine the capacity and capability of the device in terms of session scalability and raw packet-switching performance.

FWLB is necessary when multiple parallel firewalls are deployed to overcome performance limitations in terms of throughput, session rate, and session capacity. FWLB allows you to scale firewall protection by distributing traffic across multiple firewalls on a per-connection basis. In a load-balanced solution, all packets between a pair of IP addresses for a particular session, in either direction, traverse the same firewall. The firewall then allows or denies transmission of individual packets across its interfaces.

Redundancy

One of the primary reasons for FWLB is high availability of the secure path provided by the firewall. Typical firewalls, like Cisco Private Internet Exchange (PIX) firewall, do provide redundancy capability in active/backup fashion. In these scenarios, one firewall is functional and active while the other is in silent mode. Both the firewalls share an interface IP address, thus enabling continuance of traffic flow in case of a device failure.

FWLB takes the firewall redundancy to the next level by load balancing traffic to a group of active and functional firewalls. A firewall failure is detected within seconds by the load balancer, which takes that specific firewall out of rotation. As long as a single firewall within the load-balanced group is functional, the secure path stays connected.

Manageability

Firewall rule and policy changes have always been a difficult task that requires careful planning and change window allocation. This is because a firewall provides security between the public and secure segment, and an improper change can completely block user access or create a bypass of security. The same difficulty also applies to a firewall software upgrade.

FWLB solves this problem and enables easy management of the devices. Since the firewalls are being load balanced in a group, an individual firewall can be taken out of rotation for management purposes. This ensures that the user traffic is not interrupted by firewall changes.

Firewalls can be taken out of rotation by removing them from the firewall farm configured on the CSM or by blocking the probe sent by the CSM. By blocking or dropping the probe packets, the firewall is taken out of rotation dynamically by the CSM.

Types of Firewalls

As we discussed before, firewalls are physical devices that enforce security policies between network segments. There are several types of firewalls, namely:

- Packet-based firewalls
- Application-based firewalls

- Application gateway or proxy firewalls
- Layer 2 or stealth firewalls

Packet-Based Firewalls

Packet-based firewalls are first-generation devices that enforce policies on per-packet bases. They do not have any concept of session and have no application layer understanding. A simple form of packet-based firewall is an access control list (ACL) on a router. The ACL blocks or permits IP packets based on source or destination IP addresses or both. There are more complex ACLs available now on routers that can provide stateful inspection.

Load balancing of packet-based firewalls is simple because session state is not maintained on a firewall, so potentially the same TCP connection can be load balanced on a per-packet basis across multiple firewalls. In other words, asymmetric flows are allowed in this environment.

Figure 5-1 shows an example of load–balancing packet-based firewalls. Since these firewalls are stateless, a TCP SYN for a particular connection can go through the first firewall while the TCP SYN ACK from the server to the client goes through the the second firewall.

Figure 5-1   *Load-Balancing, Packet-Based Firewalls*

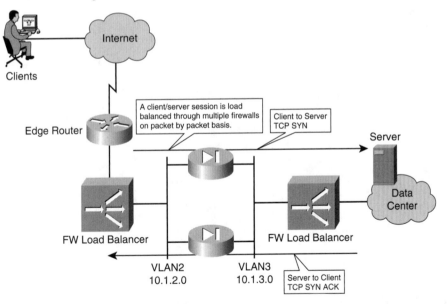

Application-Based Firewalls

Application-based firewalls that are commonly available now can provide stateful inspection of sessions along with network address translation (NAT) functionality. The PIX and Firewall Services Module (FWSM) on the Catalyst 650000 are application-based firewalls. Similar to hardware-based load balancers, application-based firewalls install permitted session information in hardware memory. These firewalls do not allow any packets through them other than those that belong to the inspected and installed sessions in the firewall.

Load balancing of application-based firewalls is complex, as it requires a particular user session to be sent through the same firewall. In other words, if a client TCP SYN is sent through firewall A to reach the server, the TCP SYN ACK from the server to the client should go through firewall A also. Path symmetry needs to be maintained, and this is typically done by using a source or destination address. A hash of the source and destination address is calculated to maintain the symmetry for the client TCP SYN and server TCP SYN ACK response. We will discuss this further in the case study.

Figure 5-2 shows an example of load balancing application-based stateful firewalls. Notice that a particular TCP connection needs to go through the same firewall in this case.

Figure 5-2 *Load-Balancing Application-Based Firewalls*

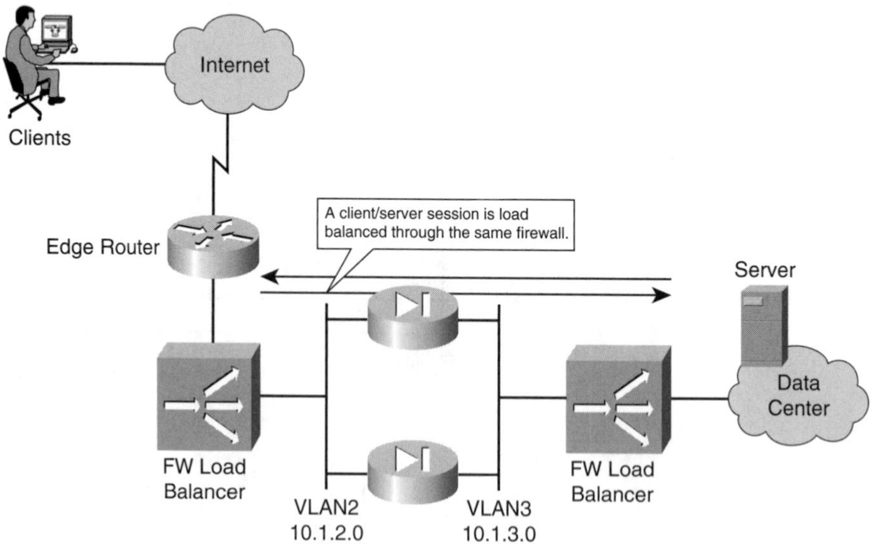

Application Gateway or Proxy Firewalls

Application gateway–based firewalls provide stateful inspection of sessions. They are not only session aware, but are also familiar with the application protocols that create sessions; for example, HTTP, SMTP, and FTP. The application-level gateway does more than just filter packets and sessions. It acts as a gateway between the protected network and the Internet. As a gateway, it does not allow any packets to travel directly between the Internet and the protected network.

Application gateway firewalls proxy all user requests and fetch the data by initiating a new connection to the end server. The end server sees the request coming from the firewall's IP address. The firewall splices the client-side and server-side TCP connection such that the client gets the data from the end server without the Internet-based end server having knowledge of the client's IP address. This functionality looks similar to NAT but is really above and beyond because the firewall is not just hiding the internal client's IP address; it is also implementing application-based security policies.

Application gateway firewalls can be implemented transparently, but most are implemented in a *proxy* fashion. This is why they are also referred to as *proxy firewalls*.

Load-balancing proxy firewalls require the load balancing of sessions from the internal network to the Internet only. From the Internet to the internal network, packets always make it to the correct firewall, as the destination IP is the firewall's physical IP. Thus, dynamic symmetry of sessions is ensured.

Figure 5-3 shows an example of load-balancing proxy firewalls. Notice, in this case, the firewall proxies the client requests and then sets up a separate connection to the end server. In this case, a client/server session is load balanced through the same firewall. The firewall proxies the client connection and issues a connection to the Internet server. The client sends the initial request to a VIP on the load balancer, and the request is translated to the firewall IP on VLAN 3.

Figure 5-3   *Load-Balancing Proxy Firewalls*

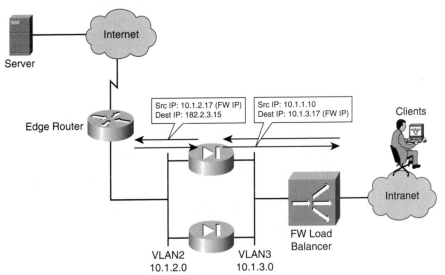

Layer 2 or Stealth Firewalls

Layer 2 or stealth firewalls are also known as "bump on the wire" firewalls. These firewalls do not have any IP addresses, and they simply bridge traffic between two segments or VLANs. Both segments or VLANs share the same IP subnet and broadcast domain. In other words, these are undetectable Layer 2 devices that can perform Layer 2 forwarding together with packet and session inspection.

Load balancing stealth firewalls is fairly complex but is supported by the Cisco CSM module. For load-balancing stealth firewalls, the firewalls are connected to unique VLANs on either side—that is, the public or private side. The public-side VLANs connect to a particular CSM pair, and the private or internal VLANs connect to another CSM pair. The firewall bridges traffic between the private and public VLANs. That means, even though they are different VLANs, they are the same broadcast domains. CSMs are configured with alias IP addresses on all VLANs, and they balance traffic across the firewalls by forwarding packets to the remote CSM's alias IP addresses. In other words, the firewall server farm consists of the alias IP addresses on the remote CSM pairs. A stealth firewall is configured so that all traffic moving in both directions across that VLAN moves through the firewall.

Figure 5-4 shows an example of load balancing Layer 2 or stealth firewalls. Notice each Layer 2 firewall exists on a separate VLAN pair and subnet. A VLAN pair (for example, VLAN 2 and VLAN 12) is used to merge a broadcast domain, servicing subnet 10.1.2.0/24.

Figure 5-4   *Load-Balancing Stealth Firewalls*

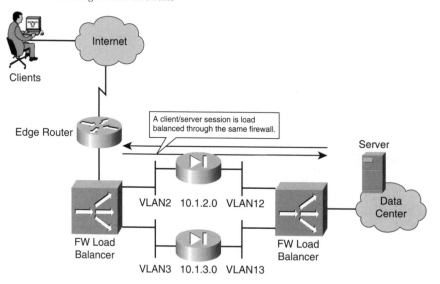

Case Study: Firewall Load Balancing

Now that you understand the different types of firewalls and the motivations behind FWLB, you can learn how to deploy a fairly complex FWLB solution over multiple secure segments. When deploying FWLB, it's critical to learn about the applications flows that would be load balanced to the firewall, whether they are outbound to the Internet or inbound to the DMZ. Applications that require multiple connections, also called *buddy connections,* such as FTP, need to be considered and accounted for in the design. For these applications, you need to ensure that both the connections belonging to the same user session go through the same firewall.

In this case study, we will examine a specific customer deployment where CSM is used to load balance firewalls with three secure segments, namely an INET, a DMZ, and a LAN segment. The idea behind the following case study is to understand not only the concepts but the implementation details. To fully understand the sample deployment, we will look at:

- Server and application requirements
- Security requirements
- Infrastructure requirements
- Design options
- Test and verification

Server and Application Requirements

Server and application requirements for this case study are defined as follows:

- The servers should be directly managed in the DMZ from management stations in the LAN segment.
- Servers should also be able to initiate sessions for application software patches and driver upgrades.
- The number of servers in the DMZ is about 300.
- The primary application that is being load balanced in the DMZ is HTTP and HTTPS based.
- Persistence is needed for the HTTPS-based application.
- TCP-based probes are OK.
- Direct access to the DMZ servers from the LAN is made using long-lived flows a minimum of three hours of idle timeout.
- FTP is used between LAN and DMZ segment servers.

Security Requirements

The security requirements for this case study are as follows:

- The main requirement is to load balance flows to the firewalls from all the three segments.

- It is critical that each network path through the firewall be verified before sending connections over it; that is, a LAN's user traffic should only be sent toward the DMZ over a firewall that has its DMZ segment interface functional.

- FTP and other applications with multiconnections should be sent across the same firewall.

- High availability is critical.

- Firewalls do not share state tables; that is, each firewall is unaware of the session states of the other firewalls.

Infrastructure Requirements

Layer 2 and Layer 3 infrastructure requirements for this case study are as follows:

- Minimal disruption to the Interior Gateway Protocol (IGP) domain

- Seamless integration of the CSM in the current Layer 2 and Layer 3 infrastructure

- Robust failover necessary in case of firewall failure

In the data center design, to meet the previously mentioned requirements, the CSMs are configured in a combination of bridge and router modes. Figure 5-5 shows the physical topology being deployed.

FWLB Design Considerations

Following are some of the key aspects of the design that you need to consider for a successful deployment:

- Use appropriate ICMP probes to track all links of the firewalls. One can easily drop traffic if all paths are not watched.

- Configure the port-channel between the Catalysts for the server and client VLANs. This port-channel should exclude the CSM fault-tolerant (FT) VLAN.

- Configure another port-channel with at least two Fast Ethernet interfaces for the CSM FT VLAN.

- The Multilayer Switching Feature Card (MSFC) should only have Layer 3 presence on either the client- or server-side VLAN of the CSM. As discussed in Chapter 3, this restriction can be removed by using policy-based routing (PBR) on the MSFC.

Figure 5-5   *Physical Topology of the Multiple-Segment FWLB Design*

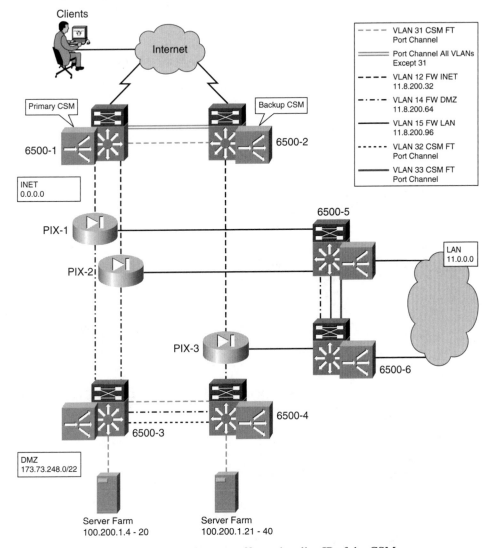

- MSFC should route relevant traffic to the alias IP of the CSMs.

- CSMs should route relevant traffic to the HSRP group IP of the MSFC.

- Distribute the firewalls and the servers across both the Catalyst 6500s. Must not have single point of failure. Measures, such as port-channeling, are required to avoid split brains, which occurs when both devices in an active/standby pair become active.

- In FWLB, virtual IPs (VIPs) within the virtual server configuration act as the routes. Make sure proper subnetting and so on are used. It is very easy to create routing loops.

- The VLAN X option in the virtual server configuration is highly significant. This is to ensure that connections from appropriate VLANs hit the VIP address. In other words, this provides you with more control in enhancing security and in preventing routing loops.

Figure 5-6 shows the logical topology of the FWLB design in consideration.

Figure 5-6 *Logical Topology of the Multiple-Segment FWLB Design*

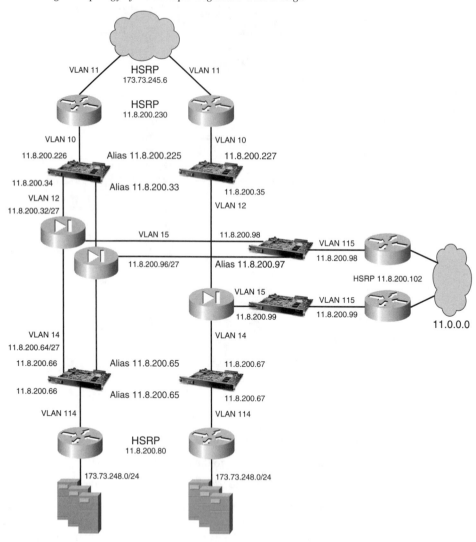

FWLB Probes

In order to ensure that the path through a firewall is available, ICMP probes are used. ICMP probes are configured with the **address** command within the probe to define which address needs to be pinged. The **address** keyword enables the CSM to send the probe to the defined address and not to the real IP (the firewall's IP). CSM uses the real server's MAC address to send the probe across each firewall. In the following example, the address is the alias IP address of the CSMs in the DMZ segment. The CSM makes sure it sends the ICMP echo across all the links of the firewalls. The receiving CSM sends back the response on the link on which the request was received. This way, all the paths are monitored by the CSM.

Within the probe configurations, *interval*, *failed*, and *retries* values can be adjusted to achieve the desired effect. For example, a probe with an interval value of 5, a retries value of 3, and a failed value of 30 sends a probe every 3 seconds, and a failure of 3 consecutive probes results in the server being marked as failed or down. So it takes 15 seconds to mark a server down. The probes are sent again after a delay of 30 seconds to see if the server is back in service or not.

```
Cat6500_01(config-module-csm)#probe DMZ icmp
Cat6500_01(config-slb-probe-icmp)#?
SLB ICMP probe config
  address    probe destination IP address
  default    Set a command to its defaults
  exit       exit probe submode
  failed     time in seconds between probes of failed server
  interval   time in seconds between probes
  no         Negate a command or set its defaults
  receive    maximum time in seconds to wait for a reply from real server
  retries    number of consecutive errors before marking real server failure
Cat6500_01(config-slb-probe-icmp)#
!
 probe DMZ icmp
   address 11.8.200.65
   interval 5

!
serverfarm OUT_DMZ
  no nat server
  no nat client
  real 11.8.200.43
   inservice
  real 11.8.200.44
   inservice
  real 11.8.200.45
   inservice
   probe DMZ
!
```

Traffic to the Firewalls

To load balance traffic across the firewalls, create a server farm with the IP addresses of the firewalls. Firewalls *must* be Layer 2-adjacent to the CSM. MSFC *must* not have a Layer 3 interface on the firewall VLAN. To route traffic across the firewalls, the user needs to create a virtual server with a VIP that defines the route through the firewall. Traffic destined to the specified VIP would be load balanced across the firewall group. Notice that in the following configuration example, a VLAN tag 10 is configured on the virtual server DMZ. This configuration command ensures that only traffic from VLAN 10 (client VLAN) should be considered by the virtual server. This is used for security purposes and also to prevent routing loops.

```
!
serverfarm OUT_DMZ
  no nat server
  no nat client
  real 11.8.200.43
   inservice
  real 11.8.200.44
   inservice
  real 11.8.200.45
   inservice
  probe DMZ
!
 vserver DMZ
  virtual 173.73.248.0 255.255.248.0 any
  vlan 10
  serverfarm OUT_DMZ
  replicate csrp sticky
  replicate csrp connection
  persistent rebalance
  inservice
!
```

The **replicate csrp sticky** command is not needed in the above configuration, as there is no sticky group configured. This command is used to synchronize sticky data tables between active and standby CSMs.

Traffic from the Firewalls

CSM is not a router. It would not know what to do with any IP packet unless configured using virtual servers or static routes and gateways. We need the following configuration to make the CSM handle the traffic originated from the firewall VLAN (12) appropriately. This is a catch-all virtual server that says the following: predictor-forward any packet that comes in from VLAN 12 for which I do not have a flow. Predictor-forward means route as defined; in this case, it's the default gateway. The **any** key word in the virtual configuration refers to any IP protocol.

```
!
 serverfarm OUT_FW_CSM
  no nat server
  no nat client
  predictor forward
!
vserver OUT_FW_CSM
  virtual 0.0.0.0 0.0.0.0 any
  vlan 12
  serverfarm OUT_FW_CSM
  replicate csrp sticky
  replicate csrp connection
  persistent rebalance
  inservice
!
```

Router or Secure Mode

Router mode (also known as *Secure mode*) is configured on the CSM by having two different subnets on the client and server VLANs respectively. Direct access to the servers from the client VLAN is not allowed in Router mode. An example can be seen on CSM1 and CSM2. Router mode is used in the Internet segment for security enhancement. Similarly, Bridge mode would have worked as well.

```
module ContentSwitchingModule 2
  vlan 10 client
   ip address 11.8.200.226 255.255.255.224
   gateway 11.8.200.230
   alias 11.8.200.225 255.255.255.224
!
  vlan 12 server
   ip address 11.8.200.34 255.255.255.224
   alias 11.8.200.33 255.255.255.224
!
```

The configuration shows that alias IP 11.8.200.33 is used by the PIXs as their upstream default gateway.

Bridge Mode

Bridge mode is configured on the CSM by having the same subnet and IP address on both the client and server VLANs. Examples can be seen on both the DMZ CSM and the LAN CSM. Bridge mode enables broadcast traffic to seamlessly pass through the CSM and also allows direct access of the servers from the front end.

```
module ContentSwitchingModule 2
 vlan 14 client
  ip address 11.8.200.66 255.255.255.224
  alias 11.8.200.65 255.255.255.224
!
 vlan 114 server
  ip address 11.8.200.66 255.255.255.224
  route 173.73.248.0 255.255.248.0 gateway 11.8.200.80
!
```

FWLB Algorithms

Any load-balancing method available on the CSM can be used for FWLB. Typically, the default balancing method, round robin, is used. Since support of multiconnection protocols, such as FTP, is required in this design, we will be using predictor IP hash in our configuration. For multiconnection protocols where some connections are open by clients and others by servers and you need to make sure all the connections belonging to the same session go through the same firewall, you will have to use **source IP hash** for incoming connection and **destination IP hash** for outgoing, or vice versa.

```
Cat6500_01(config-module-csm)#serverfarm OUT_DMZ
Cat6500_01(config-slb-sfarm)#pre
Cat6500_01(config-slb-sfarm)#predictor ?
  forward     forwarding based on destination lookup
  hash        hashing algorithms
  ip-hash     Source IP address hash algorithm (Please use hash address source)
  leastconns  least connections algorithm
  roundrobin  roundrobin algorithm (default)
Cat6500_01(config-slb-sfarm)#predictor ha
Cat6500_01(config-slb-sfarm)#predictor hash ?
  address  IP source/dest address hash algorithm
  url      URL hash algorithm
Cat6500_01(config-slb-sfarm)#predictor hash add
Cat6500_01(config-slb-sfarm)#predictor hash address ?
  /nn or A.B.C.D  IP address hash network mask
  destination     Destination IP address hash algorithm
  source          Source IP address hash algorithm
  <cr>
Cat6500_01(config-slb-sfarm)#predictor hash address
```

Configuration Details of the INET Segment

Following are detailed CSM and Catalyst 6509 configurations of the INET segment.

CSM Configurations

Following is the complete CSM configuration, which is used in the INET segment. This configuration shows the VLAN configuration, probes, server farms, and virtual servers.

```
module ContentSwitchingModule 2
 vlan 10 client
  ip address 11.8.200.226 255.255.255.224
  gateway 11.8.200.230
  alias 11.8.200.225 255.255.255.224
!
 vlan 12 server
  ip address 11.8.200.34 255.255.255.224
  alias 11.8.200.33 255.255.255.224
!
 probe DMZ icmp
  address 11.8.200.65
  interval 5
!
 probe LAN icmp
  address 11.8.200.97
  interval 5
!
 serverfarm OUT_DMZ
  no nat server
  no nat client
  predictor hash address source
  real 11.8.200.43
   inservice
  real 11.8.200.44
   inservice
  real 11.8.200.45
   inservice
  probe DMZ
!
serverfarm OUT_LAN
  no nat server
  no nat client
  predictor hash address source
  real 11.8.200.43
   inservice
  real 11.8.200.44
   inservice
  real 11.8.200.45
   inservice
  probe LAN
!
 serverfarm OUT_FW_CSM
  no nat server
  no nat client
  predictor forward
!
 vserver DMZ
  virtual 173.73.248.0 255.255.248.0 any
  vlan 10
  serverfarm OUT_DMZ
  replicate csrp sticky
  replicate csrp connection
```

```
   persistent rebalance
   inservice
 !
 vserver DMZ_V2
   virtual 11.8.200.64 255.255.255.224 any
   vlan 10
   serverfarm OUT_DMZ
   replicate csrp sticky
   replicate csrp connection
   persistent rebalance
   inservice
 !
 vserver LAN
   virtual 11.0.0.0 255.0.0.0 any
   vlan 10
   serverfarm OUT_LAN
   replicate csrp sticky
   replicate csrp connection
   persistent rebalance
   inservice
 !
 vserver OUT_FW_CSM
   virtual 0.0.0.0 0.0.0.0 any
   vlan 12
   serverfarm OUT_FW_CSM
   replicate csrp sticky
   replicate csrp connection
   persistent rebalance
   inservice
 !
```

Catalyst 6509 Layer 3 Configurations

Following are the Layer 3 configurations on the Catalyst 6509. The interface VLAN 10 is the one that links the CSM with the MSFC. VLAN 11 connects the MSFC with the edge router.

```
 !
interface Vlan10
 ip address 11.8.200.231 255.255.255.224
 no ip redirects
 standby 1 ip 11.8.200.230
 standby 1 priority 105
 standby 1 preempt
 standby 1 track Vlan11
 !
interface Vlan11
 ip address 173.73.245.6 255.255.255.0
 no ip redirects
 standby 2 ip 173.73.245.10
 standby 2 priority 105
 standby 2 preempt
```

```
    standby 2 track GigabitEthernet1/1
    standby 2 track Vlan10
   !
   ip default-gateway 173.73.245.1
   !
   ip classless
   ip route 0.0.0.0 0.0.0.0 173.73.245.1
   ip route 11.0.0.0 255.0.0.0 11.8.200.225
   ip route 173.73.0.0 255.255.0.0 11.8.200.225
```

Configuration Details of the DMZ Segment

Following are detailed CSM and Catalyst 6500 configurations of the DMZ segment.

CSM Configurations

Following is the CSM configuration used in the DMZ segment. Notice in this segment that the CSM performs dual tasks. It load balances server-originated traffic to the LAN and INET segment across the firewalls and also load balances inbound HTTP and HTTPS requests across the application server farm.

```
   module ContentSwitchingModule 2
    vlan 14 client
      ip address 11.8.200.66 255.255.255.224
      alias 11.8.200.65 255.255.255.224
    !
    vlan 114 server
      ip address 11.8.200.66 255.255.255.224
      route 173.73.248.0 255.255.248.0 gateway 11.8.200.80
    !
    probe INTERNET icmp
      address 11.8.200.33
      interval 5
    !
    probe LAN icmp
      address 11.8.200.97
      interval 5
    !
    probe WEB tcp
      interval 10
    !
    !
    serverfarm DMZ_INTERNET
      no nat server
      no nat client
      predictor hash address destination
      real 11.8.200.75
       inservice
      real 11.8.200.76
       inservice
```

```
    real 11.8.200.77
     inservice
     probe INTERNET
  !
   serverfarm DMZ_LAN
    no nat server
    no nat client
    predictor hash address destination
    real 11.8.200.75
     inservice
    real 11.8.200.76
     inservice
    real 11.8.200.77
     inservice
     probe LAN
  !
   serverfarm WEB
    nat server
    no nat client
    real 173.73.248.121
     inservice
    real 173.73.248.122
     inservice
    real 173.73.248.123
     inservice
     probe WEB
  !
   serverfarm OUT_FW_CSM
    no nat server
    no nat client
    predictor forward
  !
  !
   vserver DMZ_INTERNET
    virtual 0.0.0.0 0.0.0.0 any
    vlan 114
    serverfarm DMZ_INTERNET
    replicate csrp sticky
    replicate csrp connection
    persistent rebalance
    inservice
  !
   vserver DMZ_LAN
    virtual 11.0.0.0 255.0.0.0 any
    vlan 114
    serverfarm DMZ_LAN
    replicate csrp sticky
    replicate csrp connection
    persistent rebalance
    inservice
  !
   vserver WEB-80
    virtual 173.73.248.120 tcp www
```

```
   serverfarm WEB
   replicate csrp sticky
   replicate csrp connection
   persistent rebalance
   inservice
 !
 vserver WEB-443
   virtual 173.73.248.120 tcp https
   serverfarm WEB
   sticky 240
   replicate csrp sticky
   replicate csrp connection
   persistent rebalance
   inservice
 !
  vserver OUT_FW_CSM
   virtual 173.73.248.0 255.255.248.0 any
   vlan 14
   serverfarm OUT_FW_CSM
   replicate csrp sticky
   replicate csrp connection
   persistent rebalance
   inservice
 !
```

Catalyst 6509 Layer 3 Configurations

Following are the Layer 3 configurations on the Catalyst 6509. Interface VLAN 114 is the one that links the CSM with the MSFC. VLAN 248 is the server VLAN that exists on the MSFC. Since the default gateway of the MSFC is the CSM, all traffic from the servers going toward the INET or LAN segment passes through the CSM.

```
interface Vlan114
 ip address 11.8.200.81 255.255.255.224
 no ip redirects
 standby 3 ip 11.8.200.80
 standby 3 priority 105
 standby 3 preempt
!
interface Vlan248
 ip address 173.73.248.2 255.255.255.0
 no ip redirects
 standby 1 ip 173.73.248.1
 standby 1 priority 105
 standby 1 preempt
!
interface Vlan249
 ip address 173.73.249.2 255.255.255.0
 no ip redirects
 standby 2 ip 173.73.249.1
 standby 2 priority 105
 standby 2 preempt
```

```
!
ip default-gateway 11.8.200.65
ip classless
ip route 0.0.0.0 0.0.0.0 11.8.200.65
```

Configuration Details of the LAN Segment

The following sections provide the detailed CSM and Catalyst 6500 configurations of the LAN segment. This is the segment that connects the data center with the corporate network.

CSM Configurations

Following is the CSM configuration used in the LAN segment. Notice that in the following configuration the idle timeout is increased to 3 hours. This ensures that the user sessions from the LAN to the DMZ are not removed by the CSM even when the user is idle for up to 10,800 seconds. The default idle timeout in the CSM is 1 hour. Similar idle timeout adjustments would need to be made in the DMZ CSM configuration.

```
module ContentSwitchingModule 2
 vlan 15 client
  ip address 11.8.200.98 255.255.255.224
  alias 11.8.200.97 255.255.255.224
 !
 vlan 115 server
  ip address 11.8.200.98 255.255.255.224
  route 11.0.0.0 255.0.0.0 gateway 11.8.200.102
 !
 probe INTERNET icmp
  address 11.8.200.33
  interval 5
 !
 probe DMZ icmp
  address 11.8.200.65
  interval 5
 !
 serverfarm LAN_DMZ
  no nat server
  no nat client
  predictor hash address source
  real 11.8.200.107
   inservice
  real 11.8.200.108
   inservice
  real 11.8.200.109
   inservice
  probe DMZ
 !
 serverfarm LAN_INTERNET
```

```
  no nat server
  no nat client
  predictor hash address destination
  real 11.8.200.107
   inservice
  real 11.8.200.108
   inservice
  real 11.8.200.109
   inservice
  probe INTERNET
!
 serverfarm OUT_FW_CSM
  no nat server
  no nat client
  predictor forward
!
 vserver LAN_DMZ_V1
  virtual 173.73.248.0 255.255.248.0 any
  vlan 115
  idle 10800
  serverfarm LAN_DMZ
  replicate csrp sticky
  replicate csrp connection
  persistent rebalance
  inservice
!
 vserver LAN_DMZ_V2
  virtual 11.8.200.64 255.255.255.224 any
  vlan 115
  idle 10800
  serverfarm LAN_DMZ
  replicate csrp sticky
  replicate csrp connection
  persistent rebalance
  inservice
!
 vserver LAN_INTERNET
  virtual 0.0.0.0 0.0.0.0 any
  vlan 115
  serverfarm LAN_INTERNET
  replicate csrp sticky
  replicate csrp connection
  persistent rebalance
  inservice
!
 vserver LAN_INTERNET_2
  virtual 11.8.200.224 255.255.255.224 any
  vlan 115
  serverfarm LAN_INTERNET
  replicate csrp sticky
  replicate csrp connection
  persistent rebalance
  inservice
```

```
!
 vserver OUT_FW_CSM
  virtual 11.0.0.0 255.0.0.0 any
  vlan 15
  serverfarm OUT_FW_CSM
  replicate csrp sticky
  replicate csrp connection
  persistent rebalance
  inservice
!
```

Catalyst 6509 Layer 3 Configurations

Following are the Layer 3 configurations on the Catalyst 6509. Interface VLAN 115 is the one that links the CSM with the MSFC. VLAN 200 is used to connect the MSFC to the internal corporate routers.

```
interface Vlan115
 ip address 11.8.200.103 255.255.255.224
 no ip redirects
 standby 1 ip 11.8.200.102
 standby 1 priority 105
 standby 1 preempt
 standby 1 track Vlan200
!
interface Vlan200
 ip address 11.8.200.130 255.255.255.224
 no ip redirects
 standby 2 ip 11.8.200.129
 standby 2 priority 105
 standby 2 preempt
 standby 2 track Vlan115
!
ip default-gateway 11.8.200.97
ip classless
ip route 0.0.0.0 0.0.0.0 11.8.200.97
ip route 11.0.0.0 255.0.0.0 11.8.200.135
ip route 11.8.200.32 255.255.255.224 11.8.200.97
ip route 11.8.200.64 255.255.255.224 11.8.200.97
ip route 11.8.200.224 255.255.255.224 11.8.200.97
```

Test and Verification

As mentioned before, each data center environment is unique with respect to the number of sockets used, the duration of TCP or UDP connections, activity in each session in terms of packets per second, idle timeouts, and so on. Thus, it is critical to test and verify the FWLB and SLB environments with the particular applications.

Following are a few critical test cases that you should verify after a new deployment or a major or minor infrastructure change—including a CSM or firewall code upgrade.

- Verification of the firewall path by making sure all the probes are working correctly
- Verification of traffic flow between all segments; that is, INET, DMZ, and LAN
- Verification of active and passive FTP between LAN and DMZ
- Content retrieval from the HTTP and HTTPS servers
- A server-initiated session to a back-end database or internal server
- A server-initiated backup or data replication session
- Application daemon failure and detection by the CSM
- Primary CSM failure, measurement of the recovery time
- Primary Catalyst 6509 failure, measurement of the recovery time

Summary

This chapter introduced FWLB concepts, technology, products, and implementation details. This chapter covered motivations behind FWLB, provided an overview of different flavors of firewalls, and explained how to load balance each type.

In order to combine all the concepts of FWLB from the perspective of the CSM platform, this chapter also provided a case study. This case study focused on the deployment scenario of a real-world solution using the CSM to load balance firewalls with three secure segments. The CSM configurations have been provided and explained to introduce the reader to the CLI.

Chapter 6, "Transparent and Proxy Cache Load Balancing," introduces caching terminology, technology, and methodology, together with a complete case study of cache load balancing using CSM on the Catalyst 6500.

Transparent and Proxy Cache Load Balancing

This chapter introduces the reader to the transparent and proxy cache load-balancing concepts, technology, and designs. In order to understand the load balancing of caches, the chapter provides an overview of caching technology and its benefits, and takes an in-depth look at the mechanics of HTTP caching. It explains Cisco's Application Content Networking Software (ACNS) and the Content Engine, as well as how they provide caching for clients. A case study provides detailed configuration information for a caching solution.

Benefits of Caching

Caching is based on the idea that when a particular resource is accessed, the same resource is likely to be accessed again and again by different users. Having a cache deployed helps in the following ways:

- Provides a better user experience for requesting the resource from a particular site. Since the resource is cached and resides closer to the user, the time it takes to respond back to the client with the request is much faster than the time it takes the request to be returned from the original server.

- Helps the origin server by reducing the number of requests. Since the resource is cached and is served by the cache, the origin server has fewer requests to process, reducing the load on it.

- Reduces unnecessary traffic on the network. Since the cache is able to serve the request, there is no need for the connection to traverse the Internet.

Caching Overview

As the number of users on the Internet has increased, so has network traffic, causing congestion on the links from the client to the server. This increased traffic causes servers to have to handle more requests, which directly affects the time it takes the servers to process client requests and thereby impacts the user's web browsing and online shopping experience. Network caching, illustrated in Figure 6-1, was introduced to scale server capacity with the growth of the Internet while still providing quick response to client requests.

Figure 6-1 *Caching Overview*

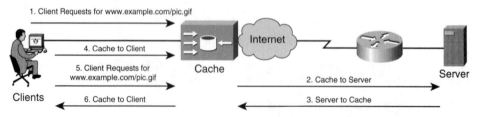

As illustrated in the diagram, caching involves the following steps:

Step 1 A user initiates requests for a resource such as http://www.example.com/pic.gif. The cache inspects the request from the client, but the cache does not have the pic.gif resource.

Step 2 The cache requests the resource from the origin server, typically using its own source IP as the initiator.

Step 3 The end server responds back to the cache.

Step 4 The cache stores the resource locally and forwards the resource to the client.

Step 5 The client refreshes his browser page and requests the http://www.example.com/pic.gif resource again.

Step 6 The cache responds to the client using a local (stored) copy of pic.gif.

Caching Terminology

On receiving a request, a cache checks to see if the response has already been cached. If not, this query is referred to as a cache *miss*, in which case the request from the client is sent to the origin server by the cache. However, if the resource is present in the cache, the query is called a cache *hit*. Before the resource can be returned to the requesting client, the resource and its expiration are validated. The resource is deemed as "fresh" if the expiration time for the resource has not expired or "stale" if it has expired. If the resource is considered stale, it must be revalidated from the origin server. The fresh or stale state of a resource is determined by the Expires header and the max-age Cache-Control directive. The Expires header is the date and time at which the resource will become stale or outdated, and the max-age Cache-Control directive specifies the number of seconds the response can take and still be considered fresh. On receiving a request, the cache may want to validate the request with the origin server. Most HTTP responses include the Last-modified header, which specifies the time when the resource was last changed on the origin server. If the response from the server is 304 (Not Modified), and the Last-modified header is still valid, the cache will return the resource and will refresh the Date and Expires headers for the content. If the server does not return a 304, the cache treats the server's response as new content, replaces the cached object, and delivers it to the client.

Many popular operating systems allow for several copies of the same document to reside in various directories of the server. Thus the cache can potentially store different versions of the same object. To uniquely identify the object, an entity tag is associated with it. The entity tag allows a cache to determine if a copy of the document has changed. If the entity tag is valid, the server will return a 304 (Not Modified) response. If the entity tag is not present, however, the object will be returned with a 200 OK response (indicating that the client request was successful), and the object will be updated on the cache.

Mechanics of HTTP Caching

Clients mostly use HTTP when communicating to caching software or hardware. Caching of FTP, HTTPS, and other protocols is also possible.

The cache's role is to store responses that it receives from the origin server. A request can be cached if it can be used to answer a request that the client might initiate in the future. The cache makes its decision to cache an object based on some of the HTTP headers, which it can find in either the request or the response. Common HTTP headers that the cache examines are as follows:

- The HTTP response status codes
- The HTTP request methods
- The HTTP Cache-Control directives
- Expiration and validation
- Request authentication

HTTP Response Status Code

The decision to cache an object can be based on the HTTP server response code. Table 6-1 lists the response status codes that allow for an object to be cached.

Table 6-1   *HTTP Response Codes*

Code	Value	Description
200	OK	The client request was successful.
203	Non-Authoritative Information	The information in the entity header is from a local or a third-party copy, not from the original server.
206	Partial Content	The server is returning partial data of the size requested. This is cacheable only if the range request is supported.
300	Multiple Choices	The entity body returned by the server could have a list of options (URLs) for the user to select from in order to view the resource.

continues

Table 6-1   *HTTP Response Codes (Continued)*

Code	Value	Description
301	Moved Permanently	This specifies the new location for the resource requested by providing a URL to the user.
410	Gone	The requested resource has been permanently removed.

HTTP Request Methods

The GET, HEAD, and POST methods are the only methods allowed to be cached by default. A successful response to a GET request is cached by default. Since the HEAD request returns header information, it is used to update previously cached resources. The response to a POST request is also cacheable if an expiration time and Cache-Control directive are associated with it.

HTTP Cache-Control Directives

HTTP Cache-Control directives allow for the caches to manage the HTTP requests and responses. They may be used to override some of the default behavior associated with the response status codes and HTTP request methods. Some of the common Cache-Control directives are as follows:

- **No-cache**—The no-cache directive allows for a cache to validate the response if it has been cached. Thus responses with this directive can be stored but cannot be sent to the client without validation.

- **Private**—The private directive allows for a particular cache to store the response but does not allow a group of shared caches to store the response. This is useful when the content being cached is customized for an individual user.

- **Public**—The public directive sets the resource being cached to be shared by both shared and nonshared caches.

- **Max-age**—The max-age directive allows a server to specify the expiration time on a cached resource. It establishes the maximum time for a resource to be cached.

RFC 2616 defines some of the Cache-Control directives and their uses.

Expiration and Validation

Expiration and validation allow the caches to verify that the response being provided to the user is up-to-date. Expiration time allows the cache to make a decision on the resource being requested and to make sure that the resource is not cached if the expiration or validation headers are not present in the response.

Request Authentication

Any HTTP connection that involves authentication is not cacheable. However, there are scenarios where a resource can be cached if a Cache-Control directive header, such as s-maxage or public, is present.

Cisco Application Content Networking and Caching

The Cisco Content Engines running the ACNS provide the caching features and can be deployed in various caching modes, which will be discussed later in the section "Transparent Caching Modes." By caching content locally, Content Engines minimize redundant network traffic that traverses WAN links. As a result, WAN bandwidth costs either decrease or grow less quickly.

Content Engines can be deployed at branch offices and can be configured for access control, filtering, and caching. The Content Engine can be used to define specific policies to determine if a content request should be denied or granted. Once access to the content is granted, the Content Engine checks its local cache for a copy of the content. If the content is already stored in its local cache, the Content Engine sends the client the cached content; otherwise, it retrieves the content from the origin server, caches the content, and sends the cached content to the client. When the Content Engine receives subsequent client requests for the same content, it sends the client the cached content instead of retrieving the same content from the origin server again.

In Figure 6-2, client requests are transparently redirected to the Content Engine at the branch office by a router running Cisco's Web Cache Communication Protocol (WCCP). Another possible caching redirection method is direct proxy routing, where web clients are explicitly configured to send their requests directly to the Content Engine.

Figure 6-2 *Caching Overview*

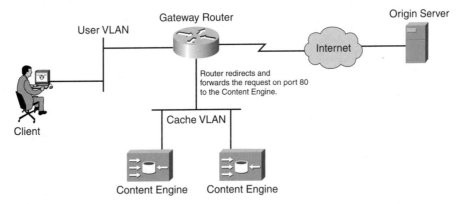

The following sections discuss the details of the various modes and roles in which the Content Engines can be configured.

ACNS Roles

The ACNS software device mode determines whether the ACNS device is functioning as a Content Distribution Manager, a Content Engine, or a Content Router. These device modes are described as follows:

- **Content Distribution Manager**—A centralized content and device management station that configures and monitors ACNS 5.*x* network devices (Content Routers and Content Engines registered with the Content Distribution Manager), acquires and distributes content, and provides services. It allows you to manage devices (Content Engines and Content Routers) centrally as groups instead of individually.

- **Content Engine**—A device that serves the requested content to the client by providing access, filtering, and caching capabilities. Content Engines can be deployed in one of two ways:
  - As stand-alone devices primarily used for transparent or proxy caching
  - As devices registered with a Content Distribution Manager to be managed collectively or based on geographic preferences for content distribution

- **Content Router**—A device that redirects content requests to the registered Content Engine closest to the client. This type of request redirection is referred to as *content routing*. With content routing, a Content Engine must be registered with a Content Distribution Manager. Stand-alone Content Engines do not support content routing.

You can specify the device mode during configuration. The default device mode is Content Engine. The following variations of the Content Distribution Manager, Content Router, and Content Engines can be used in production deployments:

- **A single stand-alone Content Engine (no Content Distribution Manager or Content Router)**—A stand-alone configuration for the Content Engine is usually done at remote sites and is implemented with transparent or proxy caching.

- **Several stand-alone Content Engines (no Content Distribution Manager or Content Router)**—The deployment of several Content Engines is usually front-ended by a load balancer to provide redundancy for a farm of Content Engines, providing caching functionality.

- **One Content Distribution Manager and several Content Engines registered with a Content Distribution Manager (no Content Router)**—This variation is usually deployed where there are large farms of Content Engines. Each Content Engine is placed strategically; for example, the Marketing department would have one set of Content Engine farms and the Engineering department would have another. To maintain and manage content according to department, the Content Distribution Manager can be used to push and pull content on the appropriate Content Engine farms.

- **One Content Distribution Manager, several Content Engines registered with a Content Distribution Manager, and one or more Content Routers**—The Content Distribution Manager and Content Engines are usually deployed in a geographically dispersed area. Thus to reduce user-experienced latency, the Content Router is deployed to service requests to the closest geographically placed Content Engine.

ACNS Content Types

The types of content supported on the Cisco ACNS platforms are as follows:

- **On-demand**—Content that is acquired, cached, and delivered in response to a user request. Cached content retrieved through HTTP is stored in the cache file system (cfs) storage partition on the Content Engine. Cached content retrieved through the two streaming protocols, Windows Media Technology (WMT) and Real Time Streaming Protocol (RTSP), is stored in the media file system (mediafs) storage partition on the Content Engine.

- **Preloaded**—Content that is retrieved and stored on a stand-alone Content Engine because a retrieval of specific content was scheduled in anticipation of user requests for that content. The following types of content can be preloaded on a stand-alone Content Engine: HTTP URLs, FTP over HTTP URLs, and MMS (Microsoft Media Server) URLs. (MMS URLs are WMT streaming media files.) All configured HTTP, FTP over HTTP, and MMS parameters and rules apply to the preloaded objects. During the preload process, the stand-alone Content Engine scans web sites several link levels down for content, retrieves the specified content, and stores it locally. When the Content Engine receives future requests for this content, it serves the content from its local storage, which results in WAN bandwidth savings as well as accelerated delivery of the content to the web client.

- **Prepositioned**—Content that is retrieved and distributed through a network of Content Engines registered with a Content Distribution Manager for the purpose of acquisition and distribution of content in anticipation of user requests. This type of content is distributed in order to populate Content Engines in a centrally managed ACNS network environment. Bandwidth-intensive content objects, such as Java applets, Macromedia Flash animations, Shockwave programs, and other file formats can be managed and scheduled for distribution to Content Engines during off-peak hours.

- **Live**—Content stream (typically streaming media) that is being broadcast from an origin server. This content is acquired as a live streaming broadcast from either a satellite or a terrestrial broadcasting source. You configure the policies associated with obtaining the live multimedia stream, such as the program listing the URL (playlist), the maximum bit rate, and so forth, as well as the distribution policies, such as the priority, the schedule, and the maximum bandwidth.

Content Engine Architecture

Content Engines enhance mostly HTTP-type requests and streaming media–type content by storing and delivering content close to the end users (web clients) on their local networks. Content Engines can service content requests from the following types of clients:

- **Web browsers**—For example, Microsoft Internet Explorer
- **Streaming media players**—For example, Windows Media Player and RealMedia players (RealPlayer and RealOne players).

Client requests for content can be routed to stand-alone Content Engines in one or more of the following ways:

- **Direct proxy routing**—Client browsers and media players are configured to send their requests directly to the Content Engine, which acts as a nontransparent forward proxy server.

- **Transparent redirection**—Routers and switches transparently intercept web requests and send them to the Content Engine for inspection and manipulation using one of the following:

  — Cisco WCCP routing

  — Layer 4 switching

With transparent redirection, the WCCP-enabled router or a Layer 4 switch transparently intercepts the client request and redirects it to the Content Engine instead of to the intended server. The Content Engine poses as the intended server, acknowledges the request, and establishes the connection with the client. The client believes that it has established a connection with the intended server even though it is actually connected to the Content Engine.

Transparent Caching Modes

The idea behind transparent caching is to intercept certain protocols that the client initiates and forward them to the transparent cache. The transparent cache can service the request or forward the connection to the origin server on behalf of the client. With the deployment of transparent caching, individual client browsers do not need to be configured to forward traffic to the cache because the decision to forward traffic from the client to the cache is determined by the transport layer (usually the default gateway for the clients).

Figure 6-3 illustrates a typical transparent caching client connection. As the client initiates the traffic, the packets pass through a router or a switch, which in turn forwards the request to the transparent cache.

Figure 6-3 *Transparent Caching Example with WCCP*

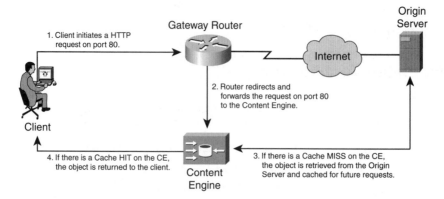

The process by which a Content Engine transparently caches a resource is as follows:

Step 1   A user requests a web page from a browser.

Step 2   The WCCP-enabled router analyzes the request and, based on the TCP port number, determines if it should transparently redirect it to a Content Engine. Access lists can be applied to control which requests are redirected.

Step 3   If a Content Engine does not have the requested content, it sets up a separate TCP connection to the end server to retrieve the content. The content is returned to the Content Engine, where it is stored.

Step 4   The Content Engine sends the content to the client. Upon receipt of subsequent requests for the same content, the Content Engine transparently fulfils the requests from its local storage.

Because the WCCP-enabled router transparently redirects content requests to a Content Engine, the Content Engine operates transparently to clients. Clients do not need to configure their browsers to point to a specific proxy cache. The Content Engine operation is transparent to the network. The router operates entirely in its normal role for nonredirected traffic.

The biggest deployment advantage for transparent caching is that no client configuration is required to provide caching functionality. Objects that the client is requesting can be returned by the Content Engine or can be fetched from the origin server. Either one of the actions is transparent to the client.

In a transparent cache, a user's request can be a cache hit or a cache miss. A cache hit signifies that the cache engine has the requested object on local storage, while a cache miss signifies that the cache engine does not have the object and has to retrieve it from the origin server.

Following is the sequence of operations and characteristics of a transparent cache miss:

1   The client's browser performs a DNS lookup to resolve the IP address of the source for the requested content.

2   With the resolved address, the client initiates a TCP session to request content from the source. Note that the client is unaware of the cache. In other words, the cache is transparent to the client.

3   The client's request is intercepted and directed to the cache.

4   In case of a cache miss, the cache will use the IP address resolved by the client and perform a request for the content from the source.

5   A copy of the content is returned from the source to the cache.

6   If the content is cacheable, it is stored on the cache.

7   The requested content is sent to the client.

Following is the sequence of operations and characteristics of a transparent cache hit:

1   The client's browser performs a DNS lookup to resolve the IP address of the source for the requested content.

2   With the resolved address, the client initiates a TCP session to request content from the source. Note that the client is unaware of the cache. In other words, the cache is transparent to the client.

3   The client's request is intercepted and directed to the cache.

4   In case of a cache hit, the requested content is retrieved from local storage and sent to the client.

WCCP Protocols

Cisco developed the Web Cache Communication Protocol (WCCP) within Cisco IOS software to enable routers and switches to transparently redirect packets to network caches. The protocol does not interfere with normal router or switch operations. Using WCCP, the router redirects requests to configured TCP ports to network caches rather than to intended hosts sites. It also balances traffic load across a cache cluster to ensure fault-tolerant and fail-safe operation. As Content Engines are added to or deleted from a cache cluster, the WCCP-aware router or switch dynamically adjusts its redirection map to reflect the currently available caches, resulting in maximized performance and content availability.

To use a WCCP-enabled router, an IP address must be configured on the interface connected to the Internet, and the interface must be visible to the Content Engine on the network.

There are two versions of WCCP, Version 1 and Version 2. The following sections discuss these protocols and their limitations.

WCCP Version 1

Following is a summary of the capabilities and limitations of WCCP Version 1:

- Only a single WCCP-enabled router is supported.
- Only a single WCCP service is supported.
- Traffic redirection is only supported on port 80.
- Each home router can support the standard web cache service for up to 32 Content Engines.
- There is no bypass support. (For example, static bypass, error bypass, and authentication bypass are not supported.)
- There is no support for generic routing encapsulation (GRE) on return.

WCCP Version 2

With Version 2, multiple routers can service a cluster. This allows any of the available routers in a service group to redirect packets to each of the Content Engines (CEs) in the cluster. A subset of CEs within a cluster and routers connected to the cluster that are running the same service is known as a service group. Available services include TCP and UDP redirection.

Following are some advantages of WCCP Version 2:

- WCCP Version 2 has the capability to adjust the load being offered to individual CEs to provide more effective use of the resources available and at the same time help to ensure the quality of service to the clients. There are three techniques for performing this task, which are as follows:
  - Hot spot handling allows an individual hash bucket, or a pool of IP addresses to which routers are mapped, to be distributed across all the CEs.
  - Load balancing allows the set of hash buckets assigned to a CE to be adjusted so that the load can be shifted from an overwhelmed CE to other CEs that have available capacity.
  - Load shedding enables the router to selectively redirect the load to avoid exceeding the capacity of the CEs.
- The Content Engine has a built-in fault tolerance. If a CE fails within a cluster, the router "heals" the system by reapportioning the load to the remaining CEs in the cluster. When the failed CE comes back online, the load is reapportioned once again.
- If a sole CE or a cluster of CEs fails, the Cisco router has the built-in intelligence to terminate redirection and forward traffic upstream instead. This is accomplished when the router no longer receives heartbeats from the CE or all CEs in the cluster and performs a WCCP shutdown.
- You can disallow rogue CEs from entering a cluster by specifying a password. This password assignment is optional and is done when referring a service to a router list number. This password performs an MD5 authentication.
- Healing mode allows for a newly added CE to query and obtain objects from other CEs in the cluster on cache misses.
- WCCP needs to include the router list for the service group as part of its messages to properly depict the view. A service group can comprise up to 32 Content Engines and 32 routers.
- All Content Engines in a cluster must include all routers servicing the cluster in its configuration. If a CE within a cluster does not include one or more of the routers in its configuration, the service group will detect the inconsistency and the CE will not be allowed to operate within the service group.
- Multicast addresses must be between 224.0.0.0 and 239.255.255.255. WCCP works in conjunction with IP networks only. The Time to Live (TTL) value of routers servicing a cluster must be 15 seconds or less.

The following sequence of events details the interaction between Content Engines and routers that have been configured to run WCCP Version 2:

1 Each Content Engine is configured with a router list.

2 Each Content Engine announces its presence to the list of all routers with which it has established communication. The routers reply with their view (list) of Content Engines in the group.

3 Routers and Content Engines become aware of one another and form a WCCP service group using a management protocol. The Content Engines also send periodic "Here I am" messages to the routers that allow the routers to rediscover the Content Engines. To properly depict the view, the protocol needs to include the list of routers in the service group as part of its messages.

4 Once the view is consistent across all the Content Engines in the Content Engine cluster, one Content Engine is designated as the lead. When there is a cluster of Content Engines, the one seen by all routers and the one that has the lowest IP address becomes the lead Content Engine. The role of this lead Content Engine is to determine how traffic should be allocated across the Content Engines in the Content Engine cluster.

5 The lead Content Engine sets the policy that the WCCP-enabled routers must adhere to when redirecting packets to the Content Engines in this cluster.

6 The assignment information is passed to the entire service group from the designated Content Engine so that the routers in the service group can redirect the packets properly and the Content Engines in the service group can better manage their load.

Figure 6-4 illustrates the service group creation between the routers and the Content Engines. Router 1, Router 2, CE 1, and CE 2 are part of a service group, and Router 1, Router 2, Router 3, CE 1, CE 2, and CE 3 are part of a service group. The routers will only redirect requests to the Content Engine that is part of the service group.

Following are some restrictions with WCCP Version 2:

- WCCP is only licensed on the caching device, not the redirecting router/switch.

- WCCP runs on UDP port 2048 within a GRE tunnel between the WCCP router and the cache.

- Routers and CEs become aware of one another and form a service group using WCCP. Once the service group has been established, one of the CEs is designated to determine load assignments among the CEs in the cluster.

- If there is a group of CEs, the one seen by all routers and the one that has the lowest IP address becomes the lead CE. The role of this CE is to determine how traffic should be allocated across CEs. The assignment information is passed to the entire service group from the designated CE so that the routers of the group can redirect the packets properly and the CEs in the group can better manage their load. Routers may be configured with an IP multicast address for use in the cluster. The **ip wccp** command must be enabled.

Figure 6-4   *CE Clustering with WCCP V2*

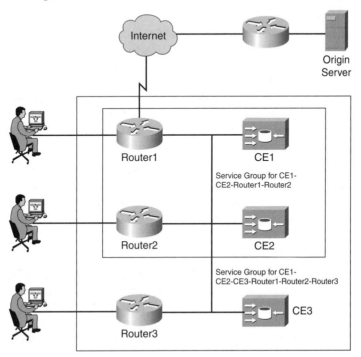

When cache support is enabled on the router and WCCP support is enabled on the Content Engine, the devices can communicate and deliver the services for which they are configured. You can disable cache support on the router to suspend proxy and caching services, rather than turning off or otherwise disabling individual Content Engines.

The router and the Content Engine are in constant communication; thus, when the router notices that the engine is no longer responding to it, the router stops sending requests to the engine. This is transparent to users. If other Content Engines are attached to the router, the router continues sending requests to the other engines.

When you remove a Content Engine, the pages that were cached on the engine are no longer available to the router or other Content Engines. Thus, you might see an increase in outgoing web traffic that might have otherwise been fulfilled by the engine you have just removed. However, after a period of time, the router and the rest of the Content Engines will have redistributed the load of web traffic.

If you remove the last Content Engine from a router, you can also disable cache support on the router. However, this is not necessary; having cache support enabled when there are no Content Engines attached has no effect on the router's performance.

Redirection with the CSS

The Cisco Content Services Switch (CSS) can be used for transparent redirection in conjunction with the Content Engine. The CSS transparently intercepts and redirects content requests to the Content Engine. With transparent interception through a CSS, the user is unaware that the request made to an origin web server is redirected to the Content Engine by the CSS. The CSS can be configured to dynamically analyze the request and determine if the requested content is cacheable or not. If the requested content is not cacheable, the CSS sends the request directly to the origin server. If the requested content is cacheable, the CSS directs the request to the Content Engine. The Content Engine either returns the requested content if it has a local copy or sends a new request to the origin web server for the content.

When Layer 4 switching is used to redirect content requests transparently to stand-alone Content Engines and the TCP SYN packet passes through the CSS that has the Layer 4 redirection feature turned on, the packet will be diverted to a Content Engine attached to the switch. In this case, the CSS changes the MAC address of the TCP SYN packet so that instead of going out to the gateway or the origin server, the MAC address is changed to that of the Content Engine.

The CSS then sends the packet to the Content Engine. The Content Engine must be prepared to accept requests that are sent to it even if the IP address of the packet is not the address of the Content Engine. The Content Engine then handles the TCP SYN packet similarly to how it handles packets redirected through WCCP. Transparent forward proxy caching with a stand-alone Content Engine and a CSS works as follows:

1 A user (web client) requests a web page from a browser. The CSS analyzes the request and determines whether the requested content is cacheable or not.

2 If the requested content is cacheable, the CSS transparently redirects the request to a Content Engine.

3 If all the Content Engines are unavailable in a transparent cache configuration, the CSS allows all client requests to progress to the origin web servers.

4 If the Content Engine has the requested content already stored in its local cache, it returns the requested content to the client.

5 If the Content Engine does not have the requested content, the following events occur:

   a The Content Engine sets up a separate TCP connection to the origin web server to retrieve the content.

   b The content is returned to, and is stored on, the Content Engine.

6 The Content Engine sends the requested content to the web client. Upon subsequent requests for the same content, the Content Engine transparently fulfills the request from its local storage (cache).

IP Spoofing

With typical transparent caching, an end user issues an HTTP request from a web browser. This request is transparently intercepted and redirected to the Content Engine (acting as a transparent proxy server) by a WCCP router. The Content Engine accepts the incoming TCP connection from the WCCP router, determines that the request is for an object not in storage (cache miss), and issues a request to the origin server for the requested object. When the Content Engine contacts the origin server, it uses its own IP address instead of the IP address of the client for which it is making the request.

If IP spoofing is configured on the WCCP Version 2–enabled routers and the Content Engines, the Content Engine (acting as a transparent proxy server) can send out the client's IP address to the origin server for authentication purposes instead of sending out the request with its own IP address. The WCCP router can also intercept packets from the server that are destined for the client's IP address and redirect those packets to the Content Engine.

By spoofing a client's IP address, the following capabilities are supported:

- The Content Engine can send out packets with the client IP (which is different from the Content Engine's own IP address).

- The Content Engine can receive packets with the client IP (which is again different from the Content Engine's own IP address) and send the packets to the correct application that is waiting for the packet.

- The WCCP Version 2–enabled router can intercept the packets from both the client and the server transparently and forward those redirected packets to the same Content Engine so that the TCP connection is not broken.

In ACNS software, release 5.0.7 and later, IP address spoofing is performed for transparently intercepted proxy-style requests when the Content Engine is configured to use the proxy server from the original request to fetch the content.

Proxy Caching Overview

Proxy caching deployment requires the cache server to be defined for a group of clients. The proxy settings are usually specified in the client browser. The browser directs all requests, for the protocols specified, toward the configured proxy cache. The proxy cache returns the content for the request. One of the challenges in deploying this solution is that each client browser needs to be configured with the correct proxy cache settings, thus making the solution difficult to manage and maintain. However, there are various scripts that can be used to automate the process of upgrading the client browsers with the appropriate settings.

With forward proxy caching, the stand-alone Content Engine acts as a proxy server for web clients. The Content Engine (forward proxy server) provides internal clients with access to the Internet. The client browsers and media players are explicitly configured to send their content requests to the Content Engine (forward proxy server). This is referred to as *direct proxy routing*. When direct proxy routing is used to direct client requests to the Content

Engine, the Content Engine is operating in nontransparent mode; that is, the clients are aware that their requests are being directed to the Content Engine. The Content Engine uses specific policies and rules to determine whether a client should be granted or denied access to the requested Internet content. This type of forward proxying service is usually provided as part of a larger Internet security solution in enterprise environments. By implementing this service, enterprises enable their end users (web clients) to go outside the firewall without compromising the integrity of the company's private network. The direct proxy routing method is the most straightforward routing method and is typically used when the user desktops are tightly controlled. Consequently, direct proxy routing is generally used in enterprise environments as opposed to service provider environments.

In deployments that use direct proxy routing to route content requests to the Content Engine, the Content Engine acts a network gateway device optimized to retrieve content on behalf of web clients. If the requested content is already in the Content Engine's local storage (cache hit), the Content Engine sends the content to the web client. If the requested content is not already stored in the Content Engine's local cache (cache miss), the Content Engine retrieves the requested content from the origin server, stores a local copy of the content if the content is cacheable, and sends the requested content to the web client. When the Content Engine receives subsequent requests for the same content, it serves the content from its local storage.

Figure 6-5 illustrates how the Content Engine's directly proxies connections from the web client, and initiates the connections to the origin server on behalf of the client.

Figure 6-5 *Proxy Caching Example*

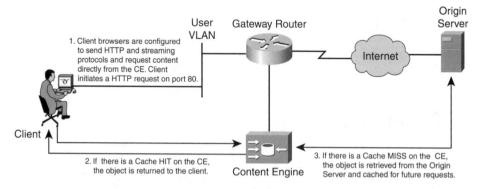

Some significant advantages to deploying nontransparent (proxy) caching services on stand-alone Content Engines are:

- Internet access for user populations can be regulated by the Content Engine that is acting as a gateway device for these end users.

- Internet requests all appear to be sourced from the proxy cache (Content Engine), thereby hiding internal network addressing.

- Frequently requested cacheable content is cached locally, which results in significant WAN bandwidth savings and accelerated delivery of content to web clients.

For HTTP proxy caching, there is a primary proxy failover option that you can configure on stand-alone Content Engines. This feature is referred to as the HTTP proxy failover feature. With this feature, you can configure the forward proxy server to contact up to eight other outgoing proxy servers when an HTTP cache miss occurs (that is, when the requested HTTP content is not already stored locally in the Content Engine cache).

These outgoing proxy servers can be other Content Engines or standard proxy servers that can be contacted to process HTTP cache misses without using the Internet Cache Protocol (ICP) or WCCP. The function of these outgoing proxy servers is to process the HTTP cache misses that have been forwarded to them by the forwarding proxy server. One outgoing proxy server functions as the primary server to receive and process all cache miss traffic. If the primary outgoing proxy server fails to respond to the HTTP request, the server is noted as failed and the requests are redirected to the next outgoing proxy server until one of the proxies services the request.

Failover occurs in the order in which the proxy servers were configured. If all of the configured proxy servers fail, the Content Engine can optionally redirect HTTP requests to the origin server specified in the HTTP header.

Server Proxy (Reverse Proxy Caching)

To ensure fast response times, maximized service availability, and the ability to withstand an excessive number of URL hits or an excess of bandwidth requested, Content Engines can be deployed in front of a web server farm to offload traffic from busy firewalls and servers, helping to optimize the entire web server infrastructure. This type of deployment is called web server acceleration, or reverse proxying.

A Content Engine deployed in this manner is called a reverse proxy cache because the Content Engine is operating at the opposite end of the transaction, in front of the origin server. By having the Content Engine (the reverse proxy cache) transparently handle inbound requests for content instead of having the origin servers (the servers in the server farms) handle these requests, web server traffic load is significantly reduced. Reverse proxy servers are an effective method for scaling server farms. In a reverse proxy cache configuration, the proxy server is configured with an Internet-routable IP address. Clients are directed to the proxy server based on DNS resolution of a domain name. To a client, the reverse proxy server appears like a web server.

Reverse proxy caching also enables a stand-alone Content Engine to provide external clients access to internal content (for example, content on a company's intranet) through a firewall. Typically, this reverse proxy caching is used for secure web publishing. In a reverse proxy cache configuration, the proxy server is configured with an Internet-routable IP address. Web clients are directed to the proxy server based on DNS resolution of a domain name. To a web client, the reverse proxy server appears to be the origin web server.

Some significant advantages to deploying reverse proxy caching on stand-alone Content Engines are:

- It provides an alternative to web server expansion by offloading the processing of static images from the server farm. By having the reverse proxy server transparently handle inbound requests for content, web server traffic load is significantly reduced.

- It provides a possible way of replicating content to geographically dispersed areas by deploying Content Engines in these areas.

- It does not require any client configuration changes (that is, you do not need to configure the client browsers to point to the Content Engine functioning as the reverse proxy server).

Consequently, both the router and the Content Engine must be configured to run the reverse proxy service.

ACNS 5.x software provides reverse proxy caching by allowing traffic redirection or interception to be performed by two types of devices: a WCCP Version 2–enabled router or a Layer 4 CSS switch.

Figure 6-6 shows a typical reverse proxy caching deployment with a WCCP-enabled router. In this type of deployment, the Content Engine interoperates with the WCCP Version 2–enabled router to bring the reverse proxy service (service 99) within the web server environment. The Content Engine is deployed in front of a web server farm. Unlike transparent and nontransparent forward proxy servers, the reverse proxy server proxies requests on behalf of a server farm, and it only caches content from servers in the server farm.

Figure 6-6 *Reverse Proxy Caching Example*

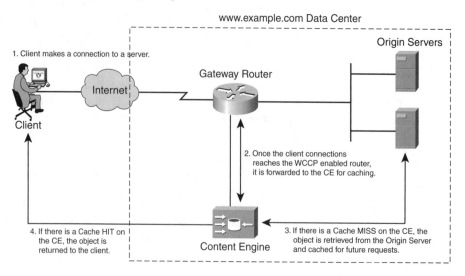

As Figure 6-6 shows, All HTTP requests destined for web servers are routed to the router. Upon receiving the HTTP request at this interface, the router transparently intercepts and redirects the request to the Content Engine. Thus, the Content Engine is logically in front of web servers, offloading web server HTTP traffic. Web clients who are requesting content from the origin server receive the static web pages from the Content Engine acting in reverse proxy mode. This frees up the back-end infrastructure from processing this HTTP traffic.

Supported Protocols on the Content Engine

The following protocols are supported on the Content Engine:

- **HTTP**—All Internet browsers including Microsoft Internet Explorer, Netscape, and all others that conform to HTTP 1.0 or HTTP 1.1 specifications.

- **FTP over HTTP**—Client browsers issuing FTP requests (support added in the ACNS 5.1 software release).

- **TFTP**—Support for Trivial File Transfer Protocol (TFTP) clients was added in the ACNS 5.1 software release.

- **RTSP**—RealPlayer (Version 8.*x* and later) and RealOne players are supported. (These media players are collectively referred to as "RealMedia players.")

- **MMS**—Supported are MMS over TCP (MMST), MMS over UDP (MMSU), Windows Media Player (Version 6.*x* and later), and Windows Media Series 9 Player (support added in the ACNS 5.2 software release). (The media players are collectively referred to as "WMT players.")

Authentication and Management on the Content Engine

ACNS 5.*x* software provides authentication, authorization, and accounting (AAA) support for users who have external access servers (for example, RADIUS or TACACS+ servers) and for users who need a local access database with AAA features. The AAA components are described here:

- *Authentication* (or "login") is the action of determining who the user is. It checks the username and password.

- *Authorization* (or "configuration") is the action of determining what a user is allowed to do. It permits or denies privileges for authenticated users in the network. For example, if you log in to a stand-alone Content Engine with a superuser administrator account, it permits you access to all the commands you are allowed to execute; or if you log in as a defined user, it permits you only limited access to commands. Thus authorization defines the roles for a user.

- *Accounting* is the action of keeping track of administrative user activities for system accounting purposes. In ACNS 5.2 software, support for AAA accounting through TACACS+ was added.

In ACNS 5.*x* environments, there are two main types of authentication:

- **Content authentication**—Controls end user access to content that is served by Content Engines.

- **Administrative login authentication**—Controls administrative login authentication methods (local, RADIUS, or TACACS+) for processing administrator requests to log on to the Content Engine for monitoring, configuration, or trouble-shooting purposes.

Content Engine Models

There are three Content Engine models available, the differences among them being the amount of disk capacity available. The smaller disk capacity Content Engines are those in the CE 5*xx* series, which range in their hard drive capacity up to 160 GB. Figure 6-7 shows a picture of the CE 5*xx*.

Figure 6-7   *Cisco Content Engine 5xx Series Platform*

Image courtesy of Cisco Systems, Inc. Unauthorized use not permitted

The Content Engines in the CE 73*xx* series have higher-capacity hard drives, up to 432 GB. Figure 6-8 shows a picture of the CE 73*xx*.

Figure 6-8   *Cisco Content Engine 73xx Series Platform*

Image courtesy of Cisco Systems, Inc. Unauthorized use not permitted

In addition, integrated Content Engine Modules are available on the 26*xx*, 36*xx*, and 37*xx* routers. Figure 6-9 shows the integrated Content Engine Module.

Figure 6-9   *Cisco Content Engine Network Modules*

Image courtesy of Cisco Systems, Inc. Unauthorized use not permitted

Case Study: Content Engine in a Transparent Caching-Based Solution

Now that we have covered the details of how transparent caching functions and the features and functionality of the Content Engine, we will discuss how the CE can be deployed. Placement of the CE in the existing or new network requires planning and understanding of the application, security, and underlying infrastructure requirements. There are many applications with different caching and security policies, and we will examine some specific ones in the following case study.

We will look at a customer deployment where the CE is implemented to provide caching via WCCP. The case study will help you understand not only the concepts but also the implementation details.

Design Requirements

The requirements for the design are as follows:

- Application requirement
  - Provide transparent caching for HTTP traffic
- Security requirement
  - Filtering of URLs to certain web sites
- Infrastructure requirement
  - Use the Layer 2 redirection method for optimized WCCP support

Design Options

To fulfill the preceding requirements, the Content Engine and the routers are enabled for WCCP.

When transparent redirection with a WCCP-enabled router is used to redirect requests to a Content Engine, the web clients send their content requests to the source and are not aware that their requests are being redirected to the Content Engine by a WCCP-enabled router. Because this interception and redirection process is completely invisible, or transparent, to the client requesting the content, no desktop changes are required. The WCCP-enabled router operates and performs other configured routing functionality, in addition to servicing WCCP requests.

Figure 6-10 shows the case study scenario. The figure illustrates a client with an IP address of 172.21.55.201 making connections to the Internet via the router, which has an IP address of 172.21.55.194. The router is running WCCP Version 2 to the Content Engine CE 511-2, which has an IP address of 172.21.55.203.

Figure 6-10 *Case Study for Caching*

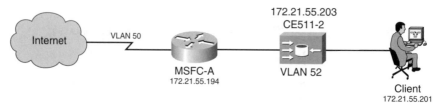

Layer 2 Redirection

In the scenario illustrated in Figure 6-10, because the router and the Content Engine are Layer 2 adjacent to each other and are configured for WCCP, they can take advantage of switching hardware that implements the traffic interception and redirection functions of WCCP in router hardware at Layer 2. This type of redirection is currently supported only with the Cisco Catalyst 6000 and 6500 series switches. With Layer 2 redirection, the first redirected traffic packet is handled by the router software. The rest of the traffic is handled by the router hardware. The redirection process is accelerated in the switching hardware, which makes Layer 2 redirection more efficient.

Two load-balancing schemes exist between WCCP Version 2–enabled routers or switches and Content Engines when the Layer 2 forwarding method is chosen:

- **Hash assignment**—For the Catalyst 6000 and 6500 series switches, this load-balancing method is called WCCP Layer 2 Policy Feature Card (PFC) redirection. This method is intended to achieve forwarding performance of up to 3 Gbps using a combination of the Supervisor Engine 1A and the Multilayer Switch Feature Card 2 (MSFC2).

- **Mask assignment**—This type of load balancing is called WCCP Layer 2 Policy Feature Card 2 (PFC2) redirection. It uses a combination of the Supervisor Engine 2 and the MSFC2.

You can use the Content Engine graphical user interface (GUI) or command-line interface (CLI) commands to specify the load-balancing schemes for a specific WCCP service on a Content Engine. You can specify one load-balancing method (hashing and masking) per WCCP service in a Content Engine cluster. For example, if you define three WCCP services for Content Engine cluster A, two of the services in cluster A could be using the hash load-balancing method, whereas the third service in cluster A could be using the mask load-balancing method.

The following steps show how to configure a Content Engine to receive Layer 2 redirected traffic from a Catalyst 6500 series switch with a Multilayer Switch Feature Card (MSFC) using a hash assignment method for load balancing.

1 Enable WCCP Version 2 on the Content Engine.

```
ContentEngine#configure terminal
ContentEngine(config)#wccp version 2
```

2 Create a router list on Content Engines CE 511-1 and CE 511-2. In the following example, router list 1 is created and contains only a single WCCP Version 2–enabled router (the router with an IP address of 1.1.3.1 for CE 511-1 and 1.1.2.1 for CE 511-2).

```
ce511-2(config)#wccp router-list 2 172.21.55.194
```

3 Configure the standard web cache service (service 0) on the Content Engine. Configure this WCCP service to use the router list you just created in step 2. Enter the Layer 2-redirect option to specify Layer 2 redirection as the packet-forwarding method for this service. The following is the configuration used on CE 511-1 and CE 511-2:

```
ce511-2(config)#wccp web-cache router-list-num 2 l2-redirect
```

4 Use the **show wccp services detail** EXEC command to display the configuration so that you can verify it. (The negotiated forwarding protocol is Layer 2 instead of the standard GRE.)

```
ContentEngine# show wccp services detail

ce511-2#show wccp services detail

Service Details for Web Cache Service
  Service Enabled             : Yes
  Service Priority            : 240
  Service Protocol            : 6
  Application                 : Caching
  Service Flags (in Hex)      : 512
  Service Ports               :     80    0    0    0
                              :      0    0    0    0

  Security Enabled for Service : No
  Multicast Enabled for Service : No
  Weight for this Web-CE      : 0
  Negotiated forwarding method : L2
  Negotiated assignment method : HASH
```

```
         Received Values:
Source IP mask (in Hex)              : 0
        Destination IP mask (in Hex)     : 0
        Source Port mask (in Hex)        : 0
        Destination Port mask (in Hex)   : 0
        Calculated Values:
Source IP mask (in Hex)              : 0
        Destination IP mask (in Hex)     : 1741
        Source Port mask (in Hex)        : 0
        Destination Port mask (in Hex)   : 0
```

HTTP Configuration

Prior to defining the caching policies on the Content Engine, the first task you need to be accomplished is to specify the disk partitions for the Content Engine. Disk space in ACNS software is allocated on a per–file system basis. You can configure your overall disk storage allocations according to the kinds of client protocols you expect to use and the amount of storage you need to provide for each of the functions. The disk on the Content Engine can be partitioned as follows:

```
ce511-2#sh disk
Local disks:
   SYSFS            3.0GB      4.4%
   CFS             30.0GB     43.8%
   MEDIAFS         33.4GB     48.8%
   CDNFS            1.0GB      1.5%
   FREE             0.0GB      0.0%
```

The sysfs (system file system) partition is used to store log files, including transaction logs, syslogs, and internal debugging logs. The sysfs also can be used to store image files and configuration files. The cfs (cache file system) is used to cache HTTP and FTP objects. The mediafs (media file system) is used to cache content from streaming proxy servers, such as WMT servers. The cdnfs (content file system) is used for storing content for prepositioning. In this particular example, the cfs partition is 30 GB for caching HTTP objects.

When transparent redirection with a WCCP-enabled router is used to redirect requests to a Content Engine, the web clients send their content requests to the source and are not aware that their requests are being redirected to the Content Engine by a WCCP-enabled router. Because this interception and redirection process is completely invisible, or transparent, to the client requesting the content, no desktop changes are required. (Clients do not have to configure their browsers or media players to point to a specific proxy server.) The Content Engine operation is transparent to the network; the WCCP-enabled router operates entirely in its normal role for nonredirected traffic.

To use WCCP transparent redirection, you must first define a WCCP service on the WCCP-enabled router. The parameters for a given service are its name, service identifier (service number), and the router interface to be used to support this WCCP service. In this scenario, because we are using the standard web cache service 0, the router intercepts HTTP traffic with a destination of port 80. The following configuration on the router enables WCCP Version 2:

```
Router(config)#ip wccp version 2
Router(config)#ip wccp web-cache
```

Once WCCP has been enabled globally on the router, the interface where the traffic will be redirected to the Content Engine is defined by specifying the **redirect** command. Since the client is forwarding the traffic to VLAN 52, this is the incoming interface and that's why the **redirect in** command is used.

```
interface Vlan52
 description STATIC LAB VLAN
 ip address 172.21.55.194 255.255.255.224
 ip wccp web-cache redirect in
```

On the Content Engine, the standard web cache service (service 0) permits a single WCCP Version 1–enabled router or one or more WCCP Version 2–enabled routers to redirect HTTP traffic to stand-alone Content Engines on port 80 only. The following configuration outlines how to enable WCCP for the web cache service on the Content Engine:

```
ce511-2(config)#wccp web-cache router-list-num 2 l2-redirect
```

In the last configuration example, the router list is defined on the cache such that the cache can accept connections from the configured routers (for example 172.21.55.194).

The following sequence of events occurs between the Content Engines and the single WCCP-enabled router:

1 The Content Engine records the IP address of the WCCP-enabled router servicing the Content Engine.

2 The Content Engines then transmit their IP addresses to the WCCP-enabled router, indicating their presence to one another.

3 The WCCP-enabled router then replies to the Content Engines, establishing that each can connect to the other and that both can recognize one another.

4 Once the view has been established, one Content Engine indicates to the WCCP-enabled router that IP packet redirection should be performed for port 80 HTTP traffic.

```
ce511-1(config)#wccp custom-web-cache router-list-num 1 port 32
```

The following show commands on the Content Engine show the defined service:

```
ce511-2#sh wccp services detail
Service Details for Web Cache Service
        Service Enabled                 : Yes
        Service Priority                : 240
        Service Protocol                : 6
        Application                     : Caching
        Service Flags (in Hex)          : 512
        Service Ports                   :      80    0    0    0
                                        :       0    0    0    0
        Security Enabled for Service    : No
        Multicast Enabled for Service   : No
        Weight for this Web-CE          : 0
        Negotiated forwarding method    : L2
        Negotiated assignment method    : HASH
        Received Values:
Source IP mask (in Hex)            : 0
        Destination IP mask (in Hex)    : 0
```

```
                    Source Port mask (in Hex)        : 0
                    Destination Port mask (in Hex)   : 0
                    Calculated Values:
          Source IP mask (in Hex)          : 0
                    Destination IP mask (in Hex)     : 1741
                    Source Port mask (in Hex)        : 0
                    Destination Port mask (in Hex)   : 0
```

Similarly, on the router:

```
Router#sh ip wccp
Global WCCP information:
    Router information:
        Router Identifier:             172.21.55.226
        Protocol Version:              2.0

    Service Identifier: web-cache
        Number of Cache Engines:       1
        Number of routers:             1
        Total Packets Redirected:      25004
        Redirect access-list:          -none-
        Total Packets Denied Redirect: 0
        Total Packets Unassigned:      0
        Group access-list:             -none-
        Total Messages Denied to Group: 0
        Total Authentication failures: 0
```

Next, we will look at how the Content Engine performs caching as the client in Figure 6-10 initiates HTTP connections. As the client makes connections to web servers, we will see how the objects get cached on the Content Engine. First, we will clear all statistics:

```
ce511-2#clear statistics all
```

And when we look at the HTTP statistics, everything shows up as clear:

```
ce511-2#show statistics http savings
                         Statistics - Savings
                    Requests                            Bytes
         -------------------------------------------------------------
Total:                      0                               0
Hits:                       0                               0
Miss:                       0                               0
Savings:                    0.0 %                           0.0 %
```

Now the client will browse to the site wwwin-eng.cisco.com and we will turn on HTTP logging using the transactional logging command on the Content Engine to view the transactions:

```
ce511-2(config)#transaction-logs enable
```

Following is a cache-miss when the user visits the site wwwin-eng for the first time:

```
ce511-2#type working.log
1131670996.080 60 172.21.55.201 TCP_MISS/302 423 GET http://wwwin-
   eng/ - DIRECT/wwwin-eng
   -
```

Following is the cache-hit when the user visits the same site again:

```
ce511-2#type working.log
1131671085.342 19 172.21.55.201 TCP_IMS_HIT/304 165 GET http://wwwin-
   eng.cisco.com/Eng/Cn
tlSvcs/InfoFrwk/GblEngWWW/Public/eng-home.html - NONE/- -
1131671085.382 20 172.21.55.201 TCP_IMS_HIT/304 165 GET http://wwwin-
```

```
    eng.cisco.com/Public
/EngWeb/eng_styles.css - NONE/- -
1131671085.442 20 172.21.55.201 TCP_IMS_HIT/304 166 GET http://wwwin-
    eng.cisco.com/Public
/EngWeb/Images/ce-banner.gif - NONE/- -
```

Following is the HTTP savings statistics after the user browsing site wwwin-eng:

```
ce511-2#show statistics http savings
                    Statistics - Savings
                    Requests                        Bytes
         -------------------------------------------------------
    Total:              21                          4344
     Hits:              18                          2971
     Miss:               3                          1373
  Savings:            85.7 %                        68.4 %
ce511-2#
```

When defining the criteria for caching HTTP objects, various rules can be defined using the pattern-list. For example, to block GIF and JPG images, you can use a pattern as follows:

```
ce511-2(config)#rule pattern-list 1 header-field request-line /*.gif
ce511-2(config)#rule pattern-list 1 header-field request-line /*.jpg
ce511-2(config)#rule action block pattern-list 1 protocol http
ce511-2(config)#rule enable
```

Because the logs show the .css extension file as an If-Modified-Since (IMS) hit, however, the .gif is denied:

```
1131672346.733 21 172.21.55.201 TCP_IMS_HIT/304 165 GET http://www-
    tac.cisco.com/images/dashboard/cent
ral-unet4.css - NONE/- -
1131672346.772 21 172.21.55.201 TCP_DENIED/403 0 GET http://www-
    tac.cisco.com/images/dashboard/topmenu
.gif - NONE/- -
```

With HTTP 1.1, you can configure the Content Engine to check the freshness of its cached objects before serving the requested content to a client browser. A cached object is considered fresh under any of the following conditions:

- The Content Engine has freshly retrieved the object from the origin server.

- The Content Engine contacts the origin server to check about the freshness of the cached object, and the origin server confirms that the cached object has not been modified since the Content Engine cached it.

- The age of the cached object has not exceeded its freshness lifetime. The age of a cached object is the time that the object has been stored in the Content Engine's cache without the Content Engine explicitly contacting the origin server to check if the object is still fresh. You can use the IMS feature to configure a stand-alone Content Engine to revalidate the freshness of the content stored in its local cache before serving the content to a client browser. The Content Engine checks the freshness of its cached content under the following conditions:

- The Content Engine receives an IMS message from the client browser. This occurs if the setting for the local cache on the client browser is configured to check for newer versions of the cached pages each time the pages are accessed.

- The Content Engine receives a request for expired content.

When a client clicks its Refresh or Reload browser button to reload the requested content into its browser, this causes all Content Engines located between the client and the origin servers containing the requested content to refresh their cached objects.

The Content Engine validates the freshness of requested content in its cache by sending an IMS request to the origin web server. The Content Engine also sends an IMS request to the origin web server when the maximum Time to Live (TTL) has expired. Content freshness is based on a conditional GET feature of the HTTP protocol. The Content Engine retrieves the requested information from the origin server again if the content has changed since it was cached. In HTTP, the conditional GET request uses the value of the Last-Modified response header received with the document when the header was retrieved and stored in the Content Engine cache. This value (the last modification date and time of the cached document) is sent in the IMS request header. The conditional GET request uses the time stamp from the Last-Modified header and sends it along with the request in the IMS header.

The following example shows an IMS request that a Content Engine would send to an origin web server:

```
GET /index.html HTTP/1.1
Server: www.cisco.com
Connection: keep-alive
```

If the content has not changed, the origin web server responds with a 304 Not Modified message and does not send the content:

```
304 Not Modified
(end-of-request)
```

If the content has changed, the new version is transferred to the Content Engine again. Typically, the origin web server also sends the Content Engine a 200 OK response along with the new version of the content:

```
200 OK
(response headers)
(data)
(end-of-request)
```

The Expires response, which indicates the time that the response expires, also affects caching. This response header indicates the time that the response becomes stale and should not be sent to the client without an up-to-date check (using a conditional GET operation). If the HTTP header of a cached object does not specify an expiration time, the Content Engine can age out cached objects with the **http age-multiplier** and **http max-ttl** global configuration commands.

The Content Engine can also calculate an expiration time for each web object before it is written to disk. The Content Engine's algorithm for calculating an object's cache expiration date is as follows:

Expiration date = (today's date – object's last modified date) * freshness factor

The last modified date is provided by the end server's file system. The freshness factor is tunable and derived from the text and binary percentage parameters of the

http age-multiplier global configuration command. Valid age-multiplier values are from 0 to 100 percent of the object's age. Default values are 30 percent for text (HTML) and 60 percent for binary objects (GIF files, for example). After the expiration date has passed, the object is considered stale and subsequent requests cause the Content Engine to make a fresh retrieval of the content.

When configuring the HTTP cache freshness settings on stand-alone Content Engines, note the following:

- You can specify the maximum size of an HTTP object that can be stored in the cache. The maximum size limit for an HTTP object is 204,799 KB. An object with a size above the configurable upper limit is not stored by the Content Engine.

- Use the minimum and maximum TTL settings to limit the duration of HTTP objects in the cache. By default, HTTP cacheable objects are kept for five minutes minimum and three to seven days maximum (three days for text-type objects, seven days for binary). If an object has an explicit expiration date, this takes precedence over the configurable TTL. The default values are three days for text files and seven days for binary objects.

- For HTTP and FTP objects, use the **http min-ttl** and **ftp min-ttl** global configuration commands to set the minimum TTL.

- Use the **http cache-cookies** global configuration command to enable the Content Engine to cache binary objects that are served with HTTP set-cookies headers and no explicit expiration information but that might be cacheable.

You can use the Content Engine CLI or GUI to configure the freshness settings for an HTTP cache on a stand-alone Content Engine with one of the following steps:

Step 1   Use the **http age-multiplier** global configuration command to specify the freshness factor for HTTP cached objects, as shown in the following example:

```
ContentEngine(config)# http age-multiplier text 50% bin 70%
```

Step 2   Use the **http min-ttl** global configuration command to set the minimum amount of time that the HTTP cached object is stored in the Content Engine cache. In the following example, this minimum time is set to ten minutes:

```
ContentEngine(config)# http min-ttl 10
```

Step 3   Use the **http max-ttl** global command to set the upper limit on the estimated expiration dates for HTTP cached objects, as shown in the following examples:

```
ContentEngine(config)# http max-ttl days text 2 binary 4
ContentEngine(config#) http max-ttl hours text 1 hours binary 4
```

The TTL sets a ceiling on estimated expiration dates. An explicit expiration date in the HTTP header takes precedence over the configured TTL.

Step 4   Use the **http reval-each-request** global configuration command to specify the method the Content Engine uses to handle requests to revalidate the content freshness of the HTTP objects in its cache. The following example configures the Content Engine to revalidate all HTTP objects for every HTTP request:

```
ContentEngine(config)# http reval-each-request all
```

Step 5   Set the upper limit of the HTTP object size in KB. The Content Engine does not store an object if the size of the object exceeds the specified limit. The default is 204,800 KB for HTTP objects. The following example sets the maximum size for an HTTP object to 500 KB:

```
ContentEngine(config)# http object max-size 500
```

Step 6   Configure the Content Engine to cache binary objects and associated cookies that are served with HTTP set-cookies headers and no explicit expiration information but that might be cacheable:

```
ContentEngine(config)# http cache-cookies
```

Step 7   Use the **show http ttl** EXEC command to display the TTL configuration changes made to HTTP objects in the Content Engine's cache:

```
ContentEngine# show http ttl
Maximum time to live in days: text 3 binary 7
Minimum time to live for all objects in minutes: 5
```

URL Filtering Configuration with Local Lists

Some enterprises have a requirement to monitor, manage, and restrict employee access to nonbusiness and objectionable content on the Internet. Using a URL filtering scheme on Content Engines, companies can allow or deny access to web sites.

You can configure stand-alone Content Engines to deny client requests for URLs listed in a badurl.lst file or configure them to fulfill only requests for URLs in a goodurl.lst file. The use of local list files (URL lists) applies to HTTP (HTTP, HTTPS over HTTP, and FTP over HTTP) as well as streaming media protocols such as MMS and RTSP. This type of URL filtering is referred to as *local list URL filtering*. Only one good sites file or one bad sites file can be active at one time per protocol. The local list file for each protocol should not contain URLs that belong to other protocols. For instance, the HTTP local list file should contain only HTTP, HTTPS, or FTP URLs, and the WMT local list file should contain only MMS URLs. If the size of the local list file becomes too large, it can adversely affect proxy performance because the local list file is loaded into memory when local list filtering is enabled. If the file size is larger than 5 MB, a warning message appears, but the ACNS software does not enforce size limits for the local list file. It is the administrator's responsibility to track the local list file size and ensure that it does not become so large that it degrades performance.

You can configure a stand-alone Content Engine to use local list URL filtering to filter the following types of client requests for content:

- Requests over HTTP (HTTP, FTP over HTTP, and HTTPS over HTTP requests)

- Requests over RTSP

- WMT requests

Filtering for native FTP and native HTTPS requests is not supported. To use the Content Engine CLI to configure local list URL filtering on a stand-alone Content Engine, use the **url-filter** global configuration commands, as shown here:

```
ContentEngine(config)# url-filter ?
http For requests over HTTP
rtsp For requests over RTSP
wm For WMT requests
```

The following example describes the Content Engine CLI commands for configuring a stand-alone Content Engine to use local list URL filtering for HTTP requests (HTTP, FTP over HTTP, and HTTPS over HTTP requests):

- **url-filter http bad-sites-deny enable**—Configures the Content Engine to deny client requests to URLs in the HTTP bad site list.

- **url-filter http bad-sites-deny file** *filename*—Specifies the filename of the HTTP bad site list.

- **url-filter http good-sites-allow enable**—Configures the Content Engine to permit client requests to URLs in the HTTP good site list.

- **url-filter http good-sites-allow file** *filename*—Specifies the filename of the HTTP good site list.

Following is an example of how to deny client requests for specific HTTP URLs:

1 Create a plain text file named badurl.lst. In this file, enter the URLs that you want to block. The list of URLs in the badurl.lst file must be written in the form http://www.*domain*.com/ and be delimited with carriage returns. The file in our example has the following content:

```
http://www.test123.com/
http://www.test456.com/
http://www.badurl.com/
```

2 Copy the badurl.lst file to the /local1 system file system (sysfs) directory of the stand-alone Content Engine. We recommend creating a separate directory under local1 to hold the bad lists; for example, /local1/filtered_urls. The following example illustrates this:

```
ce511-2#pwd
/local1/logs
ce511-2#ls
acqdist
apache
badurl.lst
```

3 Use the **url-filter http bad-sites-deny** global configuration command to point to the bad URL list and enable it:

```
ce511-2(config)#url-filter http bad-sites-deny file /local1/logs/badurl.lst
ce511-2(config)#url-filter http bad-sites-deny enable
```

Once the badurl.lst file has been enabled and the client tries to browse, there are no restrictions as to the sites they are allowed to go to, as defined here:

```
ce511-2#debug url-filter local-list
Nov 11 00:36:49 ce511-2 cache: urlfilter.c:142:
Nov 11 00:36:49 ce511-2 cache: find_url(): Given url http://wwwin-eng/
Nov 11 00:36:49 ce511-2 cache: urlfilter.c:163:
Nov 11 00:36:49 ce511-2 cache: find_url (): no match is found for
   http://wwwin-eng/
```

However, client access is denied when the URL in the badurl.lst command is matched, as shown here:

```
ce511-2#Nov 11 00:37:50 ce511-2 cache: urlfilter.c:129:
Nov 11 00:37:50 ce511-2 cache: find_url(): look for url match for
   http://www.badurl.com/
Nov 11 00:37:50 ce511-2 cache: urlfilter.c:142:
Nov 11 00:37:50 ce511-2 cache: find_url(): Given url http://www.badurl.com/
Nov 11 00:37:50 ce511-2 cache: urlfilter.c:149:
Nov 11 00:37:50 ce511-2 cache: find_url (): found matching URL
   http://www.badurl.com/
```

Configuration Details

Example 6-1 shows the completed configurations for the Content Engines and the MSFC for the case study discussed.

Example 6-1 *Content Engine Configurations for CE 511-2 and Router*

```
ce511-2#sh run
! ACNS version 5.2.3
!
!
hostname ce511-2
!
http cache-cookies
!
!
!
!
!
ip domain-name cisco.com
!
exec-timeout 0
!
!
!
!
!
interface GigabitEthernet 1/0
 ip address 172.21.55.203 255.255.255.224
 exit
```

Example 6-1   *Content Engine Configurations for CE 511-2 and Router (Continued)*

```
interface GigabitEthernet 2/0
 shutdown
 exit
!
!
ip default-gateway 172.21.55.194
!
!
!
!
no auto-register enable
!
!
!
!
ip name-server 171.68.10.140
!
!
logging console enable
!
!
!
!
!
!
!
wccp router-list 1 1.1.2.1
wccp router-list 2 172.21.55.194
wccp web-cache router-list-num 2 l2-redirect
wccp custom-web-cache router-list-num 2 port 32
wccp version 2
!
!
!
rule enable
rule action block pattern-list 1 protocol http
rule pattern-list 1 header-field request-line /*.gif
rule pattern-list 1 header-field request-line /*.jpg
!
!
!
!
!
transaction-logs enable
!
!
username admin password 1 bVmDmMMmZAPjY
username admin privilege 15
!
!
!
!
```

continues

Example 6-1 *Content Engine Configurations for CE 511-2 and Router (Continued)*

```
!
authentication login local enable primary
authentication configuration local enable primary
!
!
!
!
!
url-filter http bad-sites-deny file /local1/logs/badurl.lst
url-filter http bad-sites-deny enable
!
!
!
!
!
!
!
! End of ACNS configuration
ce511-2#
ce511-2#
```

Example 6-2 *Cat 6509 Layer 3 Configurations for Router*

```
MSFC-A
version 12.1
service timestamps debug uptime
service timestamps log uptime
no service password-encryption
!
hostname MSFC-A
!
enable password test
!
ip subnet-zero
ip wccp 90
!
ip multicast-routing
ip ssh time-out 120
ip ssh authentication-retries 3
!
interface Vlan52
 description STATIC LAB VLAN
 ip address 172.21.55.194 255.255.255.224
ip wccp web-cache redirect in
interface Vlan102
 ip address 10.23.2.2 255.255.255.0
 no ip redirects
 ip pim sparse-dense-mode
 ip route-cache same-interface
 standby 2 ip 10.23.2.1
 standby 2 priority 110
 standby 2 preempt delay sync 60
 !
```

Example 6-2 *Cat 6509 Layer 3 Configurations for Router (Continued)*

```
interface Vlan103
 ip address 10.23.6.2 255.255.255.0
 no ip redirects
 ip pim sparse-dense-mode
 standby 1 ip 10.23.6.1
 standby 1 priority 120
 standby 1 preempt delay sync 60
!
interface Vlan104
 ip address 10.23.4.2 255.255.255.0
 no ip redirects
 ip pim sparse-dense-mode
 standby 2 ip 10.23.4.1
 standby 2 priority 110
 standby 2 preempt delay sync 60
!
interface Vlan201
 ip address 10.201.2.11 255.255.255.0
 ip wccp 90 redirect out
!
!
ip classless
no ip http server
!
line con 0
line vty 0 4
 password test
 login
!
end
```

Summary

This chapter introduced the Cisco ACNS software, the Content Engine platform, and its capabilities for caching. We discussed the software and hardware architecture, caching features and benefits, and introduced basic entities used in caching. We also introduced key concepts of transparent caching using WCCP with redirection, as well as fundamentals of proxy caching and its use. We discussed how the Content Engine caches objects and explained the various headers required for HTTP.

In order to combine all the concepts of caching from the perspective of the Content Engine platform, this chapter presented a case study detailing a deployment scenario using the Content Engine with WCCP. The case study covered various features and functionalities of the Content Engine, such as URL filtering, Layer 2 redirection, and caching based on specific HTTP patterns. It also provided various configuration examples to help you understand the features and capabilities of the Cisco Content Engine.

In Chapter 7, "Load Balancing Streaming Video Servers," we will look at how video streaming is used in a load-balanced infrastructure.

CHAPTER **7**

Load Balancing Streaming Video Servers

This chapter introduces the reader to the concept of load balancing streaming video servers. We will look at the benefits of using load balancing with streaming video servers, and also review video streaming technology. We will examine streaming video servers with the Application and Content Networking System (ACNS) and the types of servers used. In order to understand the load balancing of streaming video servers, we will take an in-depth look at the protocols used for this purpose. Since ACNS software on the Cisco Content Engine (CE) possesses extensive video streaming functionality, we will be using CE as a video proxy example in the case study section of this chapter.

Benefits of Load Balancing Streaming Video Servers

As more and more streaming video applications and services are deployed, the load balancing of streaming video servers has become critical. Short movie, movie advertisements, and music video web sites are in abundance. In order to scale to user demand, these sites require hundreds of streaming servers. These are typically deployed with each server having a unique domain name. Two of the key motivations of load balancing streaming video servers are scalability and redundancy.

Scalability

Load balancing web servers has proven to be a practical and cost-effective method of scaling services. Similarly, load balancing of streaming video servers provides scaling capabilities. The application is hosted on a single domain that maps to a virtual IP (VIP) address on the server load balancing (SLB) device. The SLB device receives client requests for movies or video files and load balances them across the streaming servers.

Redundancy

One of the primary reasons for load balancing streaming video servers is to ensure high availability of video content. The SLB device performs extensive health checks of the servers and only uses operational servers in load-balancing decisions.

Introduction to Streaming

As technology has created a way to bring higher bandwidths to the end user, the content on the Internet has also shifted from text and static content to rich data sprinkled with audio and video.

Streaming is a technology that allows content to be accessed or viewed before all the media packets have been received, whereas caching requires the content to be received in its entirety before it can be accessed. Streaming media can be delivered as live or on-demand content, such as video on demand (VOD).

Streaming media files are sent to the user and played on the user's media player as the files are received from the network. Streaming media files avoid a waiting period for viewing these files because they are immediately available as a continuous stream of data packets. This eliminates the need to store large media files for viewing purposes or to allocate storage space for these files before playing them. A video stream is made up of a sequence of images, and these images in turn are represented in terms of pixels. For example, an image of 200 x 300 dimensions consists of a width of 200 pixels and a height of 300 pixels. The color and intensity of each pixel is also represented by a number that defines the pixel's color and intensity. The representation of many of these images and audio samples over time comprises a video stream. The development of a video stream consists of capturing the video and audio via a camera. Once a camera records a video, it is stored in analog format, and the encoding process can convert the analog format into digital format. There are many commercial software and hardware solutions available for encoding and editing the digitally captured video stream. Once converted to digital format, it can be stored or delivered as live video to the clients. The encoder software and hardware compresses the signal into streamable files, which are then sent to a media file server. The streaming media server in turn delivers the media files on a live or on-demand basis to the users who are running a particular media software (for example, the Windows Media Player) on their personal computers or other electronic devices.

Video Streaming Clients and Protocols

Client browsers mainly use HTTP to fetch contents, and streaming media players mainly use various streaming protocols to fetch and display contents. For example, the Windows Media Player uses the Microsoft Media Server (MMS) protocol to stream audio and video contents, QuickTime players use the IETF standard Real Time Streaming Protocol (RTSP) protocol to stream multimedia contents, and RealMedia players use the Real Networks RTSP protocol, which includes proprietary extensions to the IETF standard RTSP protocol, to stream audio and video content. The media player on the client desktop can be started directly by the end user, or it can be automatically launched by the client browser.

Methods of Video Stream Initiation

The two primary ways for the client browser to start a streaming media player on a client desktop are:

- Through JavaScript embedded in the web page.

- For the browser to start a streaming media player through a MIME–type association. A MIME-type association is a browser capability that enables the browser to invoke a particular application when it encounters an object with a particular MIME-type suffix. A set of default association rules covers the common object types on the Internet. Users can edit, add, or delete these MIME-type association rules in their browsers. For example, through MIME-type association, the client browser launches Adobe Reader when it encounters a .pdf file and it launches the Windows Media Player when it encounters a .asf or .asx file.

Client browsers can launch media players on a client desktop in a variety of situations. For example, if the HTML page contains a link to a video encoded in ASF format, the client browser launches the Windows Media Player on the client desktop while processing this HTML page in order to retrieve the .asf file from the server. The MMS protocol is used to retrieve the .asf file for the Windows Media Player.

Once the media player has been launched, it is given a media file to play, and the player follows procedures similar to those of the browser:

1 The media player looks up the IP address of the streaming server through the DNS resolution server configured on the client desktop. If a proxy is configured for the media player, the media player does not perform this DNS lookup; the player requests that the proxy perform the lookup for the IP address.

2 The media player tries to establish a connection to the media server on the default port—port 1755 for Windows Media Technology (WMT) and port 554 for RTSP—or a specified port. In the case of a proxy, it will establish a connection to the proxy on the specified port.

3 Once the connection is established between the media player and the media server or the proxy, the media player exchanges information with the media server or the proxy to establish the sessions.

Typically, the first packet the media player sends to the server or the proxy contains the IP address of the intended media server or the domain of the server. This is different from HTTP, where the first packet contains not only the domain information but also the object information. In the case of both the WMT and RTSP streaming protocols, the first packet carries server information only. The object information (pathname) is not available until the second or the third packet exchange between the client media player and the server.

Types of Streaming Video Servers

There are multiple vendors and applications providing streaming services today. Some of the most popular ones are Apple QuickTime, RealMedia, and WMT. These will be discussed in the following sections.

Apple QuickTime

Apple QuickTime is developed as an open standard and allows for streaming features and functionalities. QuickTime video format supports AVI, MPEG-1, and OpenDML (Open Digital Media), among others. The underlying protocols support web streaming, including HTTP, RTP, and RTSP.

QuickTime has support for integration among cross-platforms with applications developed on other operating systems. QuickTime movies are supported on both Windows and Mac operating systems. QuickTime movies have standard web browser support, including Microsoft Internet Explorer and Netscape. Since QuickTime is an open standard, integration with various media types on other platforms becomes simple. QuickTime 4 extends this capability to any RTP/RTSP standards-based server running a QuickTime streaming server. QuickTime uses HTTP and RTP protocols to provide streaming functionality. In order to provide real-time streaming (which means that as video frames arrive they are displayed by the QuickTime player), RTSP and RTP are used. There is a timestamp associated with the packets, so they can be viewed in the sequence in which they arrived.

The streams that are created can be sent out as unicast or multicast. When QuickTime employs unicast, the client initiates a connection to the server using RTSP. The server marks the session as a streaming session and responds back to the client. The streaming server tells the client the number of data stream connections that will be established to deliver the stream to the client. In addition, description of the individual data stream connection, such as the description of a specific codec or media type used for the stream, is sent to the client. Since there could be multiple tracks associated with the stream, each track is sent as a separate stream.

With multicast, one copy of each stream is sent over a specific group or channel on the network. A client can join the group or the channel to view the stream. Multicast is much more efficient, as a single stream session is set up on a per-group basis and many clients can join that group, thus reducing the overhead of unicast streaming. If the underlying network does not support mulitcast, the client can request the stream from an RTSP server, which will convert the stream back to unicast (the server will be deployed in a unicast-in or multicast-out manner).

Following are some advantages of using RTP with QuickTime:

- RTP can be used for live transmission and multicast.
- With RTP's real-time streaming, there is no need to store the stream on the local disk, which frees up disk space.

- Using RTP transmission under RTSP control, forwarding, rewinding, and pause features can be accomplished.

- RTP uses the UDP/IP protocol, allowing it to ignore lost packets and thus eliminating the need to retransmit them. This allows for multicasts as well as live streams, both cases where retransmission would not be practical.

RealMedia

RealMedia is the streaming media solution from RealNetworks, Inc. RealMedia uses the RealNetworks RTSP protocol (the IETF standard RTSP protocol plus proprietary extensions) to deliver streaming media content to RealMedia clients (for example, the RealPlayer 8.0 and RealOne players). RealSystem is the Internet solution for audio and video streaming proposed by RealNetworks. It provides tools such as RealServer, RealPlayer, and Real Producer, which are the media server, client, and codec, respectively. The RealSystem architecture supports both real-time and on-demand streaming. The RealAudio and RealVideo contents are created in advance using RealProducer, and are stored in RealMedia File Format (RMFF). RealMedia has two main software components (RealProxy and RealSubscriber). The RealProxy software from RealNetworks, Inc., included as a software option in the ACNS version 5 .x software, enables you to deploy the following RealMedia services:

- Live splitting (distributing live feeds)
- Streaming VOD files in an RTSP-based format
- Caching VOD files

Windows Media Technology

Windows Media Services is Microsoft's set of streaming solutions for creating, distributing, and playing back digital media files on the Internet. The WMT feature uses MMS, Microsoft's proprietary protocol. With the WMT feature enabled on the Cisco CE, the CE provides a native (integrated) WMT server that delivers Microsoft's standard streaming formats (.asf, .wma, and .wmv files) through either unicast or multicast streams. The integrated WMT server has the ability to serve the streams to the clients by VOD, broadcast (live), and multicast. The WMT feature also enables a stand-alone CE to support WMT transparent caching and WMT proxy caching.

Following is the list of components for WMT:

- *Windows Media Player* is a desktop application the end user runs to play requested digital media files (for example, Windows Media Player versions 6.4 and 7.0 or the Windows Media Player 9 series). These clients can take advantage of the VCR-like controls in the Windows Media Player to pause the stream or to skip backward or forward.

- *Windows Right Manager and Encoder* is a content-creation application.

- *Windows Media Server,* such as Windows Media 4.1 Server and Windows Media 9 Server, is an application and distribution software that uses an application-level protocol called MMS to send Active Streaming Format (ASF) files across the Internet.

Streaming Video Protocols

In this section, we will cover the details of streaming video protocols, such as MMS, RTSP, and RTP.

Microsoft Media Server (MMS)

MMS is a proprietary protocol designed by Microsoft for streaming media content. The media content format used by Microsoft is called the ASF. The MMS protocol is an application-level protocol that runs over UDP, TCP, or HTTP. MMS can also utilize IP multicast in order to broadcast media contents.

The MMS protocol automatically looks for the optimal transport method to deliver the streaming media in the following order:

- UDP
- TCP
- HTTP

Microsoft Media Server - Universal Datagram Protocol (MMSU)

MMSU is the MMS protocol with transport over UDP. UDP is a connectionless, transport-layer protocol that is ideal for real-time media because it does not guarantee delivery. Although this sounds like a drawback rather than an advantage, it is a characteristic particularly suited for streaming media. Unlike data, such as files or e-mail, which must be delivered in their entirety no matter how long the transmission time, the value of streaming media data is constrained by time. If a frame of video is lost, it is worthless because it will not arrive within the correct time frame. By default, MMS tries MMSU first.

Microsoft Media Server - Transmission Control Protocol (MMST)

MMST is the MMS protocol with transport over TCP. TCP is a connection-oriented transport-layer protocol, and it is the desired protocol when the client is behind a firewall. Because TCP is reliable, an MMS proxy will fetch the video stream from the origin server using MMST via TCP so that the cached item is reliable and complete for future delivery.

Microsoft Media Server over HTTP

MMS over HTTP is another protocol that can be used by clients to MMS streams. The client, the Windows Media Player, attempts to retrieve a file using all of these protocols—MMSU, MMST, and MMS over HTTP. The general rule for selecting the protocol is as follows:

- If the URL is http://*xxx*, the Windows Media Player attempts to retrieve the file using MMS over HTTP (also called *streamed HTTP*).

- If the URL is mms://*xxx*.asf, the player attempts to retrieve the file using MMSU, then MMST, and then finally MMS over HTTP, in that order.

- If the URL is http://*xxx*.nsc, then the player first fetches the *xxx*.nsc file through regular HTTP, and then fetches the stream described in the *xxx*.nsc file using MMS over IP multicast.

Because the MMS protocol can also run over HTTP, the Cisco CE acting as a streaming video proxy needs to distinguish MMS requests from regular HTTP requests. The CE accomplishes this by examining the User-Agent header in the request. If the User-Agent is the Windows Media Player, then the CE assumes it is an MMS request; otherwise, it considers it a regular HTTP request.

RTP and RTSP

The underlying transport protocol to support multimedia streaming should allow for the stream to be delivered in a timely manner and in sequence to the clients. The two protocols that support the transport of streaming are RTP and RTSP. RTP divides the packets and associates a timestamp, a sequence number, and information related to the client initiating the session with the packets. In addition, RTP maintains the state of the connection. RTP facilitates the timing and sequencing between the client and the server without having to use a common clock source. RTP header has a 32-bit timestamp field that identifies the specific time when the first byte of data was viewed. All subsequent packets associated with the stream have the same timestamp marked in their 32-bit timestamp field. However, the initial choice for the actual value of the timestamp is a random number, and it increases constantly as the number of packets is processed. With this consistent increase in the timestamp value, the timing between the streams can be maintained without having to rely on a common clock source.

In viewing a video stream, if there is a single frame loss, the user experience does not get interrupted by not having that one frame retransmitted. Working under this assumption, RTP relies on UDP as the underlying protocol, as there are no error control checking and retransmission capabilities in UDP. TCP can also be used as the underlying transport in case it is needed. Just like the TCP sequence number, the RTP header includes a sequence number in order to process the packets in a proper order and to adjust the transmission rate based on the sequence of the packets arriving. In addition to timing and sequencing, the encoding format for the data is included as one of the RTP headers for the proper encoding type for the stream to be used.

The RTSP defines the parameters for the session between the server and the client. RTSP allows applications and streaming servers to provide streaming as multicast and unicast in "one to many" form. In addition, RTSP also supports inter-operability between different operating systems. RTSP manages the bandwidth between the client and the server, and allows for applications to download, play, and decompress the packets all at once, without having to store the file. RTSP relies on RTP for the underlying transport. One of the advantages of using RTSP is that it is similar to HTTP but builds on top of the protocol to provide added parameters for extensibility and for maintaining and managing the client and server connection throughout the length of the stream.

RTSP requests are issued by the client, and the video stream is returned by the server. This is similar to HTTP 1.1, where HTTP requests are also issued by the client and returned by the server. In RTSP, however, the transfer of data is delegated to a separate connection. This allows RTSP to continue its messaging during the data transfer in order to make changes to the stream or to make new connections for additional streams. Common implementation of RTSP is over UDP, but TCP is also supported. UDP or TCP port 554 is reserved for RTSP, and the underlying transport—whether UDP or TCP—is specified as part of the request. For example, the request rtsp://www.cisco.com would use TCP as the underlying protocol, and the request rtspu://www.cisco.com would use UDP. Just like HTTP 1.1, the hostname tag with the requested URI must be provided with the RTSP request.

The RFCs for the RTP and RTSP are as follows:

- RTP is the data transfer protocol for multimedia data over both unicast (TCP and UDP) and multicast (RFC 1889).

- RTSP is a standard Internet streaming control protocol (RFC 2326).

Case Study: Load-Balancing Solution for Video Streaming

Now that we understand the different types of streaming video technology, the motivations behind streaming video load balancing, we will start our discussion on how a streaming video load-balancing solution can be deployed. This case study uses the Darwin Streaming Server, the open source version of Apple's QuickTime Streaming Server, and uses RTP or RTSP as the streaming mechanism. No source code changes were performed on the Darwin Streaming Server. The server was installed and used "as is." For testing purposes, a copy of this server can be found at http://developer.apple.com/darwin/projects/streaming/.

We will present two different solutions for load balancing a QuickTime Streaming Server. The first solution will use the Cisco Content Services Switch (CSS), and the second will use the Cisco Content Switching Module (CSM).

CSS-Based Solution

The CSS topology presented in this section contains two load-balanced server clusters. The first is the web server farm, and the second is the video streaming server farm. Both farms use different VIP addresses. The farms are physically connected to the Catalyst 6500 and reside in separate VLANs. The CSS interface IP is the default gateway of the servers. The topology in Figure 7-1 shows the functional view of the solution and does not incorporate any infrastructure redundancy.

Figure 7-1   *CSS-Based QT SLB Solution*

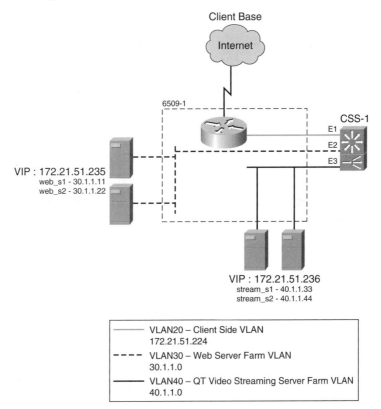

In this scenario, the client's initial web request is directed to the *web_farm* VIP address on the CSS (172.21.51.235). The CSS load balances the request to the appropriate available web server. The client's web browser displays the content of the html page. Embedded in this page is a QuickTime movie clip, which is essentially an RTSP request to the address of the QuickTime server that contains the QuickTime stream. This IP address is defined as the *streamer_farm* VIP address on the CSS (172.21.51.236).

When the user clicks this clip, the QT plug-in in the web browser sends an RTSP request to the CSS, which directs the request to the appropriate server. Once the RTSP control (TCP port 554) session is established, the QT server starts streaming the movie to the client using the UDP ports negotiated during the SETUP phase of RTSP.

In the following sections, we will cover a typical RTSP session as well as several dysfunctional scenarios. This will help you understand how the solution works and the reasoning behind it.

QuickTime Video Stream: Session Flow

Following are the steps that take place when a QT session is established:

Step 1   The client initiates a TCP SYN (port 554) to the QT server/.

Step 2   The server responses with a SYN_ACK.

Step 3   The client acknowledges the SYN_ACK.

Step 4   The client sends TCP data containing an ASCII RTSP request; for example:

DESCRIBE rtsp://172.21.51.236/j4.mov

Step 5   The server acknowledges the RTSP request and sends back an RTSP OK.

Step 6   The client and server move into the RTSP SETUP phase and negotiate the streaming parameters, that is, the UDP ports to be used for the UDP data streams and for the UDP keepalives. During this phase, the server informs the client of the *Source_IP* that it will be using when streaming.

Step 7   The client sends the PLAY request to the server.

Step 8   The server acknowledges the PLAY request.

All of the above is done within the TCP control connection. Following are the steps for the UDP data stream:

Step 1   The server initiates the UDP stream to the client using the negotiated ports.

Step 2   The client and server exchange keepalives every 5 seconds.

QuickTime Load Balancing: First Failure Scenario

The typical directed mode load-balanced configuration does not work because of embedded IP information used by RTSP and because QT streaming is based on dual sessions. Directed mode is when the real IP is used on the server by the load balancer. In essence, the SLB device NATs the destination IP from the VIP address to the server's real IP address.

As defined in the preceding section, TCP is used for session control and UDP for data. Another issue that we have to deal with in streaming applications is the fact that the data stream is initiated by the server.

In our initial configuration, directed mode is used on the CSS, and with that the control session (TCP, port 554) is not established.

In the Sniffer capture in Figure 7-2, look for "DESCRIBE rtsp://172.21.51.236/f4.mov." This is the VIP for the streaming server farm. The server gets the request with an embedded IP of 172.21.51.236 and does not recognize it. The server sends back a FIN ACK to the client.

Figure 7-2   *Sniffer Capture of First Failure Scenario*

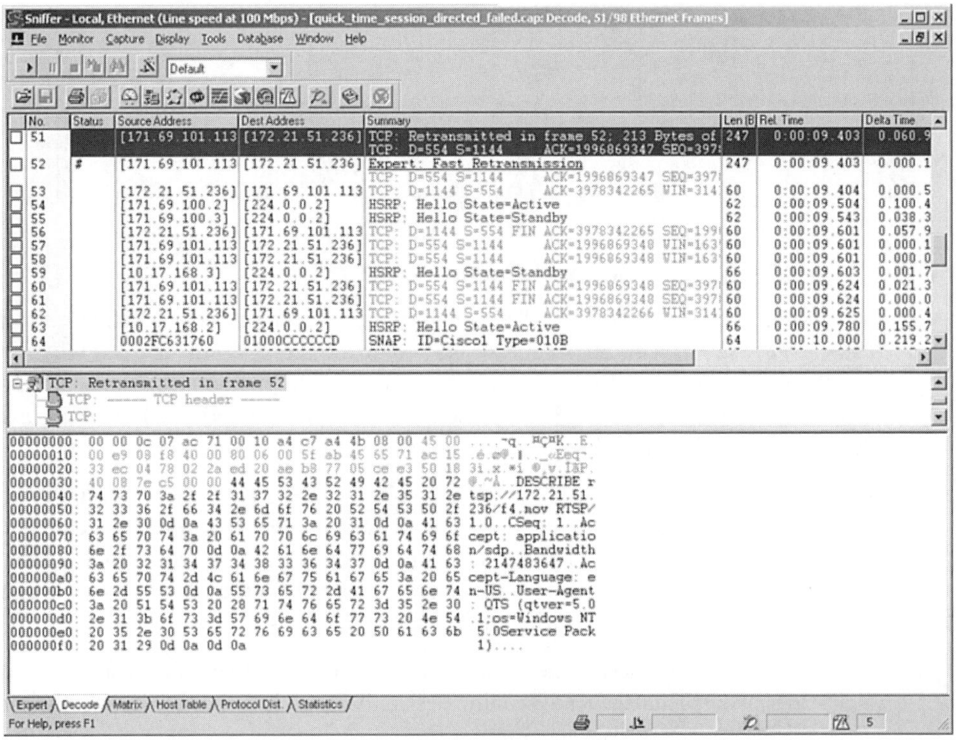

Figure 7-3 shows the client view of this failure scenario. Notice in this figure that the video session fails in the initial negotiation. The client keeps trying and then times out.

Figure 7-3 *Client Browser View of the First Failure Scenario*

QuickTime Load Balancing: Second Failure Scenario

The load-balancing mode on the CSS is changed to dispatch (the configuration keyword is **transparent-cache**). This allows for the CSS to do a Layer 2 rewrite and send the request with the VIP address to the server. Keeping all server configurations the same, secondary IP addresses are added to the server so that it will recognize the VIP address as its own IP. Please see eth0:1 in Figure 7-4.

After the secondary IP addresses have been added to the streaming server, RTSP negotiations succeed as the server recognizes the IP address as self. Since the request came in on the server's *Real_IP* (40.1.1.44), it streams back using that IP address. The client does not recognize this IP address, and the session fails. Furthermore, the server's real IP address subnet 40.1.1.0 is nonroutable from the client network.

On the client window, you see the status change from negotiating to requested data, and finally, to timeout. Thus the RTSP control session's issues have been fixed, but the server to client UDP stream needs some more work.

Figure 7-4   *Streaming Server IP Configuration*

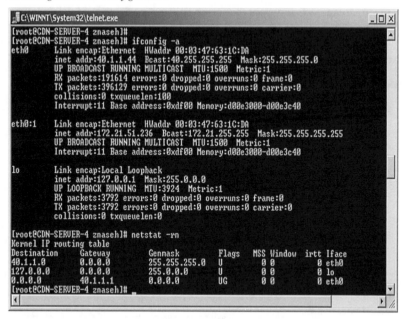

Figure 7-5 shows the client view of this failure scenario. Notice that the client session goes on to the requested data phase.

Figure 7-5   *Client Browser View of the Second Failure Scenario*

The Sniffer trace in Figure 7-6 shows that the control session is established and that the UDP streaming is started from the server side but using its Real_IP address of 40.1.1.44.

Figure 7-6 *Sniffer Capture of Second Failure Scenario*

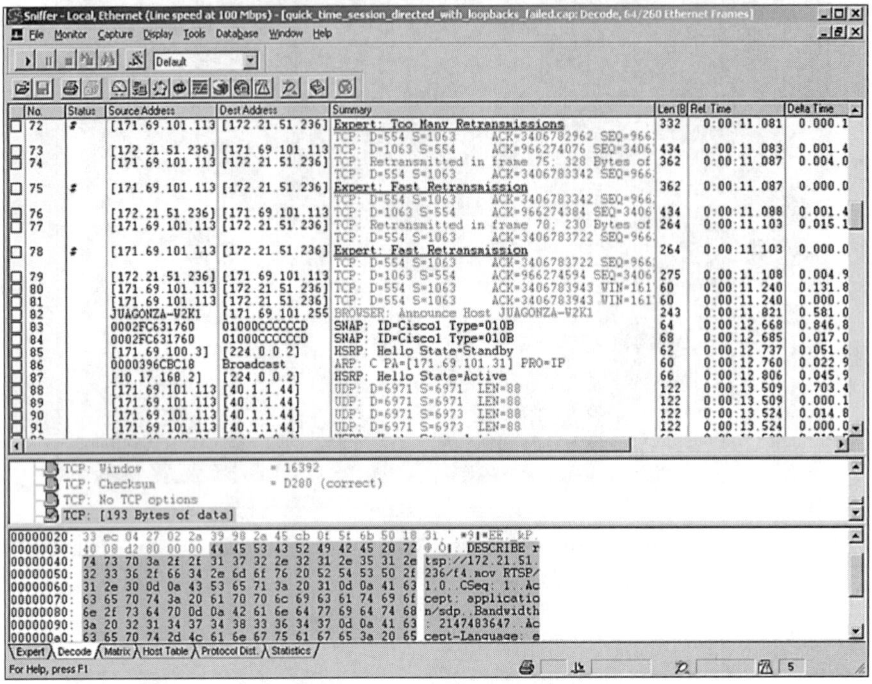

QuickTime Load Balancing

Here are the working design requirements:

- Web server farm with a Layer 4 (TCP:80) content rule definition.

- Streaming server farm with a Layer 3 content rule definition. This covers both TCP control and UDP data streams.

- Both server farms on separate VLANs.

- CSS as the default gateway for the servers in both the VLANs.

- Streaming services configured as type transparent-cache (dispatch mode).

- Secondary IP addresses or loopbacks on the streaming servers.

- Source NAT for the server-initiated UDP stream is accomplished by using the source group.

- SRC-IP sticky part of the streaming server Layer 3 content rule definition.

Stickiness is a *must* and is configured in order to make sure the client sends the UDP keepalives to the same streaming server to which the initial TCP (port 554) request was made. In other words, sticky is a linker between the TCP and UDP sessions and makes sure that the same server is used for both sessions.

CSS Configuration Details

Example 7-1 shows the CSS configuration that was used for the working test scenario.

Example 7-1   *CSS Configuration Template for QuickTime SLB Solution*

```
!
Configure
  ip route 0.0.0.0 0.0.0.0 172.21.51.230 1
!
interface e1
  bridge vlan 20
interface e2
  bridge vlan 30
interface e3
  bridge vlan 40
interface e10
  bridge vlan 40
!
circuit VLAN20
  ip address 172.21.51.231 255.255.255.224

circuit VLAN30
  ip address 30.1.1.1 255.255.255.0
circuit VLAN40
  ip address 40.1.1.1 255.255.255.0
!

service stream_s1
  ip address 40.1.1.33
  type transparent-cache
  active

service stream_s2
  ip address 40.1.1.44
  type transparent-cache
  active

service web_s1
  ip address 30.1.1.11
  active

service web_s2
  ip address 30.1.1.22
  active
!
```

continues

Example 7-1 *CSS Configuration Template for QuickTime SLB Solution (Continued)*

```
owner znaseh

  content streamer_farm
    add service stream_s1
    add service stream_s2
    vip address 172.21.51.236
    advanced-balance sticky-srcip
    sticky-inact-timeout 1
    active

  content web_farm
    add service web_s1
    add service web_s2
    vip address 172.21.51.235
    protocol tcp
    port 80
    active
!
  group nat-data-stream
    vip address 172.21.51.236
    add service stream_s1
    add service stream_s2
    active
!
```

MSFC Configuration Details for the CSS-Based Solution

Example 7-2 shows the Multilayer Switch Feature Card (MSFC) configuration that was used for the working test scenario.

Example 7-2 *MSFC Configuration Template for QuickTime SLB Solution*

```
!
!
version 12.1
service timestamps debug uptime
service timestamps log uptime
no service password-encryption
!
hostname Cat6506-2-MSFC
!
enable password test
!
ip subnet-zero
no ip domain-lookup
!
!
interface Vlan20
 ip address 172.21.51.230 255.255.255.224
!
interface Vlan111
```

Example 7-2   *MSFC Configuration Template for QuickTime SLB Solution (Continued)*

```
 ip address 172.21.51.20 255.255.255.128
 !
ip classless
ip route 0.0.0.0 0.0.0.0 172.21.51.15
 !
```

HTML Code Used in the Solution

Example 7-3 shows the simple HTML code that was used for the working test scenario.

Example 7-3   *HTML File Template for QuickTime SLB Solution*

```html
<HTML>
<HEAD>
<TITLE>Zeeshan's Qtime Web Server - 1</TITLE>
</HEAD>
<!-- Background white, links blue (unvisited), navy (visited), red (active) -->
<BODY BGCOLOR="#FFFFFF">
<P><BR>
<H3><I>CDN-SERVER-1</I></H3>
</CENTER>
<P><BR>
Tests performed using Darwin Streaming Server which uses Quick Time code base and
   the same protocols, i.e., RTP & RTSP.
<BR>
<HR>
QuickTime Movie Clips :
<BR><I>Now Showing !</I>
<P><LI><A HREF=#f4>Horror Flick 1</A>
<BR><LI><A HREF=#j4>Horror Flick 2</A>
<P>
<CENTER>
<A NAME=f4> </A>
<embed width="470" src="qtstart.mov" height="310" controller="false"
href="rtsp://172.21.51.236/f4.mov" border="0" target="myself">
</EMBED>
<BR>
<A NAME=j4> </A>
<embed width="470" src="qtstart.mov" height="310" controller="false"
href="rtsp://172.21.51.236/j4.mov" border="0" target="myself">
</EMBED>
</CENTER>
<HR>
<P><BR><P><BR>
<B><I>
<A HREF="mailto:znaseh@cisco.com">Zeeshan Naseh</A>
<BR>Network Design Consultant
</I></B>
</BODY>
</HTML>
```

CSM-Based Solution

The CSM can be used in fairly similar fashion as the CSS to provide load balancing for video streaming servers. The key difference in the design is the use of the *direct server return* (DSR) feature on the CSM. This feature enables the bypass of the CSM for the data stream. The SLB device makes the load-balancing decision and forwards the request using dispatch mode to the real servers. The server's default gateway is the MSFC and not the CSM. The server responds directly to the client using the VIP address as the source IP address.

In the following CSM-based solution topology, there are two load-balanced server clusters. The first is the web server farm, and the second is the video streaming servers. Both farms use different VIP addresses. The farms are physically connected to the Cat6500 and reside in separate VLANs. The default gateway of the servers is the MSFC interface IP address. The topology in Figure 7-7 shows the functional view of the solution and does not incorporate any infrastructure redundancy.

Figure 7-7 *CSM-Based QuickTime SLB Solution*

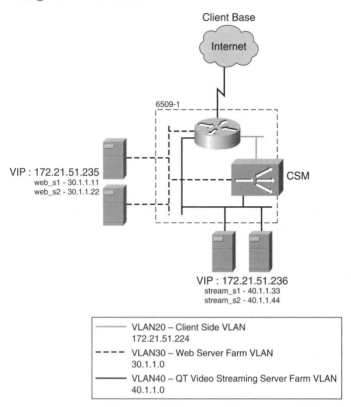

Client Base

Internet

6509-1

VIP : 172.21.51.235
web_s1 - 30.1.1.11
web_s2 - 30.1.1.22

CSM

VIP : 172.21.51.236
stream_s1 - 40.1.1.33
stream_s2 - 40.1.1.44

——— VLAN20 – Client Side VLAN
172.21.51.224

- - - - VLAN30 – Web Server Farm VLAN
30.1.1.0

——— VLAN40 – QT Video Streaming Server Farm VLAN
40.1.1.0

QuickTime Load Balancing

The design would stay the same as load balance streaming with the CSS, except now we use CSM on the CAT6500 to load balance traffic across the streaming video servers. Following are the key QuickTime application load-balancing design requirements:

- Web server farm with a Layer 4 (TCP:80) virtual server definition

- Use of TCP probe for the web servers

- Streaming server farm with a control session virtual server (TCP:554)

- Streaming server farm with a data session virtual server (UDP:any)

- Both server farms on separate VLANs with the CSM being Layer 2 adjacent to the servers

- MSFC as the default gateway for the servers in both VLANs

- Streaming services configured as type dispatch mode (configuration keyword: **no nat server**)

- Secondary IP addresses or loopbacks configured on the streaming servers

- TCP and UDP streaming virtual servers part of the same sticky group

CSM Configuration Details

Example 7-4 shows the CSM configuration that was used for the working solution.

Example 7-4 *CSM Configuration Template for QuickTime SLB Solution*

```
!
!
module ContentSwitchingModule 6
 vlan 20 client
  ip address 172.21.51.231 255.255.255.224
  gateway 172.21.51.230
 !
 vlan 30 server
  ip address 30.1.1.10 255.255.255.0
 !
 vlan 40 server
  ip address 40.1.1.10 255.255.255.0
 !
 probe TCP_80 tcp
  interval 5
  failed 3
  port 80
 !
 probe TCP_554 tcp
  interval 5
  failed 3
  port 554
 !
```

continues

Example 7-4   *CSM Configuration Template for QuickTime SLB Solution (Continued)*

```
 serverfarm STREAMER_FARM
  no nat server
  no nat client
  real 40.1.1.33
   inservice
  real 40.1.1.44
   inservice
  probe TCP_554
 !
 serverfarm WEB_FARM
  nat server
  no nat client
  real 10.70.1.11
   inservice
  real 10.70.1.22
   inservice
  probe TCP_80
 !
 sticky 10 netmask 255.255.255.255 timeout 30
 !
 vserver STREAMER_CTRL
  virtual 172.21.51.251 tcp rtsp
  unidirectional
  serverfarm STREAMER_FARM
  idle 120
  sticky 30 group 10
  persistent rebalance
  inservice
 !
 vserver STREAMER_DATA
  virtual 172.21.51.251 udp 0
  unidirectional
  serverfarm STREAMER_FARM
  idle 120
  sticky 30 group 10
  persistent rebalance
  inservice
 !
 vserver WEB_FARM
  virtual 172.21.51.250 tcp www
  serverfarm WEB_FARM
  persistent rebalance
  inservice
 !
 !
```

MSFC Configuration Details for the CSM-Based Solution

Example 7-5 shows the MSFC configuration that is used for the CSM-based solution.
Notice that the default gateway of the servers now exists as Layer 3 interfaces on the MSFC.
On VLAN 30, the server's default gateway is 30.1.1.1, and on VLAN 40, the server's
default gateway is 40.1.1.1.

Example 7-5 *MSFC Configuration Template for CSM-Based QuickTime SLB Solution*

```
!
!
version 12.1
service timestamps debug uptime
service timestamps log uptime
no service password-encryption
!
hostname Cat6506-2-MSFC
!
enable password test
!
ip subnet-zero
no ip domain-lookup
!
!
interface Vlan20
 ip address 172.21.51.230 255.255.255.224
!
interface Vlan30
 ip address 30.1.1.1 255.255.255.0
!
interface Vlan40
 ip address 40.1.1.1 255.255.255.0
!
interface Vlan111
 ip address 172.21.51.20 255.255.255.128
!
ip classless
ip route 0.0.0.0 0.0.0.0 172.21.51.15
!
!
```

Summary

This chapter introduced streaming video technology. You learned about the different types of streaming video servers, such as Apple QuickTime, RealMedia, WMT, and streaming protocols, such as MMS and RTSP. The chapter also covered the motivation behind load balancing streaming video servers.

In order to combine all the concepts of streaming video SLB from the perspective of the CSS and CSM platforms, this chapter presented a case study. This case study focused on the deployment scenario of streaming video servers using both the CSS and CSM. The CSS and CSM configurations were provided and explained to introduce you to the command-line interface.

Chapter 8, "Virtual Private Network Load Balancing," introduces virtual private networks and details of IPsec protocol components, such as Internet Key Exchange (IKE) and Encrypted Security Payload (ESP). The chapter addresses how IPsec tunnels can be load balanced by an SLB device.

Virtual Private Network Load Balancing

VPN load balancing (VPNLB) provides the scalability and availability that enterprise and service provider customers are looking for. VPN load balancing allows customers to scale their VPN infrastructures easily by simply adding new devices while at the same time improving the redundancy level.

The idea behind VPNLB is to use a load balancer device to distribute the VPN sessions across a group of IP Security (IPsec) protocol devices, thus allowing customers to add or remove devices as needed.

This chapter introduces the concept of load balancing in VPNs, providing an overview of the technology, and discusses its benefits as well as the VPN protocols in depth. To help you understand VPN load balancing, this chapter includes a case study with design and configuration details.

Benefits of VPN Load Balancing

Some of the benefits of VPN load balancing include scalability, monitoring, and the ability to scale the IPsec end points terminating the connections.

Conceptually, IPsec devices are grouped in farms, and each farm represents a virtual device, which is the only element known in the external world. The outside world is only knows about the virtual IP (VIP) address representing the VPN device farm and not the internal secure network of the enterprise. Depending on the requirements, multiple farms can be defined; for example, one farm of VPN concentrators to attend to *access* VPNs and another farm of routers for *site-to-site* connections. Each virtual device has an IP address associated, which is called a VIP address and which resides in the Content Switching Module (CSM). Remote VPN peers are only aware of this VIP and the real IP addresses of the VPN devices, and when a peer initiates a connection to a virtual device, the load balancer decides which real device within the farm will serve the session based on the load-balancing algorithm in use. There are multiple load-balancing algorithms that can be used to distribute VPN traffic, from a simple round robin to more sophisticated algorithms based on the concurrent number of connections, server load, and weight.

The load balancer is also responsible for monitoring the status of the real devices to make sure VPN traffic is only distributed along active units. Failing devices are transparently removed from the farm, and are only returned once they are back in service.

Figure 8-1 shows an example in which two farms are defined, one for *access* VPNs, and another for *site-to-site* connections.

Figure 8-1 *Logical Example of IPsec Distribution*

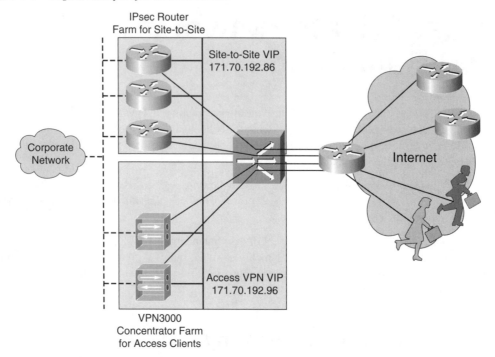

As processing of IPsec connections is very CPU intensive (with Internet Key Exchange, or IKE, negotiations first and then the actual encryption and decryption), the need to offload these connections and load balance them over a farm of IPsec end points becomes crucial. In addition, as connections are being made from Internet clients or remote sites, providing persistency for the connections to the original IPsec peer becomes necessary. The IKE security associations (SAs) and the IPsec SAs cannot be load balanced to two different peers and have to be persistent to the same IPsec end point.

Figure 8-2 shows how a traditional single VPN concentrator solution becomes a single point of resource exhaustion or failure. Using multiple concentrators can help scale the environment and make it more redundant.

It should be noted that the VPN 3000 concentrator already provides a native load-balancing mechanism without the use of any external load-balancing device, but allows only farms composed by VPN 3000 concentrators. This native mechanism is very easy to deploy and is the solution we recommend when you are implementing only VPN 3000 concentrators. For more information regarding VPN 3000 load balancing, please refer to the document "Load Balancing Cisco VPN Clients," available at http://www.cisco.com/univercd/cc/td/doc/product/vpn/vpn3000/4_7/config/lbssf.htm.

Figure 8-2   *Redundancy and Scalability as Key Advantages of VPN Load Balancing*

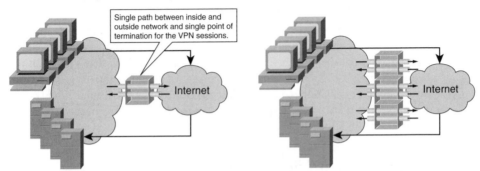

Introduction to Virtual Private Networks

A VPN is a network solution deployed on a shared infrastructure, such as the Internet, employing the same security, management, and throughput policies applied in a private network. Remote access VPNs connect telecommuters, mobile users, or even smaller remote offices, utilizing the Internet to access the corporate intranet resources.

As customers realize the benefits of deploying intranets and extranets, the more they rely on the VPN foundation and the more they are concerned about the scalability and availability of the deployed technologies. In the enterprise space, many organizations have deployed intranets and extranets as the natural communication medium for telecommuters, remote offices, and partners. In the service provider space, VPNs have opened up a great opportunity to expand the service offerings by selling VPN services and setting a value differentiator in an extremely competitive market. Each market space has particular needs in driving the implementation of VPNs; however, both spaces have something in common: the VPN infrastructure. This infrastructure has become a critical medium, and organizations rely on it for some of their most important operations.

VPNs offer many advantages over traditional, leased-line networks. The primary benefits include:

- Lower cost than private networks. Users trying to connect to the corporate network remotely use the Internet to connect. There is no need to pay for leased lines or Plain Old Telephone System (POTS) services similar to dial-up through remote access.

- Ease of use and manageability. The addition of users and managing their connections becomes very simple, as VPNs are usually integrated with the existing remote access solution, or integration is easily implemented. Connections can now be provided to remote offices, international locations, telecommuters, roaming mobile users, and external business partners.

- Simplified network topologies while still providing the choice of high-speed access to intranet resources. The IP backbone does not require static permanent virtual circuits (PVCs) usually associated with connection-oriented protocols, such as Frame Relay and ATM, thereby creating a fully meshed network topology while actually decreasing network complexity and cost.

Even though the VPN solution provides many benefits, there are some risks involved. Providing remote access on a shared network, such as the Internet, creates a security risk associated to the data being transferred over the VPN connections. The VPN solution needs to be secure from hackers observing or tampering with confidential data passing over the network and from unauthorized users gaining access to network resources and proprietary information. The IPsec protocol was created to provide the security needed for transferring confidential information over the Internet.

Virtual Private Network Protocols

IPsec is a protocol developed by the Internet Engineering Task Force (IETF) to provide encryption and authentication for the data that the IP packets carry.

IETF RFC 2401 defines IPSec as follows:

> IPsec provides security services at the IP layer by enabling a system to select required security protocols, determine the algorithm(s) to use for the service(s), and put in place any cryptographic keys required to provide the requested services.

> The set of security services that IPsec can provide includes access control, connectionless integrity, data origin authentication, rejection of replayed packets (a form of partial sequence integrity), confidentiality (encryption), and limited traffic flow confidentiality. Because these services are provided at the IP layer, they can be used by any higher layer protocol, e.g., TCP, UDP, ICMP, BGP, etc.

As most of the connections on the Internet and on intranets use IP as the standard protocol for communication, it seems fit to use IPsec as the underlying protocol to provide authentication and encryption for VPN services. Since IPsec is an IETF standard, it allows for interoperability among the various vendor implementations of the protocol. In addition to the network equipment (mostly routers and switches), applications, such as Microsoft Windows and UNIX, are implementing IPsec to provide end-to-end encryption and authentication. IPsec also has support for the IKE protocol and for digital certificates. IKE provides negotiation services and key derivation services for IPsec, thus allowing it to scale better on the Internet, by the use of digital signatures.

IPsec relies on three protocols:

- Internet Key Exchange (IKE) protocol—used primarily for key negotiation used in encryption

- Authentication Header (AH)—used within the IP header to authenticate the data and the IP headers

- Encapsulating Security Protocol (ESP)—used for encapsulation of the IP packet with IPsec headers and the actual encryption of the payload

Internet Key Exchange Protocol (IKE)

IKE is the first protocol that gets negotiated when an IPsec connection is initiated. IKE is responsible for negotiating the SAs. The SA defines the set of policies and keys that the two peers need to agree on before the data can be encrypted, and how these keys will be authenticated and managed once the connection is established. There are different modes for IKE to be deployed, and one of the biggest advantages that IKE has is its ability to automate the key exchange process. This scales very well on the Internet and forgoes the problems of having to do preconfiguration of keys and policies between the peers.

IKE is a result of three different protocols:

- **ISAKMP**—The Internet Security Association and Key Management Protocol. A protocol framework that defines payload formats, the mechanics of implementing a key exchange protocol, and the negotiation of a SA

- **Oakley**—A key exchange protocol that defines how to derive authenticated keying material

- **SKEME**—A key exchange protocol that defines how to derive authenticated keying material with rapid key refreshment

IKE protocols operate in two modes, each of which operates in one of two phases. Phase 1 establishes an ISAKMP SA and derives shared secrets used to protect Phase 2 exchanges. The Phase 1 mode is called Main mode or Aggressive mode. The primary objective of Main mode is to agree on a set of parameters that allow the two peers to be authenticated by each other and to generate a session key. These negotiations are what constitute an SA for each peer.

Phase 2 negotiates SAs on behalf of IPsec or other security services and generates fresh keying material. Phase 2 is called Quick mode. Quick mode enables the two peers to negotiate attributes associated with the IPsec SAs. For example, if one of the peers has Perfect Forward Secrecy (PFS) configured, the two peers need to agree on it. PFS ensures that a given IPsec SA key was not derived from any other secret (such as from another key). In other words, if someone breaks a key, PFS ensures that the attacker is not able to derive any other key. If PFS is not enabled, someone can potentially break the IKE SA secret key, copy all the IPsec protected data, and then use knowledge of the IKE SA secret in order to compromise the IPsec SAs set up by this IKE SA. With PFS, breaking IKE does not give an attacker immediate access to IPsec. The attacker needs to break each IPsec SA individually. The Cisco IOS IPsec implementation uses PFS group 1 (D-H 768-bit) by default.

The following attributes are used by IKE and are negotiated as part of the ISAKMP SA. (These attributes pertain only to the ISAKMP SA and not to any SAs that ISAKMP may be negotiating on behalf of other services.)

- Encryption algorithm
- Hash algorithm

- Authentication method
- Information about a negotiated Diffie-Hellman group

All of these attributes are mandatory and *must* be negotiated before the IPsec SAs are negotiated and before the data can be used for encryption. IKE is layered on User Datagram Protocol (UDP) and uses UDP port 500 to exchange IKE information between the two peers.

ESP and AH

The security services for IPsec are provided by the Authentication Header (AH) and the Encapsulating Security Payload (ESP) protocols along with cryptographic key management. Some of the services are defined here:

- *Data integrity* ensures that the data going over the public network hasn't been changed while in transit. For example, IPsec does a hash, validating the hash value generated before and after transit, to ensure that the encrypted portion of the packet, or the entire header and data portion of the packet, has not been tampered with. If the hash value is not the same, the packet is dropped.

- *Authentication* verifies the identity of the source of the data being sent to guard against a number of attacks that depend on spoofing the identity of the sender.

- *Anti-replay* is the ability to detect and reject replayed packets. This helps in preventing IP address spoofing.

- *Packet encapsulation, or tunneling,* is the process of encapsulating an entire packet within another packet and sending it over a network. In order to support multiple users on the IPsec tunnel, it hides the source of the client originating the traffic. For example, a single device using IPsec encapsulates traffic belonging to a number of hosts behind it and adds its own header on top of the existing packets. By encrypting the original packet and header (and routing the packet based on the additional Layer 3 header added on top), the tunneling device effectively hides the actual source of the packet.

AH and ESP provide integrity checking and encryption for the packet. Encryption on the packet is performed using the Data Encryption Standard (DES) or a stronger version of it called 3DES.

Authentication Header (AH)

AH mode provides authentication for as much of the IP header as possible, as well as the data; however, there is no encryption provided by AH. AH provides a hash value, which it computes based on the IP header and the payload it is carrying. AH is different from ESP because AH checks the entire IP header for integrity rather than just the payload. This becomes an issue when the IP packet needs to be NATed. AH is defined as IP protocol 51.

The Encapsulating Security Payload (ESP)

ESP is the protocol used for encapsulating the IPsec packet in an IP header and also provides encryption and authentication. ESP uses DES or 3DES to provide encryption and provides data integrity using the MD5 and SHA hashes on the encrypted data portion of the packet. Once ESP finishes encrypting the packet, it adds a new IP header to the packet using the local crypto end point's IP address as the source address and the remote crypto end point's IP address as the destination address. ESP is defined as IP protocol 50.

Case Study: VPN Load-Balanced Solution

In this case study, we will analyze the IPsec protocols and go into detail on how a load-balancing solution can be provided for them. Each component of the protocols will be analyzed to cover their specific requirements.

IPsec services are provided by different protocols that can be combined according to the security services selected by the user. As indicated earlier in the chapter, standard protocols used by IPsec include IKE, ESP, and AH. The IKE is a UDP protocol that provides the key management and allows the dynamic negotiation of SAs. IKE is also often referred to as ISAKMP, which is the name of the protocol it is based on. ESP is an IP protocol (50) that provides encryption services plus optional authentication and integrity services. AH is another IP protocol (51), and it provides authentication and integrity services.

AH and ESP packets are usually not supported by firewalls or routers implementing Port Address Translation (PAT). To overcome this problem, the Cisco VPN Unity client allows the encapsulation of IPsec over UDP, which is called "IPsec through NAT."

In this case study, we will cover configurations for load balancing both raw IPsec (IKE and ESP) and IPsec over UDP traffic. The following sections describe the nature of each protocol to be supported and provide details about how load balancing should be implemented.

IKE Requirements

IKE is a UDP protocol used for key management and the negotiation of the SAs. When an IPsec peer needs to establish a VPN tunnel with another peer, first it must initiate an IKE session. IKE acts like the control session where peers authenticate each other, agree on policies, and negotiate IPsec tunnels. IKE traffic has the following peculiarities:

- IKE traffic is sent over UDP with source and destination ports 500. Usually, in UDP-based applications, the source port is randomly chosen from the non-well-known range. IKE traffic is different because it always uses the same source port (UDP/500).

- The UDP source port may change if packets go through a PAT/NAT device.
- IKE flows are usually long term; for example, in Cisco IOS implementation, the default lifetime for an IKE session is 24 hours.
- In Cisco IOS, peers send keepalive packets every 10 seconds by default. A keepalive is retransmitted every 2 seconds if no response has been received. And once three packets are missed, the IPsec termination point concludes that it has lost connectivity with its peer. The keepalive interval can be between 10 and 3600 seconds, while the retry interval can be between 2 and 10 seconds.

ESP Requirements

ESP is IP protocol 50, and it provides the main encryption services, plus some optional authentication and integrity services. ESP can be described briefly as the protocol used to transport users' encrypted data.

Since the CSM supports load balancing of IP, traffic load balancing for ESP traffic is possible. Following are the most relevant characteristics of ESP traffic:

- ESP traffic is directly transported over IP protocol 50. It is not encapsulated in TCP or UDP.
- ESP flows (IPsec SAs) are unidirectional, so multiple flows can exist between two IPsec peers.
- ESP flows should be directed to the same VPN concentrator as their associated IKE sessions; otherwise, IPsec will fail. An IPsec VPN can be described as a bundle composed of an IKE session and multiple IPsec sessions.
- ESP flows are usually long term; for example, in our IOS implementation, the default lifetime for an IPsec SA is 1 hour. The lifetime of an IOS IPsec SA can be configured to any value between 2 minutes and 24 hours.

IPsec over UDP Requirements

As it was explained in the "Virtual Private Network Protocols" section, IPsec packets are usually not supported by PAT/NAT devices. To overcome this problem, vendors have developed some proprietary solutions, such as the one found in the Cisco Unity VPN client. The Cisco Unity client solves the problem by encapsulating IPsec over UDP, which is also called *IPsec through NAT* or *UDP wrapping*.

IPsec over UDP traffic has the following characteristics:

- The flow is always initiated from the client and uses the same number for source and destination ports. The port number is predefined in the IPsec server; by default, it is 10000, but it can be changed to any value within the 4001–49151 range. Note that the source port is not randomly chosen and that subsequent flows share the same source port number.

- The UDP source port may change if packets go through a PAT/NAT device.

- Only ESP is encapsulated; IKE is already UDP traffic.

- IPsec over UDP flows should be directed to the same VPN concentrator as their associated IKE sessions; otherwise, IPsec will fail.

- Flows inherit the nature of ESP and are usually long term; for example, in IOS implementation, the default lifetime for an IPsec SA is 1 hour. The lifetime of an IOS IPsec SA can be configured to any value between 2 minutes and 24 hours.

Design Options

This section builds two solutions to meet the requirements of the supported protocols. From the requirements, it is evident that we need the following features on the load balancer:

- UDP load balancing with bidirectional flow management

- IP protocol 50 and 51 load balancing with bidirectional flow management

- Idle timeout commands to modify default flow cleanup timers

- Cleanup of flows when an associated VPN concentrator fails probes

- Dispatch mode to support protocols like AH (IP protocol 51), which does not work with network address translation (NAT) (directed mode)

- Source IP–based stickiness across multiple virtual servers to ensure the binding of IKE and ESP sessions with the same VPN concentrator

The first design solution uses Directed mode as the method of sending packets from the load balancer to the VPN device, and the second solution uses Dispatch mode as the method of rewriting headers of packets before forwarding them to the IPsec-enabled IOS router.

Directed Mode Solution

Directed mode is simple to deploy. The load balancer, in this case the CSM, performs NAT when sending packets to the IOS-based VPN concentrator. Figure 8-3 illustrates how the address translation will happen.

Figure 8-4 defines the infrastructure used in this solution. For simplicity's sake, infrastructure redundancy is not shown. A deployed solution will have appropriate high availability, such as redundant CSMs, built in. In this design, CSM is used in Bridge mode with VLAN 51 being the client-side VLAN and VLAN 61 being the server-side VLAN. The VPN concentrators are IOS-based routers with IPsec enabled. The VIP address on the CSM is 172.21.51.253. In the testing of this solution, CSM-adjacent routers R1 and R2 are used as remote VPN clients. Typically, VPN clients come in from the Internet and are not in the same subnet as the CSM.

Figure 8-3 *VPNLB Using Directed Mode on the CSM*

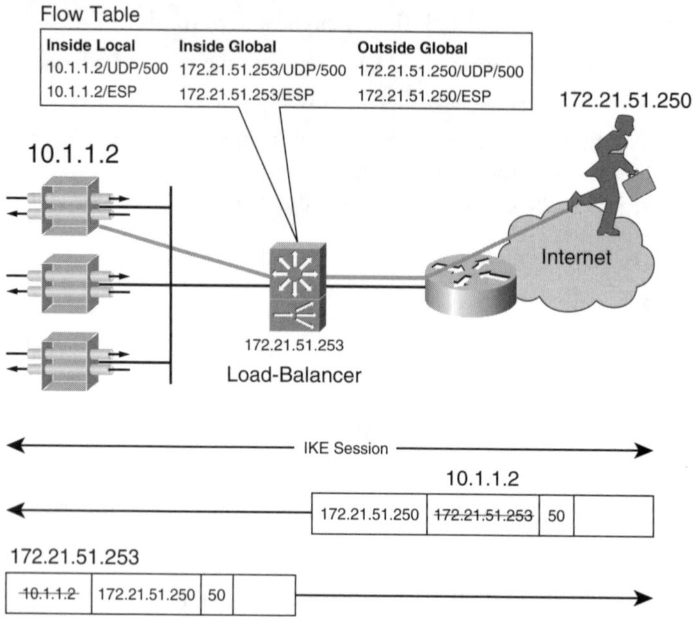

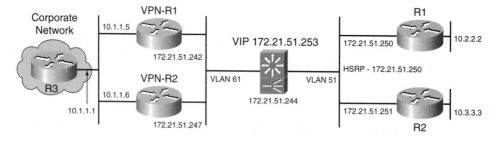

Figure 8-4 *VPNLB Directed Mode Solution Topology*

CSM Configurations for Directed Mode

As mentioned in the section "Design Options," one of the key elements in VPNLB is the stickiness of the client's IKE and ESP sessions to the same concentrator. Figure 8-5 highlights the composition of a VPN session. The stickiness is achieved by using the same sticky group for both the IKE and ESP virtual servers. This methodology is also known as *buddy group* or *buddy sticky*.

Figure 8-5   *Session Stickiness Is Required on the CSM*

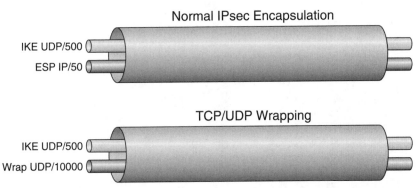

Example 8-1 shows the CSM configuration used in this solution. One of the key features used in this example is the purging of connections when the associated server fails. This feature is enabled by the keyword **failaction purge** within the server farm configuration. In this solution, the health check method used is ICMP to the VPN router's public-side interface. This can be further improved by sending a ping to the inside interface of the VPN router to ensure that both the public and inside interfaces are verified before sending user requests to a particular VPN router.

Notice in the configuration how sticky group 11 is used for both the IKE and ESP virtual servers.

Example 8-1   *CSM Configuration Example for Directed Mode Solution*

```
module ContentSwitchingModule 6
vlan 51 client
  ip address 172.21.51.244 255.255.255.240
  gateway 172.21.51.250
  alias 172.21.51.241 255.255.255.240
!
 vlan 61 server
  ip address 172.21.51.244 255.255.255.240
!
 probe ICMP_PROBE icmp
  interval 5
  retries 2
!
 serverfarm VPN_IOS
  nat server
  no nat client
  failaction purge
  real 172.21.51.242
   inservice
  real 172.21.51.247
   inservice
  probe ICMP_PROBE
```

continues

Example 8-1 *CSM Configuration Example for Directed Mode Solution (Continued)*

```
!
 sticky 11 netmask 255.255.255.255 timeout 60
!
 policy VPNIOS
  sticky-group 11
  serverfarm VPN_IOS
!
 vserver VPN_IOS_ESP
  virtual 172.21.51.253 50
  persistent rebalance
  slb-policy VPNIOS
  inservice
!
 vserver VPN_IOS_IKE
  virtual 172.21.51.253 udp 500
  persistent rebalance
  slb-policy VPNIOS
  inservice
!
```

CSM show Commands for Directed Mode

Example 8-2 demonstrates **show** command output from the CSM, showing proper functioning of the VPNLB solution. The first output shows the connection table from the CSM, and the second output shows proper stickiness behavior.

Example 8-2 *Connection and Sticky Tables on the CSM for the Directed Mode Solution*

```
Cat6506-1-Native#show module contentSwitchingModule all conns
-------------------- CSM in slot 6 --------------------
    prot vlan source                 destination          state
--------------------------------------------------------------------
In   UDP  51   172.21.51.250:500     172.21.51.253:500    ESTAB
Out  UDP  61   172.21.51.242:500     172.21.51.250:500    ESTAB
In   50   51   172.21.51.251         172.21.51.253        ESTAB
Out  50   61   172.21.51.247         172.21.51.251        ESTAB
In   50   51   172.21.51.250         172.21.51.253        ESTAB
Out  50   61   172.21.51.242         172.21.51.250        ESTAB
In   UDP  51   172.21.51.251:500     172.21.51.253:500    ESTAB
Out  UDP  61   172.21.51.247:500     172.21.51.251:500    ESTAB
Cat6506-1-Native#
Cat6506-1-Native#show module contentSwitchingModule all sticky
-------------------- CSM in slot 6 --------------------
client IP:     172.21.51.250
real server:   172.21.51.242
connections:   0
group id:      11
timeout:       38
sticky type:   netmask 255.255.255.255
client IP:     172.21.51.251
real server:   172.21.51.247
```

Example 8-2 *Connection and Sticky Tables on the CSM for the Directed Mode Solution (Continued)*

```
connections:  0
group id:     11
timeout:      40
sticky type:  netmask 255.255.255.255
```

IPsec Router Configurations for Directed Mode

Example 8-3 shows the IOS-based IPsec router configuration used in the solution verification.

Example 8-3 *IOS IPSec Configuration Example*

```
crypto isakmp policy 10
 authentication pre-share
crypto isakmp key cisco123 address 0.0.0.0
!
crypto ipsec transform-set myset esp-3des esp-sha-hmac
crypto mib ipsec flowmib history tunnel size 200
crypto mib ipsec flowmib history failure size 200
!
crypto dynamic-map mydyn 10
 set transform-set myset
 reverse-route
!
crypto map mymap 10 ipsec-isakmp dynamic mydyn
!
interface FastEthernet0/0
ip address 172.21.51.247 255.255.255.240
crypto map mymap
!
interface FastEthernet2/0
 ip address 10.1.1.6 255.255.255.0
router eigrp 1
 redistribute static
 network 10.0.0.0
 no auto-summary
 no eigrp log-neighbor-changes
!
ip classless
ip route 0.0.0.0 0.0.0.0 172.21.51.241
 !
```

Dispatch Mode Solution

Dispatch mode is used for load balancing when NAT is not appropriate for protocols using embedded IP address or Layer 4 port information. In this mode, the VPN devices are configured with a loopback address that is the same as the VIP address on the CSM. The CSM performs a Layer 2 rewrite (a MAC address change) when it needs to forward traffic to a selected VPN device. Figure 8-6 illustrates how a MAC address rewrite is performed.

Figure 8-6   *VPNLB Using Dispatch Mode on the CSM*

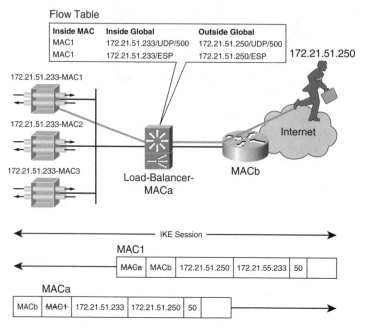

Figure 8-7 defines the infrastructure used in this solution. Again, for simplicity's sake, infrastructure redundancy is not shown. A deployed solution will have appropriate high availability, such as redundant CSMs, built in. In this design, CSM is used in Bridge mode with VLAN 51 being the client-side VLAN and VLAN 61 being the server-side VLAN. The VPN concentrators are IOS-based routers with IPsec enabled. The VIP address on the CSM is 172.21.51.233.

Figure 8-7   *VPNLB Dispatch Mode Solution Topology*

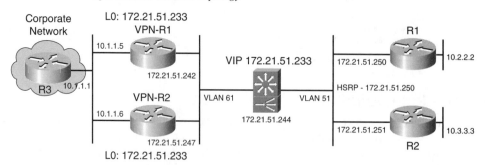

CSM Configurations for Dispatch Mode

Example 8-4 shows the CSM configuration with inline comments on the features being used.

Example 8-4 *CSM Configuration Example for Dispatch Mode Solution*

```
module ContentSwitchingModule 6
 vlan 51 client
  ip address 172.21.51.244 255.255.255.240
  gateway 172.21.51.250
  alias 172.21.51.241 255.255.255.240
 !
 vlan 61 server
  ip address 172.21.51.244 255.255.255.240
 !
 probe ICMP_PROBE icmp
  interval 5
  retries 2
 !
 serverfarm VPN_IOS
  no nat server
  no nat client
  failaction purge
  real 172.21.51.242
   inservice
  real 172.21.51.247
   inservice
  probe ICMP_PROBE
 !
 sticky 11 netmask 255.255.255.255 timeout 60
 !
 policy VPNIOS
  sticky-group 11
  serverfarm VPN_IOS
 !
 vserver VPN_IOS_AH_2
  virtual 172.21.51.233 51
  persistent rebalance
  slb-policy VPNIOS
  inservice
 !
 vserver VPN_IOS_ESP_2
  virtual 172.21.51.233 50
  persistent rebalance
  slb-policy VPNIOS
  inservice
 !
 vserver VPN_IOS_IKE_2
  virtual 172.21.51.233 udp 500
  persistent rebalance
  slb-policy VPNIOS
  inservice
 !
```

CSM show Commands for Dispatch Mode

Example 8-5 demonstrates **show** output from the CSM, showing proper functioning of the Dispatch mode VPNLB solution. The first output shows the connection count on the configured virtual server on the CSM, and the second output shows proper stickiness behavior.

Example 8-5 *Vserver and Sticky Tables on the CSM for the Dispatch Mode Solution*

```
Cat6506-1-Native#show module c 6 vser
slb vserver       prot  virtual                    vlan  state         conns
---------------------------------------------------------------------------
VPN_IOS_ESP       50    172.21.51.253/32:0         ALL   OPERATIONAL   0
VPN_IOS_IKE       UDP   172.21.51.253/32:500       ALL   OPERATIONAL   0
VPN_IOS_ESP_2     50    172.21.51.233/32:0         ALL   OPERATIONAL   0
VPN_IOS_IKE_2     UDP   172.21.51.233/32:500       ALL   OPERATIONAL   2
VPN_IOS_AH_2      51    172.21.51.233/32:0         ALL   OPERATIONAL   2
Cat6506-1-Native#show module c 4 sticky
client IP:     172.21.51.250
real server:   172.21.51.247
connections:   0
group id:      11
timeout:       39
sticky type:   netmask 255.255.255.255
client IP:     172.21.51.251
real server:   172.21.51.242
connections:   0
group id:      11
timeout:       39
sticky type:   netmask 255.255.255.255
```

IPsec Router Configurations for Dispatch Mode

Example 8-6 shows the IOS-based IPsec router configuration used in the solution verification. Notice the loopback address configured. The IP address of the loopback0 interface is the same as the VIP address used in the CSM.

Example 8-6 *IOS IPSec Configuration Example Used for Testing*

```
crypto isakmp policy 10
 authentication pre-share
crypto isakmp key cisco123 address 0.0.0.0
crypto isakmp keepalive 10
!
!
crypto ipsec transform-set myset ah-sha-hmac esp-3des esp-sha-hmac
crypto mib ipsec flowmib history tunnel size 200
crypto mib ipsec flowmib history failure size 200
!
crypto dynamic-map mydyn 10
 set transform-set myset
 reverse-route
```

Example 8-6 *IOS IPSec Configuration Example Used for Testing (Continued)*

```
!
!
crypto map mymap local-address Loopback0
crypto map mymap 10 ipsec-isakmp dynamic mydyn
!
interface Loopback0
 ip address 172.21.51.233 255.255.255.255
!
interface FastEthernet0/0
 ip address 10.1.1.5 255.255.255.0
!
interface FastEthernet0/1
 ip address 172.21.51.242 255.255.255.240
 crypto map mymap
!
router eigrp 1
 redistribute static
 network 10.0.0.0
 no auto-summary
 no eigrp log-neighbor-changes
!
ip route 0.0.0.0 0.0.0.0 172.21.51.241
```

Summary

This chapter introduced the concept of the VPN and how IPsec protocol components like IKE and ESP function. The load-balancing motivations for VPNs and the specific requirements of IKE, ESP, and IPsec over UDP were covered. Keeping these requirements in mind, the chapter presented two solutions for load balancing VPNs. The first solution focused on IKE and ESP, and the second on IKE, ESP, and AH.

The load balancer used in the case studies in this chapter was the CSM, which is recommended due its support of load balancing for IP any protocol traffic. The case studies consist of the CSM and IPsec-enabled Cisco IOS router configurations.

Chapter 9, "Content Switching Device Migrations," introduces the concepts, methods, and reasoning behind migration of a server environment from one SLB device to another. The chapter provides migration planning techniques followed by a detailed case study.

Content Switching Device Migrations

As applications become increasingly sophisticated with the variety of features and functionality they offer for clients, so has the growth in the number of clients accessing these applications. From online banking to delivery tracking of packages, for businesses to offer such detailed services over the Internet, load balancing has also had to evolve over time.

Cisco's load-balancing solutions have also evolved over time. Initially, there was the Local Director, followed by the Content Services Switch (CSS), and then the Content Switch Module (CSM). Whichever platform was chosen, migrating from an existing load-balancing solution to another became necessary.

This chapter looks at the evolution of load-balancing devices and provides information about how to plan a migration. A case study provides the configuration information for a sample migration from a CSS solution to a CSM solution.

Motivation Behind Migration

There are several key reasons behind the migration of server environments from one SLB device to another. These reasons range from the evolution of load balancers in terms of features, performance, and scalability to the need for advanced load-balancing methods like HTTP cookie insert.

Evolution of Load Balancing

The Local Director's load balancing for applications was accomplished using the basic information about the clients and the application services they were trying to reach. The Local Director made these decisions at the IP and TCP layers, which included looking at either the source or destination IP address or the source or destination TCP port number.

However, as the applications and services offered became more complex, there was an increasing need to provide load-balancing decisions at layers above the transport layer (TCP layer). This is where the CSS came into the picture. The CSS not only provided the capability to provide load balancing at the basic TCP layer packets, but also provided inspection into the packet payload and identified headers and fields to allow for more intelligent traffic load balancing. The decision could be based on HTTP protocol headers or URL matches and other fields embedded within the payload of the packet.

As the load-balancing platforms evolved, they allowed the data center managers to choose either appliance-based load balancing or an integrated solution within their distribution switches. Depending on which particular platform they chose, there was always a need for migrating from their existing load-balancing solution to the new one.

Advanced Load-Balancing Methods

Some additional motivations for migrating to CSS load balancing was that it provided session persistence, content customization, and application acceleration. Session persistence helped solve the problem of maintaining a client session to a server during the length of the session. Content customization allowed for inspection at the Layer 7 level (HTTP protocol) and allowed a connection to be redirected to a geographically or linguistically appropriate site. As the user experience became more and more important, the CSM was developed to provide application acceleration while still providing optimization. Application acceleration refers to low user response times—that is, faster download of content.

Scalability and Performance

Scalability and performance in server load balancing (SLB) devices is crucial in a data center. As the number of users of applications increases, more traffic goes through the SLB device, which in turn requires more available resources in the load balancer. If you look at the matrix in Table 9-1, you can decide which platform will meet the need for the supported throughput and which one will support connections for the number of applications in your system.

Table 9-1 *Product Comparison*

Platform→ Decision Points↓	Cisco CSS 11501	Cisco CSS 11503	Cisco CSS 11506	Cisco CSM for Catalyst 6500
Form Factor	Fixed	Stand-alone modular	Stand-alone modular	Integrated module
Port Density*	8 FE 0–1 GE	0–32 FE 2–6 GE	0–80 FE 2–12 GE	46–528 FE 8–178 GE
Site Activity	Low	Medium	High	Highest
Hardware Scalability	✓	✓✓	✓✓✓	✓✓✓✓
Hardware Redundancy	No	No	Yes	Yes
Session Redundancy	Yes	Yes	Yes	Yes
Layer 2–3 Networking	✓	✓	✓	✓✓✓

Table 9-1   *Product Comparison (Continued)*

Platform→ Decision Points↓	Cisco CSS 11501	Cisco CSS 11503	Cisco CSS 11506	Cisco CSM for Catalyst 6500
Management/Control	✓✓✓	✓✓✓	✓✓✓	✓✓✓
SSL Termination	CSS11501S	Module	Module	Cisco Catalyst 6500 SSL module
Load Balancing	Applications, servers, caches, firewalls	Applications, servers, caches, firewalls	Applications, servers, caches, firewalls	Applications, servers, caches, firewalls, virtual private networks (VPNs)

*Fast Ethernet (FE), Gigabit Ethernet (GE)

Software Features and Functionality

Improved features and functionality in hardware-based SLB devices like CSS and CSM have lead to migration from software-based load balancers like the Local Director. Many times the requests for functionality like HTTP Cookie sticky is requested by the application team, and in order to honor the requests the data center managers have to migrate from their current SLB device to one that optimally supports HTTP Cookie–based persistence. The Cisco CSS and the CSM Series offer the following features for any SLB environment:

- Complete access control list (ACL) functions
- Secure Shell (SSH) protocol version 2 configurability
- Secure Sockets Layer (SSL) GUI
- Extensible Markup Language (XML) capability or Simple Network Management Protocol (SNMP) configuration
- Expandability and scalability (ports and performance)
- Out-of-band health checking (keepalives include Internet Control Message Protocol [ICMP], HTTP, and scripted)
- Support for persistent HTTP 1.1 connections
- HTTP connection persistence across multiple rules
- Robust set of URL load-balancing features
- Session persistence based on URL parameters
- Algorithms balanced specifically for caches
- Hashed domain names for cache load balancing
- Global SLB solution
- Support for Direct Server Return mode

- Large depth of header inspection (20 x 1460 bytes)
- Up to 2048 bytes of actual cookie value inspection
- Integrated SSL termination and back-end SSL support

Migration Planning

Once the decision to migrate to a particular load-balancing platform has been determined, the actual plan of how the migration will happen needs to be laid out. As part of the migration plan, there are a number of factors that need to be considered, such as the dates and timelines for the migrations to be complete, what the fallback plans are in case the migration doesn't happen successfully, and other factors, which are discussed in the following sections.

Migration Team

Because load balancers are an integral part of the data center and interface with the applications and the Layer 2/Layer 3 infrastructure, much personnel across many different groups within an organization will be involved. For this reason, a migration team needs to be developed. The migration team consists of the following members:

- Project Manager
- Content Engineer
- Network Operations Engineer
- Core (Layer 2/Layer 3) Engineer
- Application Administrator

Project Manager

The Project Manager needs to be a fairly technical individual with knowledge of the overall objective of the migration. Following are some critical responsibilities the Project Manager manages:

- The Project Manager must understand how other teams within the data center function, such as how the security team handles requests or how the network operations center (NOC) monitors devices and what are the escalation paths of those devices. Who the vendor contacts are for the load-balancing devices and what other infrastructure teams are needed for the migration. This is necessary because the Project Manager is the single point of contact for all the engineering resources and the single point of contact for providing management updates.

- The Project Manager needs to be aware of the timelines and the milestones associated with the project. It is essential for the Project Manager to be fluent in applications, such as Microsoft Project, which help lay out the details of the migration plan. The Project Manager needs to handle all resources, assign action items to the appropriate engineers, and update the project timelines and milestones as they are completed.

- One of the key activities the Project Manager conducts is coordination of the times for the various resources and the project milestones. Migration projects can last months, so planning and setting the right expectations for all the engineers is the key. Having the same set of individuals from the start to the end of the project is a key success factor for the migration.

- The Project Manager should take charge of the project and take the lead in helping the resources with the challenges they face throughout the project.

- The Project Manager should also assign a backup project manager and update that individual on the key activities as the migration project progresses.

Content Engineer

The dedicated content engineer is responsible for providing assistance in the migration process and also for managing the new content networking infrastructure. Some of the key responsibilities for the Content Engineer working in collaboration with the content device vendor are as follows:

- The Content Engineer must understand the existing load balancing mode of operation. For example, if there is a migration required from the Local Director to the CSS, there are some key differences. The Local Director is deployed as a bridge, and the CSS can be deployed either in Bridge mode (as a bridge, merging two distinct VLANs) or in Routed mode (creating a Layer 3 boundary between the client and server VLANs). Thus, having such knowledge of the platforms helps in designing and preparing for the migration. Since the Local Director is deployed in Bridge mode, it would be easier and simpler to migrate to the CSS in Bridge mode also, without having to make too many changes to the server environment. However, if a Layer 3 boundary is required and the server's default gateways can point to the CSS, it would be easier to implement Routed mode on the CSS. Therefore, the Content Engineer's understanding of the existing environment and the capabilities of the new platform is critical.

- The Content Engineer needs to understand the feature parity between the devices. The current functionality, features, and parameter values that are set in the existing infrastructure should be maintained when migrating to the new load-balancing platform. For example, the default keepalive frequency on the CSS is 5 seconds; however, the default keepalive frequency on the CSM is 120 seconds.

- The redundancy and failover should be configured with the same functionality as the existing load-balancing platform. For example, if moving from CSS 11000 in box-to-box redundancy mode to CSS 11500 with Virtual Router Redundancy Protocol (VRRP), the Content Engineer must make sure that the critical scripts are specified to provide interface tracking.

- The Content Engineer is required to interface with the application team to understand the application requirements. Even though the load-balanced configurations and features are the same, other administrative access that needs to traverse the load balancer should also be properly understood. For example, if the CSS is deployed in Routed mode, it routes the traffic between the circuit VLANs by default; however, the CSM will drop it unless specifically configured with a catch all vserver (virtual 0.0.0.0 0.0.0.0 any), or the variable ROUTE_UNKOWN_FLOW_PACKETS is enabled. So, when migrating from one platform to another, non-load-balanced traffic through the load balancer should be understood. A basic survey can be provided to the application team before migrating their application from one platform to the other.

The survey may ask the following questions:

1 What are the mission-critical applications being load balanced?

2 What TCP/UDP ports are required for these applications?

3 What is the average time for the application connection?

4 What is the average time for the application session?

5 Who is the client/user of this application?

6 Are there internal users only? (These are users whose source IP address is known, and includes partners.)

7 Are there external (Internet) users only?

8 Are there both internal and external users?

9 Does the application handle the TCP/IP stack properly? (It should not have problems with TCP reset [RST].)

10 What kind of persistence (stickiness) is required for these applications?

11 What kind of back-end traffic is used (for example, sessions to and from the database, authentication servers, and so on)?

12 Is the application HTTP based (TCP:80)?

13 Is the application SSL based (TCP:443)?

14 Does the application track/log the client's source IP address?

15 What level of keepalive capability is required (for example, ICMP, UDP, TCP, HTTP, or scripted)?

- The Content Engineer, along with the vendor for the new load-balancing platform, is responsible for the conversion of the existing load-balancing configurations as well as the configurations for the new load-balancing platform. All the devices, Active and Standby, need to be converted and tested. The configurations are tested in collaboration with the application engineers to verify that the converted configurations work and function similarly to the existing load balancer.

- The migration cutover scripts and the commands to be entered on the load balancer are conducted by the Content Engineer.

- Providing a test plan for the success of the migration is also provided by the Content Engineer. This is mainly a checklist to make sure the administrators for the applications are satisfied that the application is working in its production capacity and that no issues have been encountered when moving the application from one platform to the other.

Network Operations Engineer

A dedicated Network Operations Engineer is needed to monitor the applications once they have been migrated and to report any failures to the Content Engineer.

Core (Layer 2/Layer 3) Engineer

The Core Engineer provides any routing information for the load balancers, any new IP addressing schemes, the default gateway for the servers and load balancers, the VLAN numbers and the ports to which the servers and new load balancers get attached. The Core Engineer works closely with the Content Engineer in providing the necessary information for the load-balancing virtual IPs (VIP) and in ensuring that load-balanced traffic passes through symmetrically via the load balancer.

Application Administrator

The Application Administrator provides the information needed to load balance the application. The administrator is also responsible for verifying and conducting tests with the Content Engineer to make sure the application is functioning, in its feature and functionality, similar to the features and functionality of the application as it is deployed in the production environment. Any new features offered by the new load-balancing platform are discussed with the application team to determine how they can be leveraged for the application. Together with the Content Engineer, success criteria are created for the application migration.

Table 9-2 presents a sample migration form based on the assumption that the customer is migrating from the CSS to the CSM.

Table 9-2   *Sample Migration Plan with Area Owners*

Data Center	San Jose
Application	Web hosting
Application Administrator	John Doe
Content Engineer	Mr. Content
Vendor Contact	Mr. Cisco

continues

Table 9-2   *Sample Migration Plan with Area Owners (Continued)*

Data Center	San Jose
Core Engineer	Mr. Core
NOC Engineer	Mr. NOC
Project Manager	Mr. Manager
Questionnaire gaps	<date>
CSM team/customer meeting date	5/6/05 4:00 PM
Application freeze	5/1/2005 — 5/3/2005
Premigration test date	5/15/05 12:00 PM
Premigration test CRs	TBD
Premigration test completed successfully?	Yes
Migration date	5/20/03 2:00 PM
Migration cutover	TBD
Migration completed successfully?	Yes
CSS configuration removal for application	5/23/2005

Fallback Plan

Because the migration is done on an application-by-application basis, having a fallback plan of action is important in case the migration for the application fails. As these changes are happening to a live production network and an already properly working application, it is important to make sure that the application works when it is migrated to the new load-balancing device and that it also works if it is switched back to the existing load-balancing platform in case it does not function properly on the new load-balancing platform. Given the fact that there is a limited time for the changes to happen, it is always a good idea for the team to be aware of the activities and to establish a cutoff time for implementation of the fallback plan. If the cutoff time for the migration of an application is three hours and the application is not working properly within two hours of that period, the Project Manager must decide to migrate that application back to the existing load balancer. Following is a sample list of steps that take place if a failure in the application migration occurs when migrating from the CSS to the CSM.

1 The application is not working properly on the CSM.

2 The migration team authorizes fallback.

3 The Project Manager implements a fallback from the CSM to the CSS.

4 The Application Administrator changes the gateways back to the CSS.

5 The application is rebooted to clear ARP entries.

6 The application is confirmed to be fully functional after fallback to the CSS.

7 The Application Administrator verifies that the application is working properly on the CSS.

8 Logs and statistics are captured on the CSM to determine failure.

9 The configuration on the CSM is disabled.

10 The Content Engineer works with the vendor to resolve issue(s).

11 The CSM is reloaded.

12 A schedule is made up for retesting the application.

The preceding checklist helps ensure that not only are the steps for the fallback followed but that logs and statistics are also gathered to determine why the failure occurred. There are key lessons to be learned from the failure scenario so that they are not repeated for other applications migrated in the future.

Methods and Procedures for the Maintenance Window

During migration, all team members have to be ready to follow a script detailing the exact commands to be issued on the devices and in what order. This is critical no matter what the migration path is. For example, following is a sample script that lists the steps to take when migrating from the CSS 11000 platform to the CSS 11500 platform.

Step 1 Change and mirror the configuration on the CSS 11500 for the interfaces and the ports because the CSS 11000 numbers its ports as e1, e2. . .e14; however, the CSS 11500 numbers its ports as 2/1, 2/2, and so on. So you need to make sure that the CSS 11500 configurations are preconfigured; otherwise, the configuration from the CSS 11000 will give syntax errors on the CSS 11500. The CSS 11500 will be added as a Standby (Backup) CSS to the production Active CSS 11000 first. We will create an Active/ Backup relationship between the CSS 11000 and the CSS 11500, respectively.

Step 2 Ensure that the CSS 11000 stays Master when adding the CSS 11500 as a Backup. To guarantee mastership of the CSS 11000, you configure the CSS 11000 with the **ip redundancy master** command. In order for this command to take effect, the **redundancy-phy** commands from the interfaces on the CSS 11000 need to be removed. Once the CSS 11500 is added, the **redundancy-phy** command will be added back under the interface and the **ip redundancy** command (without the **master** keyword) will be re-issued.

Step 3 Don't use the commit_redundancy configuration script to copy the configuration from the Active to the Standby because the configuration will be different between the Active (CSS 11000) and Backup (CSS 11500).

Step 4 Shut down the interfaces for the Backup CSS 11000 and remove the Backup from the Layer 2 infrastructure.

Step 5 Make sure that the configuration for the Backup CSS 11500 is preloaded and that the interfaces being used (including the redundancy interface) are admin-shutdown, as described in the following example:

```
interface  2/8
  bridge vlan 99
  admin-shutdown
interface  2/9
  bridge vlan 102
  redundancy-phy
  admin-shutdown
interface  2/10
  bridge vlan 102
  redundancy-phy
  admin-shutdown
```

Step 6 The current state of the CSS 11500 should be Master, because nothing is connected to it. It cannot send a GARP (Gratuitous Address Resolution Protocol) out for the VIPs because the interfaces are down.

```
CSS500-1# sh redundancy
Redundancy:             Enabled   Redundancy Protocol:    Not Running
Redundancy State:       Master    MasterMode:             No
Number of times redundancy state changed to Master:     9
                                        to Backup:      9
Current State Duration:   0 days 00:00:34
Last Fail Reason:         Other Switch Asserted Mastership
Physical Link Failure Monitor on :
Interface:              State
 2/9                    Down
 2/10                   Down
```

Step 7 Now bring up only the redundancy interface on the CSS 11500. (The CSS 11000 should stay as Master, and the CSS 11500 will attain Backup.)

```
CSS500-1(config-if[ 2/8])# no admin-shutdown
CSS500-1(config-if[ 2/8])#
```

Step 8 The CSS 11500 redundancy status should go to Backup.

```
CSS500-1# sh redundancy
Redundancy:             Enabled   Redundancy Protocol:    Running
Redundancy State:       Backup    MasterMode:             No
Number of times redundancy state changed to Master:     9
                                        to Backup:      10
```

```
Redundancy interface:      172.16.1.2
Current State Duration:    0 days 00:00:12
Last Fail Reason:          Other Switch Asserted Mastership
VRID:                      128        Priority:            100
Physical Link Failure Monitor on :
Interface:                 State
 2/9                       Down
 2/10                      Down
CSS500-1#
```

Step 9   The CSS 11000 redundancy status should stay as Master.

```
css-256-1# sh redundancy
Redundancy:                Enabled    Redundancy Protocol:      Running
Redundancy State:          Master     MasterMode:               Yes
Number of times redundancy state changed to Master:           15
                                        to Backup:            15
Redundancy interface:      172.16.1.1
Current State Duration:    0 days 00:10:14
Last Fail Reason:          No Fail
VRID:                      128        Priority:             255
css-256-1#
```

Step 10   Now bring up the interfaces on the CSS 11500, and they will stay Backup. (Make sure to place the **redundancy-phy** commands under the interface.)

```
CSS500-1# sh redundancy
Redundancy:                Enabled    Redundancy Protocol:      Running
Redundancy State:          Backup     MasterMode:               No
Number of times redundancy state changed to Master:           9
                                        to Backup:            10
Redundancy interface:      172.16.1.2
Current State Duration:    0 days 00:01:57
Last Fail Reason:          Other Switch Asserted Mastership
VRID:                      128        Priority:             100
Physical Link Failure Monitor on :
Interface:                 State
 2/9                       Up
 2/10                      Up
```

Step 11   At this point, all traffic should still be flowing through the CSS 11000 (Active), and the CSS 11500 should still be the Backup.

Step 12   Similarly, to bring up the second CSS 11500, take the CSS 11000 offline by first doing a redundancy force-master on the CSS 11500 so it will become Master. Also change the **ip redundancy** command to **ip redundancy master** and remove the **redundancy-phy** commands from the interfaces on the CSS 11500 so it always stays Master.

Step 13   Shut down the interfaces on the CSS 11000 and remove the CSS 11000 from the Layer 2 infrastructure.

Step 14   Next, attach the other CSS 11500, with all the interfaces as admin shut down. Then bring up just the redundancy interface.

Step 15   Make sure that the first CSS 11500 stays Master and the just-added CSS 11500 stays Backup.

Step 16   Bring up the interfaces on the just-added CSS 11500.

Step 17   On the first CSS 11500, issue the **ip redundancy** command (without the **master** keyword) and add the **redundancy-phy** commands to the interfaces.

Step 18   Verify that the first CSS 11500 is Master and that the just-added CSS 11500 is Backup.

The following is the testing log:

```
ARP ENTRIES FOR VIPs on 11000
0010.5803.ee42
ARP ENTRIES FOR VIPs on 11500
0007.8543.313d
MAKING CONNECTIONS:
CAT-Native-1#telnet 12.29.100.70 80
Trying 12.29.100.70, 80 ... Open
get
<!DOCTYPE HTML PUBLIC "-//IETF//DTD HTML 2.0//EN">
<HTML><HEAD>
<TITLE>501 Method Not Implemented</TITLE>
</HEAD><BODY>
<H1>Method Not Implemented</H1>
get to /index.html not supported.<P>
Invalid method in request get<P>
<HR>

<ADDRESS>Apache/1.3.20 Server at localhost Port 80</ADDRESS>
</BODY></HTML>
[Connection to 12.29.100.70 closed by foreign host]
```

In addition to the script, there is an overall migration task list to follow during the actual migration cutover. The following task list covers a sample migration from the CSS to the CSM:

1   Set up a conference call for the migration.

2   Schedule the application team to be available.

3   Schedule the Core/CDN/NOC Engineer to be available.

4   Check ARP entries on the core switch for Active CSS VIPs.

5 Suspend CSS Active content rules.

6 Enter all vserver configurations.

7 Enable all vservers.

8 Check ARP entries on the core switch for Active CSS/CSM VIPs.

9 On core switches, clear ARP entries for CSS, if necessary.

10 Perform a Migration Verification Test.

11 Provide the NOC with a detailed description of services hosted by the CSM.

Application Testing

The following list defines the activities associated with the testing of the application before migration. There are test VIPs and DNS names defined for the application. Complete client-to-server testing is conducted, with the addition of Sniffer traces on the client and server side of the CSM in case the test does not work and also to identify the kind of traffic being produced by the application.

1 DNS A records changes for the test domain; that is, www.test.example.com should point to the new VIP address.

2 Complete the test plan.

3 Schedule team participation and the migration team to be available.

4 Set up Sniffer capture software.

5 Complete the CSM configuration changes and verify their functionality by testing the changes.

6 Ensure the DNS delegation is working properly.

7 Execute the test plan.

8 Perform a Premigration Verification Test.

The application system administrator is responsible for testing to ensure that all functionality for the application is working and that the testing has been verified. Following is a testing checklist that the application system administrator can use to verify the various features, functionality, and administrative access for the application.

❑ Verify that Telnet, SSH, and FTP is working for a period of time without timing out. The Telnet, SSH, and FTP connections should be made to the application servers.

❑ Verify that Backup, SNMP, NFS, and SYSLOGGING applications are working from the server.

❑ Verify that multiple clients are able to access the application via the DNS name and the VIP address.

❏ Verify SSL persistency content rules.

❏ Verify primary sorry server content rules.

❏ Verify HTTP 1.1 persistency content rules.

❏ Verify all application functionality.

❏ Agree on the test results.

Once the application testing has been verified, the application is ready to be migrated to the new load-balancing platform.

Case Study: Migration from CSS to CSM

Now that the basic migration plan has been discussed in detail, examination of a sample migration from the CSS platform to the CSM platform follows.

Figure 9-1 illustrates the existing topology of the currently deployed CSSs.

Figure 9-1 *Existing Infrastructure of the CSS*

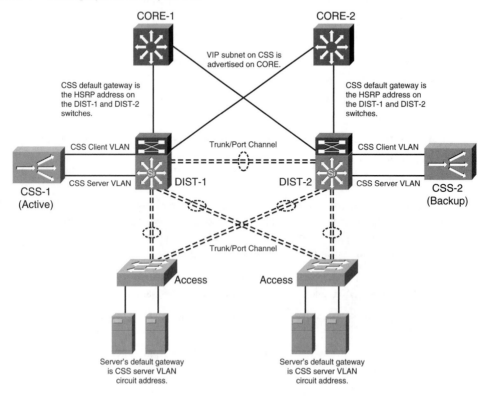

Figure 9-1 illustrates the Routed mode design for the CSS. The default gateway for the servers is the CSS server VLAN circuit address. The CSS's default gateway is the Hot Standby Router Protocol (HSRP) address shared on the DIST-1 and DIST-2 switches. Using this topology, the case study will examine the following:

- Infrastructure requirements
- Server and application requirements
- Configuration and design details

Infrastructure Requirements

A successful SLB device migration depends on a clear understanding of the current networking infrastructure. Some of the critical infrastructure requirements that we will discuss are:

- CSS and CSM modes of operation
- The server's default gateway
- Redundancy and fault tolerance

CSS and CSM Mode of Operation

As the migration happens from the CSS to the CSM, the mode of operation should be consistent. Thus, in our example, because the CSS is currently deployed in Routed mode, the CSM is also required to be deployed in Routed mode.

Server's Default Gateway

The default gateway will be required to be changed when the CSS and CSM server VLANs are the same. If different server VLANs are selected, the default gateway for the servers need not change, and the same IP address can be shared between the CSS and the CSM server VLAN address; however, they are required to be on different VLANs. In our example, the server's default gateway will be changed. (It previously was pointing to the CSS circuit VLAN, and after the migration will point to the CSM alias IP address.)

Redundancy and Fault Tolerance

In the design presented, because the CSS was deployed in box-to-box redundancy mode, the CSM will maintain a similar redundancy mechanism, which is called the Content Switch Replication Protocol (CSRP). With CSRP, the CSM maintains an Active and Backup relationship and exchanges Hello messages for the current Active and Standby state. These Hello messages are carried over a fault-tolerant VLAN between the two CSMs.

Server and Application Requirements

The following requirements are from the applications being load balanced currently on the CSS, and the same must be handled by the CSM:

- **Sticky source IP**—Because the applications being load balanced behind the CSS requires a client connection to be stuck to a particular server based on the source IP address for a certain period of time, a similar requirement will be met by the CSM.

- **Layer 5 content rules**—The CSS is capable of looking at the HTTP headers and the URL of the packet and making load-balancing decisions based on those headers. Similar functionality will be provided by the CSM. For example, if the URL for the header request contains *.gif, then the request should be sent to the GIF server or to the next available server.

- **Port mapping**—Most applications have multiple servers listening on multiple ports. The CSS accepts connections to a VIP address on a particular port and then forwards that request to the server on a different port. Similar functionality will be provided by the CSM.

- **TCP and HTTP keepalives**—The CSS allows for probes to be sent to the server to check for availability of that particular application. Based on the response from the server, the CSS brings the server in or out for load-balancing rotation. Similar functionality will be required by the CSM for health checks to the server.

Migration Configuration and Design Details

Now that the requirements are defined, we will discuss details of the implementation of the requirements. Figure 9-2 illustrates the process of migration from the CSS to the CSM. For the migration to happen in a smooth and nondisruptive fashion, the following criteria must be met:

- A down time is required for making changes to the applications and to the distribution switches.

- Both the CSS and the CSM must reside in a parallel fashion, so that the migration of the application can be accomplished one at a time. This is to make sure that if there is a failure in the application migration to the CSM, that particular application can fall back to the CSS and still be operational after the down time window expires.

- Sniffer software should be available to capture any traffic for analysis in case an application does not function properly on the CSM.

- The CSM can be placed in the distribution switch chassis. In Figure 9-2, each CSS will be replaced by a CSM.

- The VLANs for the CSS and the CSM can be shared; however, unique IP addresses for the client and server VLAN will be required.

Figure 9-2 *Topology During Migration*

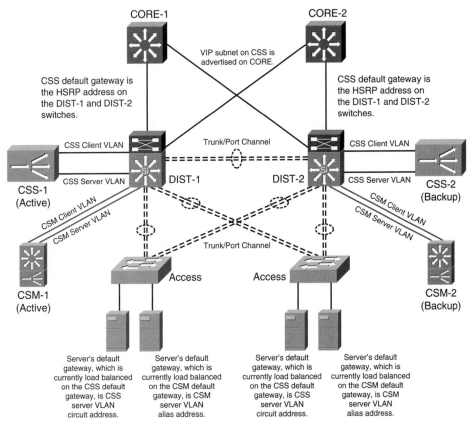

In the following sections, we will discuss the migration configurations in details. Following are the topics that will be covered:

- CSS and CSM mode of operation
- Redundancy and fault tolerance
- Ready for migration
- Source IP sticky configuration
- Layer 5 content rules
- Port redirection
- Keepalives
- CSS configurations
- CSM configurations

CSS and CSM Mode of Operation

Example 9-1 shows the CSS circuit VLAN configuration deployed in Routed mode.

Example 9-1 *CSS Layer 3 Configuration*

```
ip route 0.0.0.0 0.0.0.0 10.10.10.100 1
circuit VLAN100
   description "CSS Client VLAN"
   redundancy
   ip address 10.10.10.1 255.255.255.0

circuit VLAN200
   description "CSS Server VLAN"
   redundancy
   ip address 20.20.20.1 255.255.255.0
```

The CSS configuration defines two separate circuits and two separate subnets. The client VLAN is VLAN 100 in the subnet 10.10.10.0, and the server VLAN is VLAN 200 in the subnet 20.20.20.0. The **ip route** statement specifies the default gateway for the CSS.

To maintain the same mode deployed for the CSS, the CSM is deployed in Routed mode, as shown in Example 9-2.

Example 9-2 *CSM Layer 3 Configuration*

```
vlan 100 client
   ip address 10.10.10.3 255.255.255.0
   alias  10.10.10.4 255.255.255.0
   gateway 10.10.10.100
 !
 vlan 200 server
   ip address 20.20.20.3 255.255.255.0
   alias 20.20.20.4 255.255.255.0
```

The equivalent of the circuit VLANs on the CSS are the VLAN commands on the CSM. The gateway command on the CSM is the equivalent of the **ip route** command on the CSS. VLAN 100 and VLAN 200 need to be created as Layer 2 VLANs. The gateway address is 10.10.10.100, and it is usually the HSRP address on the Layer 3 interface on VLAN 100 or could be an upstream router. You should be careful that VLAN 100 and VLAN 200 both do not have Layer 3 interfaces on the Multilayer Switch Feature Card (MSFC) hosting the CSM. The **alias** command is used for redundancy and will be discussed in the next section, "Redundancy and Fault Tolerance." VLAN 100 and VLAN 200 on the switch can be port-channeled and included as part of the trunk. The preceding configuration can be configured on the CSM without any changes to the CSS (as long as the IP addresses are unique on both devices). The Standby CSM should not be placed in the DIST-B chassis because fault tolerance and redundancy need to be configured; otherwise, an IP address conflict will be detected on VLAN 100 and VLAN 200 (because the alias IP address will be the same).

Redundancy and Fault Tolerance

The configuration shown in Example 9-3 is required to configure box-to-box redundancy on the CSS.

Example 9-3 *CSS Redundancy Configuration*

```
! ACTIVE CSS
circuit VLAN300
   description "Fault Tolerance VLAN"
   ip address 30.30.30.1 255.255.255.0
   redundancy-protocol
! STANDBY CSS
circuit VLAN300
   description "Fault Tolerance VLAN"
   ip address 30.30.30.2 255.255.255.0
   redundancy-protocol
```

After VLAN 300 is configured on the Standby CSS, VLANs 100 and 200 can be configured. The redundancy role on the CSS is Active/Standby, where the IP addresses for VLANs 100 and 200 are the same (since only one CSS is Active at a time). Example 9-4 shows the configuration for the circuit addresses on the CSS.

Example 9-4 *CSS Layer 3 Circuit Configurations*

```
circuit VLAN100
   description "CSS Client VLAN"
   redundancy
   ip address 10.10.10.1 255.255.255.0

circuit VLAN200
   description "CSS Server VLAN"
   redundancy
   ip address 20.20.20.1 255.255.255.0
```

Example 9-5 shows the equivalent configuration on the CSM. Make sure to put the fault-tolerant configuration on the Standby CSM first and than configure the client and server VLANs.

Example 9-5 *CSM Redundancy Configuration*

```
! ACTIVE CSM
ft group 1 vlan 300
! STANDBY CSM
ft group 1 vlan 300
vlan 100 client
  ip address 10.10.10.3 255.255.255.0
  alias address 10.10.10.4
  gateway 10.10.10.100
!
 vlan 200 server
  ip address 20.20.20.3 255.255.255.0
  alias address 20.20.20.4
```

With the Standby CSM, once the fault-tolerant VLAN 300 is configured, it will go into Standby mode. Following are some general guidelines that should be followed when configuring the fault-tolerant VLAN:

- Have a dedicated fault-tolerant (FT) VLAN link between the Active and the Standby CSM.

- Disable preemption because if a CSM fails, returns to service, and becomes Active, the existing connections on the Standby CSM need to be re-established on the Active CSM.

- Leave the FT failover interval at a default of 3 seconds. The FT failover time does not need to correspond to the Spanning Tree failover time for the client and server VLANs, because in the scenario where both port-channel links fail, the Active CSM will still stay Active. It is only in the scenario with a module and supervisor failure that the FT VLAN port-channel will be brought down automatically in the recommended chassis configuration.

- The FT VLAN heartbeat should also be left at the default of 1 second.

- The FT VLAN priority values should be set to default on both the Active and Standby CSM. This priority value is used with preemption and since preemption is set to off, you do not need to change these values. The default is 10.

- It is recommended to disable IGMP snooping only for the FT VLAN, not the whole chassis. The reason is that turning it off on the whole chassis will cause multicast flooding. To turn it off on the FT VLAN, create an interface FT VLAN and *do not assign an IP address to it*; then type in **no ip igmp snooping**:. For example:

```
interface Vlan300
 no ip address
 no ip igmp snooping
end
```

  The reason for turning off IGMP snooping is that CSRP uses a Multicast Type destination address with its own IP address (unicast). If IGMP snooping is turned on, the switch listens for the Internet Group Messaging Protocol (IGMP) to find the multicast group membership and builds its database of the groups and the members that it has learned off. If the switch does not find any group members, it can prune its database and drop the packets. Thus the switch can potentially tag the CSRP address to be a multicast group without any members since it has a unicast source address. This could lead the CSM to drop the CSRP packet causing inconsistent redundancy between the active and standby CSM. That is why its recommended to have IGMP snooping turned off.

- When you configure multiple fault-tolerant CSM pairs, do not configure multiple CSM pairs to use the same FT VLAN. Use a different FT VLAN for each fault-tolerant CSM pair (for example, FT VLAN 950 for CSM 1 pair and FT VLAN 951 for CSM 2 pair).

- Enable the calendar in the switch Cisco IOS software so that the CSM state change gets stamped with the correct time. The following command enables the calendar:

```
Cat6k-2# conf t
Cat6k-2(config)# clock timezone WORD offset from UTC
Cat6k-2(config)# clock calendar-valid
```

The following **show** command indicates that the configuration between the Active and Standby CSMs is not the same:

```
CAT-Native-3#sh mod c 9 ft
FT group 1, vlan 300
 This box is in standby state
 Configuration is out-of-sync
 priority 10, heartbeat 1, failover 3, preemption is off
```

The CSM does not have a full configuration-checking mechanism between the Active and Standby CSMs. The CSM does only a quick server farm and real servers configuration check. This checking is required for the purpose of "sticky states" replication. For example, if the IP addresses of real servers are different in Active/Standy CSM configuration, you will see this out-of-sync message. In CSM software version 4.2(1), a configuration synchronization feature that performs a complete configuration synch from the Active to Standby CSM was released.

The following message indicates that a CSM has become Active:

```
*Feb 18 20:45:59.183: %CSM_SLB-6-REDUNDANCY_INFO: Module 9 FT info:
State Transition Standby -> Active
*Feb 18 20:45:59.187: %CSM_SLB-4-REDUNDANCY_WARN: Module 9 FT warning:
Standby is Active now (no heartbeat from active unit)
```

Ready for Migration

Once the CSM mode and redundancy have been configured, you are ready to migrate the applications from the CSS to the CSM. Example 9-6 is a CSS service and content rule configuration example.

Example 9-6 *CSS Service and Content Rule that Needs to Be Migrated*

```
service First_Service
    ip address 20.20.20.20
    port 80
    protocol tcp
    keepalive type tcp
    active

content First_Content
    protocol tcp
    vip address 33.33.30.30
    port 80
    add service First_Service
    active
```

On the CSS, we currently have a content rule called First_Content, with a VIP of 33.33.30.30 listening on port 80, and those connections are load balanced to the server 20.20.20.20 on port 80. Following is a sample content rule configuration:

- Suspend the content rule on the CSS by issuing the **suspend** command under the content rule configuration, thus making the content rule on the CSS inactive.

- Cut and paste the equivalent CSM configuration on the Active CSM first (DIST-1) and then copy the configuration onto the Standby CSM (DIST-2).

```
probe TCP tcp
!
 serverfarm First_Service
  nat server
  no nat client
  real 20.20.20.20 80
   inservice
   probe TCP
!
vserver First_Vserver
  virtual 33.33.30.30 tcp 80
   serverfarm First_Service
   inservice
  !
```

- From the CSM, you should be able to ping server 20.20.20.20. Issue the **ping mod CSM** *module_number Server_IP* command. This will help update the ARP entry in the CSM and in the access and distribution layer switches. Also, from the CORE switch, try to ping the VIP address 33.33.30.30 and clear ARP for the Layer 3 VLAN and the CSS, such that the ARP entries are cleared out and refreshed and updated to the ARP entries of the CSM.

- As a precautionary measure, clear the ARP on the DIST-1 and DIST-2 switches and on the access switches to which the servers are connected. If the ARP table for all the VLANs is a concern, use the **arp-timeout** command under the VLAN interface for that VLAN and set it to something low, such as 3 seconds. Once the ARP is refreshed, remove the **arp-timeout** command from the VLAN interface.

- Change the default gateway of the server from 20.20.20.1 (CSS server VLAN address) to 20.20.20.4 (CSM server VLAN address).

- The application administrator at this time should verify the functionality of the application via the CSM.

- Once everything is verified, remove the configuration from the CSS for this application.

These rules should be followed for other applications that are being migrated from the CSS to the CSM. As you can see, while the specific features might be different, the process of migrating an application should follow these rules.

Source IP Sticky Configuration

The following is the CSS configuration for source IP sticky load balancing:

Example 9-7 *CSS Service and Content Rule Configuration with Source IP Sticky*

```
service Second_Service
    ip address 20.20.20.21
    port 80
    protocol tcp
    keepalive type tcp
    active

content Second_Content
    protocol tcp
    vip address 33.33.30.31
    port 80
    add service Second_Service
    advance-balance sticky-srcip
    active
```

When migrating a similar service and content rule to the CSM, the configuration will be as shown in Example 9-8.

Example 9-8 *CSM Server Farm and Virtual Server Configuration with Source IP Sticky*

```
sticky 4 netmask 255.255.255.255 address source timeout 1440
!
probe TCP
!
 serverfarm Second_Service
  nat server
  no nat client
  real 20.20.20.20 80
   inservice
  probe TCP
!
vserver Second_vserver
  virtual 33.33.30.31   tcp http
  serverfarm Second_service
  replicate csrp connection
  persistent rebalance
  sticky 1440 group 4
  inservice
```

The sticky group 4 is applied to the vserver Second_vserver (the server farm Second_Service stays the same), and the sticky group is configured in the Global CSM mode. Leave the sticky table timeout values at the default of 1440 minutes (one day) unless a specific application has a need for a longer timeout. Also note that this timeout is an idle timeout; reset its value to 1440 once the connection is refreshed.

Layer 5 Content Rules

Layer 5 content rules on the CSS are also supported on the CSM. The Layer 5 content rule shown in Example 9-9 is configured on the CSS.

Example 9-9 *CSS Service and Layer 5 Content Rule Configuration*

```
service third_Service
    ip address 20.20.20.22
    port 80
    protocol tcp
    keepalive type tcp
    active

content third_Content
    protocol tcp
    vip address 33.33.30.32
    port 80
    add service third_Service
    url "/*.gif"
    active
```

This content rule accepts traffic on the VIP 33.33.30.32 on port 80, but also matches to see if the URL in the HTTP request has anything followed by a .gif extension; if it does, the request would be sent to the server 20.20.20.22. The similar Layer 5 content rule definition for the vserver on the CSM can be configured as follows:

```
map THIRD_MAP url
    match protocol http url *.gif
!
```

The map is then applied to a policy:

```
policy THIRD
    url-map THIRD_MAP
    serverfarm THIRD_SERVER
!
```

The policies are then defined under the vserver as demonstrated in Example 9-10.

Example 9-10 *CSM Server Farm and Layer 5 Virtual Server Configuration*

```
serverfarm THIRD_SERVER
    nat server
    no nat client
    real 20.20.20.22 80
     inservice
    probe TCP
!
vserver THIRD_VSERVER
    virtual 33.33.30.32 tcp www
    serverfarm THIRD_SERVER
    persistent rebalance
    slb-policy THIRD
    inservice
!
```

Port Mapping or Port Redirection

The port mapping or port redirection functionality on the CSS is the same on the CSM. The servers are listening on ports, such as 8080–8085, but the vserver is listening on a well-known port, such as 80. So, when the client makes a connection, it hits the vserver on port 80, but the CSM maps that port to the server port in the range 8080–8085. The CSS configuration in Example 9-11 defines how port redirection happens.

Example 9-11 *CSS Service and Content Rule Configuration with Port Address Translation from 80 to 8080 and 8081*

```
service Fourth_Services
    ip address 20.20.20.24
    port 8080
    protocol tcp
    keepalive type tcp
    active
service Fifth_Services
    ip address 20.20.20.25
    port 8081
    protocol tcp
    keepalive type tcp
    active
content Fourth_Content
    protocol tcp
    vip address 33.33.30.34
    port 80
    add service Fifth_Services
    add service Fourth_Services
    active
```

Thus, connections being load balanced to 20.20.20.24 will be forwarded to port 8080, and connections being load balanced to 20.20.20.25 will be forwarded to 8081. Example 9-12 shows the similar configuration on the CSM.

Example 9-12 *CSM Server Farm and Virtual Server Configuration with Port Address Translation from 80 to 8080 and 8081*

```
serverfarm FORTH_FIFTH
  nat server
  no nat client
  real 20.20.20.24 8080
   inservice
  real 20.20.20.25 8081
   inservice
  probe TCP
 !
vserver 4N5th
  virtual 33.33.30.35 tcp www
  serverfarm FORTH_FIFTH
  persistent rebalance
  inservice
 !
```

Thus, the configuration on the CSM for the services (in CSS terminology) is a lot simpler than the configuration on the CSS because we only have to create server farms and add real servers to them. Also note that even though the servers are listening on port 8080 and 8081, the vserver is accepting connections on port 80. So the CSM does a port redirection from 80 to 8080 or 8081 when sending the traffic to the server for it to be load balanced.

Keepalives

There are many forms of keepalives that are supported on the CSM, such as TCP, HTTP, SCRIPTED, and FTP. TCP keepalives on the CSS have the following defaults: 5 second Frequency, 3 Max Failure, and 5 second Retry period. Examples 9-13 and 9-14 show the keepalives for TCP and HTTP that are defined on the CSS.

Example 9-13 *CSS Service Configuration with TCP Keepalive*

```
! TCP Keepalives
service Sixth_Services
    ip address 20.20.20.26
    port 8080
    protocol tcp
    keepalive type tcp
    active
```

This keepalive will perform a TCP negotiation on port 8080 for server 20.20.20.26, as Example 9-14 shows.

Example 9-14 *CSS Service Configuration with HTTP Keepalive*

```
service seventh_Services
    ip address 20.20.20.27
    port 8081
    protocol tcp
    keepalive type http
    keepalive uri "/index.html"
    active
```

This keepalive will send an HTTP GET request for /index.html on port 8081 for server 20.20.20.27 and wait for a response back. These keepalives are defined on the CSM, as demonstrated in Example 9-15.

Example 9-15 *CSM TCP and HTTP Probe Configurations*

```
! TCP Probe
probe TCP2 tcp
 interval 5
 failed 5
 retries 3
! HTTP Probe
```

Example 9-15 *CSM TCP and HTTP Probe Configurations (Continued)*

```
probe HTTP http
  request method head url /index.html
  expect status 200
  interval 5
  retries 3
  failed 5
```

These probes can be applied to the server farm, and all the reals for the server farm with their corresponding ports will be probed.

For the mixed keepalives where there are multiple ports being checked, the CSM offers a unique solution for specifying multiple probes under the server farm. For example, if you wanted to check port 80 and port 443 and perform an HTTP head probe on a server farm, you can use the configuration shown in Example 9-16.

Example 9-16 *CSM Probe and Server Farm Configuration*

```
probe TCP tcp
 interval 5
 failed 5
 retries 3
 port 80
probe SSL tcp
 interval 5
 failed 5
 retries 3
port 443
probe HTTP http
  request method head url /index.html
  expect status 200
  interval 5
  retries 3
  failed 5
serverfarm TEST
 nat server
  no nat client
  real 4.4.4.4
   inservice
  probe SSL
  probe TCP
  probe HTTP
```

This configuration checks for all the ports and performs an HTTP head request on a file for all the real servers specified in the server farm.

Figure 9-3 illustrates the migration completion to the CSM.

Figure 9-3 *Topology After Migration*

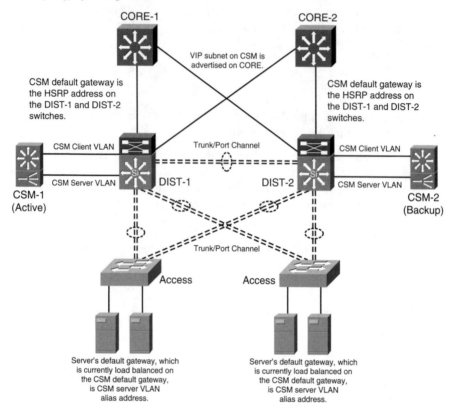

CSS Configurations

Example 9-17 shows the complete configuration for the CSS. The exact same configuration is on the Standby box, except that for circuit VLAN 300, the IP address is 30.30.30.2 255.255.255.0

Example 9-17 *Complete CSS Configuration*

```
css-256-2# sh run
!Generated on 05/12/2005 02:07:12
!Active version: ap0500403
configure
!*************************** GLOBAL ***************************
  ip redundancy
  ip route 0.0.0.0 0.0.0.0 10.10.10.100 1
!*********************** INTERFACE ***********************
interface e1
  bridge vlan 100
```

Example 9-17 *Complete CSS Configuration (Continued)*

```
interface e2
  bridge vlan 200
interface e3
  bridge vlan 300
!************************* CIRCUIT *************************
circuit VLAN100
  redundancy
  ip address 10.10.10.1 255.255.255.0
circuit VLAN200
  description "CSS Server VLAN"
  redundancy
  ip address 20.20.20.1 255.255.255.0
circuit VLAN300
  description "Fault Tolerance VLAN"
  ip address 30.30.30.1 255.255.255.0
    redundancy-protocol
!************************* SERVICE *************************
service Fifth_Services
  ip address 20.20.20.25
  port 8081
  protocol tcp
  keepalive type tcp
  active
service First_Service
  ip address 20.20.20.20
  port 80
  protocol tcp
  keepalive type tcp
  active
service Fourth_Services
  ip address 20.20.20.24
  port 8080
  protocol tcp
  keepalive type tcp
  active
service Second_Service
  ip address 20.20.20.21
  port 80
  protocol tcp
  keepalive type tcp
  active
service Sixth_Services
  ip address 20.20.20.26
  port 8080
  protocol tcp
  keepalive type tcp
  active
service Seventh_Services
  ip address 20.20.20.27
  port 8081
  protocol tcp
  keepalive type http
```

continues

Example 9-17 *Complete CSS Configuration (Continued)*

```
     keepalive uri "/index.html"
     active
   service Third_Service
     ip address 20.20.20.22
     port 80
     protocol tcp
     keepalive type tcp
     active
   !*************************** OWNER ***************************
   owner Book
     content First_Content
       vip address 33.33.30.30
       protocol tcp
       port 80
       add service First_Service
       active
     content Fourth_Content
       vip address 33.33.30.34
       protocol tcp
       port 80
       add service Fifth_Services
       add service Fourth_Services
       active
     content Second_Content
       vip address 33.33.30.31
       protocol tcp
       port 80
       add service Second_Service
       advanced-balance sticky-srcip
       active
     content Third_Content
       vip address 33.33.30.32
       add service Third_Service
       protocol tcp
       port 80
       url "/*.gif"
       active
   css-256-2#
```

CSM Configurations

Example 9-18 shows the migrated configuration of the CSM. The exact same
configuration is on the Standby CSM, except that for VLAN 100 the client IP address is
10.10.10.5 255.255.255.0 and for VLAN 200 the server IP address is 20.20.20.5
255.255.255.0.

Example 9-18 *Complete CSM Configuration*

```
module ContentSwitchingModule 2
ft group 1 vlan 300
!
 vlan 100 client
  ip address 10.10.10.3 255.255.255.0
  gateway 10.10.10.100
  alias 10.10.10.4 255.255.255.0
!
 vlan 200 server
  ip address 20.20.20.3 255.255.255.0
  alias 20.20.20.4 255.255.255.0
!
 probe TCP tcp
!
 probe TCP2 tcp
  interval 5
  failed 5
!
 probe HTTP http
  request  method head  url /index.html
  expect status 200
  interval 5
  failed 5
!
 probe SSL tcp
  interval 5
  failed 5
  port 443
!
 map THIRD_MAP url
  match protocol http url *.gif
!
 serverfarm FIRST_SERVICE
  nat server
  no nat client
  real 20.20.20.20 80
   inservice
  probe TCP
!
 serverfarm FOURTH_FIFTH
  nat server
  no nat client
  real 20.20.20.24 8080
   inservice
  real 20.20.20.25 8081
   inservice
  probe TCP
!
 serverfarm SECOND_SERVICE
  nat server
  no nat client
```

continues

Example 9-18 *Complete CSM Configuration (Continued)*

```
    real 20.20.20.20 80
     inservice
    probe TCP
 !
  serverfarm TEST
   nat server
   no nat client
   real 4.4.4.4
    inservice
   probe SSL
   probe TCP
   probe HTTP
 !
  serverfarm THIRD_SERVER
   nat server
   no nat client
   real 20.20.20.22 80
    inservice
   probe TCP
 !
  sticky 4 netmask 255.255.255.255 address source
 !
  policy THIRD
   url-map THIRD_MAP
   serverfarm THIRD_SERVER
 !
  vserver 4N5TH
   virtual 33.33.30.35 tcp www
   serverfarm FOURTH_FIFTH
   persistent rebalance
   inservice
 !
  vserver FIRST_VSERVER
   virtual 33.33.30.30 tcp www
   serverfarm FIRST_SERVICE
   persistent rebalance
   inservice
 !
  vserver SECOND_VSERVER
   virtual 33.33.30.31 tcp https
   serverfarm SECOND_SERVICE
   sticky 1440 group 4
   replicate csrp connection
   persistent rebalance
   inservice
 !
  vserver THIRD_VSERVER
   virtual 33.33.30.31 tcp www
   serverfarm THIRD_SERVER
   persistent rebalance
   slb-policy THIRD
   inservice
 !
```

Summary

This chapter examined the processes related to migration planning and implementation. It highlighted the roles and responsibilities of the migration project team and provided pointers for making a migration task successful. The migration process is very complex and critical because these changes are happening in the live production data center; therefore, planning, testing, and teamwork are the key to success.

Chapter 10, "SSL Offloading," introduces the SSL protocol and reviews the SSL modules (SSLMs) available for the Cisco Catalyst 6500, the CSM, and the CSS.

Secure Socket Layer

SSL Offloading

More users today are using e-commerce applications to carry out a variety of financial or confidential transactions over the Internet, and securing those connections has become a must. Because HTTP inherently does not have any form of encryption or strong authentication, there is a need to provide confidentiality, authentication, and encryption so that e-commerce applications can be trusted and used confidently by consumers.

The Secure Socket Layer (SSL) protocol was introduced to fill the security gap left by HTTP. SSL provides not only encryption for the packets sent between the client and the server, it provides authentication between them. The processes for this authentication are CPU intensive and are a bottleneck for availability of actual resources on the server. To offload authentication and encryption processing from the servers, SSL termination on dedicated devices was implemented on SSL offload appliances. Clients initiating SSL connections would terminate their SSL connections on the SSL offload devices, and the SSL offload devices would forward packets to the server. Since the SSL offload devices were placed behind firewalls, the connection from the SSL offload to the server (even though in clear text) was in the trusted network.

This chapter provides an introduction to the SSL protocol and reviews the SSL Modules (SSLMs) available for the Cisco Catalyst 6500, as well as integration of the SSLMs with the Content Services Module (CSM). The SSLM solution for the Content Services Switch (CSS) is also reviewed. A case study looks at a deployment solution using the CSM and SSLM, including design and configuration details. Before discussing the details of the SSLMs, we present an overview of the SSL protocol.

Introduction to SSL

The Secure Socket Layer (SSL) was designed to provide a secure connection from the client to the server. In addition to encrypting the data being transferred between the two communicating devices, SSL ensures the authenticity of the connections (that is, it ensures that the client knows that the server to which it is connecting is the right one). The underlying transport protocol that SSL uses is the TCP, and the reason for this was not only to provide encryption for the HTTP protocol but other protocols, such as FTP and SMTP, which use TCP as the transport protocol for communication. SSL is based on cryptography, and as

Figure 10-1 illustrates, a shared key between the client and the server is used to encrypt and decrypt the data.

Figure 10-1 *Shared Key (Symmetric Encryption)*

As Figure 10-1 shows, in order to encrypt and decrypt a message, the key between the client and the server needs to be shared; that is, the client and server must use the same key. This mechanism is called *symmetric encryption* because the keys for encrypting and decrypting are the same and are shared between the communicating client and server. Symmetric key encryption and decryption is very fast, as no CPU cycles are needed to verify the keys. However, a problem with symmetric key encryption is key sharing between the communicating devices, especially over a medium such as the Internet. This problem is resolved by using some common symmetric encryption algorithms such as Data Encryption Standard (DES), Triple-DES (3DES), and Rivest Cipher (RC2 and RC4).

To overcome the problem of key distribution, another encryption mechanism known as *asymmetric encryption* was introduced, where one key is used for encrypting the packet and another key is used for decrypting it. If key A is used to encrypt a packet and key B is used to decrypt it, then key B cannot be used to encrypt the packet and key A cannot be used to decrypt. The keys used in the encryption cannot be derived from each other. Asymmetric encryption is part of the public key cryptography method.

Public Key Cryptography

Public key cryptography, just like asymmetric encryption, allows for the client and the server to use two separate keys, one for encryption and the other for decryption. One of the keys in the key pair is called a private key and should be kept as a secret and never disclosed by the owner of the key. The other key is called the public key and can be disclosed. Each of the two communicating parties, the client and the server, has its own set of public and private keys. The client and server advertise their public keys to each other and to other general clients and servers for communication with them. However, the private keys for both the client and server are kept a secret by each one. As the client initiates a connection to the server, it uses the server's public key to encrypt the message and send it to the server. Once the server receives the message, it will decrypt it using its private key. Since the server's private key is not shared, only the server can successfully decrypt the information. Figure 10-2 illustrates the process of public key cryptography.

Figure 10-2 *Public Key Cryptography (Asymmetric Encryption)*

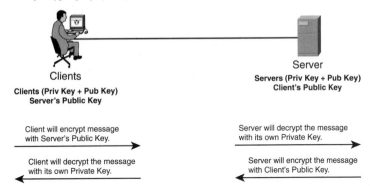

SSL uses both asymmetric encryption for the key exchanges and symmetric encryption based on the keys exchanged to provide a secure connection. In the scenario where a client wants to initiate a secure connection to a server, it will first generate a key for the session based on some random number. In order for the client to make a connection to the server, it needs to know the server's public key, which it uses to encrypt the session key. Once the server has decrypted the key with its own private key, both the client and the server share a secret key that they can use to encrypt and decrypt the data, after which point there is no need to do the asymmetric encryption for the length of the session.

One of the problems with public key is identity. How does the client or the server receiving the message verify the identity of the server or client that sent the message? In order to overcome this issue, the public key cryptography can be applied such that instead of using the public key to encrypt the message, the private key can be used to encrypt the message and the public key can be used to decrypt it. If a client encrypts a message using its private key and sends it to the server, the only way the server can possibly decrypt it is by using the client's public key. This way, the server is assured that the message it receives is from the client because it uses the client's public key to decrypt the message. This method allows for a digital signature of the message from the client to the server, and one algorithm for accomplishing this is the Digital Signature Algorithm (DSA).

SSL Certificates

In order to establish trusted third parties from which public keys for a server could be obtained, organizations called *certificate authorities* (including VeriSign and Entrust, for example) were created to issue public key, or SSL, certificates. An SSL certificate is a digital representation of the public key associated with a client or server. The certificate contains the public key, identifies the client or server name, and asserts that the public key is legitimate and authorized by a known certificate authority (CA) managing certificates on the Internet.

Some of the important fields within a certificate are the issuer, the expiration, and the signature fields. The issuer field identifies the organization that certified and issued the certificate. The issuer certifies the legitimacy of the certificate and allows the receiver of the certificate to trust it. The expiration field specifies when the certificate expires. The signature field is created by first calculating a hash of the certificate and then encrypting it with the issuer's private key. If a particular server presents its certificate to a client, the client uses the issuer's public key to decrypt the signature and verify the hash on the certificate. This allows the client to validate the authenticity of the certificate by verifying that it was signed by a trusted CA.

The CA is the entity usually responsible for issuing SSL certificates, and it digitally signs all certificates to certify the validity of the certificate and the public key it contains. A public CA often acts as a service for a public CA server on the Internet. The CA validates the authenticity of a particular server as legitimate based on the credentials it provided to the CA. Important credentials could be the business license or SEC filings that legitimize the company to which the server belongs. Modern-day browsers come prepackaged with a long list of CAs whose certificates are already trusted. In order to manage certificates and their validity, the CAs maintain a list of revoked certificates called the Certificate Revocation List (CRL). If a previously valid certificate becomes invalid due to expiration or lost private keys, the certificate is revoked and put on the CRL list. A domain that wishes to use SSL presents a certificate request to a CA. After verifying the validity and source of the certificate request, the CA creates a certificate and encrypts it with its private key. This is known as the signature. The certificate is then returned to the requester.

Following is a summary of the various steps that take place to allow key exchange between the communicating devices:

1 When a client browser initiates an SSL (HTTPS) connection to the domain, the SSLM presents the certificate (also called the server or ID certificate) to the client browser.

2 The client browser, which trusts the CA, uses the CA's public key to validate the certificate, as well as the signature and hash on the certificate, and the certificate's expiration. The other value in the certificate that client validates is the expiration time of the certificate. The issuer of the certificate is the CA and the certificate offered by the SSLM must match the URL to which the client browser connects.

3 After validating the certificate, the client extracts the server's public key.

4 The client browser then generates a session key, encrypts it with the SSLM's public key, and sends it to the SSLM. The SSLM decrypts the key using its private key in order to extract it for encryption.

5 The SSLM and the client browser use this shared key to encrypt all traffic, which is part of the SSL negotiation.

Figure 10-3 illustrates the preceding process.

Figure 10-3 *Key Exchange with SSL Certificates*

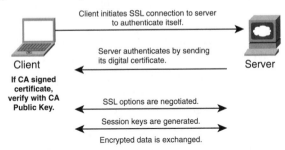

Once the keys between the client and the server are exchanged in a secure manner and each entity (the client and the server) trust each other's identity, the actual encryption of the data is conducted by the SSL protocol. The next section discusses the steps involved in SSL communication.

SSL Protocol Communication

As the client initiates an SSL connection to the server, both the client and server go through various message exchanges before they start encrypting the data between them. As part of the initiation of an SSL connection to the server, the client presents the server with a list of options for SSL and the server decides which of the options it will use for the connection. Figure 10-4 illustrates some of the messages that are exchanged between the client and server.

Figure 10-4 *SSL Message Exchange*

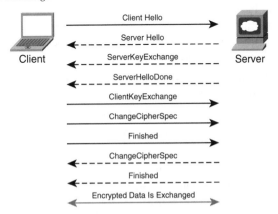

Let us review these messages in detail. The SSL ClientHello is the first message that gets exchanged and is the indication to the server that the client wants to negotiate an SSL connection to it. Following are the fields that are contained as part of the SSL ClientHello packet:

- The Version Number field is used to identify the version of the SSL protocol that the client can support.

- The Random Number field contains the value used during the encryption and decryption of packets between the server and the client.

- The SessionID is used to track the session with a particular number. The SessionID can also be used with load balancers to provide persistency for a client to a particular SSL server for the length of the connection.

- The CipherSuite field lists the variety of encrypting algorithms and key sizes supported by the client. These are presented to the server, and the server chooses which ones to use for encryption of the data.

- The CompressionMethod field defines the various compression methods that can be used for the data before encrypting the packets. Similar to the CipherSuite field's presentation of algorithms for the server to choose from, the compression methods are presented for the server to choose from.

The ServerHello fields are very similar to the ClientHello fields and are defined here:

- The Version Number field specifies the SSL version the server will use for the communication. The server must pick a version of SSL that the client supports. (This must be a number at or lower than the version specified in the ClientHello packet.)

- The Random Number field contains the value used during the encryption and decryption of packets between the server and the client.

- The SessionID is used to track the session with a particular value. The SessionID can also be used with load balancers to provide persistency for a client to a particular SSL server for the length of the connection. In addition, the SessionID value can be used as a means to reuse a connection. If the SSL SessionID is still valid, it can be included as part of the ClientHello and ServerHello packets and the session can be resumed without having to perform the key negotiation again.

- The CipherSuite field is used to select the ciphers that the client presents to the server, as well as the algorithms used and the key size.

- Similarly, the CompressionMethod field is used to select the compression methods that the client presents to the server.

The ServerKeyExchange is the next message to be exchanged and contains the public key information for the server. The client uses the server's public key to encrypt the SSL session key used for the symmetric encryption and decryption of the data. The client verifies the certificate from the server by confirming that it is signed by a trusted CA. The CA's public key is usually part of a popular client browser like Netscape or Internet Explorer and is used to decrypt the digital signature on the certificate that is encrypted with the CA's private key. The client can also authenticate the SSL certificate by checking to make sure the domain name it is trying to communicate with is the same as the one on the SSL certificate.

Next, the server sends the ServerHelloDone message to the client, indicating that it has completed the initial negotiation messages and is ready to establish an encrypted connection. The client then sends the ClientKeyExchange message, encrypted with the server's public key, and provides the session key information to be used for the data encryption phase.

After the key information between the server and the client has been exchanged, the data encryption phase should be ready to start based on the parameters negotiated. As part of the ChangeCipherSpec message, the client and server agree on the algorithm used for encryption, as well as the message integrity algorithm and the key used for the encryption process. The key used for the encryption is different when the data is encrypted from client to server than when it is encrypted from server to client; however, the algorithms used for encryption and message integrity are the same. From this point on, the server expects to see data encrypted with the algorithms specified in the ChangeCipherSpec message from the client. Similarly, when the server sends its own ChangeCipherSpec message to the client, the client expects to see data encrypted with the algorithms indicated in that message.

The Finished message follows the ChangeCipherSpec message and is the first message encrypted with the new negotiated encryption algorithms and keys. This message allows both the client and server to test that the negotiation is successful and that the security between the devices has not been compromised. The following steps summarize the SSL negotiation:

1 The client initiates an SSL connection to the server and sends the ClientHello message, which includes the version number, random number, session ID, cipher suites, and compression methods.

2 The server responds to the ClientHello with a ServerHello, indicating the values it picked from the list presented by the client. (The list includes the version number, random number, session ID, cipher suites, and compression methods.)

3 The server then sends its public key as part of the ServerKeyExchange message.

4 The server sends the ServerHelloDone message, notifying the client that it has completed its initial part of the SSL negotiation.

5 The client encrypts the session key information with the server's public key in the ClientKeyExchange message.

6 The client follows with the ChangeCipherSpec message, informing the server that it has agreed on the algorithms for encryption and authentication and that it will use these options for future communication of data.

7 The client then sends the Finished message to verify the negotiated algorithms and options. The Finished message is the first message encrypted with the algorithms agreed on for data encryption.

8 The server follows with the ChangeCipherSpec message, informing the client that it has agreed on the algorithms for encryption and authentication and that it will use these options for future communication of data.

9 The server then sends the Finished message to verify the negotiated algorithms and options. The Finished message is the first message encrypted with the algorithms agreed on for data encryption.

Similar to the server authentication required by the client, some servers might request client authentication to enhance security. The server requests client authentication as part of a CertificateRequest during the ServerHello phase. The client has to comply with this request and send its public key as part of the Certificate message. The client then sends a Certificate-Verify message to the server, which includes the session information (such as key information and contents of the previous SSL handshake messages) encrypted using the client's private key. The server decrypts this private key using the client's public key, which it received in the previous Certificate message. Figure 10-5 illustrates these additional messages for client authentication.

Figure 10-5 *SSL Message Exchange with Client Authentication*

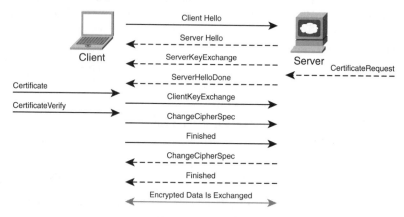

The following section defines how the SSL protocol layer interacts with the application and the underlying TCP layer.

SSL Protocol Structure

Part of the SSL handshake that is defined includes the various key negotiations and encryption mechanisms between the server and the client. The encapsulation of the various SSL protocol headers, which include handshake and change cipher messages, alerts, and application data, is done via the SSL Record Protocol. The Record Protocol layer interfaces with the underlying TCP transport layer by accepting all of the messages and framing them to be sent down to the TCP transport layer. Figure 10-6 illustrates the Record Protocol.

Figure 10-6 *SSL Record Protocol*

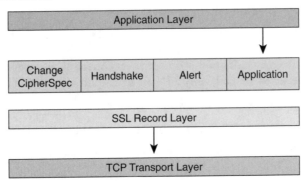

SSL wraps or encrypts application layer protocols used by the end user software or client. For example, HTTP wrapped by SSL becomes HTTPS. As you can see in the figure, SSL sits between the TCP layer and the application layer.

The ChangeCipherSpec shown in the figure is the same message that is covered in the SSL handshake negotiation. This ChangeCipherSpec is the indication to the client or server that the agreed on algorithms for encryption and key information will be used.

The Alert Protocol is used for error detection and signaling. If a particular SSL handshake has errors, those errors are carried in the Alert signals, such as handshake failures or BadCertificate errors.

The SSL handshake as described in the previous sections is crucial to the SSL negotiations. The SSL handshake messages like the HelloRequest, ClientHello, ServerHello, Certificate, ServerKeyExchange, ClientKeyExchange, ServerHelloDone, and Finished are some of the messages that are exchanged between the client and the server.

The Record Layer header contains the following fields:

- The Protocol field specifies which higher layer protocol is being encapsulated.
- The Version field specifies which version of SSL is being used.
- The Length field specifies the length of the application data that is carried as part of SSL.
- The Application field specifies the actual protocol packets, such as HTTP or FTP, that are being transmitted over SSL.

SSL Protocol Versions

SSL version 2 was designed by Netscape primarily to provide encryption over the Internet and to secure e-commerce transactions. This version supports the following:

- Rivest-Shamir-Adelman (RSA) public key algorithm

- RC2, RC4, DES, and 3DES encryption algorithms
- Message Digest Algorithm 5 (MD5)

SSL version 3 is an enhancement to SSL version 2 and supports more algorithms. It provides SSL version 2 compatibility. Most SSL applications should run in both SSL version 2 and SSL version 3 modes to support either version for the browsers. However, if either the client or the server supports only SSL version 2, only that version is used.

SSL version 3 supports the following:

- RSA and Diffie-Hellman/Digital Signature Standard (DH/DSS) public key algorithms
- RC2, RC4, DES, and 3DES encryption algorithms
- MD5 and Secure Hash Algorithm (SHA) (also known as SHA-1) message digest algorithms
- Authentication mode only, which means information is not encrypted

Some of the enhancements to SSL version 3 over 2 are as follows:

- Handshake flows are different than version 2 handshake flows.
- Has a fixed number of time-based security vulnerabilities and provides support for the SHA-1 hashing algorithm, which is more secure than the MD5 hashing algorithm. Having SHA-1 allows version 3 to support additional Cipher Suites that use SHA-1 instead of MD5.
- Allows support for DSS, DH, and the National Security Agency's Fortezza cryptographic ciphers. Support for closing the handshake messages is also provided to limit other security vulnerability. (SSL version 2 has some possibilities where the ciphers used can be weakened, thus potentially compromising the SSL session keys.) Transport Layer Security (TLS) protocol version 1 was developed by the Internet Engineering Task Force (IETF) to standardize an SSL-like protocol for the industry. TLS in its current implementation is similar to SSL version 3 and has built-in support for the most popular browser versions and SSL server implementations.

Introduction to SSLMs

Offloading authentication and encryption processing is an important strategy to ensure that server resources are not overwhelmed. Some of the key benefits of SSL offloading devices are:

- They serve as a single point for key and certificate management. Because the servers are front ended by the SSL offload device to manage the domains being hosted for SSL communication, there is no need to obtain a certificate for each server. Instead, a single certificate for the domain can be managed and maintained on the SSL offload.

- SSL termination at the SSL offload allows for load-balancing to be a lot more effective. Once the packets are decrypted at the SSL offload, they can be inspected for HTTP persistence based on cookies or other HTTP headers before being forwarded to the servers.

- They handle all the processing for the SSL key and encryption/decryption, and they offload the CPU-intensive processes from the servers. With a combination of SSL offload and load balancers like the CSM, equal load balancing to the servers can be achieved for SSL traffic.

As part of the SSL offloading portfolio, Cisco offers multiple solutions. The appliance-based solutions are the SSLM for the Catalyst 6500 and the SSLM as part of the CSS. Discussion on these solutions follows.

SSLM for the Catalyst 6500

The SSLM is a Layer 4–through–Layer 7 service module that you can install into the Catalyst 6500 series switch. The module terminates SSL transactions and accelerates the encryption and decryption of data used in SSL sessions.

The module operates either in a stand-alone configuration or with the CSM. When used with the CSM, only encrypted client traffic is forwarded to the module, while clear text traffic is forwarded to the real servers. The SSLM uses the SSL protocol to enable secure transactions of data through privacy, authentication, and data integrity; the protocol relies on certificates, public keys, and private keys.

Some of the features the SSLM supports are:

- SSL 3, SSL 3.1/TLS 1, and SSL 2
- Configuration of client/server NAT/PAT
- Symmetric algorithms (RC4, DES/3DES)
- Asymmetric algorithms (RSA, DH, DSA)
- Hash algorithms (MD5, SHA-1)
- Centralized key and certificate storage management
- Generation of key pairs (private and public)
- 3000 new SSL transactions per second and 60,000 concurrent SSL connections
- 256,000 cached SSL sessions and 300 Mbps symmetric throughput
- 256 SSL proxy services and 356 certificates

Figure 10-7 shows a picture of the SSLM.

Figure 10-7 *SSLM for the Catalyst 6500*

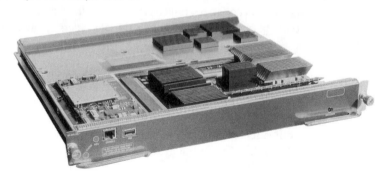

SSLM support on the Catalyst 6500 requires Supervisor Engine 2 with MSFC2 and PFC2 or Supervisor Engine 720 with MSFC3 and PFC3.

SSLM Deployments

The SSLM can be deployed in conjunction with the CSM, where the CSM forwards traffic to the SSLM classified as SSL traffic. Once the traffic has been decrypted by the SSLM, the SSLM can then forward the decrypted traffic back to the CSM to be forwarded to the server. This is illustrated in Figure 10-8.

Figure 10-8 *SSLM Deployment with the CSM*

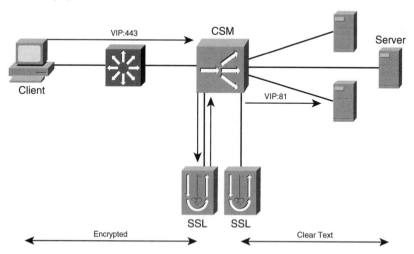

As the figure shows, the connection from the client is made to the virtual IP (VIP) of the CSM on port 443. Once the CSM receives the traffic on the VIP for 443, it forwards that traffic to the SSLM. The SSLM decrypts that traffic and forwards the clear text traffic back to the CSM on the VIP on port 81. Once the CSM receives the traffic on the port 81 VIP, it load balances that traffic to the real server.

The SSLM can be deployed with the CSM in two different modes, one in Bridge mode and the other in Routed mode.

SSLM in Bridge Mode with the CSM

Figure 10-9 illustrates the SSLM in a Bridge mode deployment with the CSM.

Figure 10-9 *SSLM Bridge Mode Deployment with the CSM*

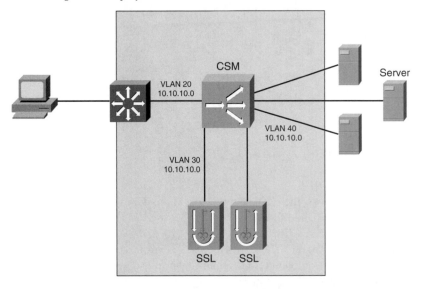

As Figure 10-9 illustrates, the CSM and the SSLM are deployed in Bridge mode. The subnet for the VIPs and the client and server VLANs on the CSM and the SSLM is 10.10.10.0; however, the VLANs between them are separate. One of the biggest advantages of deploying the CSM with the SSLM in Bridge mode is that the VIP address between the CSM and the SSLM can be shared, simplifying routing of SSL traffic between the CSM and the SSLM. The following addresses are configured on the CSM virtual servers:

- Client clear text traffic: 10.10.10.100:80
- Client SSL traffic: 10.10.10.100:443
- Decrypted traffic from SSLMs : 10.20.10.100:80

The 10.10.10.100:443 address is configured on the SSL virtual server. (This IP address is configured with the secondary keyword to allow for sharing of the same VIP between the CSM and the SSLM.) As noted, the VIP address and the port are the same on the CSM and the SSLM.

SSLM in Routed Mode with the CSM

Figure 10-10 illustrates the SSLM in a Routed mode deployment with the CSM.

Figure 10-10 *SSLM Routed Mode Deployment with the CSM*

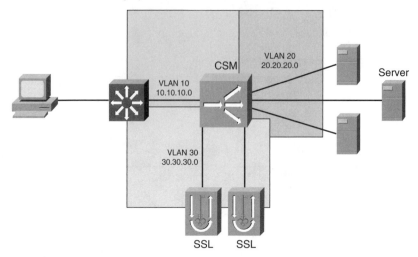

As the figure shows, the CSM and the SSLM are deployed in Routed mode. The subnet between the CSM and the server is 20.20.20.0 on VLAN 20. The subnet between the MSFC and the CSM is 10.10.10.0 on VLAN 10, and the subnet between the CSM and SSLM is 30.30.30.0 on VLAN 30. The SSLM in Routed mode have to be configured such that they can make outbound connections for key management. The following addresses are configured on the CSM virtual servers:

- Client SSL traffic: 10.10.10.100:443 sent to SSLM on 30.30.30.0
- Decrypted traffic from SSLMs: Sent to CSM on 30.30.30.0
- CSM forwarding of decrypted SSL traffic: Sent to server on 20.20.20.0

The address configured on the SSL virtual server is 30.30.30.100:443. Note that the VIP addresses on the CSM and the SSLM have to be different, as the VLAN between the CSM and the SSLM resides on a different subnet.

SSLM on the CSS

The CSS uses the SSL Acceleration Module and a special set of SSL commands to perform the SSL cryptographic functions between a client and a server. The SSL functions include client and server authentication, private key and public key generation, certificate management, and data packet encryption and decryption.

The SSLM supports SSL version 3 and TLS version 1. The module understands and accepts an SSL version 2 ClientHello message to allow dual version clients to communicate with the CSS through the SSLM.

The CSS SSLM has support for the following public key exchange and key agreement algorithms:

- **RSA**—512 bit, 768 bit, 1024 bit, and 2048 bit (key exchange and key agreement algorithm)
- **DSA**—512 bit, 768 bit, and 1024 bit (certificate signing algorithm)
- **DH**—512 bit, 768 bit, 1024 bit, and 2048 bit (key agreement algorithm)

The following encryption types are supported:

- DES
- 3DES
- RC4

The following hash types are supported:

- SSL MAC-MD5
- SSL MAC-SHA-1

The following are some highlights of the throughput capacity on the CSS SSLM:

- 800 SSL transactions per second per module
- 20,000 simultaneous SSL sessions per module
- Full and transparent proxy modes
- SSL session reuse
- 256 digital certificates
- Support for import of Apache, Microsoft IIS, and Netscape certificates
- Personal information exchange syntax standard no. 12 (PKCS12)

The CSS 11503 and CSS 11506 support multiple SSLM—a maximum of two in a CSS 11503 and a maximum of four in a CSS 11506. The CSS 11501 supports a single integrated SSLM.

The SSLM is responsible for all user authentication, public/private key generation, certificate management, and packet encryption and decryption functions between the client and server. It is dependent on the Switch Module to provide the interface for processing network traffic and the Switch Control Module (SCM) to send and receive configuration information.

The CSS stores all certificates and keys on the SCM disk. The CSS supports a maximum of 256 certificates and 256 key pairs per SSLM. This equals approximately 3 MB of storage space on the disk. The CSS stores all certificates and key-related files in a secure location on the disk. When processing connections, the CSS loads the certificates and keys into volatile memory on the SSLM for faster access.

No network traffic is sent to an SSLM from the SCM until an SSL content rule is activated to:

- Define where the content physically resides
- Specify the service to which to direct the request for content
- Specify which load-balancing method to use

An SSL proxy list determines the flow of information to and from an SSLM. An entry in the proxy list defines the flow from a client to an SSLM. An entry also defines a flow from an SSLM to a back-end SSL server. To define how an SSLM processes SSL requests for content, add an SSL proxy list to an SSL service.

SSL Flows on the CSS-SSLM

To terminate SSL flows, the SSLM functions as a proxy server, meaning that it is the TCP end point for inbound SSL traffic. The SSLM maintains a separate TCP connection for each side of the communications, the client side and the server side. The proxy server can perform both TCP and SSL handshakes. Figure 10-11 illustrates the SSL connections that are terminated on the CSS-SSLM.

Figure 10-11 *CSS-SSLM Flows*

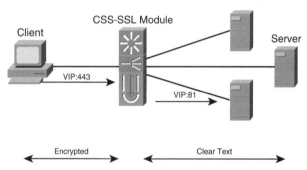

As the figure shows, the client initiates an encrypted SSL connection to the CSS VIP address on port 443. When the client connection reaches the CSS, it load balances the connection to the SSLMs. When the inbound TCP SYN connection reaches the SSLM, it terminates the SSL connections from the client.

As the CSS forwards the SSL packet to that module, the CSS saves the SSL session ID sticky table for subsequent SSL connections from the same client (if SSL persistence is on). Once this SSL flow is mapped, the CSS forwards all subsequent packets for this connection to the SSLM. If there are additional SSL connections associated with this transaction (as determined by the SSL session ID), the CSS also forwards and maps the packets to the same SSLM.

The SSLM terminates the SSL connection and decrypts the packet data. The SSLM then initiates an HTTP connection to a content rule configured on the CSS. The data in this HTTP connection is clear text.

If configured for persistency on cookies, the CSS uses the Layer 5 HTTP cookies or URL sticky content rule on this HTTP request. The cookie or URL string in this clear text HTTP request is used to locate the same server as the one initially used by the non-SSL HTTP connection in the transactions. The CSS forwards the request to the server and maps this flow. Once the flow is mapped, the return HTTP response from the server is sent to the same SSLM that sent the original request. The SSLM encrypts the response as an SSL packet (it translates flows from HTTP to HTTPS for outbound packets) and sends the packets back to the client through the correct SSL connection.

When the TCP connection is finished, the four flows (the two flows between the client and the SSLM and the two flows between the SSLM and the server) are removed.

Another feature that the SSLM provides is the SSL-transparent proxy server, which allows the client source IP address to be maintained. When you configure an SSL-transparent proxy on the CSS, the CSS intercepts and redirects client requests to an HTTP server on the network without changing the source IP address in the IP header. This is useful for applications that use the client source IP address for logging or other statistics.

Case Study: CSM and SSLM–Based Solution

Now that you understand the various steps required to make SSL connections via the SSLM, this section covers a design with the connection to the SSLM in a load-balanced environment using the CSM.

Design Requirements

The requirements for the design are as follows:

- Server and application requirements
    - All connections should be load balanced to a single domain.
    - A single certificate should be purchased for the domain.
    - Four servers that are load balanced and use sticky cookies should be provided for client connections for all HTTP and HTTPS connections.
    - Clients making connections on port 80 (HTTP) should be redirected to port 443 for HTTPS connections.
    - Only a single VIP address should be used for the domain.
    - Port 80 should be used for HTTP traffic and port 443 should be used for SSL traffic.

- Management and security requirements

  — The strongest possible cipher should be used for all SSL connections.

- Infrastructure requirements

  — The default gateway for the servers should be pointing to the CSM.

  — A single VLAN should be configured for the SSL implementation.

Design Details of a CSM and an SSLM–Based Solution

This section provides an overview of the connection the client makes when an SSL connection is initiated to the SSLM. The domain used in this design is www.test.com. The VIP address that domain resolves to is 172.21.55.149 for HTTPS traffic and 172.21.55.145 for HTTP traffic. The CSM client VLAN is 50, and the server VLAN is 80. The VLAN for the SSLM is 150. The server's IP addresses are in the subnet 80.80.80.0 /24.

Figure 10-12 illustrates the topology between the CSM, the SSLM, and the servers.

Figure 10-12 *Design Topology*

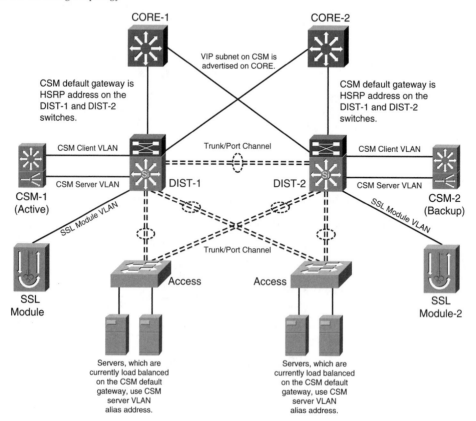

As the figure shows, two SSLMs are directly attached to the Catalyst 6500. Figure 10-13 illustrates the logical connections.

Figure 10-13 *Logical Connections for the Design*

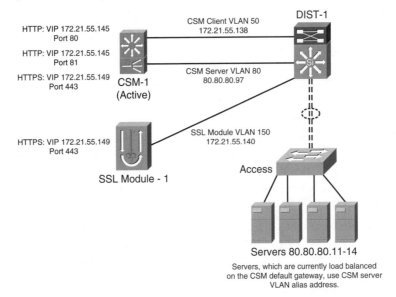

SSLM Certificate Management

Before the design discussion begins, the SSL certificates need to be imported on the SSLM. The following steps walk you through the process.

First, a private and public key pair needs to be generated for the exchange of the SSL session key used for encryption. Because these keys and certificates will be used on other SSLMs, they must be exportable. To generate the key pair, use the following instructions:

```
ssl-proxy-3(config)#crypto key generate rsa general-keys exportable
% You already have RSA keys defined named ssl ssl-module-5.cisco.com
% Do you really want to replace them? [yes/no]: yes
Choose the size of the key modulus in the range of 360 to 2048 for your General
   Purpose Keys. Choosing a key modulus greater than 512 may take a few minutes.
How many bits in the modulus [512]: 1024
% Generating 1024 bit RSA keys ...[OK]
```

Now that the RSA keys are generated, you can view the RSA public key (only the public key can be viewed) with the following command:

```
ssl-module-5#show crypto key mypubkey rsa
% Key pair was generated at: 14:12:22 UTC Jun 6 2004
Key name: ssl-module-5.cisco.com
 Usage: General Purpose Key
 Key is exportable.
 Key Data:
  30819F30 0D06092A 864886F7 0D010101 05000381 8D003081 89028181 00E2ADA1
```

```
3B916878 80BBBCC1 698B5943 B724CA9B EC5E6030 EF891FC2 5F603DFA C53B1F1F
2C1786F7 2F0D7A26 C628027A 4394AD60 1CD73A9A 9B535768 1CFD47A0 FC2D5254
C8BD1C12 E0913025 318A696E 8925FC5C E028F43D 1A55B1F9 60A9A2B6 9C419C7A
3D0103EB 6460F34B DE990D14 A9BE15C4 7110D688 F7FD87D9 D34D14A8 7B020301 0001
% Key pair was generated at: 14:12:22 UTC Jun 6 2004
```

The key name is important, as this name will be used in the later steps.

The following command on the SSLM creates an entity called the *trust point* with the label testcert. The trust point is used to generate and handle all SSL certificate requests for a particular SSL-hosted domain. In order for the SSLM to offer a client an SSL certificate, the trust point labeled testcert, which is used in this example, must be associated with the SSL proxy service, as explained in later sections.

```
crypto ca trustpoint testcert
```

Now that a trust point has been established, it's time to request a certificate from a CA server. In our testing, we have used test certificates issued by VeriSign. Anyone can apply for these certificates at www.verisign.com. When applying for a certificate, VeriSign will ask the user for a Certificate Signing Request (CSR) and will request that the user cut and paste the CSR onto their web site.

In the trust point submode configuration, you provide information that will be included in the CSR request. The enrollment method could be via HTTP or terminal (we can cut and paste it to the SSL module console or terminal session); the terminal method is what we have used in this example. The subject name portion of the CSR is important, and you must make sure that the CN value or string matches the name for the site to which the client is going to connect. The state name has to be entered in its entirety because an abbreviated state name will generate an error. A CRL optional is configured on the SSLM, as the SSLM will try to contact the CA every time to check to see the list for revoked certificates, in this case study, we have made it optional. The certificate we are requesting has been associated with the RSA key pair we generated. The rsakeypair name of ssl-module-5 is used.

```
ssl-proxy-3(ca-trustpoint)#enrollment terminal
ssl-proxy-3(ca-trustpoint)#rsakeypair ssl-module-5
ssl-proxy-3(ca-trustpoint subject-name C=US; ST=California; L=San Jose;
  O=Cisco; OU=Lab; CN=www.test.com
ssl-proxy-3(ca-trustpoint)# crl optional
ssl-proxy-3(ca-trustpoint)#exit
```

After the trust point has been created, you need to enroll the trust point and the CSR request. The CSR request must be sent to VeriSign. Choose Apache as the platform when requesting a certificate for the SSLM from VeriSign.

```
ssl-module-5(config)#crypto ca enroll testcert
% Start certificate enrollment ..
% The subject name in the certificate will be: C=US; ST=California; L=San Jose;
  O=Cisco; OU=Lab; CN=www.test.com
% The fully-qualified domain name in the certificate will be: ssl-module-5.cisco.com
% The subject name in the certificate will be: ssl-module-5.cisco.com
% Include the router serial number in the subject name? [yes/no]: no
% Include an IP address in the subject name? [no]: no
Display Certificate Request to terminal? [yes/no]: yes
Certificate Request follows:
MIIB9zCCAWACAQAwgZUxGTAXBgNVBAMTEHd3dy5zc2wtbGFiMy5jb20xDDAKBgNV
```

```
BAsTA0xhYjEOMAwGA1UEChMFQ2lzY28xETAPBgNVBAcTCFNhbiBKb3NlMRMwEQYD
VQQIEwpDYWxpZm9ybmlhMQswCQYDVQQGEwJVUzE1MCMGCSqGSIb3DQEJAhYWc3Ns
LW1vZHVsZS01LmNpc2NvLmNvbTCBnzANBgkqhkiG9w0BAQEFAAOBjQAwgYkCgYEA
4q2hO5FoeIC7vMFpi1lDtyTKm+xeYDDviR/CX2A9+sU7Hx8sF4b3Lw16JsYoAnpD
lK1gHNc6mptTV2gc/Ueg/C1SVMi9HBLgkTAlMYppbokl/FzgKPQ9GlWx+WCporac
QZx6PQED62Rg80vemQ0Uqb4VxHEQ1oj3/YfZ000UqHsCAwEAAaAhMB8GCSqGSIb3
DQEJDjESMBAwDgYDVR0PAQH/BAQDAgWgMA0GCSqGSIb3DQEBBAUAA4GBALp3jeMH
klDmjNw+Ho+MO+EQTgztxwBIK+WckyyrYU6WVjNv1do6b4+CXv4BfV7a2bXxYp7+
We1e7T/buDxkmVGR1FhnwNS4ME988uf32gWnKeMhrc4KlFDBgfrCX7N9p+dE8qwv
IwJd1dkA0B7ImJ9WQRK36+I0Fo/Q1Yw05FC/
---End - This line not part of the certificate request---
Redisplay enrollment request? [yes/no]: no
```

As seen in this example, the CSR is displayed and you can use it to request the certificate from VeriSign. When requesting certificates from VeriSign for multiple SSLMs, a single certificate is used, so make sure to purchase a license for a certificate that allows for installation on multiple SSLMs. Once you have the certificate from VeriSign, which usually sends the certificate details via e-mail, import it into the SSLM. However, before you can start using the certificate, you also have to authenticate the CA's root certificate on the SSLM. VeriSign should be able to provide you with this. (The CA's root certificate information is usually available in the e-mail sent along with the server certificate.) On our test certificate, the root certificate authentication is as follows:

```
ssl-proxy-3(config)#crypto ca authenticate testcertroot
Enter the base 64 encoded CA certificate.
End with a blank line or the word "quit" on a line by itself
-----BEGIN CERTIFICATE-----
MIICTTCCAfcCEFKp9CTaZ0ydr09TeFKr724wDQYJKoZIhvcNAQEEBQAwgakxFjAU
BgNVBAoTDVZlcmlTaWduLCBJbmMxRzBFBgNVBAsTPnd3dy52ZXJpc2lnbi5jb20v
cmVwb3NpdG9yeS9UZXN0Q1BTIEluY29ycC4gQnkgUmVmLiBMaWFiLiBMVEQuMUYw
RAYDVQQLEz1Gb3IgVmVyaVNpZz24gYXV0aG9yaXplZCB0ZXN0aW5nIG9ubHkuIE5v
IGFzc3VyYW5jZXMgKEMpVmVyaVNpZ24sMB4XDTk4MDYwNzAwMDAwMFoXDTA2MDYwNjIz
NTk1OVowgakxFjAUBgNVBAoTDVZlcmlTaWduLCBJbmMxRzBFBgNVBAsTPnd3dy52
ZXJpc2lnbi5jb20vcmVwb3NpdG9yeS9UZXN0Q1BTIEluY29ycC4gQnkgUmVmLiBM
aWFiLiBMVEQuMUYwRAYDVQQLEz1Gb3IgVmVyaVNpZz24gYXV0aG9yaXplZCB0ZXN0
aW5nIG9ubHkuIE5vIGFzc3VyYW5jZXMgKEMpVmVyaVNpZ24wXDANBgkqhkiG9w0BAQEB
BQADSwAwSAJBAMak6xImJx44jMKcbkACy5/CyMA2fqXK4PlzTtCxRq5tFkDzne7s
cI8oFK/J+gFZNE3bjidDxf07O3JOYG9RGx8CAwEAATANBgkqhkiG9w0BAQQFAANB
AKWnR/KPNxCglpTP5nzbo+QCIkmsCPjTCMnvm7KcwDJguaEwkoi1gBSY9biJp9oK
+cv1Yn3KuVM+YptcWXLfxxI=
-----END CERTIFICATE-----
quit
Certificate has the following attributes:
Fingerprint: 40065311 FDB33E88 0A6F7DD1 4E229187
% Do you accept this certificate? [yes/no]: yes
Trustpoint CA certificate accepted.
% Certificate successfully imported

ssl-module-5(config)#crypto ca import testcert certificate
% The fully-qualified domain name in the certificate will be: ssl-module-5.cisco.com
Enter the base 64 encoded certificate.
End with a blank line or the word "quit" on a line by itself
-----BEGIN CERTIFICATE-----
MIIDLjCCAtigAwIBAgIQfxLUGE62jMAEGxEVKdpWDDANBgkqhkiG9w0BAQUFADCB
qTEWMBQGA1UEChMNVmVyaVNpZz24sIEluYzFHMEUGA1UECxM+d3d3LnZlcmlzaWdu
LmNvbS9yZXBvc2l0b3J5L1Rlc3RDUFMgSW5jb3JwLiBCeSBSZWYuIExpYWIuIExU
RC4xRjBEBgNVBAsTPUZvciBWZXJpU2lnbiBhdXRob3JpemVkIHRlc3Rpbmcgb25s
eS4gTm8gYXNzdXJhbmNlcyAoQylWZXJpU2lnbiwhhcNMDQwNjA3MDAwMDAwWhcNMDQw
NjIxMjM1OTU5WjBuMQswCQYDVQQGEwJVUzETMBEGA1UECBMKQ2FsaWZvcm5pYTER
MA8GA1UEBxQIU2FuIEpvc2UxDjAMBgNVBAoUBUNpc2NvMQwwCgYDVQQLFANMYWIx
```

```
GTAXBgNVBAMUEHd3dy5zc2wtbGFiMy5jb20wgZ8wDQYJKoZIhvcNAQEBBQADgY0A
MIGJAoGBAOKtoTuRaHiAu7zBaYtZQ7ckypvsXmAw74kfwl9gPfrFOx8fLBeG9y8N
eibGKAJ6Q5StYBzXOpqbU1doHP1HoPwtUlTIvRwS4JEwJTGKaW6JJfxc4Cj0PRpV
sflgqaK2nEGcej0BA+tkYPNL3pkNFKm+FcRxENaI9/2H2dNNFKh7AgMBAAGjgdEw
gc4wCQYDVR0TBAIwADALBgNVHQ8EBAMCBaAwQgYDVR0fBDswOTA3oDWgM4YxaHR0
cDovL2NybC52ZXJpc2lnbi5jb20vU2VjdXJlU2VydmVyVGVzdGluZ0NBLmNybDBR
BgNVHSAESjBIMEYGCmCGSAGG+EUBBxUwODA2BggrBgEFBQcCARYqaHR0cDovL3d3
dy52ZXJpc2lnbi5jb20vcmVwb3NpdG9yeS9UZXN0Q0Q1BTMB0GA1UdJQQWMBQGCCsG
AQUFBwMBBggrBgEFBQcDAjANBgkqhkiG9w0BAQUFAANBAGs5b4PSrVbp0EJTvOOv
kgvMp5PzsSaJmJh8TWIcnrmacEGk7e3I6g8gA6JIPnM0PtnQoiIvb3qjVsNRp5aU
91c=
-----END CERTIFICATE-----
quit
% Router Certificate successfully imported
```

Let's view the certificate that we have downloaded and make sure that the root certificate and the server certificate are associated.

```
ssl-module-5#sh crypto ca certificates testcert
Certificate
  Status: Available
  Certificate Serial Number: 7F12D4184EB68CC0041B111529DA560C
  Certificate Usage: General Purpose
  Issuer:
    OU = For VeriSign authorized testing only. No assurances (C)VS1997
     OU = www.verisign.com/repository/TestCPS Incorp. By Ref. Liab. LTD.
     O = "VeriSign
     Inc"
  Subject:
    Name: www.test.com
    CN = www.test.com
     OU = Lab
     O = Cisco
     L = San Jose
     ST = California
     C = US
  CRL Distribution Point:
    http://crl.verisign.com/SecureServerTestingCA.crl
  Validity Date:
    start date: 00:00:00 UTC Jun 7 2004
    end   date: 23:59:59 UTC Jun 21 2004
    renew date: 00:00:00 UTC Jan 1 1970
  Associated Trustpoints: testcert
CA Certificate
  Status: Available
  Certificate Serial Number: 52A9F424DA674C9DAF4F537852ABEF6E
  Certificate Usage: General Purpose
  Issuer:
    OU = For VeriSign authorized testing only. No assurances (C)VS1997
     OU = www.verisign.com/repository/TestCPS Incorp. By Ref. Liab. LTD.
     O = "VeriSign
     Inc"
  Subject:
    OU = For VeriSign authorized testing only. No assurances (C)VS1997
     OU = www.verisign.com/repository/TestCPS Incorp. By Ref. Liab. LTD.
     O = "VeriSign
     Inc"
  Validity Date:
    start date: 00:00:00 UTC Jun 7 1998
    end   date: 23:59:59 UTC Jun 6 2006
  Associated Trustpoints: testcert
```

Now that we have imported the server certificate for the domain http://www.test.com and imported it on both the SSLMs, we will discuss how the client connections get terminated on the SSLM and how the SSLM forwards the connection to the server via the CSM.

SSLM and CSM Flow Overview

Figure 10-14 identifies the traffic path when deploying the SSLM in the data center. Clear text traffic, such as regular HTTP GETs, goes to the CSM and the CSM distributes the requests to the servers listening on port 80. The CSM is also used to intercept encrypted HTTP (HTTPS) traffic, and it forwards this traffic to the SSLM. The SSLM returns the decrypted traffic to the CSM for load balancing. Because this traffic is clear text, the CSM keeps persistence between HTTPS and HTTP, after which the CSM forwards the request to the real server. We will discuss the details of the flow from client to server in the following order in the next sections:

- Client connection to the CSM
- CSM connection to the SSLM
- SSLM connection to the CSM
- CSM connection to the server

The configuration details for each section will also be discussed.

Figure 10-14 illustrates the sequence of flows that take place when performing load balancing for SSL traffic on the CSM.

Figure 10-14 *HTTPS Connection Flow*

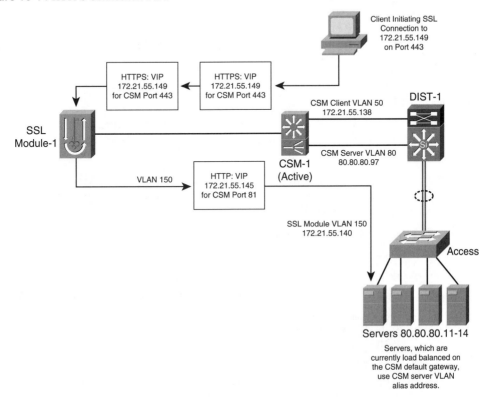

Client Connection to the CSM

As the client initiates a connection to the SSL domain, the connection is forwarded to the CSM. Following is the CSM client and server VLAN configuration used in this example. VLAN 50 is the client VLAN on the CSM. All connections from the client side will enter the CSM on VLAN 50:

```
module ContentSwitchingModule 9
!
 vlan 50 client
   ip address 172.21.55.138 255.255.255.224
   gateway 172.21.55.130
 !
```

The following VLAN is the server VLAN on the CSM. All connections from the CSM to the server will enter the CSM on VLAN 80:

```
 vlan 80 server
   ip address 80.80.80.97 255.255.255.0
 !
```

As the client connects to the VIP address on the CSM using an SSL-enabled browser, the traffic is load balanced to one of the two configured SSLMs. In our testing, the VIP address is defined as 172.21.55.149 listening on port 443:

```
 vserver ATT-CLIENT-443
   virtual 172.21.55.149 tcp https
   serverfarm SSL-MOD
   persistent rebalance
   inservice
```

The server farm definition has the IP addresses of the SSLMs, and their role is defined in the next section.

CSM Connection to the SSLM

Before we describe the connection from the CSM to the SSLM, the following steps for defining VLAN 150, which is used for the communication between the SSLM and the CSM, need to be accomplished.

In order for the MSFC to forward VLAN 150 traffic between the CSM and the SSLM, VLAN 150 (carried from the Catalyst 6500 to the SSLM) must be allowed to the SSLM using the following command:

```
 ssl-proxy module 6 allowed-vlan 150
```

This command also needs to be configured on the second SSLM, as follows:

```
 ssl-proxy module 7 allowed-vlan 150
```

Issue the following command to check the state of the VLANs allowed to the SSLM:

```
 sh ssl-proxy module 6 state
 SSL-proxy module 6 data-port:
 Switchport: Enabled
 Administrative Mode: trunk
 Operational Mode: trunk
 Administrative Trunking Encapsulation: dot1q
 Operational Trunking Encapsulation: dot1q
```

```
Negotiation of Trunking: Off
Access Mode VLAN: 1 (default)
Trunking Native Mode VLAN: 1 (default)
Trunking VLANs Enabled: 150
Pruning VLANs Enabled: 2-1001
Vlans allowed on trunk:150
Vlans allowed and active in management domain: 150
Vlans in spanning tree forwarding state and not pruned:
    150
Allowed-vlan : 150
```

This command verifies that VLAN 150 is carried to the SSLM. Additionally, VLAN 150 is defined on the CSM for communication to the SSLM as follows:

```
vlan 150 server
  ip address 172.21.55.138 255.255.255.224
!
```

VLAN 150 is the communication VLAN between the SSLM and the CSM. All connections from the client to the SSLM, the connection from the CSM to the SSLM, and the connection from the SSLM to the server side will use VLAN 150. Note that the IP address is the same as the client VLAN 50 on the CSM, indicating that VLAN 50 and VLAN 150 on the CSM are configured in Bridge mode. This allows simpler configuration for maintenance of the SSLMs and for import/export of certificates to and from the SSLMs. The solution can also be achieved by using Routed mode, but in that case virtual servers with predictor forward need to be configured on the CSM to route traffic to and from the SSLM. Since the SSLM needs to download certificates or access the TFTP/FTP server for software upgrades or downloading archived configurations, it is important to use a routable IP for the management VLAN.

Similarly, VLAN 150 is defined on the SSLM to accept the traffic. VLAN 150 on the SSLM is defined as an administrative VLAN (admin) also, where the IP address 172.21.55.140 can be used for Telnet, SNMP, and other types of administrative access:

```
ssl-proxy vlan 150
  ipaddr 172.21.55.140 255.255.255.224
  gateway 172.21.55.138 forward
```

This exact same configuration would reside on the second SSLM with the IP address 172.21.55.150:

```
ssl-proxy vlan 150
  ipaddr 172.21.55.150 255.255.255.224
  gateway 172.21.55.138 forward
```

The default gateway for the SSLMs is the CSM.

Now that the communication on VLAN 150 has been set up, we will continue where the CSM has load balanced traffic to the server farm SSL-MOD. The client is load balanced to one of the real servers defined for the SSLM that has IP addresses of 172.21.55.140 and 172.21.55.150, as configured here on the CSM:

```
serverfarm SSL-MOD
  no nat server
  no nat client
  real 172.21.55.140
   inservice
  real 172.21.55.150
   inservice probe ICM
```

Notice that Dispatch mode (**no nat server**) is used to send load-balanced traffic from the CSM to the SSLM. This enables us to use the same VIP address for the SSL proxy service on the SSLM as we used on the CSM (that is, 172.21.55.149). In Dispatch mode, only a Layer 2 rewrite is performed.

The CSM forwards the client connection to VLAN 150 based on the real server it selected (in our example, 172.21.55.140). The SSL traffic enters the SSLM and hits the SSL proxy service (the same IP address as defined on the vserver for port 443 on the CSM):

```
ssl-proxy service csm-ssl-443-in
  virtual ipaddr 172.21.55.149 protocol tcp port 443 secondary
```

This command in the SSLM allows it to start listening and proxying for connections to 172.21.55.149 on port 443. The **secondary** keyword is optional and is needed when the address is also used elsewhere. (In our example, notice that the **virtual ipaddr** on the SSLM and the vserver IP on the CSM are the same: 172.21.55.149.) You do not want the SSLM to respond to Address Resolution Protcol (ARP) requests because there would be a similar vserver addressconfigured on the CSM. (The **secondary** keyword allows us to host a similar VIP address on the SSLM and the CSM).

Now that the SSLM has accepted the connection on port 443, it's ready to present the certificate we imported in the section "SSLM Certificate Management" to the client. In order to associate our certificate with the SSL proxy of 172.21.55.140, the following command is issued under the SSL proxy configuration submode:

```
certificate rsa general-purpose trustpoint testcert
```

This command in the SSLM allows for the testcert (in our testing, we are using a test certificate) to be presented to the client. Once the client accepts the certificate and completes the SSL handshake, the data from the client is ready to be decrypted and sent to the CSM in clear text. This is discussed in the next section.

SSLM to the CSM

Now that the SSLM has decrypted the connection, it is ready to send the connection back to the CSM on virtual server 172.21.55.145 on port 81. The following command under the SSL proxy service configuration allows for the SSLM to forward the decrypted packet to the CSM on vserver 172.21.55.145 on port 81:

```
server ipaddr 172.21.55.145 protocol tcp port 81
```

The SSLM will use VLAN 150, also defined as the admin VLAN on the SSLM for administration purposes (Telnet, SNMP, SSH, import/export, and so on). The default gateway is the CSM on VLAN 150. The **admin** keyword is used to define this VLAN as the admin VLAN:

```
ssl-proxy vlan 150
  ipaddr 172.21.55.140 255.255.255.224
  gateway 172.21.55.138 forward
  admin
```

Similarly, on the second SSLM the configuration is as follows:

```
ssl-proxy vlan 150
  ipaddr 172.21.55.150 255.255.255.224
  gateway 172.21.55.138 forward
admin
```

Now that the SSLM has forwarded the decrypted HTTP packet to the CSM, we will discuss how the CSM forwards this connection to the server.

CSM Connection to the Server

Following is the configuration on the CSM for the VIP address to which the SSLM sends the decrypted traffic:

```
vserver CSM-SSL-81
  virtual 172.21.55.145 tcp 81
```

Once the CSM receives the decrypted traffic, it forwards that traffic to the servers listening for HTTP clear text traffic, but before doing this, the CSM can look at the HTTP headers and make persistence decisions based on cookies.

The CSM matches the cookie apache=*whatever_the_random_string* and associates it to a real server. The next time the user connects with the same cookie, the CSM will remember to stick the user to the same real server. The string used in this testing is apache=*some_random_string*, and the CSM stores it until the cookie expires. The following configuration defines the cookie persistence on the CSM:

```
sticky 1440 group 11
```

This is the sticky cookie group used for the vserver for cookie persistence. To match this sticky group for vserver 172.21.55.145, sticky group 11 is defined, and it matches on the cookie string of "apache", as the following configuration shows:

```
sticky 11 cookie apache
```

Once the sticky table is set up, the connection is forwarded to the server, as defined in the following configuration:

```
serverfarm CSM-SERVER
  nat server
  no nat client
  real 80.80.80.10
   inservice
  real 80.80.80.11
   inservice
  real 80.80.80.12
   inservice
  real 80.80.80.13
   inservice
probe ICMP
```

As the client connection reaches the server, the server responds back. The connection reaches the CSM, where it updates its sticky table for persistency and sends the traffic back to the SSLM. At the SSLM, the traffic is re-encrypted using the SSL protocol parameters defined in the SSL handshake. The SSLM then forwards the traffic back to the CSM, which in turn forwards it to the client.

Configuration Details

The following sections list the complete configurations for the CSM and the SSLM that have been discussed in preceding sections.

CSM Configuration

```
module ContentSwitchingModule 9
 variable ROUTE_UNKNOWN_FLOW_PKTS 1
 !
 vlan 50 client
  ip address 172.21.55.138 255.255.255.224
  gateway 172.21.55.130
 !
 vlan 80 server
  ip address 80.80.80.97 255.255.255.0
 !
 vlan 150 server
  ip address 172.21.55.138 255.255.255.224
 !
 probe ICMP icmp
  interval 5
  retries 2
  failed 5
 !
 serverfarm SSL-MOD
  no nat server
  no nat client
  real 172.21.55.140
   Inservice
  real 172.21.55.150
   inservice
  probe ICMP
 !
 serverfarm CSM-SERVER
  nat server
  no nat client
  real 80.80.80.10
   inservice
  real 80.80.80.11
   inservice
  real 80.80.80.12
   inservice
  real 80.80.80.13
   inservice
 probe ICMP
 !
 sticky 11 cookie apache
 !
 vserver CLIENT-443
  virtual 172.21.55.149 tcp https
  vlan 50
  serverfarm SSL-MOD
  persistent rebalance
  inservice
```

```
!
vserver CSM-SSL-81
  virtual 172.21.55.145 tcp 81
  vlan 150
  serverfarm CSM-SERVER
  sticky 1440 group 11
  persistent rebalance
  inservice
!
 ft group 90 vlan 90
!
 xml-config
  port 8080
  vlan 50
  credentials znaseh password znaseh
  inservice
!
!
```

SSLM Configuration—Primary

```
version 12.2
no service pad
service timestamps debug datetime msec
service timestamps log datetime msec
no service password-encryption
!
hostname ssl-proxy
!
no logging buffered
!
spd headroom 512
ip subnet-zero
ip tftp source-interface Ethernet0/0.150
no ip domain lookup
!
!
!
ssl-proxy service csm-ssl-443-in
 virtual ipaddr 172.21.55.149 protocol tcp port 443 secondary
trusted-ca test_pool
 server ipaddr 172.21.55.145 protocol tcp port 81
 certificate rsa general-purpose trustpoint testcert
 inservice
!
ssl-proxy vlan 150
 ipaddr 172.21.55.140 255.255.255.224
 gateway 172.21.55.138 forward
admin
ssl-proxy mac address 000d.29f0.b9b7
!
ssl-proxy pool ca test_pool
 ca trustpoint testcertroot
!
crypto ca trustpoint testcert
 rsakeypair testcert
!
!
crypto ca certificate chain testcert
 certificate ca 00
  30820353 308202BC A0030201 02020100 300D0609 2A864886 F70D0101 04050030
  7F310B30 09060355 04061302 55533113 30110603 55040813 0A43616C 69666F72
```

```
  6E696131 11300F06 03550407 13085361 6E204A6F 7365311A 30180603 55040A13
  11436973 636F2053 79737465 6D732049 6E633111 300F0603 55040B13 08536563
  75726974 79311930 17060355 04031310 74657374 63612E63 6973636F 2E636F6D
  301E170D 30333131 31313231 35353038 5A170D31 34313032 34323235 3530385A
  307F310B 30090603 55040613 02555331 13301106 03550408 130A4361 6C69666F
  726E6961 3111300F 06035504 07130853 616E204A 6F736531 1A301806 0355040A
  13114369 73636F20 53797374 656D7320 496E6331 11300F06 0355040B 13085365
  63757269 74793119 30170603 55040313 10746573 7463612E 63697363 6F2E636F
  6D30819F 300D0609 2A864886 F70D0101 01050003 818D0030 81890281 8100B57D
  1C000D5E CBAE09D9 C6836E77 744DDC4C 4C8E9A2F A2F591BE 7492368F CAF22C63
  7BD622B4 89C47148 E1D3BB2E CD870DB1 43AB1DFF 43122FF3 87BA50F9 114A35BE
  A76303CA B74FC306 7845CBBA 5B3227EB 101EA2E1 29109CE1 F9214B95 EA83C45C
  A77D6EEC FB8BE256 3305F512 4E653787 C2A0F74C 30D27037 171A7589 5E030203
  010001A3 81DE3081 DB301D06 03551D0E 04160414 32F4122B 3C7C38D7 FDFC2440
  D04E6448 233F0C9C 3081AB06 03551D23 0481A330 81A08014 32F4122B 3C7C38D7
  FDFC2440 D04E6448 233F0C9C A18184A4 8181307F 310B3009 06035504 06130255
  53311330 11060355 0408130A 43616C69 666F726E 69613111 300F0603 55040713
  0853616E 204A6F73 65311A30 18060355 040A1311 43697363 6F205379 7374656D
  7320496E 63311130 0F060355 040B1308 53656375 72697479 31193017 06035504
  03131074 65737463 612E6369 73636F2E 636F6D82 0100300C 0603551D 13040530
  030101FF 300D0609 2A864886 F70D0101 04050003 8181002E FD07F050 E903D217
  C7F4A2D4 2F15C153 DD9FE072 68925B1E A62EEA31 13FDCFD9 ED25F406 61EE7E82
  FB0C9936 E91F8488 2EF12458 FE34F6F0 EBC1C307 E6ED0DDD 98CEED20 9C4371C9
  1F7749CF 2DC8A3A4 A1A8692D 1185CA1D A2D17723 A6E27AE4 53BCB8EB 15309E52
  DCC3BB5F 522EDB2B 8C60FD15 9054B86D 53A41E44 A5DF9E
  quit
certificate 01
  30820265 308201CE 02010130 0D06092A 864886F7 0D010104 0500307F 310B3009
  06035504 06130255 53311330 11060355 0408130A 43616C69 666F726E 69613111
  300F0603 55040713 0853616E 204A6F73 65311A30 18060355 040A1311 43697363
  6F205379 7374656D 7320496E 63311130 0F060355 040B1308 53656375 72697479
  31193017 06035504 03131074 65737463 612E6369 73636F2E 636F6D30 1E170D30
  33313131 31323135 3632335A 170D3133 31313038 32313536 32335A30 77310B30
  09060355 04061302 55553113 30110603 55040813 0A43616C 69666F72 6E696131
  11300F06 03550407 13085361 6E204A6F 7365311A 30180603 55040A13 11436973
  636F2053 79737465 6D732049 6E633111 300F0603 55040B13 08536563 75726974
  79311130 0F060355 04031308 74657374 63657274 30819F30 0D06092A 864886F7
  0D010101 05000381 8D003081 89028181 00C57FA1 5C598047 D862D87D 6D9E70F1
  ACF0BFDA 3FE23685 F7B11340 0BD8092D E982DBB1 7C9BCE35 588F8A1F 12A66DB3
  7066E0D1 E7B78F8B 4D519C18 E13A7C33 5DDECE9E C26CB060 1A9097CB 18D7DB2E
  FFA0B74D 3934A4AF B9956D52 4AEFE06D 6A0084A4 E1F82349 E15976DA C55320D6
  103643DC 715E8E3D F9C01362 F224DA88 45020301 0001300D 06092A86 4886F70D
  01010405 00038181 00610373 C6BB39C4 BD34BC3E 6FEE179F 81ED0AB2 CB1D8EFD
  0DECF3EC CB764717 DFDE555F 2E968324 DE667118 7031C9E0 C26A8FA4 BE3B0BF8
  C5DF437B 61C1ACAD D4FAC602 2848FCA8 628B65BD 6A64EC46 D2C1A47F 7BD8A2FB
  1594917C 4B7F0E2A AF72B7FE EF114CED 2BCDFDB1 A03C22EF 29709E41 D3A6D238
  C6EF54A1 F2A321A5 D6
  quit
!
ip classless
ip route 0.0.0.0 0.0.0.0 172.21.55.138
ip http server
no ip http secure-server
!
!
snmp-server community public RW
snmp-server queue-length 256
snmp-server contact The Superman and Batgirl
snmp-server chassis-id
no snmp-server enable traps tty
snmp-server enable traps ssl-proxy oper-status
snmp-server enable traps ssl-proxy cert-expiring
snmp-server host 171.69.100.148 version 2c ssl-proxy
!
```

```
            line con 0
            line 1 3
             no exec
             transport input all
             flowcontrol software
            line vty 0 4
             password ww
             login
            !
            end
            ssl-proxy#
```

SSLM Configuration—Secondary

```
            version 12.2
            no service pad
            service timestamps debug datetime msec
            service timestamps log datetime msec
            no service password-encryption
            !
            hostname ssl-proxy
            !
            no logging buffered
            !
            spd headroom 512
            ip subnet-zero
            ip tftp source-interface Ethernet0/0.150
            no ip domain lookup
            !
            !
            !
            ssl-proxy service csm-ssl-443-in
             virtual ipaddr 172.21.55.149 protocol tcp port 443 secondary
            trusted-ca test_pool
             server ipaddr 172.21.55.145 protocol tcp port 81
             certificate rsa general-purpose trustpoint testcert
             inservice
            !
            ssl-proxy vlan 150
             ipaddr 172.21.55.150 255.255.255.224
             gateway 172.21.55.138 forward
            admin
            ssl-proxy mac address 000d.29f0.b9b7
            !
            ssl-proxy pool ca test_pool
             ca trustpoint testcertroot
            !
            crypto ca trustpoint testcert
             rsakeypair testcert
            !
            !
            crypto ca certificate chain testcert
             certificate ca 00
              30820353 308202BC A0030201 02020100 300D0609 2A864886 F70D0101 04050030
              7F310B30 09060355 04061302 55533113 30110603 55040813 0A43616C 69666F72
              6E696131 11300F06 03550407 13085361 6E204A6F 7365311A 30180603 55040A13
              11436973 636F2053 79737465 6D732049 6E633111 300F0603 55040B13 08536563
              75726974 79311930 17060355 04031310 74657374 63612E63 6973636F 2E636F6D
              301E170D 30333131 31313231 35353038 5A170D31 34313032 34323135 3530385A
              307F310B 30090603 55040613 02555331 13301106 03550408 130A4361 6C69666F
              726E6961 3111300F 06035504 07130853 616E204A 6F736531 1A301806 0355040A
              13114369 73636F20 53797374 656D7320 496E6331 11300F06 0355040B 13085365
```

```
  63757269 74793119 30170603 55040313 10746573 7463612E 63697363 6F2E636F
  6D30819F 300D0609 2A864886 F70D0101 01050003 818D0030 81890281 8100B57D
  1C000D5E CBAE09D9 C6836E77 744DDC4C 4C8E9A2F A2F591BE 7492368F CAF22C63
  7BD622B4 89C47148 E1D3BB2E CD870DB1 43AB1DFF 43122FF3 87BA50F9 114A35BE
  A76303CA B74FC306 7845CBBA 5B3227EB 101EA2E1 29109CE1 F9214B95 EA83C45C
  A77D6EEC FB8BE256 3305F512 4E653787 C2A0F74C 30D27037 171A7589 5E030203
  010001A3 81DE3081 DB301D06 03551D0E 04160414 32F4122B 3C7C38D7 FDFC2440
  D04E6448 233F0C9C 3081AB06 03551D23 0481A330 81A08014 32F4122B 3C7C38D7
  FDFC2440 D04E6448 233F0C9C A18184A4 8181307F 310B3009 06035504 06130255
  53311330 11060355 0408130A 43616C69 666F726E 69613111 300F0603 55040713
  0853616E 204A6F73 65311A30 18060355 040A1311 43697363 6F205379 7374656D
  7320496E 63311130 0F060355 040B1308 53656375 72697479 31193017 06035504
  03131074 65737463 612E6369 73636F2E 636F6D82 0100300C 0603551D 13040530
  030101FF 300D0609 2A864886 F70D0101 04050003 8181002E FD07F050 E903D217
  C7F4A2D4 2F15C153 DD9FE072 68925B1E A62EEA31 13FDCFD9 ED25F406 61EE7E82
  FB0C9936 E91F8488 2EF12458 FE34F6F0 EBC1C307 E6ED0DDD 98CEED20 9C4371C9
  1F7749CF 2DC8A3A4 A1A8692D 1185CA1D A2D17723 A6E27AE4 53BCB8EB 15309E52
  DCC3BB5F 522EDB2B 8C60FD15 9054B86D 53A41E44 A5DF9E
  quit
certificate 01
  30820265 308201CE 02010130 0D06092A 864886F7 0D010104 0500307F 310B3009
  06035504 06130255 53311330 11060355 0408130A 43616C69 666F726E 69613111
  300F0603 55040713 0853616E 204A6F73 65311A30 18060355 040A1311 43697363
  6F205379 7374656D 7320496E 63311130 0F060355 040B1308 53656375 72697479
  31193017 06035504 03131074 65737463 612E6369 73636F2E 636F6D30 1E170D30
  33313131 31323135 3632335A 170D3133 31313038 32313536 32335A30 77310B30
  09060355 04061302 55553113 30110603 55040813 0A43616C 69666F72 6E696131
  11300F06 03550407 13085361 6E204A6F 7365311A 30180603 55040A13 11436973
  636F2053 79737465 6D732049 6E633111 300F0603 55040B13 08536563 75726974
  79311130 0F060355 04031308 74657374 63657274 30819F30 0D06092A 864886F7
  0D010101 05000381 8D003081 89028181 00C57FA1 5C598047 D862D87D 6D9E70F1
  ACF0BFDA 3FE23685 F7B11340 0BD8092D E982DBB1 7C9BCE35 588F8A1F 12A66DB3
  7066E0D1 E7B78F8B 4D519C18 E13A7C33 5DDECE9E C26CB060 1A9097CB 18D7DB2E
  FFA0B74D 3934A4AF B9956D52 4AEFE06D 6A0084A4 E1F82349 E15976DA C55320D6
  103643DC 715E8E3D F9C01362 F224DA88 45020301 0001300D 06092A86 4886F70D
  01010405 00038181 00610373 C6BB39C4 BD34BC3E 6FEE179F 81ED0AB2 CB1D8EFD
  0DECF3EC CB764717 DFDE555F 2E968324 DE667118 7031C9E0 C26A8FA4 BE3B0BF8
  C5DF437B 61C1ACAD D4FAC602 2848FCA8 628B65BD 6A64EC46 D2C1A47F 7BD8A2FB
  1594917C 4B7F0E2A AF72B7FE EF114CED 2BCDFDB1 A03C22EF 29709E41 D3A6D238
  C6EF54A1 F2A321A5 D6
  quit
!
ip classless
ip route 0.0.0.0 0.0.0.0 172.21.55.138
ip http server
no ip http secure-server
!
!
snmp-server community public RW
snmp-server queue-length 256
snmp-server contact The Superman and Batgirl
snmp-server chassis-id
no snmp-server enable traps tty
snmp-server enable traps ssl-proxy oper-status
snmp-server enable traps ssl-proxy cert-expiring
snmp-server host 171.69.100.148 version 2c ssl-proxy
!
line con 0
line 1 3
 no exec
 transport input all
 flowcontrol software
line vty 0 4
 password ww
```

```
 login
!
end
ssl-proxy#
```

Summary

As part of the portfolio for Cisco SSL solutions, this chapter looked at the SSLM design with the CSM in detail and the overall functionality of the SSLM on the CSS. SSL is a requirement for e-commerce, and SSL offloading is a must in order to make sure the servers have the capability to provide the resources and the CPU cycles needed to operate optimally. In conjunction with the CSM or the CSS, SSL offloading provides a variety of solutions, such as Bridge mode or Routed mode and other functionality, making integration in the existing environment easy.

Chapter 11, "Back-End SSL Offloading," will look at back-end encryption for SSL.

Back-End SSL Offloading

As described in detail in Chapter 10, "SSL Offloading," secure encrypted connections are established between the client and the SSL offload. The data still passes unencrypted from the SSL offload to the server. Even though the unencrypted traffic from the SSL offload is usually forwarded on to the internal network, many network and security administrators consider parts of the internal network not to be as secure and would like all client traffic to be encrypted end to end. The back-end SSL offloading solution provides the SSL termination functionality from the client to the server. In addition, after decrypting the session, the SSL offload device re-encrypts it and sends it back to the server.

This chapter introduces the Cisco back-end SSL solution implemented on the SSL Module (SSLM) for the Cisco Catalyst 6500 Switch and the SSLM for the Content Services Switch (CSS). A case study explains the details of the back-end SSL solution on the SSLM for the Catalyst 6500 switch.

Back-End SSL on Modules

As part of the back-end SSL offloading portfolio, Cisco offers multiple solutions. The appliance-based solution is the SSLM as part of the CSS and the SSLM for the Catalyst 6500. Some of the key benefits of back-end SSL connections are as follows:

- End-to-end encryption from the client to the server.

- With the SSL offload terminating the front-end connection, the load balancer can still be used to inspect the clear text traffic that allows for load-balancing decisions based on persistency or other HTTP-related headers. This functionality treats all SSL traffic with the same policies as clear text HTTP traffic.

- As explained in Chapter 10, the SSL session reuse feature is designed to reduce the burden of establishing a new SSL session by reusing a previously established SSL session ID. The SSL session ID is a 32-byte sequence used to uniquely identify an SSL session. Once the SSL session is established between the offload and the server, the SSL offload and servers maintain an index of the SSL session ID and the keying material used for that session. During the initial SSL negotiation, the server presents the client with an SSL session ID to use. If the same TCP session is used after the SSL handshake, the key does not have to be renegotiated and subsequent communication will use the same key. However, if a new TCP connection is established, the client has the option of reusing the previously negotiated SSL session ID, telling the server to reuse the previously negotiated key for communication. This helps in foregoing asymmetric encryption, which is usually the most CPU-intensive process of an SSL handshake.

• To optimize the back-end connection, the SSL session reuse takes advantage of the HTTP Connection Keepalive feature provided by HTTP/1.0 and HTTP/1.1. This helps avoid multiple TCP handshakes from the SSL offload to the server. The SSL offload maps multiple client connections into a few back-end TCP/SSL connections. The same TCP connection from the SSL offload is used to send and receive multiple requests/responses, as opposed to opening a new one for every single client request.

Discussion on these solutions follows.

Back-End SSL on the SSLM for the Catalyst 6500

The SSLM is a Layer 4–through–Layer 7 service module that can be installed into the Catalyst 6500 series switch. The module terminates SSL transactions and accelerates the encryption and decryption of data used in SSL sessions.

For back-end SSL encryption support, the module operates either in a stand-alone configuration or with the Content Switching Module (CSM). In a stand-alone configuration, secure traffic is directed to the module and the module re-encrypts and forwards it to the server. With the CSM, only encrypted client traffic is forwarded to the module, while clear text traffic is forwarded to the real servers.

Figure 11-1 illustrates how back-end encryption flows work with the CSM.

Figure 11-1 *SSLM Back-End Encryption with the CSM*

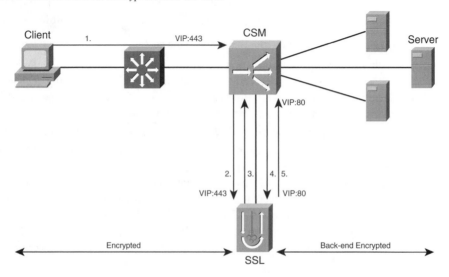

Following is a description of each of the steps that take place during back-end SSL processing:

1 The client initiates SSL traffic to a virtual address defined on the CSM on port 443. The following sample configuration on the CSM is needed for traffic to be accepted:

```
serverfarm SSL_MOD
  no nat server
  no nat client
  real 172.21.55.148
   inservice
  probe ICMP
!
vserver SSL_FRONT
  virtual 172.21.55.149 tcp https
  serverfarm SSL_MOD
  persistent rebalance
  inservice
!
```

2 In the preceding example, the client makes a connection to the virtual IP (VIP) address 172.21.55.149 on port 443 and forwards the traffic to the SSLM on 172.21.55.148. Server network address translation (NAT), which is enabled by default on the CSM, is disabled. This is required if the vserver IP address on the CSM and the SSLM is shared. The CSM load balances to the SSLMs, rewriting the destination MAC address to that of the SSLM.

3 The SSLM decrypts the incoming connection and maintains the original source and destination of the IP packet. After the SSLM decrypts the packet, it forwards it to the CSM as clear text on port 80 to vserver 172.21.55.151, such that the load-balancing decisions and policies can also be applied to the SSL traffic. The following configuration on the SSLM illustrates the decryption and forwarding of the clear text traffic to the CSM:

```
ssl-proxy service AUTH
  virtual ipaddr 172.21.55.149 protocol tcp port 443 secondary
  server ipaddr 172.21.55.151 protocol tcp port 80
  certificate rsa general-purpose trustpoint verisign
  inservice
!
```

As noted in the preceding proxy configuration, the VIP on the CSM and on the SSLM is the same. Once the SSLM accepts the connections from the CSM, the SSL connection is decrypted with the algorithms defined in the trust point verisign. Once decrypted, the SSLM forwards the traffic to 172.21.55.151 on port 80, which is a vserver defined on the CSM.

```
ssl-proxy vlan 32
  ipaddr 172.21.55.148 255.255.255.224
```

```
gateway 172.21.55.150
route 40.40.40.0 255.255.255.0 gateway 172.21.55.150
!
```

As noted, VLAN 32 is defined on the SSLM, and the IP address defined for the SSLM is the same as the real IP address defined for the server farm on the CSM. There is a route configured to reach the server which is pointing to the CSM.

4 Once the CSM has done the inspection in clear text, it forwards the traffic back to a VIP (the virtual SSL proxy 172.21.55.152) on the SSLM on port 80. This time around, since the traffic is forwarded to the SSLM VIP address, the CSM does destination NAT on the IP packet. The following sample configuration illustrates this:

```
serverfarm BACK_SSL
  nat server
  no nat client
  real 172.21.55.152
    inservice
!
vserver BACK
  virtual 172.21.55.151 tcp www
  serverfarm BACK_SSL
  persistent rebalance
  inservice
!
```

As this configuration shows, the CSM receives the decrypted packet from the SSLM on port 80 on VIP 172.21.55.151 and, if needed, will perform any HTTP policy decisions. The CSM then forwards the packet back to the SSLM on VIP 172.21.55.152. This time, the CSM performs a server NAT when forwarding the packet back to the SSLM.

5 The SSLM receives the packet in clear text, and re-encrypts the traffic based on the certificates and keys established between the SSL offload and the server. The SSL offload then forwards the encrypted packet to the server. The following sample configuration illustrates this:

```
ssl-proxy service BACK client
  virtual ipaddr 172.21.55.152 protocol tcp port 80
  server ipaddr 40.40.40.40 protocol tcp port 443
  trusted-ca test
  authenticate verify all
  inservice
```

As the configuration shows, the SSLM accepts the traffic from the CSM on port 80, re-encrypts it to be forwarded back to the CSM, and then sends it to server 40.40.40.40 on port 443.

```
serverfarm FWD
  no nat server
```

```
        no nat client
        predictor forward
    !
    vserver SSL_FWD
        virtual 40.40.40.0 255.255.255.0 any
        serverfarm FWD
        persistent rebalance
        inservice
    !
```

As the preceding configuration demonstrates, once the SSLM forwards the encrypted packet to server 40.40.40.40 on port 443, the CSM accepts the traffic and forwards it to the server, using the predictor forward algorithm.

With the back-end SSLM design, the SSLM is acting as a client initiating an SSL connection to the server, so you need to import the certificate authority's root certificate onto the SSLM. (This is similar to having the certificate authority's root certificates on a client browser in order for the client to be able to verify the digital signature on the server certificate being presented to it by the server for the back-end SSL communication.) The configuration shown in Example 11-1 illustrates how the server's certificate authority (CA) root certificate can be imported onto the SSLM.

Example 11-1 *CA Root Certificate Import*

```
crypto ca trustpoint test3
 enrollment terminal
 crl optional
!
ssl-proxy-3(config)#crypto ca authenticate test3
Enter the base 64 encoded CA certificate.
End with a blank line or the word "quit" on a line by itself
-----BEGIN CERTIFICATE-----
MIICTTCCAfcCEFKp9CTaZ0ydr09TeFKr724wDQYJKoZIhvcNAQEBBQAwgakxFjAU
BgNVBAoTDVZlcmlTaWduLCBJbmMxRzBFBgNVBAsTPnd3dy52ZXJpc2lnbi5jb20v
cmVwb3NpdG9yeS9UZXN0Q1BTIEluY29ycC4gQnkgUmVmLiBMaWFiLiBMVEQuMUYw
RAYDVQQLEz1Gb3IgVmVyaVNpZ24gYXV0aG9yaXplZCB0ZXN0aW5nIG9ubHkuIE5v
IGFzc3VyYW5jZXMgKEMpVlMxOTk3MB4XDTk4MDYwNzAwMDAwMFoXDTA2MDYwNjIz
NTk1OVowgakxFjAUBgNVBAoTDVZlcmlTaWduLCBJbmMxRzBFBgNVBAsTPnd3dy52
ZXJpc2lnbi5jb20vcmVwb3NpdG9yeS9UZXN0Q1BTIEluY29ycC4gQnkgUmVmLiBM
aWFiLiBMVEQuMUYwRAYDVQQLEz1Gb3IgVmVyaVNpZ24gYXV0aG9yaXplZCB0ZXN0
aW5nIG9ubHkuIE5vIGFzc3VyYW5jZXMgKEMpVlMxOTk3MFwwDQYJKoZIhvcNAQEB
BQADSwAwSAJBAMak6xImJx44jMKcbkACy5/CyMA2fqXK4PlzTtCxRq5tFkDzne7s
cI8oFK/J+gFZNE3bjidDxf07O3JOYG9RGx8CAwEAATANBgkqhkiG9w0BAQQFAANB
AKWnR/KPNxCglpTP5nzbo+QCIkmsCPjTCMnvm7KcwDJguaEwkoi1gBSY9biJp9oK
+cv1Yn3KuVM+YptcWXLfxxI=
-----END CERTIFICATE-----
quit
Certificate has the following attributes:
Fingerprint: 40065311 FDB33E88 0A6F7DD1 4E229187
% Do you accept this certificate? [yes/no]: yes
Trustpoint CA certificate accepted.
% Certificate successfully imported
```

Multiple CA root certificates can be imported on the SSLM and can be referred to via a trust point pool. The trust points can refer to the trust point pool, which point to the imported CA root certificates, as shown in Example 11-2.

Example 11-2 *CA Trust Point Pool Example*

```
ssl-proxy pool ca test
 ca trustpoint test
 ca trustpoint test3
 !
```

The configuration in Example 11-3 shows how the SSL proxy refers to the SSL proxy pool by using the **trusted-ca** command.

Example 11-3 *SSL Proxy's Reference to Trust Point Pool for CA Root Certificates*

```
ssl-proxy service BACK client
 virtual ipaddr 172.21.55.152 protocol tcp port 80
 server ipaddr 40.40.40.40 protocol tcp port 443
 trusted-ca test
 authenticate verify all
 inservice
```

Use the commands in Example 11-4 to import the server certificate on the SSLM. (The server certificates on the SSLM need to be imported along with the CA root certificate.)

Example 11-4 *server Certificate Import*

```
ssl-module-5(config)#crypto ca import verisign certificate
% The fully-qualified domain name in the certificate will be: www.backend.com
Enter the base 64 encoded certificate.
End with a blank line or the word "quit" on a line by itself
-----BEGIN CERTIFICATE-----
MIIDLjCCAtigAwIBAgIQfxLUGE62jMAEGxEVKdpWDDANBgkqhkiG9w0BAQUFADCB
qTEWMBQGA1UEChMNVmVyaVNpZ24sIEluYzFHMEUGA1UECxM+d3d3LnZlcmlzaWdu
LmNvbS9yZXBvc2l0b3J5L1Rlc3RRUFMgSW5jb3JwLiBCeSBBSZWYuIExpYWIuIExU
RC4xRjBEBgNVBAsTPUZvciBWZXJpU2lnbiBhdXRob3JpemVkIHRlc3Rpbmcgb25s
eS4gTm8gYXNzdXJhbmNlcyAoylWUzE5OTcwHhcNMDQwNjA3MDAwMDAwWhcNMDQw
NjIxMjM1OTU5WjBuMQswCQYDVQQGEwJVUzETMBEGA1UECBMKQ2FsaWZvcm5pYTER
MA8GA1UEBxQIU2FuIEpvc2UxDjAMBgNVBAoUBUNpc2NvMQwwCgYDVQQLFANMYWIx
GTAXBgNVBAMUEHd3dy5zc2wtbGFiMy5jb20wgZ8wDQYJKoZIhvcNAQEBBQADgY0A
MIGJAoGBAOKtoTuRaHiAu7zBaYtZQ7ckypvsXmAw74kfwl9gPfrFOx8fLBeG9y8N
eibGKAJ6Q5StYBzXOpqbU1doHP1HoPwtUlTIvRwS4JEwJTGKaW6JJfxc4Cj0PRpV
sflgqaK2nEGcej0BA+tkYPNL3pkNFKm+FcRxENaI9/2H2dNNFKh7AgMBAAGjgdEw
gc4wCQYDVR0TBAIwADALBgNVHQ8EBAMCBaAwQgYDVR0fBDswOTA3oDWgM4YxaHR0
cDovL2NybC52ZXJpc2lnbi5jb20vU2VjdXJlU2VydmVyVGVzdGluZ0NBLmNybDBR
BgNVHSAESjBIMEYGCmCGSAGG+EUBBxUwODA2BggrBgEFBQcCARYqaHR0cDovL3d3
dy52ZXJpc2lnbi5jb20vcmVwb3NpdG9yeS9UZXN0UFMNTBTMB0GA1UdJQQWMBQGCCsG
AQUFBwMBBggrBgEFBQcDAjANBgkqhkiG9w0BAQUFAANBAGs5b4PSrVbpOEJTvOOv
kgvMp5PzsSaJmJh8TWIcnrmacEGk7e3I6g8gA6JIPnM0PtnQoiIvb3qjVsNRp5aU
91c=
-----END CERTIFICATE-----
quit
% Router Certificate successfully imported
```

The **show** command in Example 11-5 demonstrates the SSL certificates and the appropriate chained root certificates for front-end SSL termination.

Example 11-5 *show Command for Imported Certificates*

```
SSL-Cat4-Slot7#show crypto ca certificates
CA Certificate
  Status: Available
  Certificate Serial Number: 20A897AEDB8202DEC136A04E26BD8773
  Certificate Usage: General Purpose
  Issuer:
    CN = VeriSign Trial Secure Server Test Root CA
    OU = For Test Purposes Only.  No assurances.
    O = "VeriSign
    Inc."
    C = US
  Subject:
    CN = VeriSign Trial Secure Server Test Root CA
    OU = For Test Purposes Only.  No assurances.
    O = "VeriSign
    Inc."
    C = US
  Validity Date:
    start date: 00:00:00 UTC Feb 9 2005
    end   date: 23:59:59 UTC Feb 8 2025
  Associated Trustpoints: test3 test verisign
Certificate
  Status: Available
  Certificate Serial Number: B3753950BA12FCF55BFC95FC5615A9
  Certificate Usage: General Purpose
  Issuer:
    CN = VeriSign Trial Secure Server Test Root CA
    OU = For Test Purposes Only.  No assurances.
    O = "VeriSign
    Inc."
    C = US
  Subject:
    Name: www.frontendssl.com
    CN = www.frontendssl.com
    OU = Terms of use at www.verisign.com/cps/testca (c)05
    OU = Lab
    O = Cisco
    L = San Jose
    ST = California
    C = US
  CRL Distribution Point:
    http://SVRSecure-crl.verisign.com/SVRTrialRoot2005.crl
  Validity Date:
    start date: 00:00:00 UTC Jun 20 2005
    end   date: 23:59:59 UTC Jul 4 2005
    renew date: 00:00:00 UTC Jan 1 1970
  Associated Trustpoints: verisign
```

Back-End SSL on the SSLM on the CSS

Back-end SSL allows a CSS to initiate a connection with an SSL server. When used with SSL termination, back-end SSL provides a secure end-to-end connection between a client and an SSL server.

Since the SSLM is integrated with the CSS as a module, the configuration for the SSLM is done via WebNS software. To manage the connections for back-end and front-end SSL, an SSL proxy list determines the flow of SSL information among the SSLM, the client, and the server. An SSL proxy list comprises one or more back-end SSL servers. The back-end SSL server entry initiates the connection to an SSL server. You can define a maximum of 256 virtual or back-end SSL servers for a single SSL proxy list.

After you create and configure the entries in a proxy list, you must activate the list and then add the SSL proxy list to a service to initiate the transfer of SSL configuration data to the SSLM. When you activate the service, the CSS transfers the data to the module. Then you need to add each SSL service to an SSL content rule. Figure 11-2 illustrates how back-end encryption flows work with the CSS SSLM.

Figure 11-2 *CSS SSLM Back-End Encryption*

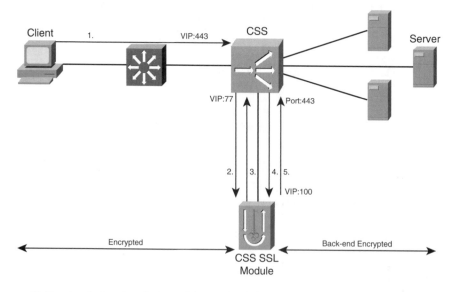

Following is the description of the each of the steps that take place during back-end CSS SSLM processing.

1 The client initiates SSL traffic to a virtual address defined on the CSS on port 443.

```
service SSL-p
  type ssl-accel
  keepalive type none
  slot 4
```

```
    add ssl-proxy-list SSL-TEST
    active
content SSL-FRONT
    protocol tcp
    vip address 172.21.55.147
    port 443
    add service SSL-p
    active
```

The service SSL-p references the SSL proxy list SSL-TEST, which allows the connections to be forwarded to the SSLM. Since multiple SSLMs can be installed on the CSS, the slot number for the appropriate SSLM needs to be specified.

2 Once the traffic is forwarded to the SSLM via the SSL proxy list, the SSLM decrypts the packets from the client, as the following configuration shows:

```
ssl-proxy-list SSL-TEST
    ssl-server 100
    ssl-server 100 rsakey mykey
    ssl-server 100 cipher rsa-with-rc4-128-md5 77.77.77.77 77
    ssl-server 100 rsacert testassoc
    ssl-server 100 vip address 172.21.55.147
    backend-server 10
    backend-server 10 ip address 172.21.55.145
    backend-server 10 port 100
    backend-server 10 server-ip 172.21.55.145
    backend-server 10 server port 443
    backend-server 10 cipher rsa-with-rc4-128-md5
    active
```

The thing to note here is that the VIP address is shared between the SSL proxy list and the content rule. Port 443 needs to be the same also. The SSL proxy list accepts connections, decrypts them with the cipher specified (in this case, it is a 128-bit RC4 with MD5 encryption), and forwards the traffic to another VIP address of 77.77.77.77 on port 77. This is an internal VIP address for communication between the SSLM and the CSS.

The Rivest-Shamir-Adleman (RSA) algorithm key pairs and the certificates are generated and imported in the SSL proxy list configuration. In order to generate an RSA key pair, the following command should be entered:

```
ssl genrsa  mykeyfile keylength "password"
```

The generated keys will be saved in a file called mykeyfile. Once the RSA key pair has been generated, an association for it needs to be created for verification:

```
ssl associate rsakey mykey mykeyfile
```

This association is specified in the SSL proxy list and associates the imported certificate with the key pair. The certificate is imported on the CSS SSLM using the following command:

```
copy ssl ftp DEFAULT_FTP import frontend3.crt PEM "cisco"
```

Other formats supported for the certificate are Public Key Cryptography Standard 12 (PKCS12) and Distinguished Encoding Rules (DER).

Once the certificate is imported, an association is created with the name also and verified, as follows:

```
CSS500-4(config)# ssl associate cert testassoc frontend3.crt
CSS500-4(config)# ssl verify testassoc mycert
Certificate and key match
```

(Note that frontend3.crt is the name of the certificate acquired from the CA.)

3   After the traffic is processed by the internal VIP 77.77.77.77 on port 77 between the CSS and SSLM, the traffic is forwarded back to the SSL proxy list to be re-encrypted and forwarded to the server, as shown:

```
ssl-proxy-list SSL-TEST
  ssl-server 100
  ssl-server 100 rsakey mykey
  ssl-server 100 cipher rsa-with-rc4-128-md5 77.77.77.77 77
  ssl-server 100 rsacert testassoc
  ssl-server 100 vip address 172.21.55.147
  backend-server 10
  backend-server 10 ip address 172.21.55.145
  backend-server 10 port 100
  backend-server 10 server-ip 172.21.55.145
  backend-server 10 server port 443
  backend-server 10 cipher rsa-with-rc4-128-md5
  active
service backend-ssl
  ip address 172.21.55.145
  port 100
  type ssl-accel-backend
  add ssl-proxy-list SSL-TEST
  keepalive type ssl
  keepalive port 443
  active
content SSL-OFFLOAD
    protocol tcp
    vip address 77.77.77.77
    port 77
    add service backend-ssl
    active
```

The traffic would be forwarded to the service defined on the SSL proxy list at 172.21.55.145 on port 100. It would be re-encrypted using the cipher and sent to real server 172.21.55.145 on port 443. The internal service address could have been different and listening on a different port. However, to preserve IP addresses the server's own IP address is used in this example.

Example 11-6 shows the full configuration of the preceding defined example with the CSS and back-end SSL.

Example 11-6 *CSS SSLM Configuration*

```
CSS500-4(config)# sh run
!Generated on 06/19/2005 18:39:08
!Active version: sg0720305
configure
!*************************** GLOBAL ***************************
  ip redundancy
  bridge spanning-tree disabled
  app session 172.16.1.2
  app
  ssl associate rsakey mycert mykeyfile
  ssl associate cert testassoc frontend3.crt
  ip route 0.0.0.0 0.0.0.0 172.21.55.131 1
 ftp-record DEFAULT_FTP 171.68.173.10 nsa des-password sdqdqhkaxafgdfle /tftpboot
!************************* INTERFACE *************************
interface  2/1
  bridge vlan 50
interface  2/3
  bridge vlan 117
interface  2/4
  bridge vlan 117
interface  2/9
  bridge vlan 501
interface  2/15
  bridge vlan 99
!************************* CIRCUIT *************************
circuit VLAN50
  ip address 172.21.55.146 255.255.255.224
circuit VLAN117
  redundancy
  ip address 148.173.180.101 255.255.255.0
circuit VLAN99
  ip address 172.16.1.1 255.255.255.0
    redundancy-protocol
!********************** SSL PROXY LIST **********************
ssl-proxy-list SSL-TEST
  ssl-server 100
  ssl-server 100 rsakey mycert
  ssl-server 100 cipher rsa-with-rc4-128-md5 77.77.77.77 77
  ssl-server 100 rsacert testassoc
  ssl-server 100 vip address 172.21.55.147
  backend-server 10
  backend-server 10 ip address 172.21.55.145
  backend-server 10 port 100
  backend-server 10 server-ip 172.21.55.145
  backend-server 10 cipher rsa-with-rc4-128-md5
  active
!************************* SERVICE *************************
```

continues

Example 11-6 *CSS SSLM Configuration (Continued)*

```
service TEST
  ip address 148.173.180.72
  active
service SERVER-CLEAR
  ip address 172.21.55.145
  port 80
  keepalive type tcp
  active
service SSL-p
  type ssl-accel
  keepalive type none
  slot 4
  add ssl-proxy-list SSL-TEST
  active
service backend-ssl
  ip address 172.21.55.145
  port 100
  type ssl-accel-backend
  add ssl-proxy-list SSL-TEST
  keepalive type ssl
  keepalive port 443
  active
!*************************** OWNER ***************************
owner TEST
  content SSL-FRONT
    protocol tcp
    vip address 172.21.55.147
    port 443
    add service SSL-p
    active
  content SSL-OFFLOAD
    protocol tcp
    vip address 77.77.77.77
    port 77
    add service backend-ssl
    active
CSS500-4(config)#
```

Case Study: Back-End SSL Solution

Now that you understand the various steps required in creating an SSL back-end connection via the SSLM, this section examines a design for terminating client-initiated connections on the SSLM, after which the SSLM re-encrypts the connection and forwards it to the server via the CSM.

Requirements

The requirements are as follows.

- Application requirements

— Persistence should be maintained from the client termination to the SSLM and from the SSLM to the server. This persistence should be based on cookie persistence.

— Only a single VIP address should be used for the domain.

— Port 80 should be used for HTTP traffic and port 443 should be used for the SSL traffic.

- Management and security requirements

— The certificates should be imported on the SSLM using the cut-and-paste method.

— The strongest possible ciphers should be used for the front-end client SSL termination.

- Infrastructure requirements

— The default gateway for the servers should be pointing to the CSM.

— A single VLAN should be configured for the SSL implementation.

Design Options

The topology in Figure 11-3 illustrates the logical connections between the CSM, the SSLM, and the servers.

Figure 11-3 *Design Topology*

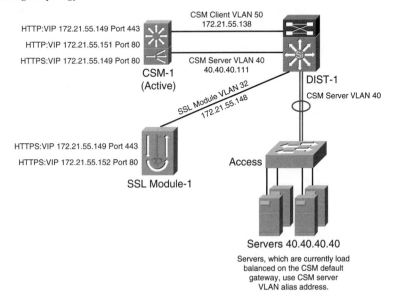

HTTP:VIP 172.21.55.149 Port 443
HTTP:VIP 172.21.55.151 Port 80
HTTPS:VIP 172.21.55.149 Port 80
CSM-1
(Active)

CSM Client VLAN 50
172.21.55.138

CSM Server VLAN 40
40.40.40.111

SSL Module VLAN 32
172.21.55.148

HTTPS:VIP 172.21.55.149 Port 443
HTTPS:VIP 172.21.55.152 Port 80
SSL Module-1

DIST-1
CSM Server VLAN 40

Access

Servers 40.40.40.40
Servers, which are currently load balanced on the CSM default gateway, use CSM server VLAN alias address.

As the figure shows, an SSLM is directly attached to the Catalyst 6500. The steps listed below give an overview of the connection the client will make when an SSL connection is initiated to the SSLM. The domain we will be using in this design is www.frontend.com. Following are the IP and VLAN configurations used in this design:

- The VIP address the domain resolves to is 172.21.55.149 for HTTPS traffic.

- The CSM client VLAN is 50, and the server VLAN is 40. The server's IP addresses are in the subnet 40.40.40.0 /24.

- The VLAN for the SSLM is 32.

The client initiates an SSL connection to the CSM that then gets forwarded to the SSLM. The SSLM decrypts that traffic and sends the clear text traffic, such as regular HTTP GETs, back to the CSM. The CSM distributes the requests to the servers listening on port 80. Because this traffic is clear text, the CSM keeps persistence between HTTPS and HTTP, after which the CSM forwards the request to the real server.

SSLM Certificate Management

Before the design discussion begins, the SSL root and server certificates need to be imported on the SSLM. The discussion below walks you through the process.

First, a private and public key pair needs to be generated for the exchange of the SSL session key used for encryption. Because these keys and certificates will be used on other SSLMs, they must be exportable so they can be used on other SSLMs for the same domain. (We are using http://www.frontend.com in this case study.) To generate the key pair, use the following instructions:

```
crypto key generate rsa general-keys label mykey exportable
Choose the size of the key modulus in the range of 360 to 2048 for your
  General Purpose Keys. Choosing a key modulus greater than 512 may take a few
  minutes.
How many bits in the modulus [512]: 1024
% Generating 1024 bit RSA keys ...[OK]
```

Now that the RSA keys are generated, you can view the RSA public key (only the public key can be viewed) with the following command:

```
ssl-module-5#show crypto key mypubkey rsa
% Key pair was generated at: 14:12:22 UTC Jun 6 2004
Key name: mykey
 Usage: General Purpose Key
 Key is exportable.
 Key Data:
  30819F30 0D06092A 864886F7 0D010101 05000381 8D003081 89028181 00E2ADA1
  3B916878 80BBBCC1 698B5943 B724CA9B EC5E6030 EF891FC2 5F603DFA C53B1F1F
  2C1786F7 2F0D7A26 C628027A 4394AD60 1CD73A9A 9B535768 1CFD47A0 FC2D5254
  C8BD1C12 E0913025 318A696E 8925FC5C E028F43D 1A55B1F9 60A9A2B6 9C419C7A
  3D0103EB 6460F34B DE990D14 A9BE15C4 7110D688 F7FD87D9 D34D14A8 7B020301 0001
```

The key name is important, as this name will be used in the later steps.

The following command on the SSLM creates an entity called the *trust point* with the label verisign. The trust point is used to generate and handle all SSL certificate requests for a particular SSL-hosted domain. In order for the SSLM to offer a client an SSL certificate, the trust point label verisign, which is used in this example, must be associated with the SSL proxy service, explained in later sections.

```
certificate rsa general-purpose trustpoint verisign
```

Now that a trust point has been established, it's time to request a certificate from a CA server. In our testing, we have used the test certificates issued by VeriSign. Anyone can apply for these certificates at http://www.verisign.com. When applying for a certificate, VeriSign will ask the user to input the Certificate Signing Request (CSR).

In the trust point submode configuration, information will be requested from the user that will be included in the CSR request. The enrollment method could be via HTTP or terminal (we can cut and paste it to the SSL module console or terminal session); the terminal method is what we have used in this example. The subject name portion of the CSR is important, and you must make sure that the CN value or string matches the name for the site to which the client is going to connect. The state name has to be entered in its entirety because an abbreviated state name will generate an error. A CRL optional is configured on the SSLM, as the SSLM will try to contact the CA every time to check to see the list for revoked certificates, in this case study we have made it optional. The certificate we are requesting has been associated with the RSA key pair we generated.

```
SSL-Cat4-Slot7 (ca-trustpoint)#enrollment terminal
SSL-Cat4-Slot7 (ca-trustpoint)#rsakeypair mykey
SSL-Cat4-Slot7 (ca-trustpoint subject-name C=US; ST=California; L=San Jose;
  O=Cisco; OU=Lab; CN=www.frontend.com
SSL-Cat4-Slot7 (ca-trustpoint)#crl optional
SSL-Cat4-Slot7 (ca-trustpoint)#exit
```

After the trust point has been created, you need to enroll the trust point and the CSR request. The CSR request must be sent to VeriSign. In the checkbox for the platform, you can select Apache as the platform when requesting a certificate for the SSLM from VeriSign.

```
ssl-module-5(config)#crypto ca enroll verisign
% Start certificate enrollment ..
% The subject name in the certificate will be: C=US; ST=California; L=San Jose;
  O=Cisco; OU=Lab; CN=www.frontend.com
% The fully-qualified domain name in the certificate will be: SSL-Cat4-
  Slot7.cisco.com
% The subject name in the certificate will be: SSL-Cat4-Slot7.cisco.com
% Include the router serial number in the subject name? [yes/no]: no
% Include an IP address in the subject name? [no]: no
Display Certificate Request to terminal? [yes/no]: yes
Certificate Request follows:
MIIB9zCCAWACAQAwgZUxGTAXBgNVBAMTEHd3dy5zc2wtbGFiMy5jb20xDDAKBgNV
BAsTA0xhYjEOMAwGA1UEChMFQ2lzY28xETAPBgNVBAcTCFNhbiBKb3NlMRMwEQYD
VQQIEwpDYWxpZm9ybmlhMQswCQYDVQQGEwJVUzElMCMGCSqGSIb3DQEJAhYWc3Ns
LW1vZHVsZS01LmNpc2NvLmNvbTCBnzANBgkqhkiG9w0BAQEFAAOBjQAwgYkCgYEA
4q2hO5FoeIC7vMFpi1lDtyTKm+xeYDDviR/CX2A9+sU7Hx8sF4b3Lw16JsYoAnpD
1K1gHNc6mptTV2gc/Ueg/C1SVMi9HBLgkTAlMYppbokl/FzgKPQ9GlWx+WCporac
QZx6PQED62Rg80vemQQUqb4VxHEQ1oj3/YfZ000UqHsCAwEAAaAhMB8GCSqGSIb3
DQEJDjESMBAwDgYDVR0PAQH/BAQDAgWgMA0GCSqGSIb3DQEBBAUAA4GBALp3jeMH
klDmjNw+Ho+MO+EQTgztxwBIK+WckyyrYU6WVjNv1do6b4+CXv4BfV7a2bXxYp7+
```

```
We1e7T/buDxkmVGR1FhnwNS4ME988uf32gWnKeMhrc4KlFDBgfrCX7N9p+dE8qwv
IwJd1dkA0B7ImJ9WQRK36+I0Fo/Q1Yw05FC/
---End - This line not part of the certificate request---
Redisplay enrollment request? [yes/no]: no
```

As seen in this example, the CSR is displayed and you can use it to request the certificate
from VeriSign. When requesting certificates from VeriSign for multiple SSLMs, a single
certificate is used, so make sure to purchase a license for a certificate that allows for
installation on multiple SSLMs. Once you have the certificate from VeriSign, which usually
sends the certificate details via e-mail, you import it into the SSLM. However, before you
can start using the certificate, you also have to authenticate the CA's root certificate on the
SSLM. VeriSign should be able to provide you with CA's root certificate. (This information
is usually available in the e-mail sent along with the server certificate.) On our test
certificate, the root certificate authentication is as follows:

```
ssl-proxy-3(config)#crypto ca authenticate verisign
Enter the base 64 encoded CA certificate.
End with a blank line or the word "quit" on a line by itself
-----BEGIN CERTIFICATE-----
MIICTTCCAfcCEFKp9CTaZ0ydr09TeFKr724wDQYJKoZIhvcNAQEEBQAwgakxFjAU
BgNVBAoTDVZlcmlTaWduLCBJbmMxRzBFBgNVBAsTPnd3dy52ZXJpc2lnbi5jb20v
cmVwb3NpdG9yeS9UZXN0IEluY29ycC4gQnkgUmVmLiBMaWFiLiBMVEQuMUYw
RAYDVQQLEz1Gb3IgVmVyaVNpZ24gYXV0aG9yaXplZCB0ZXN0aW5nIG9ubHkuIE5v
IGFzc3VyYW5jZXMgKEMpVmMxOTk3MB4XDTk4MDYwNzAwMDAwMFoXDTA2MDYwNjIz
NTk1OVowgakxFjAUBgNVBAoTDVZlcmlTaWduLCBJbmMxRzBFBgNVBAsTPnd3dy52
ZXJpc2lnbi5jb20vcmVwb3NpdG9yeS9UZXN0IEluY29ycC4gQnkgUmVmLiBM
aWFiLiBMVEQuMUYwRAYDVQQLEz1Gb3IgVmVyaVNpZ24gYXV0aG9yaXplZCB0ZXN0
aW5nIG9ubHkuIE5vIGFzc3VyYW5jZXMgKEMpVmMxOTk3MFwwDQYJKoZIhvcNAQEB
BQADSwAwSAJBAMak6xImJx44jMKcbkACy5/CyMA2fqXK4PlzTtCxRq5tFkDzne7s
cI8oFK/J+gFZNE3bjidDxf0703JOYG9RGx8CAwEAATANBgkqhkiG9w0BAQQFAANB
AKWnR/KPNxCglpTP5nzbo+QCIkmsCPjTCMnvm7KcwDJguaEwkoi1gBSY9biJp9oK
+cv1Yn3KuVM+YptcWXLfxxI=
-----END CERTIFICATE-----
quit
Certificate has the following attributes:
Fingerprint: 40065311 FDB33E88 0A6F7DD1 4E229187
% Do you accept this certificate? [yes/no]: yes
Trustpoint CA certificate accepted.
% Certificate successfully imported
```

Now we are ready to import the server certificate on the SSLM, as follows:

```
ssl-module-5(config)#crypto ca import verisign certificate
% The fully-qualified domain name in the certificate will be: SSL-Cat4-
  Slot7.cisco.com
Enter the base 64 encoded certificate.
End with a blank line or the word "quit" on a line by itself
-----BEGIN CERTIFICATE-----
MIIDLjCCAtigAwIBAgIQfxLUGE62jMAEGxEVKdpWDDANBgkqhkiG9w0BAQUFADCB
qTEWMBQGA1UEChMNVmVyaVNpZ24sIEluYzFHMEUGA1UECxM+d3d3LnZlcmlzaWdu
LmNvbS9yZXBvc2l0b3J5L1Rlc3RRDUFMgSW5jb3JwLiBCeSBSZWYuIExpYWIuIExU
RC4xRjBEBgNVBAsTPUZvciBWZXJpU2lnbiBhdXRob3JpemVkIHRlc3Rpbmcgb25s
eS4gTm8gYXNzdXJhbmNlcyAoQylWUzE5OTcwHhcNMDQwNjA3MDAwMDAwWhcNMDQw
NjIxMjM1OTU5WjBuMQswCQYDVQQGEwJVUzETMBEGA1UECBMKQ2FsaWZvcm5pYTER
MA8GA1UEBxQIU2FuIEpvc2UxDjAMBgNVBAoUBUNpc2NvMQwwCgYDVQQLFANMYWIx
GTAXBgNVBAMUEHd3dy5zc2wtbGFiMy5jb20wgZ8wDQYJKoZIhvcNAQEBBQADgY0A
MIGJAoGBAOKtoTuRaHiAu7zBaYtZQ7ckypvsXmAw74kfwl9gPfrFOx8fLBeG9y8N
eibGKAJ6Q5StYBzXOpqbU1doHP1HoPwtUlTIvRwS4JEwJTGKaW6JJfxc4Cj0PRpV
sflgqaK2nEGcejØBA+tkYPNL3pkNFKm+FcRxENaI9/2H2dNNFKh7AgMBAAGjgdEw
gc4wCQYDVR0TBAIwADALBgNVHQ8EBAMCBaAwGgYDVR0fBDswOTA3oDWgM4YxaHR0
```

```
cDovL2NybC52ZXJpc2lnbi5jb20vU2VjdXJlU2VydmVyVGVzdGluZ0NBLmNybDBR
BgNVHSAESjBIMEYGCmCGSAGG+EUBBxUwODA2BggrBgEFBQcCARYqaHR0cDovL3d3
dy52ZXJpc2lnbi5jb20vcmVwb3NpdG9yeS9UZXN0Q0EBTMB0GA1UdJQQWMBQGCCsG
AQUFBwMBBggrBgEFBQcDAjANBgkqhkiG9w0BAQUFAANBAGs5b4PSrVbpOEJTvOOv
kgvMp5PzsSaJmJh8TWIcnrmacEGk7e3I6g8gA6JIPnM0PtnQoiIvb3qjVsNRp5aU
91c=
-----END CERTIFICATE-----
quit
% Router Certificate successfully imported
```

Let's view the certificate that we have downloaded and make sure that it is chained properly. The most important field to verify is the OU field in the subject area to make sure the server certificate and the CA root certificate match. The expiration date of the certificate is also important because the certificate is only valid until that date.

```
SSL-Cat4-Slot7#show crypto  ca certificates
CA Certificate
  Status: Available
  Certificate Serial Number: 20A897AEDB8202DEC136A04E26BD8773
  Certificate Usage: General Purpose
  Issuer:
    CN = VeriSign Trial Secure Server Test Root CA
    OU = For Test Purposes Only.  No assurances.
    O = "VeriSign
    Inc."
    C = US
  Subject:
    CN = VeriSign Trial Secure Server Test Root CA
    OU = For Test Purposes Only.  No assurances.
    O = "VeriSign
    Inc."
    C = US
  Validity Date:
    start date: 00:00:00 UTC Feb 9 2005
    end   date: 23:59:59 UTC Feb 8 2025
  Associated Trustpoints: test3 test verisign
Certificate
  Status: Available
  Certificate Serial Number: B3753950BA12FCF55BFC95FC5615A9
  Certificate Usage: General Purpose
  Issuer:
    CN = VeriSign Trial Secure Server Test Root CA
    OU = For Test Purposes Only.  No assurances.
    O = "VeriSign
    Inc."
    C = US
  Subject:
    Name: www.frontend.com
    CN = www.frontend.com
    OU = Terms of use at www.verisign.com/cps/testca (c)05
    OU = Lab
    O = Cisco
    L = San Jose
    ST = California
    C = US
  CRL Distribution Point:
    http://SVRSecure-crl.verisign.com/SVRTrialRoot2005.crl
  Validity Date:
    start date: 00:00:00 UTC Jun 20 2005
    end   date: 23:59:59 UTC Jul 4 2005
    renew date: 00:00:00 UTC Jan 1 1970
  Associated Trustpoints: verisign
```

The SSLM is acting as an SSL client when it re-encrypts and sends the connection back to the server. In order for the encrypted connection from the SSLM to the server to work properly, the SSL handshake and key exchange need to happen between the server and the SSLM. To allow this exchange to take place, we will import the server root certificate on the SSLM so that when the server presents its certificate to the SSLM for the back-end connection, the SSLM can authenticate it and exchange the keys to start the SSL encryption. The following commands illustrate how to create a trust point for the back-end SSL server root certificate:

```
crypto ca trustpoint test
  enrollment terminal
```

Next, we import the server root certificate, as follows:

```
ssl-proxy-3(config)#crypto ca authenticate test
Enter the base 64 encoded CA certificate.
End with a blank line or the word "quit" on a line by itself
-----BEGIN CERTIFICATE-----
MIICTTCCAfcCEFKp9CTaZ0ydr09TeFKr724wDQYJKoZIhvcNAQEEBQAwgakxFjAU
BgNVBAoTDVZlcmlTaWduLCBJbmMxRzBFBgNVBAsTPnd3dy52ZXJpc2lnbi5jb20v
cmVwb3NpdG9yeS9UZXN0Q01BTIEluY29ycC4gQnkgUmVmLiBMaWFiLiBMVEQuMUYw
RAYDVQQLEz1Gb3IgVmVyaVNpZ24gYXV0aG9yaXplZCB0ZXN0aW5nIG9ubHkuIE5v
IGFzc3VyYW5jZXMgKEMpVlMxOTk3MB4XDTk4MDYwNzAwMDAwMFoXDTA2MDYwNjIz
NTk1OVowgakxFjAUBgNVBAoTDVZlcmlTaWduLCBJbmMxRzBFBgNVBAsTPnd3dy52
ZXJpc2lnbi5jb20vcmVwb3NpdG9yeS9UZXN0Q01BTIEluY29ycC4gQnkgUmVmLiBM
aWFiLiBMVEQuMUYwRAYDVQQLEz1Gb3IgVmVyaVNpZ24gYXV0aG9yaXplZCB0ZXN0
aW5nIG9ubHkuIE5vIGFzc3VyYW5jZXMgKEMpVlMxOTk3MFwwDQYJKoZIhvcNAQEB
BQADSwAwSAJBAMak6xImJx44jMKcbkACy5/CyMA2fqXK4PlzTtCxRq5tFkDzne7s
cI8oFK/J+gFZNE3bjidDxf07O3JOYG9RGx8CAwEAATANBgkqhkiG9w0BAQQFAANB
AKWnR/KPNxCglpTP5nzbo+QCIkmsCPjTCMnvm7KcwDJguaEwkoi1gBSY9biJp9oK
+cv1Yn3KuVM+YptcWXLfxxI=
-----END CERTIFICATE-----
quit
Certificate has the following attributes:
Fingerprint: 40065311 FDB33E88 0A6F7DD1 4E229187
% Do you accept this certificate? [yes/no]: yes
Trustpoint CA certificate accepted.
% Certificate successfully imported
```

Once the server root certificate has been imported, we make it part of the trust point pool where the root certificates can be referenced, as shown here:

```
ssl-proxy pool ca test
  ca trustpoint test
```

Now that we have imported the server certificate for the domain www.frontend.com, we will discuss how the client connections get terminated on the SSLM and how the SSLM forwards the connection to the server via the CSM.

SSLM and CSM Flow Overview

Figure 11-4 identifies the traffic path when deploying the SSLM in the data center. Clear text traffic, such as regular HTTP GETs, goes to the CSM and the CSM distributes the requests to the servers listening on port 80. The CSM is also used to intercept encrypted HTTP (HTTPS) traffic, and it forwards this traffic to the SSLM. The SSLM returns the decrypted traffic to the CSM for load balancing. Once the CSM has applied the persistency policies to the clear text traffic, it forwards it back to the SSLM to be re-encrypted. At that time, the SSLM re-encrypts the packet and sends it back to the CSM to be load balanced to the server as encrypted traffic. We will discuss the details of the flow from client to server in the following order in the next sections:

- Client connection to the CSM
- CSM connection to the SSLM (encrypted traffic)
- SSLM connection to the CSM (decrypted traffic)
- CSM connection to the SSLM (decrypted traffic with persistence)
- SSLM connection to the server via CSM (re-encrypted traffic)

The configuration details for each section will also be discussed.

Figure 11-4 illustrates the sequence of flows that take place when performing load balancing for SSL traffic on the CSM.

Figure 11-4 *HTTPS Back-End Connection Flow*

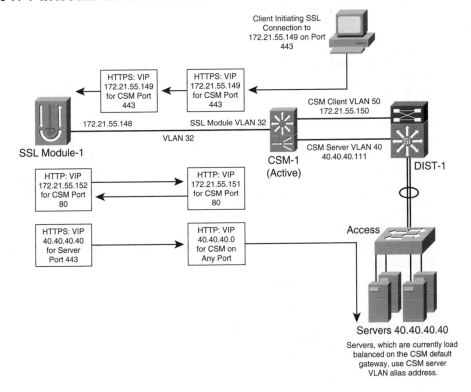

Client Connection to the CSM

As the client initiates a connection to the SSL domain www.frontend.com, the connection is forwarded to the CSM. Following is the CSM client and server VLAN configuration, used in this example. VLAN 50 is the client VLAN on the CSM. All connections from the client side will enter the CSM on VLAN 50:

```
module ContentSwitchingModule 6
!
vlan 50 client
  ip address 172.21.55.150 255.255.255.224
  gateway 172.21.55.131
!
```

VLAN 40 is the server VLAN on the CSM. All connections from the CSM to the server will enter the CSM on VLAN 40:

```
vlan 40 server
  ip address 40.40.40.111 255.255.255.0
!
```

As the client connects to the VIP address on the CSM using an SSL-enabled browser, the traffic is load balanced to the SSLM. In our testing, the VIP address is defined as 172.21.55.149 listening on port 443:

```
vserver SSL_FRONT
  virtual 172.21.55.149 tcp https
  serverfarm SSL_MOD
  persistent rebalance
  inservice
```

The server farm definition has the IP addresses of the SSLMs, and their role is defined in the next section.

CSM Connection to the SSLM

Before we describe the connection from the CSM to the SSLM, the following steps for defining VLAN 32, which is used for the communication between the SSLM and the CSM, need to be accomplished.

In order for the MSFC to forward VLAN 32 traffic between the CSM and the SSLM, VLAN 32 (carried from the Catalyst 6500 to the SSLM) must be allowed to the SSLM using the following command:

```
ssl-proxy module 7 allowed-vlan 32
```

Issue the following command to check the state of the VLANs allowed to the SSLM:

```
CAT-Native-4#sh ssl-proxy module 7 state
SSL-proxy module 7 data-port:
Switchport: Enabled
Administrative Mode: trunk
Operational Mode: trunk
Administrative Trunking Encapsulation: dot1q
Operational Trunking Encapsulation: dot1q
Negotiation of Trunking: Off
Access Mode VLAN: 1 (default)
```

```
Trunking Native Mode VLAN: 1 (default)
Trunking VLANs Enabled: 32
Pruning VLANs Enabled: 2-1001
Vlans allowed on trunk:32
Vlans allowed and active in management domain: 32
Vlans in spanning tree forwarding state and not pruned:
   32
Allowed-vlan : 32
```

This command verifies that VLAN 32 is carried to the SSLM. Additionally, VLAN 32 is defined on the CSM for communication to the SSLM as follows:

```
vlan 32 server
   ip address 172.21.55.150 255.255.255.224
```

VLAN 32 is the SSLM VLAN on the CSM. All connections from the client to the SSLM, the connection from the CSM to the SSLM, and the connection from the SSLM to the server side will use VLAN 32. Note that the IP address is the same as the client VLAN 50 on the CSM, indicating that VLAN 50 and VLAN 32 on the CSM are configured in Bridge mode. This allows simpler configuration for maintenance of the SSLMs and for import/ export of certificates to and from the SSLMs. The solution can be achieved by using Routed mode also, but in that case virtual servers with predictor forward need to be configured on the CSM to route traffic to and from the SSLM. Since the SSLM needs to download certificates, or access the TFTP/FTP server for configuration or software updates, it is important to use a routable IP for the management VLAN.

Similarly, VLAN 32 is also defined on the SSLM to accept the traffic. VLAN 32 on the SSLM is defined as an administrative VLAN (admin) also, where the IP address 172.21.55.148 can be used for Telnet, SNMP, and other types of administrative access:

```
ssl-proxy vlan 32
  ipaddr 172.21.55.148 255.255.255.224
  gateway 172.21.55.150
!
```

Now that the communication on VLAN 32 has been set up, we will continue where the CSM has load balanced traffic to the server farm SSL-MOD. The client is load balanced to the real server defined for the SSLM that has an IP address of 172.21.55.148, as configured here on the CSM:

```
serverfarm SSL_MOD
  no nat server
  no nat client
  real 172.21.55.148
   inservice
  probe ICMP
```

Notice that Dispatch mode (**no nat server**) is used to send load-balanced traffic from the CSM to the SSLM. This enables us to use the same VIP address for the SSL proxy service on the SSLM as we used on the CSM (that is, 172.21.55.149). In Dispatch mode, only a Layer 2 rewrite is performed.

The CSM forwards the client connection to VLAN 32, forwarding the connection to the SSLM at the IP address 172.21.55.140. The SSL traffic enters the SSLM and hits the

SSL proxy service (the same IP address as defined on the vserver for port 443 on the CSM):

```
ssl-proxy service AUTH
  virtual ipaddr 172.21.55.149 protocol tcp port 443 secondary
```

This command in the SSLM allows it to start listening and proxying for connections to 172.21.55.149 on port 443. The **secondary** keyword is optional and is needed when the address is also used elsewhere. (In our example, notice that the virtual ipaddr on the SSLM and the vserver IP on the CSM are the same: 172.21.55.149.) You do not want the SSLM to respond to Address Resolution Protocol requests (ARPs) because there would be a similar ip address configuration on the SSLM for an IP address already configured under the vserver on the CSM. (The reason for this is that the **secondary** keyword allows us to host a similar virtual ipaddr on the CSM.)

Now that the SSLM has accepted the connection on port 443, it's ready to present the certificate that we imported to the client in the earlier section "SSLM Certificate Management." In order to associate our certificate with the SSL proxy of 172.21.55.149, the following command is issued under the SSL proxy configuration submode:

```
certificate rsa general-purpose trustpoint verisign
```

This command in the SSLM allows for the trust point verisign to be presented to the client. (In our testing, we are using a test certificate from VeriSign with the domain www.frontend.com. This is the same trust point created in the "SSLM Certificate Management" section, earlier in this case study.) Once the client accepts the certificate and completes the SSL handshake, the data from the client is ready to be decrypted and sent to the CSM in clear text. This is discussed in the next section.

SSLM to the CSM

Now that the SSLM has decrypted the connection, it is ready to send the connection back to the CSM on virtual server 172.21.55.151 on port 80. The following command under the SSL proxy service configuration allows for the SSLM to forward the decrypted packet to the CSM on the vserver 172.21.55.151 on port 80:

```
server ipaddr 172.21.55.151 protocol tcp port 80
```

The SSLM will use VLAN 32, also defined as the admin VLAN on the SSLM for administration purposes (Telnet, SNMP, SSH, import/export, and so on). The default gateway is the CSM VLAN 32 address of 172.21.55.150. The **admin** keyword is used here to define this VLAN as the admin VLAN:

```
ssl-proxy vlan 32
  ipaddr 172.21.55.148 255.255.255.224
  gateway 172.21.55.150 forward
  admin
```

For the strongest possible encryption for the client SSL termination, we define a policy using the following command (RSA with 3DES is used):

```
ssl-proxy policy ssl test
  cipher rsa-with-3des-ede-cbc-sha
```

This gets applied under the SSL proxy configuration as a policy for SSL with the name test:

```
ssl-proxy service AUTH
  virtual ipaddr 172.21.55.149 protocol tcp port 443 secondary
  virtual policy ssl test
  server ipaddr 172.21.55.151 protocol tcp port 80
  certificate rsa general-purpose trustpoint verisign
  policy url-rewrite test
  policy http-header test
  inservice
!
```

Now that the SSLM has forwarded the decrypted HTTP packet to the CSM on vserver 172.21.55.151, in the next section we will discuss how the CSM forwards this connection back to the SSLM to be re-encrypted.

CSM to the SSLM

Following is the configuration on the CSM for the VIP address to which the SSLM sends the decrypted traffic:

```
vserver BACK
  virtual 172.21.55.151 tcp www
```

Once the CSM receives the decrypted clear text HTTP traffic, it sends that traffic back to the SSLM to be re-encrypted, but before doing this it can look at the HTTP headers and make persistence decisions based on cookies.

The CSM matches the cookie value of apache=*whatever_the_random_string* and associates it to a real server, as shown in the following configuration. The next time the user connects with the same cookie, the CSM will remember to stick the user to the same SSLM. The string used in this testing is apache=*some_random_string*, and the CSM stores it until the cookie expires. The following configuration defines the cookie persistence on the CSM:

```
sticky 1440 group 11
```

This is the sticky cookie group used for the vserver for cookie persistence. To match this sticky group for the vserver 172.21.55.151, sticky group 11 is defined, and it matches on the cookie string of "apache", as the following configuration shows:

```
sticky 11 cookie apache
```

Once the sticky table is set up, the connection is forwarded to the SSLM to be re-encrypted, as defined in the configuration under the vserver BACK, as follows:

```
serverfarm BACK_SSL
```

The following is the configuration of the server farm BACK_SSL, used under the vserver BACK:

```
serverfarm BACK_SSL
  nat server
  no nat client
  real 172.21.55.152
  inservice
```

The IP address of 172.21.55.152 is the SSL proxy service defined on the SSLM to accept connections on port 80, re-encrypt them, and forward them back to the server via the CSM. This is defined in next section.

SSLM to the Server (via CSM)

Now that the connection is forwarded back to the SSLM, it will accept the connection on the following SSL proxy service:

```
ssl-proxy service BACK client
  virtual ipaddr 172.21.55.152 protocol tcp port 80
  server ipaddr 40.40.40.40 protocol tcp port 443
  trusted-ca test
  inservice
```

The SSLM receives the traffic on port 80 from the CSM on virtual 172.21.55.152. The SSLM has a back-end SSL connection to server 40.40.40.40. In order to establish the back-end connection between the SSLM and the server, the root certificate for the server certificate is imported on the SSLM. The root certificate is referred to by using the **trusted-ca** test command, which refers to the pool of root certificates used for SSL key exchange. (This is explained in the earlier section "SSLM Certificate Management.")

Once the back-end SSL connection has been established, the unencrypted traffic that is forwarded to the SSLM from the CSM is re-encrypted based on the SSL session keys exchange with the server, and the connection is forwarded to the CSM to be forwarded to the server. In our example, the SSLM forwards the traffic to 40.40.40.40. On the CSM, the following vserver is defined to match the traffic destined for 40.40.40.40:

```
vserver SSL_FWD
  virtual 40.40.40.0 255.255.255.0 any
  serverfarm FWD
  persistent rebalance
  inservice
```

The server farm FWD simply takes the connection and forwards it to the server 40.40.40.40 on port 443 as an SSL-encrypted connection. The configuration for the server farm is as follows. The predictor forward is used simply to forward the traffic to the destination:

```
serverfarm FWD
  no nat server
  no nat client
  predictor forward
```

The following **show** command helps identify the status of the proxy service on the SSLM:

```
SSL-Cat4-Slot7#show ssl-proxy service
Proxy Service Name                     Admin   Operation
                                       status  status

AUTH                                   up      up
BACK                                   up      up
```

The status of the SSL proxy service BACK for the back-end negotiation is based on the SSL handshake it established with the server.

The following **show** command helps identify the status of the connections on the SSLM:

```
SSL-Cat4-Slot7#show ssl-proxy stats
TCP Statistics:
    Conns initiated    : 200      Conns accepted      : 218
    Conns established  : 394      Conns dropped       : 86
    Conns Allocated    : 217      Conns Deallocated   : 217
    Conns closed       : 418      SYN timeouts        : 0
    Idle timeouts      : 0        Total pkts sent     : 1925
    Data packets sent  : 768      Data bytes sent     : 188293
    Total Pkts rcvd    : 2237     Pkts rcvd in seq    : 1062
    Bytes rcvd in seq  : 266055
SSL Statistics:
    conns attempted    : 200      conns completed     : 200
    full handshakes    : 80       resumed handshakes  : 76
    active conns       : 0        active sessions     : 0
    renegs attempted   : 0        conns in reneg      : 0
    handshake failures : 0        data failures       : 0
    fatal alerts rcvd  : 0        fatal alerts sent   : 0
    no-cipher alerts   : 0        ver mismatch alerts : 0
    no-compress alerts : 0        bad macs received   : 0
    pad errors         : 0        session fails       : 0
```

The commands show the number of successful connections through the SSLM for both the TCP and SSL connections. This **show** command is a useful troubleshooting command if the connections are failing because it can help isolate whether the problem exists with the TCP layer or the SSL layer.

The following **show** command helps identify the status of the vservers on the CSM:

```
CAT-Native-4#show mod csm 6 vservers
vserver        type  prot virtual                  vlan state        conns
-----------------------------------------------------------------------------
SSL_FRONT      SLB   TCP  172.21.55.149/32:443     ALL  OPERATIONAL  5
SSL_FWD        SLB   any  40.40.40.0/24:0          ALL  OPERATIONAL  5
WWW            SLB   TCP  172.21.55.149/32:80      ALL  OPERATIONAL  0
BACK           SLB   TCP  172.21.55.151/32:80      ALL  OPERATIONAL  5
```

The **show** command highlights the various vservers that get hits on the connections. The vserver SSL_FRONT shows the client connection to the CSM, and the vserver BACK shows the connections for the unencrypted connections from the SSLM. The vserver SSL_FWD shows the connections that the SSLM forwards to server 40.40.40.40 as encrypted. The CSM simply forwards these connections to the server unchanged.

Configuration Details

Examples 11-7 and 11-8 show the configurations for the CSM and the SSLM.

Example 11-7 *CSM Configuration*

```
module ContentSwitchingModule 6
 vlan 40 server
  ip address 40.40.40.111 255.255.255.0
 !
 vlan 50 client
  ip address 172.21.55.150 255.255.255.224
  gateway 172.21.55.131
 !
 vlan 32 server
  ip address 172.21.55.150 255.255.255.224
 !
 probe TCP tcp
  interval 10
  failed 60
 !
 probe TCP_REMOTE tcp
  interval 60
 !
 probe ICMP icmp
  interval 2
  retries 2
  failed 2
 !
sticky 11 cookie apache
 !
serverfarm BACK_SSL
  nat server
  no nat client
  real 172.21.55.152
   inservice
 !
 serverfarm FWD
  no nat server
  no nat client
  predictor forward
 !
 serverfarm SERVER-1
  nat server
  no nat client
  real 40.40.40.40
   inservice
  probe TCP
 !
 serverfarm SSL_MOD
  no nat server
  no nat client
  real 172.21.55.148
   inservice
  probe ICMP
```

Example 11-7 *CSM Configuration (Continued)*

```
!
 vserver BACK
  virtual 172.21.55.151 tcp www
  serverfarm BACK_SSL
  sticky 1440 group 11
  persistent rebalance
  inservice
 !
 vserver SSL_FRONT
  virtual 172.21.55.149 tcp https
  serverfarm SSL_MOD
  persistent rebalance
  inservice
 !
 vserver SSL_FWD
  virtual 40.40.40.0 255.255.255.0 any
  serverfarm FWD
  persistent rebalance
  inservice
 !
 vserver WWW
  virtual 172.21.55.149 tcp www
  serverfarm SERVER-1
  persistent rebalance
  inservice
 !
```

Example 11-8 *SSLM Configuration*

```
SSL-Cat4-Slot7#sh run
Building configuration...
Current configuration : 9051 bytes
!
version 12.2
no service pad
service timestamps debug datetime msec
service timestamps log datetime msec
no service password-encryption
!
hostname SSL-Cat4-Slot7
!
no logging buffered
enable password ww
!
spd headroom 512
ip subnet-zero
no ip domain lookup
ip domain name cisco.com
!
!
```

continues

Example 11-8 *SSLM Configuration (Continued)*

```
ssl-proxy policy ssl test
 cipher rsa-with-3des-ede-cbc-sha
!
ssl-proxy service AUTH
 virtual ipaddr 172.21.55.149 protocol tcp port 443 secondary
 server ipaddr 172.21.55.151 protocol tcp port 80
 virtual policy ssl test
 certificate rsa general-purpose trustpoint verisign
 inservice
!
ssl-proxy service BACK client
 virtual ipaddr 172.21.55.152 protocol tcp port 80
 server ipaddr 40.40.40.40 protocol tcp port 443
 trusted-ca test
 authenticate verify all
 inservice
ssl-proxy vlan 32
 ipaddr 172.21.55.148 255.255.255.224
 gateway 172.21.55.150
 route 40.40.40.0 255.255.255.0 gateway 172.21.55.150
!
ssl-proxy pool ca test
 ca trustpoint test
!
crypto ca trustpoint verisign
 enrollment terminal
 subject-name C=US; ST=California; L=San Jose; O=Cisco; OU=Lab;
  CN=www.frontendssl.com
 crl optional
 rsakeypair mykey
!
crypto ca trustpoint test
 enrollment terminal
 crl optional
!
crypto ca certificate chain verisign
 certificate ca 20A897AEDB8202DEC136A04E26BD8773
  30820298 30820201 021020A8 97AEDB82 02DEC136 A04E26BD 8773300D 06092A86
  4886F70D 01010205 0030818C 310B3009 06035504 06130255 53311730 15060355
  040A130E 56657269 5369676E 2C20496E 632E3130 302E0603 55040B13 27466F72
  20546573 74205075 72706F73 6573204F 6E6C792E 20204E6F 20617373 7572616E
  6365732E 31323030 06035504 03132956 65726953 69676E20 54726561 6C205365
  63757265 20536572 76657220 54657374 20526F6F 74204341 301E170D 30353032
  30393030 30303030 5A170D32 35303230 38323335 3935395A 30818C31 0B300906
  03550406 13025553 31173015 06035504 0A130E56 65726953 69676E2C 20496E63
  2E313030 2E060355 040B1327 466F7220 54657374 20507572 706F7365 73204F6E
  6C792E20 204E6F20 61737375 72616E63 65732E31 32303006 03550403 13295665
  72695369 676E2054 7269616C 20536563 75726520 53657276 65722054 65737420
  526F6F74 20434130 819F300D 06092A86 4886F70D 01010105 0003818D 00308189
  02818100 9F21F7C5 3B925699 1F97049F A09210A9 8659506C 4F01C868 C00056A1
  AA0949FB 43D0B5D2 C10E2070 739F22F2 7920E332 CE4CD670 BF88003B 2820127F
```

Example 11-8 *SSLM Configuration (Continued)*

```
    FC87CF40 1D954FB5 2114A28F 01D317FD 9D612A13 4F13F618 29AD2F51 9AE22EFE
    CC30E8D3 CE95EFE3 62140189 8FE0987B 2E3BB9EE 176B7DE8 FF860E03 D3C62FCE
    E8A857BB 02030100 01300D06 092A8648 86F70D01 01020500 03818100 3AAE38EE
    B3F9103A 85125DEF 84B8604D B9F26AC9 0D6303EF C64FB482 B9D0C830 38B05FEA
    80AF2716 59EF2E60 0E1770E6 7EEA96E9 64ABE33A 93633A70 98996C9F 8F0E9BFC
    968AB2FC 1AE5917E D8ADD8F3 B14DF1D2 07C56647 E3D9C769 36E14816 519CA88C
    31B126D8 87777B63 09DA8581 38ADE0D2 B8DBD716 39C66B87 8EF178E2
  quit
certificate B3753950BA12FCF55BFC95FC5615A9
    30820437 308203A0 A0030201 02021000 B3753950 BA12FCF5 5BFC95FC 5615A930
    0D06092A 864886F7 0D010105 05003081 8C310B30 09060355 04061302 55533117
    30150603 55040A13 0E566572 69536967 6E2C2049 6E632E31 30302E06 0355040B
    1327466F 72205465 73742050 7572706F 73657320 4F6E6C79 2E20204E 6F206173
    73757261 6E636573 2E313230 30060355 04031329 56657269 5369676E 20547269
    616C2053 65637572 65205365 72766572 20546573 7420526F 6F742043 41301E17
    0D303530 36323030 30303030 305A170D 30353037 30343233 35393539 5A3081AD
    310B3009 06035504 06130255 53311330 11060355 0408130A 43616C69 666F726E
    69613111 300F0603 55040714 0853616E 204A6F73 65310E30 0C060355 040A1405
    43697363 6F310C30 0A060355 040B1403 4C616231 3A303806 0355040B 14315465
    726D7320 6F662075 73652061 74207777 772E7665 72697369 676E2E63 6F6D2F63
    70732F74 65737463 61202863 29303531 1C301A06 03550403 14137777 772E6672
    6F6E7465 6E647373 6C2E636F 6D30819F 300D0609 2A864886 F70D0101 01050003
    818D0030 81890281 8100C2DE BE8FB06C 6A5A89BC BE4B0E9F 14E862B3 220A9A2F
    A84A1051 175E2C76 611C07D1 F94A992B 7CB242C2 1CD553E6 EB67ABD4 B62BC6F7
    FD6FCEE9 4A5087FE 7674EA32 C9C84DF3 A48F7A56 C05B0DDA 070872C5 0C034356
    986D4F7E 67E7BFDE FA2361AB 69B068C8 FD66DD40 81D3A5B0 B3913EE8 45FC2FB0
    88A30196 84DC4496 97610203 010001A3 82017530 82017130 09060355 1D130402
    3000300B 0603551D 0F040403 0205A030 47060355 1D1F0440 303E303C A03AA038
    86366874 74703A2F 2F535652 53656375 72652D63 726C2E76 65726973 69676E62E
    636F6D2F 53565252 7269616C 526E6C74 32303035 2E63726C 304A0603 551D2004
    43304130 3F060A60 86480186 F8450107 15303130 2F06082B 06010505 07020116
    23687474 70733A2F 2F777777 2E766572 69736967 6E2E636F 6D2F6370 732F7465
    73746361 301D0603 551D2504 16301406 082B0601 05050703 0106082B 06010505
    07030230 3406082B 06010505 07010104 28302630 2406082B 06010505 07300186
    18687474 703A2F2F 6F637370 2E766572 69736967 6E2E636F 6D306D06 082B0601
    05050701 0C046130 5FA15DA0 5B305930 57305516 09696D61 67652F67 69663021
    301F3007 06052B0E 03021A04 148FE5D3 1A86AC8D 8E6BC3CF 806AD448 182C7B19
    2E302516 23687474 703A2F2F 6C6F676F 2E766572 69736967 6E2E636F 6D2F7673
    6C6F676F 2E676966 300D0609 2A864886 F70D0101 05050003 81810067 9A4A147F
    53A4F101 C2B3A6A2 A962A3DB 35A27A1F BF2609E2 C6FF7719 B976DDC7 D5E9C262
    9CF0A086 9A4A68F0 E5632A81 D3A12799 16732927 7AFD660D 183F7F55 12E6C9D1
    47AAF90A EB48792E 4423CF3E ACEC8167 260107E6 85348031 9CFE537D DEB42F81
    4D6BCF1A ADF40532 31736E0F 67F51AE5 729AA9B9 54425E16 49C557
  quit
crypto ca certificate chain test
 certificate ca 20A897AEDB8202DEC136A04E26BD8773
    30820298 30820201 021020A8 97AEDB82 02DEC136 A04E26BD 8773300D 06092A86
    4886F70D 01010205 0030818C 310B3009 06035504 06130255 53311730 15060355
    040A130E 56657269 5369676E 2C20496E 632E3130 302E0603 55040B13 27466F72
    20546573 74205075 72706F73 6573204F 6E6C792E 20204E6F 20617373 7572616E
    6365732E 31323030 06035504 03132956 65726953 69676E20 54726961 6C205365
```

continues

Example 11-8 *SSLM Configuration (Continued)*

```
63757265 20536572 76657220 54657374 20526F6F 74204341 301E170D 30353032
30393030 30303030 5A170D32 35303230 38323335 3935395A 30818C31 0B300906
03550406 13025553 31173015 06035504 0A130E56 65726953 69676E2C 20496E63
2E313030 2E060355 040B1327 466F7220 54657374 20507572 706F7365 73204F6E
6C792E20 204E6F20 61737375 72616E63 65732E31 32303006 03550403 13295665
72695369 676E2054 7269616C 20536563 75726520 53657276 65722054 65737420
526F6F74 20434130 819F300D 06092A86 4886F70D 01010105 0003818D 00308189
02818100 9F21F7C5 3B925699 1F97049F A09210A9 8659506C 4F01C868 C00056A1
AA0949FB 43D0B5D2 C10E2070 739F22F2 7920E332 CE4CD670 BF88003B 2820127F
FC87CF40 1D954FB5 2114A28F 01D317FD 9D612A13 4F13F618 29AD2F51 9AE22EFE
CC30E8D3 CE95EFE3 62140189 8FE0987B 2E3BB9EE 176B7DE8 FF860E03 D3C62FCE
E8A857BB 02030100 01300D06 092A8648 86F70D01 01020500 03818100 3AAE38EE
B3F9103A 85125DEF 84B8604D B9F26AC9 0D6303EF C64FB482 B9D0C830 38B05FEA
80AF2716 59EF2E60 0E1770E6 7EEA96E9 64ABE33A 93633A70 98996C9F 8F0E9BFC
968AB2FC 1AE5917E D8ADD8F3 B14DF1D2 07C56647 E3D9C769 36E14816 519CA88C
31B126D8 87777B63 09DA8581 38ADE0D2 B8DBD716 39C66B87 8EF178E2
quit
!
!
!
!
!
ip classless
ip route 40.40.40.0 255.255.255.0 172.21.55.150
ip http server
no ip http secure-server
!
!
no cdp run
!
line con 0
 exec-timeout 0 0
line 1 3
 exec-timeout 0 0
 password ww
 login
 no exec
 transport input all
 flowcontrol software
line vty 0 4
 exec-timeout 0 0
 password ww
 login
!
end
SSL-Cat4-Slot7#
```

Summary

In today's networks where security and encryption are paramount, the CSS and the SSLM provide a comprehensive solution for providing end-to-end encryption. This chapter discussed various designs for providing back-end encryption using both the CSS and the SSLM, and illustrated the complexities and caveats associated when deploying back-end encryption.

In Chapter 12, "Global Server Load Balancing," we will discuss how Global Server Load Balancing (GSLB) solutions provide redundancy and availability across geographically dispersed data centers.

PART III

Distributed Data Centers

CHAPTER 12

Global Server Load Balancing

With businesses today relying heavily on revenues from their online applications, any disruption of service to mission-critical applications can mean large losses that can be measured at thousands of dollars per minute of downtime. These losses are not simply qualified in terms of dollars but also in terms of productivity and customer dissatisfaction.

In order to minimize the downtime of these mission-critical applications, companies are looking for solutions that can guarantee that these applications stay online, regardless of any situation (natural disaster or link, hardware, or software failures). One such solution available to customers today is global server load balancing (GSLB). GSLB can make intelligent decisions by inspecting the IP packet and Domain Name Service (DNS) information and direct traffic to the best-available, least-loaded sites and servers that will provide the fastest and best response.

This chapter introduces GSLB and its benefits, provides an overview of the DNS, and discusses the Global Site Selector (GSS). The chapter also provides a case study that shows how GSLB can be deployed using GSS.

Motivation for GSLB

In the previous chapters, the discussions were focused on load-balancing traffic within a data center environment, where the CSS or the CSM was placed to provide redundancy and high availability to applications residing local to the data center. However, companies cannot rely on a single point of presence for their applications, since it's a single point of failure. To provide enhanced user experience in various geographic regions, multiple data centers or points of presence for the applications need to be built. In order to use these dispersed data centers and applications efficiently while providing redundancy and optimal end user experience, GSLB is deployed between multiple data centers.

A network using the GSLB solution will direct user requests to the most appropriate data center based on the request, thus improving the user experience. For example, if a bank has offices in North America and Europe, users accessing the bank online services in Europe will be directed to the applications in Europe, thus reducing the latency and enhancing customer experience. Since the GSLB solution directs the user traffic to a local data center, this helps in reducing the WAN traffic, thus saving costly bandwidth for WAN links. The product that Cisco offers as a solution for GSLB is called the GSS and will be the focus of this chapter.

Domain Name System (DNS) Overview

DNS is the primary technology used for GSLB, and an overview of how it functions and how it relates to the GSLB devices follows.

DNS is a distributed database of host information that maps domain names to IP addresses. Most of the clients and servers on the Internet rely on DNS for communication services like electronic mail and remote terminal access (for example, Telnet, file transfers using FTP, and HTTP web browsing). DNS makes possible the use of easy-to-remember alphanumeric host names instead of numeric IP addresses that bear no relationship to the content on the host. For example, the name www.example.com translates to an IP address of 1.2.3.4. Now a browser trying to communicate to www.example.com will use DNS to resolve the name to an IP address of 1.2.3.4 via the DNS server. So instead of the users try to remember 1.2.3.4 for the example.com web site, they can remember the name of the web site as www.example.com, which is much easier to recall.

As the users on the Internet try to connect to specific web sites, the resolution from a name to an IP address is conducted by name servers (DNS servers) distributed throughout the Internet. The need for a DNS-based solution arose because in the earlier days of the Internet the name resolution to an IP address was done based on a file that resided on the client machine; these files were called host files and had static mapping of names to IP addresses, and all changes to the file were done manually. As the Internet grew in the number of hosts and clients, these host files were not able to scale. The solution was to implement the DNS servers throughout the Internet, which can maintain and manage the name resolution process.

DNS is based on the namespace architecture. This namespace is a logical and hierarchical representation of how domains on the Internet can be named (for example, www.cisco.com or www.exampleuni.edu, and so on) and defines rules as to how these names can be created. Figure 12-1 shows an example of a DNS namespace.

Figure 12-1 *DNS Namespace Example*

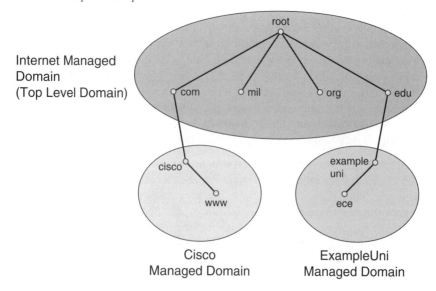

As the figure illustrates, the Internet-managed namespace starts from the root and is managed by an Internet namespace authority, responsible for delegating domains for organizations connecting to the Internet. The top-level domains are usually subdivided into organization-specific and geographically specific domains. As the figure shows, one of the organizational domains is the *.com* domain, which is usually associated with enterprise organizations in the U.S. (for example, www.cisco.com and www.example.com). The organizational domains are further divided into educational organizations, such as UC Exampleuni, represented with *.edu* (www.exampleuni.edu); government organizations, such as the State of California, represented with *.gov* (www.ca.gov); international organizations, such as UN, represented with *.int* (www.un.int); military organizations, such as the U.S. Army, represented with *.mil* (www.army.mil); noncommercial organizations, such as UNICEF, represented with *.org* (www.unicef.org); and networking organizations, such as IEEE, represented with *.net* (www.ieee.net). The DNS namespace is also divided on a specific geography basis; for example, DNS names in the United Kingdom are represented with *.uk* and in Canada are represented with *.ca*.

Similar to the namespace hierarchy, where there is the root domain followed by specific domains based on the nature of the organization (.com) and further subdivision for that specific organization (Cisco.com), the authorities for delegation of the specific domains are also hierarchical. For example, the top-level Internet domains (.com, .net, .mil, and so on) are all managed by the Internet Assigned Numbers Authority (IANA). IANA delegates which organizations get categorized as the .com domain and which ones get categorized as the .org domain. For example, *exampleuni* is an educational institution; the IANA delegates the exampleuni.edu subdomain and delegates the authority of this subdomain to Exampleuni's network administrators. Exampleuni's network administrators can further subdivide the domain into specific categories such ece.exampleuni.edu, cs.exampleuni.edu, and www.exampleuni.edu. Each organization is given authority over its specific namespace and is responsible for subdividing and managing its namespace for the entire organization.

DNS Architecture Components

The DNS architecture contains two main components, which are described here:

- **DNS clients**—Clients that access domain name servers. A very common example is when a web browser initiates a query to a web site and resolves the web site name to an IP address to which to connect. In that instance, the web browser acts as a DNS client.

- **DNS server**—A server running DNS software that has the responsibility of returning to the client a reference or a direct answer for the domain-to-IP address mapping. This is also referred to as the client D-proxy. A DNS server at different hierarchies of the DNS tree has different functions. For example, the root DNS server knows how to resolve names for all the top-level domains, such as .com, .mil, and so on. A total of 13 root servers exist on the Internet. For specific DNS queries to specific domains, intermediate DNS servers exist that forward requests that were forwarded to them by the root servers. For example, a test.cisco.com query will go to the root DNS server, the root server will forward this to the intermediate DNS server for Cisco, and the intermediate DNS server in turn will forward it to the authoritative DNS server for test.cisco.com. The authoritative DNS server will return the correct IP address for that domain. In Figure 12-1 you can see top-level DNS servers (.com, .edu, and so on) that point to intermediate DNS servers.

DNS Resolution Process

Figure 12-2 illustrates that when a client tries to connect to the domain test.cisco.com and the client's DNS server is unable to resolve that address, the local D-proxy checks with another name server that is authoritative for test.cisco.com.

Figure 12-2 *DNS Query Example*

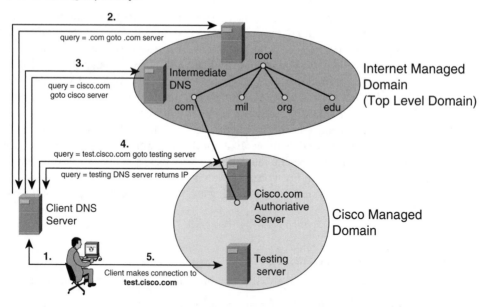

1. The client sends a query for test.cisco.com to the client's DNS server.

2. The client's DNS server does not have the IP address for test.cisco.com, so it sends a query to a root name server (".") asking for the IP address. The root name server refers the client DNS server to contact the intermediate DNS server that knows the authoritative DNS server for test.cisco.com.

3. The client DNS server sends a query to the intermediate name server, which responds by referring the client DNS server to the authoritative name server for cisco.com and all the associated subdomains.

4 The client DNS server sends a query to the test.cisco.com authoritative name server (authoritative for the requested domain), which sends the IP address to the client's DNS server. In this example, test.cisco.com is a subdomain of cisco.com.

5 The client DNS server sends the IP address to the client browser. The browser uses this IP address and initiates a connection to the test.cisco.com web site.

DNS Resource Records and Zones

The building blocks for DNS queries are based on what are called resource records and zones. By using pieces of this information, a DNS hierarchy is defined for a particular domain.

Resource Records

A *resource record* is the actual translation of a DNS domain name to an IP address and resides on the authoritative DNS server for the domain for which it is responsible. Following is an example of a resource record:

```
test.cisco.com.   IN  A   172.21.55.131
```

Some of the common resource records used to answer DNS queries are as follows:

- **SOA resource records**—The start of authority (SOA) record refers to servers that have zone files for specific domains.

- **NS resource records**—The name server (NS) record indicates a server that is authoritative for the zone and that can resolve names.

- **A resource records**—The address (A) record is responsible for mapping the host name to an IP address.

- **PTR resource records**—The pointer (PTR) record maps an IP address to a host name used for reverse name queries.

- **CNAME resource records**—The canonical name (CNAME) record creates an alias (synonymous name) for the specified host name.

- **MX resource records**—The mail exchange (MX) record specifies a mail exchange server for a DNS domain name.

Zones

DNS *zones* are files stored on the DNS server that usually contain multiple resource records. A DNS domain can be subdivided into specific logical zones. For example, the domain cisco.com is subdivided into two zones, test.cisco.com and www.cisco.com. Each of these specific zones can be controlled by two different DNS servers, and each specific server is responsible for returning queries associated to the zone for which it is authoritative. The updates for records in a particular zone are made on the primary zone, and these changes are pushed to the secondary zone. Only one particular server can be made primary or secondary for a specific zone, and no other DNS server can be primary or secondary for that zone. However, one DNS server can manage one or multiple zones.

The server that hosts the primary zone is called the primary server for that zone, and the server that hosts the secondary zone is called the secondary server for that zone. Updates to a zone are made on the primary zone files, which are replicated to the secondary zone server. The secondary zone server periodically checks with the primary server for updates and changes to the zone files. If there are changes to the zone files, the secondary server initiates a zone transfer to update its zone information. One of the key benefits of having a secondary zone server is that DNS resolution can be conducted by the secondary zone server even if the primary zone server fails. This also helps in reducing traffic on the wide area links where a secondary server for the zone can return DNS queries locally to a site.

When a query is received by a DNS server, it first tries to service the request from its local zones. However, if the server is not authoritative for that zone, it will refer the client to another DNS server to process the request. The first DNS server tries to cache the request from the other DNS server for a certain configurable amount of time, and this results in faster processing of client requests.

Types of DNS Queries

There are two kinds of DNS queries, recursive and iterative. When the client initiates a *recursive DNS query,* the client's local DNS server is responsible for returning the address to the client. The local DNS server makes this query on behalf of the client, and if the response is not available, the local DNS server forwards the query to another DNS server and waits for a response back to be forwarded to the originating client. If the request received by the other DNS server is also recursive, it will also be sent back to the server that originated the query (usually back to the client's local DNS server). Figure 12-3 illustrates the DNS recursive query process.

As the figure illustrates, when the client makes a request to the local DNS server for a name query, it forwards the request to the root DNS server. If the root DNS server does not have an answer, it forwards this request on behalf of the local DNS server to the high-level intermediate server. Once the intermediate server forwards the request to the authoritative server, the authoritative server returns the request back to the root server, which in turn forwards the request to the local DNS server. The local DNS server awaits a response from the root server for the query.

If a client issues an *iterative DNS query* and a match for the query is not found, instead of returning an error or a match for the query (as in the case of a recursive query), the DNS server can get referrals to other DNS servers, which can return an authoritative response for the query. Figure 12-4 illustrates the DNS iterative query process.

Figure 12-3 *DNS Recursive Query*

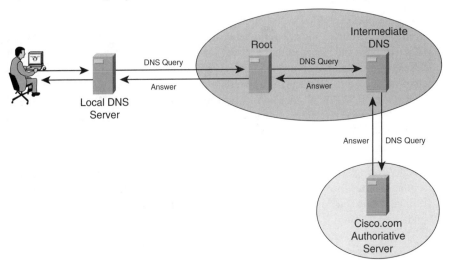

Figure 12-4 *DNS Iterative Query*

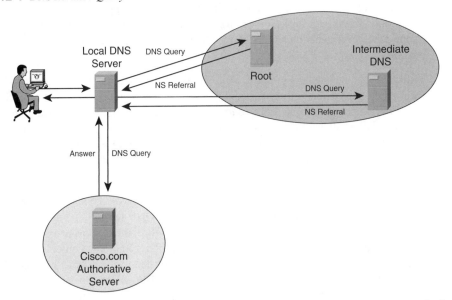

As the figure illustrates, in an iterative query, the response to an answer can be based on referrals to other DNS servers. When the client makes a query to its local DNS server, the local DNS server forwards the response to its root server. The root server refers back to the local DNS server to contact the intermediate server. When the local DNS server contacts the intermediate server, it answers back with a referral to the authoritative server. The local DNS server then contacts the authoritative DNS server to get the IP address.

Global Site Selector

The GSS platform allows customers to leverage global content deployment across multiple distributed and mirrored data centers. The GSS integrates with the existing DNS hierarchy and interfaces with the server load balancers, such as the Cisco CSS, the Cisco CSM, or third-party server load balancers to monitor the health and load of the server load-balancing (SLB) devices in the data centers. The GSS uses health probes based on TCP ports, ICMP, and other application protocols, such as HTTP to select the best possible site for the client connection. The GSS can detect application outages in a data center and allows the user to connect to the mirrored application available in another data center.

The following sections discuss the basic features and terminology used for configuring and managing the GSS for GSLB. These sections also review the DNS features of specifying domain name rules and associating them to VIP addresses for detecting application failures and site selection.

GSLB Using GSS

In today's IT environments where having resiliency for applications and services is paramount, having multiple server farms in different geographic locations is preferred. If one data center becomes unavailable, the other data center can start servicing requests.

With multiple data centers in place, DNS solutions today do not provide any insight into local application availability and load. DNS servers do not have a solution for determining if a client request should be sent to data center 1 or data center 2. They have no reference for the location of the client and so cannot redirect traffic based on client geography or latency to the appropriate data center. In addition, DNS servers cannot keep clients persistent to a particular data center if an application requires it.

Figure 12-5 illustrates how a DNS server solution runs into problems when there are two or more data centers. As shown in the figure, the DNS server is responsible for returning A records for queries it receives. The authoritative DNS server can be configured to return A records in a round robin fashion. In the figure, the authoritative DNS server is responsible for returning the A record for data center 1 and data center 2. However, as you notice in the diagram, the A record can be returned to the client by the DNS server without knowledge of the state of the applications. The client tries to connect to data center 1, even though it can potentially be redirected to data center 2 where the application is still available. There is no link or state established between the load balancers or the applications and the DNS servers to redirect client traffic to the best possible site.

Figure 12-5 *DNS with Two Data Centers*

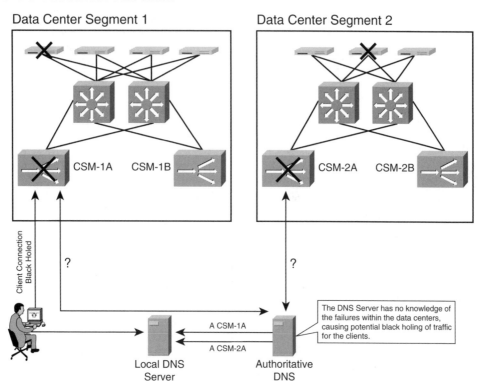

Figure 12-6 illustrates how the GSS integrates into the DNS server hierarchy, provides an answer back to the client if the application in data center 1 is down, and forwards the answer for data center 2. As the figure shows, GSS-1 and GSS-2 interact with the DNS server. GSS-1 and GSS-2 are both authoritative for the VIPs configured on CSM-1A and CSM-2A, respectively. The DNS server now has name server records that point to both the GSSs. The GSS-1 and GSS-2 also have a connection in between them to share the state of the database and report any changes they have. The GSSs also run keepalives to the load balancers to check for the availability of the applications based on response by the applications to the GSSs. In Figure 12-6, the applications in data center 1 have become nonresponsive. When a client tries to resolve DNS for those applications, the DNS server still forwards the requests of the name servers to the GSS; however, GSS-1 detects that the applications have gone down because it is running a keepalive to CSM-1A. Once the keepalives for the applications are down, the GSS-1 replies with the addresses of VIPs on CSM-2A, where the applications are still functional and where the client request is forwarded. The GSS maintains the state of the applications in both the data centers by creating communication between the GSS in data center 1 and the GSS in data center 2 and sharing its database information on a periodic basis.

Figure 12-6 *GSS with Two Data Centers*

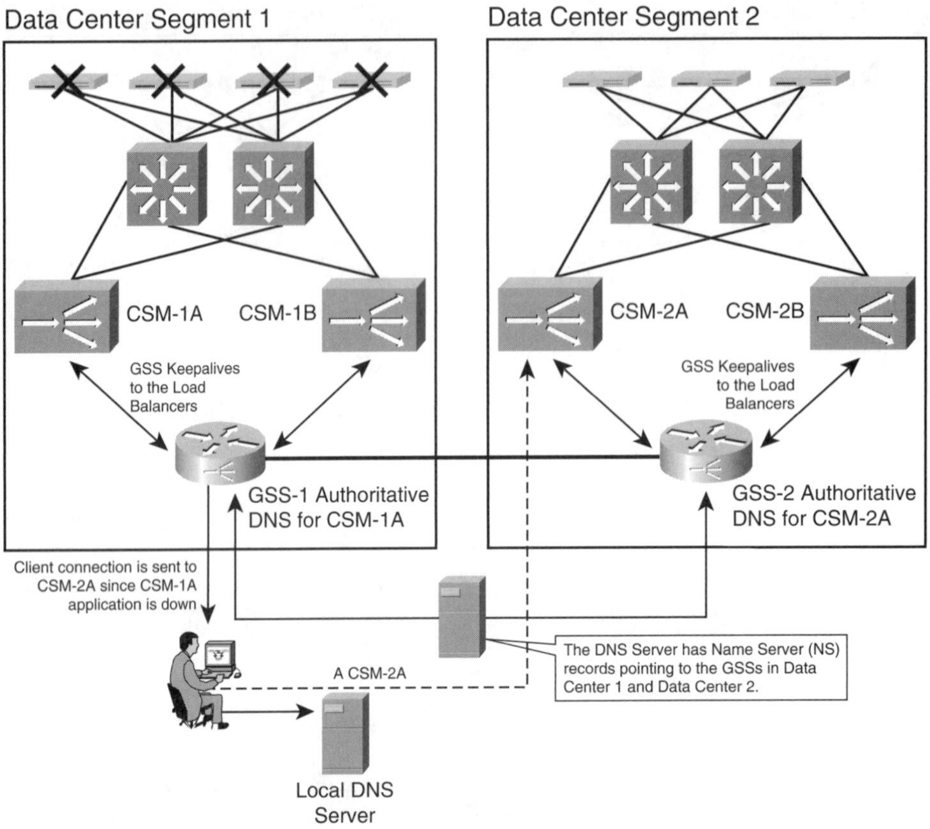

Thus the GSS builds intelligence about the state of the applications by running periodic keepalives to the load balancers or the applications and also by acting as the authoritative answer for the domain. It returns a positive response if the keepalives are responding and returns a response for other data centers if the local keepalives report a negative response.

The following sections discuss how the GSS implements solutions for the gaps that are not answered by DNS servers.

GSS Features and Performance

One of the key benefits of deploying the GSS is that it creates a link between the client request based on the DNS and the state of the applications by probing either the load balancers or the applications directly. The devices the GSS supports are as follows:

- Cisco CSS 11500, 11000, or 11150
- Cisco CSM

- Cisco LocalDirector
- Cisco IOS SLB
- Cisco router using the DRP agent for network proximity
- Any server that is capable of responding to an HTTP HEAD or TCP request
- Cisco router with cache modules
- Cisco Cache Engines

The decision the GSS makes is based on the keepalives it uses to probe the load balancers for the health of the applications. The GSS can also make decisions based on the proximity of the client or the local DNS server making the request to the GSS, the load in terms of connections on the applications, and the source of the DNS server querying the GSS. In addition, the GSS can respond with a backup site address in case the primary site is down. The GSLB features and options allow for end users always to be directed to resources that are online, and for requests to be forwarded to the optimal location to service the request.

GSS Roles

When deployed, the GSS can begin by acting in one of three roles:

- Primary GSSM
- Secondary GSSM
- Standalone GSS

The primary Global Site Server Manager (GSSM) is the GSS hardware responsible for the centralized management of the GSS network. The primary GSSM is responsible for hosting the GSS database that contains configuration information for all the devices and domains. The configuration for all other GSSs is also through the GUI interface provided through the primary GSSM. All changes that are made on the primary GSSM are pushed to other GSS devices. If a GSS is part of a particular network, it will report its status to the primary GSSM. In order to provide redundancy in case the primary GSSM becomes unavailable, a GSS takes the role of the secondary GSSM. The secondary GSSM contains a duplicate copy of the primary GSSM database. GUI support for configuration is still available via the primary GSSM, and in a case where the primary GSSM becomes unavailable, the secondary GSSM becomes the primary and GUI support becomes available through it. Any changes, such as keepalives or the addition or deletion of devices, are synchronized between the primary and the secondary GSSM. Both the primary and secondary GSSM are still responsible for returning A record queries they receive. The third role is the GSS role as a standalone. Standalone GSSs do not report their presence to one another but synchronize themselves with the primary GSSM. The thing to note about the GSS roles is that they are primarily used for administrative purposes and to be aware of the devices and domain availability. As far as the DNS functionality goes, all the GSSs, regardless of their role, are still functioning to return the DNS queries for which they are responsible based on the configurations specified.

Access to the GSS for configuration purposes is usually achieved via the GUI, which is made over a Secure Socket Layer (SSL) connection. Figure 12-7 shows a screen shot of the GUI access to the GSS.

Figure 12-7 *GSS GUI Access*

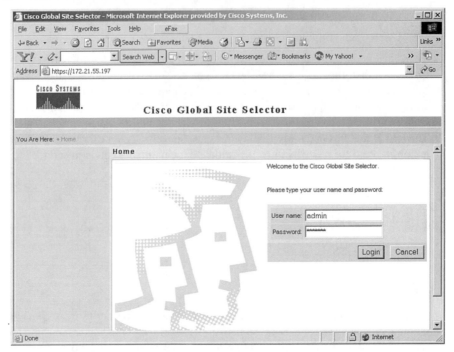

In the login screen, once the username and password are entered, the initial primary GSSM GUI is displayed, as illustrated in Figure 12-8.

The primary GSSM GUI is organized into five main functional areas. Each area is divided by tabs, which you click to navigate to a particular section of the primary GSSM. These functional areas are as follows:

- **DNS Rules**—Pages for creating and modifying DNS rules, including the creation of source address lists, hosted domain lists, answers, answer groups, and shared keepalives.

- **Resources**—Pages for creating and modifying GSS network resources, such as GSSs, locations, regions, and owners. You can also modify global keepalive properties from this tab.

- **Monitoring**—Pages for monitoring the performance of content routing on your GSS network, such as displays of hit counts, organized by source address, domain, answer method, or DNS rule.

- **Tools**—Pages for performing the administrative functions for the GSS network, such as creating login accounts, managing account passwords, and viewing system logs.

- **Traffic Mgmt**—Pages for configuring the advanced GSLB functions, DNS sticky, and network proximity.

Figure 12-8 *GSS Main GUI*

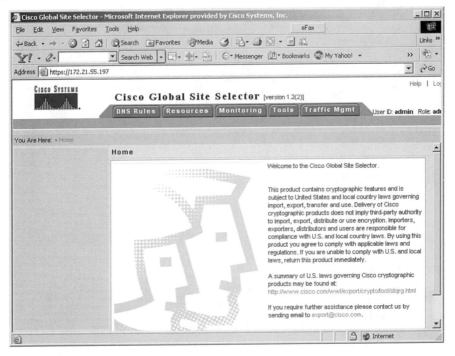

These tabs will be reviewed in the following sections.

GSS DNS Rules

The GSS GUI manages the configuration of A records via the use of DNS rules, which are configured by the administrator via the GUI on the primary GSSM. The DNS rules allow the administrators to have a central point of configuration as to how the GSS globally load balances a given hosted domain. Two of the key functionalities that the DNS rules allow the administrator to define are the IP addresses for the domains that need to be sent as part of the DNS query and the list of all the domain names. The DNS rules also allow the specification of matching criteria based on the source IP address for the requesting DNS server, matching criteria for the hosted domain, a load-balancing method to use (whether to use round robin or to prefer a VIP), DNS persistence, and proximity functionality. Each GSS supports a maximum of 4000 DNS rules. Figure 12-9 shows the GSS DNS rule interface. Figure 12-10 shows the inputs that are required when a new DNS rule is created.

Figure 12-9 *GSS DNS Rule Interface*

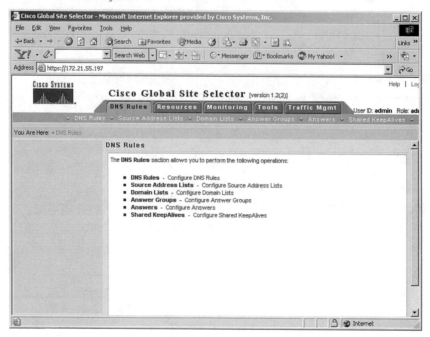

Figure 12-10 *GSS DNS Rule Options*

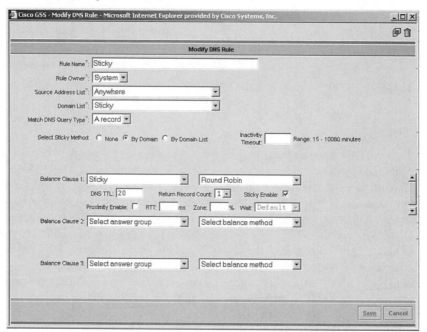

As Figure 12-10 shows, the parameters for the DNS rule configuration define the following:

- The name of the DNS rule.

- The source address list of the client DNS server that is allowed to make a request for the rule.

- The names of the domains that are members of the domain list—that is, the domains configured with this DNS rule. (The DNS list configuration will be discussed in the following sections.)

- The DNS query type, such as the A or NS record to be returned.

- The sticky parameter if necessary for connections that are required to be persistent. This is based on either a single domain name or a list of domains.

- The answers (the actual VIP addresses) associated with the domains defined as part of the domain list and the load-balancing method that should be used when returning the VIP addresses as part of the answer group. (The current default is round robin.)

- The DNS Time To Live (the TTL field, which is the time for this record to be cached) and the number of records that can be returned for a particular query.

- The second and third balance clauses can be configured with a different answer group and load-balancing pair, in case for some reason the answers in balance clause 1 go offline due to failed keepalives.

GSS Balance Methods

The GSS allows for six different load-balancing methods, which determine how the GSS responds to a particular DNS query. Each balance method provides a different algorithm for selecting one answer from a configured answer group. Figure 12-11 shows the interface for the load-balancing options to choose from in the GSS configuration. The following sections summarize the various balance methods.

Hashed

When the GSS uses the hashed balance method, the GSS creates a unique value (a hash value) based on the client's DNS proxy IP address and the requesting client's domain. The unique hash value is attached to and used to identify a VIP that is chosen to serve the DNS query. The use of hash values makes it possible to provide persistency to the traffic from a particular requesting client to a specific VIP, ensuring that future requests from that client are routed to the same VIP. This type of continuity can be used to facilitate features, such as online shopping baskets, in which client-specific data is expected to persist even when client connectivity to a site is terminated or interrupted. The GSS can do the hash based on the source address, where the GSS selects the answer based on a hash value created from the source address of the request, or based on the domain name, where the GSS selects the answer based on a hash value created from the requested domain name.

Figure 12-11 *GSS Load-Balancing Methods*

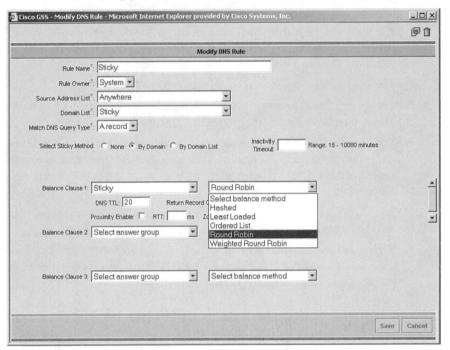

Least Loaded

With the least-loaded balance method, the GSS returns answers for the least loaded of all resources, as reported by the KAL-AP keepalive process. The least-loaded balance method resolves the request by determining the least number of connections on a CSM or the least-loaded CSS.

Ordered List

When the GSS uses the ordered list balance method, each resource within an answer group (for example, an SLB VIP or a name server) is assigned a number that corresponds to the rank of that answer within the group. The number you assign represents the order of the answer on the list. Subsequent VIPs or name servers on the list will only be used if preceding VIPs or name servers are unavailable.

Round Robin

When the GSS uses the round robin balance method, each resource within an answer group is tried in turn. The GSS cycles through the list of answers and selects the next answer in line for each request. In this way, the GSS can resolve requests by evenly distributing the load among possible answers.

Weighted Round Robin

With the weighted round robin balancing method, the GSS tries each answer in turn. However, weight is associated to specific answers, providing preference over the answers with less weight when cycling through the list. If a weight of 2 is given to an answer, the GSS will return the answer twice as opposed to once for a weight of 1.

Boomerang (DNS Race)

The boomerang method is used by the GSS and is based on the concept that instantaneous proximity can be determined if a content routing agent (CRA) within each data center sends an A record (IP address) at the exact same time to the client's DNS server. The DNS race method of DNS resolution gives all CRAs (such as Cisco Content Engines (CEs) or Content Services Switches (CSSs)) a chance at resolving a client request and allows for proximity to be determined without probing the client's DNS server. The A record received first by the client's DNS server is, by default, considered to be the most proximate.

GSS Domains

A hosted domain is any domain or subdomain that has been delegated to the GSS and configured using the primary GSSM GUI for DNS query responses. A hosted domain is a DNS domain name for which the GSS is authoritative. All DNS queries must match a domain that belongs to a configured domain list, or the GSS denies the query. Queries that do not match domains on any GSS domain lists can also be forwarded by the GSS to an external DNS name server for resolution.

Hosted domains can correspond to standard third-level domain names but cannot exceed 128 characters in length. The GSS supports domain names that use wildcards. The GSS also supports POSIX 1003.2-extended regular expressions when matching wildcards. The following examples illustrate domain or subdomain names configured on the GSS:

```
cisco.com
www.cisco.com
.*\.cisco\.com
```

Domain lists are groups of hosted domains that have been delegated to the GSS. Each GSS can support a maximum of 2000 hosted domains and 2000 hosted domain lists, with a maximum of 500 hosted domains supported for each domain list.

By using a DNS rule, requests for any member of a domain list are matched to an answer, IP address of a resource hosting the content being requested, through one of a number of balance methods. Figure 12-12 shows the GSS hosted domain interface.

As the figure shows, the domain list and the matching domains are listed. On the upper left corner of the interface is where domains can be added or deleted as domain list members.

Figure 12-12 *GSS Hosted Domain Interface*

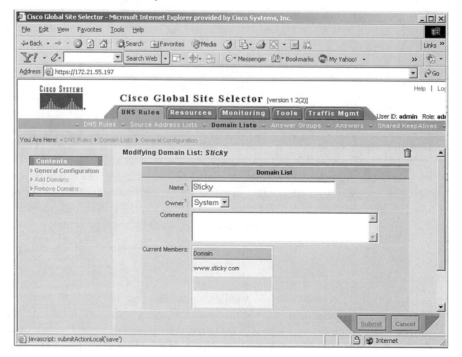

GSS Answers

Answers in the GSS configuration are used to resolve DNS requests that the GSS receives. The three types of possible answers on a GSS network are as follows:

- **VIP**—VIP addresses associated with an SLB device, such as the Cisco CSS, Cisco CSM, Cisco IOS-compliant SLB, Cisco LD, a web server, a cache, or other geographically dispersed SLBs in a global network deployment

- **NS**—Configured DNS name server on your network that can answer queries that the GSS cannot resolve

- **CRA**—CRAs that use a resolution process called DNS race to send identical and simultaneous responses back to a user's D-proxy

As with domains and source addresses, answers are configured using the primary GSSM GUI by identifying the IP address to which queries can be directed. Once created, answers can be grouped together as resource pools called answer groups.

From the available answer groups, the GSS can use up to three possible response answer group and balance method clauses in a DNS rule to select the most appropriate resource to serve a user request. Each balance method provides a different algorithm for selecting one answer from a configured answer group. Each clause specifies that a particular answer group serve the request and a specific balance method be used to select the best resource from that answer group. Figure 12-13 shows the GSS answer interface.

Figure 12-13 *GSS Answer Interface*

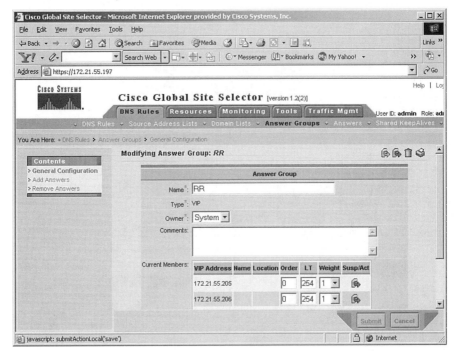

In the answers group configuration screen, the type of answers (whether it is a VIP, CRA, or NS type) and list of answers are configured. Figure 12-14 shows a screen shot of the configuration for the type of answer group.

On the upper left-hand corner, the already defined answers can be selected to be added to the answer list. When defining answers, the set of options illustrated in Figure 12-15 can be specified.

Figure 12-14 *GSS Answer Type*

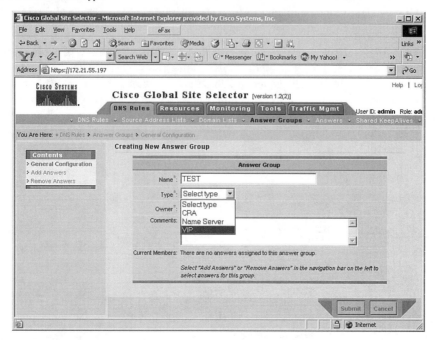

Figure 12-15 *GSS Answer Configuration*

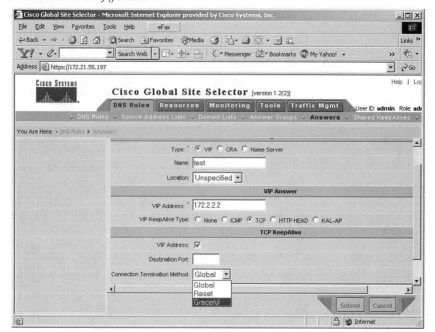

As you can see by the VIP Answer configuration, the VIP address and the keepalive type are to be specified. The kinds of keepalives and the parameters are defined in the following section.

GSS Keepalives

Associated to each answer there is a keepalive value that needs to be specified. A *keepalive* is a probe that the GSS periodically initiates to test to see if a resource is responding and a specific protocol on the device is functioning properly. If the handshake is successful, it means the device is available, active, and able to receive traffic. If the handshake fails, the device is considered to be unavailable and inactive. All answers are validated by configured keepalives and are not returned by the GSS for the DNS queries if the keepalive indicates the answer is not viable.

The sections that follow describe the different kinds of keepalives supported on the GSS.

ICMP Keepalives

The Internet Control Message Protocol (ICMP) keepalive type monitors the health of resources by issuing queries containing ICMP packets to the configured VIP address for the answer. Online status is determined by a response from the targeted address. The GSS supports up to 500 ICMP keepalives when using the standard detection method and up to 100 ICMP keepalives when using the fast detection method. Figure 12-16 shows the interface for the ICMP keepalive configuration on the GSS.

Figure 12-16 *GSS ICMP Keepalive Interface*

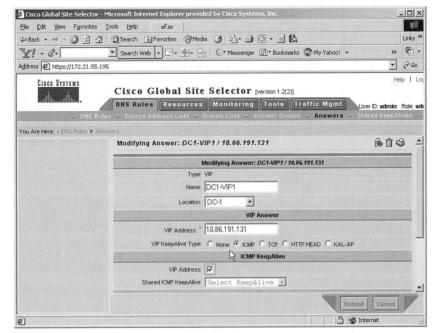

The figure shows the VIP address and the selection for the type of keepalive.

TCP Keepalives

The TCP keepalive initiates a TCP connection to the remote device by performing the three-way handshake sequence. Once the TCP connection is established, the GSS terminates the connection. The choice for the termination of the connection can be as follows:

- Reset (immediate termination using a hard reset)
- Graceful (standard three-way handshake termination)

The GSS supports up to 500 TCP keepalives when using the standard detection method and up to 100 TCP keepalives when using the fast detection method. Figure 12-17 shows the interface for the TCP keepalive configuration on the GSS.

Figure 12-17 *GSS TCP Keepalive Interface*

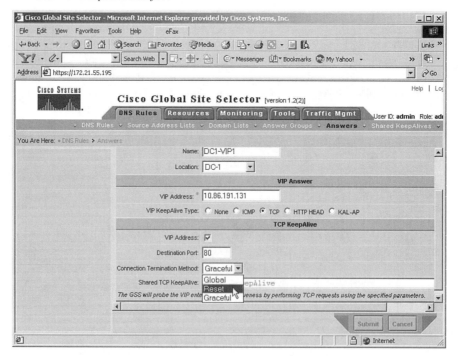

The figure illustrates the parameters for the TCP keepalive. The port and the connection close type for the keepalive are to be specified. Similarly, the rest of the keepalives have their own set of parameters that will be required when selected.

HTTP HEAD Keepalives

The HTTP HEAD keepalive type sends a TCP-formatted HTTP HEAD request to a web server at an address that you specify, returning the online status of the device in the form of an HTTP Response Status Code of 200 (for example, HTTP/1.0 200 OK). The GSS supports up to 500 HTTP HEAD keepalives when using the standard detection method and up to 100 HTTP HEAD keepalives when using the fast detection method.

KAL-AP Keepalives

The KAL-AP keepalive type sends a detailed query to both a primary (master) and an optional secondary (backup) circuit address that you specify, returning the online status of each interface as well as information on the specific VIP address or domain. The GSS supports up to 128 primary and 128 secondary KAL-AP keepalives when using the standard detection method and up to 40 primary and 40 secondary KAL-AP keepalives when using the fast detection method.

CRA Keepalives

The CRA keepalive type tracks the time required (in milliseconds) for a packet of information to reach the CRA and return to the GSS. The GSS supports up to 200 CRA keepalives.

NS Keepalives

The NS keepalive is used to query the IP address of the NS for a specified query domain (for example, www.cisco.com). The online status for the NS answer is determined by the ability of the NS for the query domain to respond to the query and assign the domain to an address. The GSS supports up to 100 NS keepalives.

None Keepalives

With the keepalive set to None, the GSS assumes that the named answer is always online.

GSS Resources, Locations, Regions, and Owners

In order to better manage the GSSs in a network, the features of specifying the resources, location, regions, and owners can be specified via the primary GSSM. The resources include other GSSs (secondary GSSMs, stand-alone GSSs), which the primary GSSM is aware of, and the keepalive properties, such as their pooling frequencies. The owners specify who manages and maintains a specific DNS rule, and the locations and regions allow better association to DNS rules and answers with respect to their actual geographic or logical locations and regions. Figure 12-18 through Figure 12-21 show examples of how the GSS resources can be assigned.

The GSS Resources tabs and options, shown in Figure 12-18, help manage other GSSs (for example, stand-alone GSSs and secondary GSSMs).

Figure 12-18 *GSS Resources*

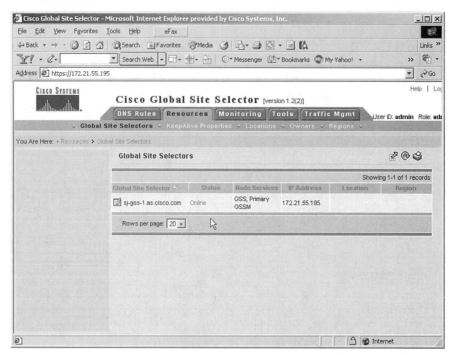

The GSS Locations options, shown in Figure 12-19, help define the administrative and organizational labels for the various GSSs in the network and where they geographically exist.

The GSS Owners options, shown in Figure 12-20, help define the administrative roles responsible for managing and maintaining the GSS.

The GSS Regions options, shown in Figure 12-21, help create the geographic regions, so that the GSS can be geographically administered by the correct owners in the specific region.

Figure 12-19 *GSS Locations*

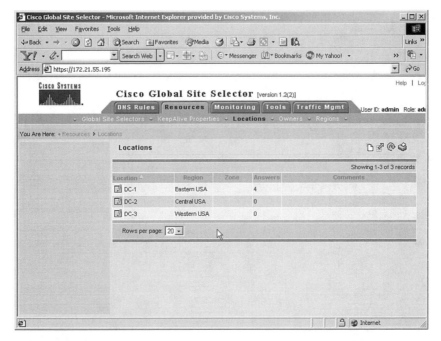

Figure 12-20 *GSS Owners*

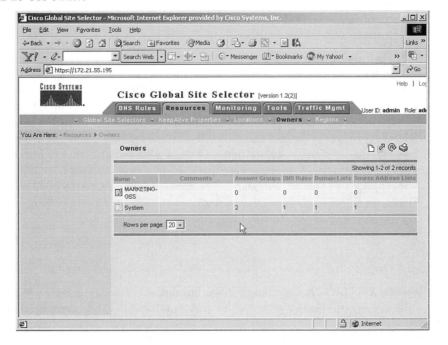

Figure 12-21 *GSS Regions*

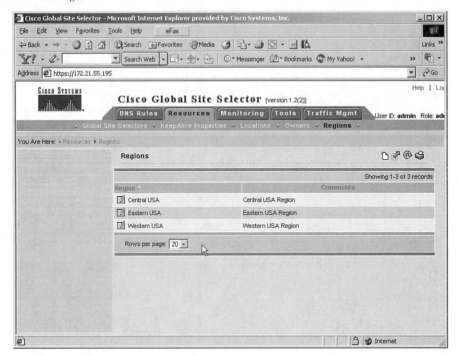

GSS DNS Stickiness

Stickiness, also known as having persistent connections or answers, allows the GSS to remember the DNS response returned for a client's DNS server and to later return that same answer when the client's DNS server makes the same request. With stickiness in a DNS rule enabled, the GSS makes a best effort to always provide identical DNS server responses to the requesting client's DNS server, assuming that the original VIP continues to be available. DNS sticky on a GSS ensures that e-commerce clients remain connected to a particular server for the duration of a transaction even when the client's browser refreshes the DNS mapping. While some browsers allow client connections to remain for the lifetime of the browser instance or for several hours, other browsers impose a connection limit of 30 minutes before requiring a DNS re-resolution. This time may not be long enough for a client to complete an e-commerce transaction.

GSS Network Proximity

With the GSS network Proximity feature, the closest or most proximate server based on measurements of round-trip time to the requesting client's DNS server location is selected. The GSS responds to DNS requests with the most proximate answers relative to the requesting client's DNS server. In this context, proximity refers to the distance or delay in terms of network topology, not geographical distance, between the requesting client's DNS server and its answer. To determine the most proximate answer, the GSS communicates with a probing device, a Cisco IOS-based router, located in each proximity zone to gather round-trip time (RTT) metric information measured between the requesting client's DNS server and the zone. Each GSS directs client requests to an available server with the lowest RTT value. Figure 12-22 is a screen shot of the network proximity configuration on the GSS.

Figure 12-22 *GSS Network Proximity*

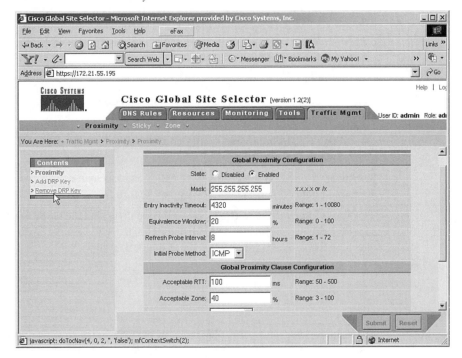

The network proximity on the GSS is based on the DRP, and the configuration for the DRP agent can be added on the upper left-hand corner.

Case Study: GSLB Solution Using GSS

Now that the various features and functionality of the GSS have been reviewed, a design study follows, explaining the detailed configurations and architecture for using GSS for GSLB deployment.

Requirements

Before examining the design details, here are the design requirements for a GSLB solution using GSS:

- Infrastructure requirements

    - **GSSM primary and secondary setup and communications**—The specific infrastructure requirements are for the primary and secondary GSSM to communicate with each other. The logical placement of the GSS should have connectivity between the DNS server and the load balancers.

    - **GSS redundancy**—The GSS should have redundancy in case the primary GSSM becomes unavailable, in which case the secondary GSSM should be able to service the DNS queries and take the role of the primary GSSM.

- Domains and application requirements

    Following are the requirements for the applications and domains configured on the GSS:

    - **Round robin load balancing**—All connections for specific domains should be load balanced equally.

    - **Stickiness for SSL connections**—All SSL connections for specific domains should be persistent to the same VIP address.

    - **TCP-based keepalives to the CSS**—All keepalives that the GSS initiates should check to see if the server is listening on the specified port, before returning the A record for the domain of that VIP address.

Topology

The topology in Figure 12-23 shows the placement of the GSS in the specific data centers. As the figure shows, this design is built around two data centers. The primary data center is where most of the applications reside, and the secondary data center contains the same applications. In the secondary data center, some applications are used for disaster recovery purposes and some are used for load sharing. The following sections describe the initial setup for the GSS and how the CSSs are configured accordingly.

Figure 12-23 *GSS Design Topology*

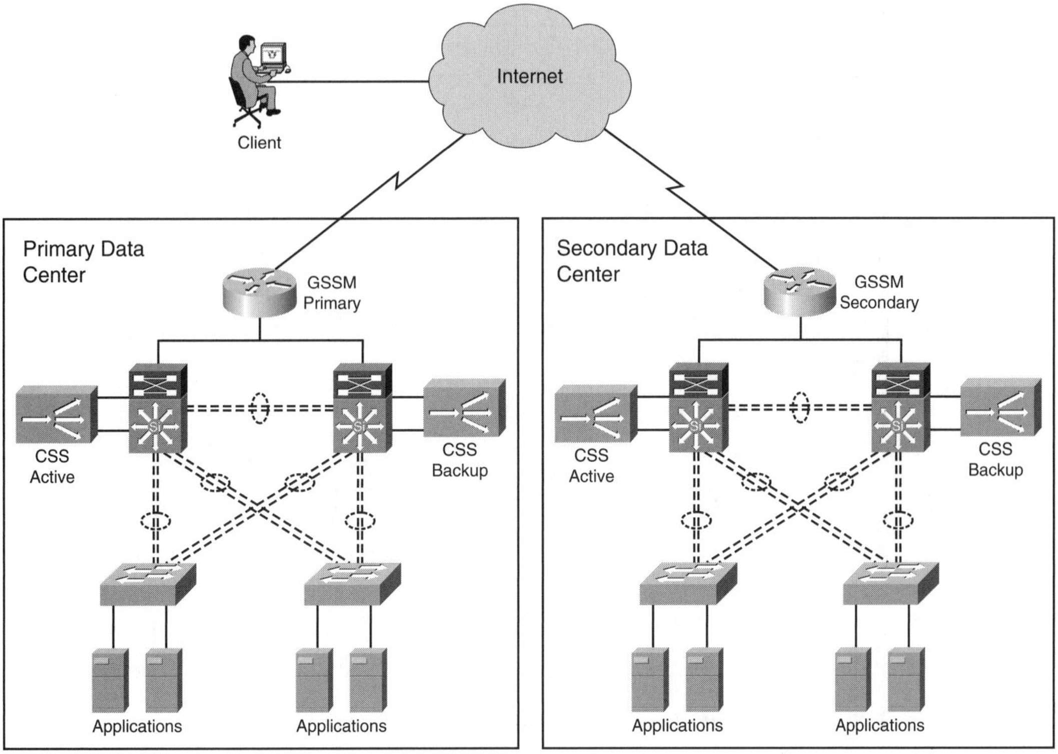

GSS Network Setup

Following are the IP addresses and domains hosted by the GSSs, as illustrated in Figure 12-24:

- **Primary GSSM**—IP address 172.21.55.197
  - 172.21.55.205 and 172.21.55.206 maps to www.roundrobin.com
  - 171.21.55.207 and 171.21.55.208 maps to www.sticky.com
- **Secondary GSSM**—IP address 172.21.55.198
  - 172.21.55.205 and 172.21.55.206 maps to www.roundrobin.com
  - 171.21.55.207 and 171.21.55.208 maps to www.sticky.com

Figure 12-24 *GSS GSSM Activation*

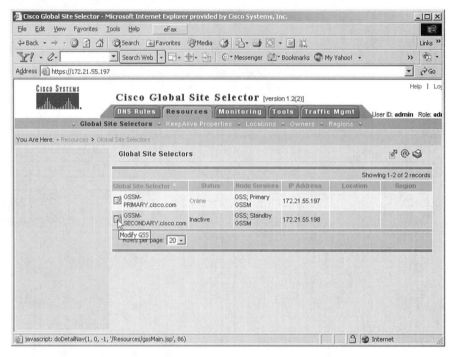

The following sections describe the initial setup for the GSSM.

Primary GSSM

The initial setup for the primary GSSM is as follows. (You can console into the GSS to start the configuration through the CLI.)

1 Specify the IP address:

```
GSSM-PRIMARY.cisco.com(config)#interface ethernet 0
GSSM-PRIMARY.cisco.com(config-eth0)#ip address 172.21.55.197 255.255.255.224
```

2 Enter these commands to use this interface for inter-GSS communication:

```
GSSM-PRIMARY.cisco.com(config)#interface ethernet 0
GSSM-PRIMARY.cisco.com(config-eth0)#gss-communications
```

3 Use the following command to specify the interface for the GSS to use to initiate the keepalives:

```
GSSM-PRIMARY.cisco.com(config)#interface ethernet 0
GSSM-PRIMARY.cisco.com(config-eth0)#gss-tcp-keepalives
```

4 Enter the following command to specify the default gateway for the primary GSSM:

```
GSSM-PRIMARY.cisco.com(config)#ip default-gateway 172.21.55.193
```

5 Enter the following command to enable the GSSM as the primary:

```
GSSM-PRIMARY.cisco.com#gss enable ?
```

```
gss          Enable GSS
gssm-primary Enable GSS as Primary GSSM
gssm-standby Enable GSS as Standby GSSM
GSSM-PRIMARY.cisco.com#gss enable gssm-primary
Note: GSSM database is required only on the primary GSSM and the
  standby GSSM.
Creating database. This may take a few minutes...
Generating certificates
Deploying certificates for interbox communications.
Generating certificates
System started. (Routing component waiting for configuration data (wait a
  minute).)
```

6 Issue the following commands to check the current status of the primary GSSM:

```
GSSM-PRIMARY.cisco.com#gss status
Cisco GSS - 1.2(2) GSSM - primary [Mon Aug 29 23:44:47 UTC 2005]
Normal Operation [runmode = 5]
 START  SERVER
 23:43  Boomerang
 23:43  Config Agent (crdirector)
 23:43  Config Server (crm)
 23:43  DNS Server
 23:43  Database
 23:43  GUI Server (tomcat)
 23:43  Keepalive Engine
 23:43  Node Manager
 23:43  Proximity
 23:43  Sticky
 23:43  Web Server (apache)
```

Secondary GSSM

The initial setup for the secondary GSSM is as follows.

1 Specify the IP address:

```
GSSM-SECONDARY.cisco.com(config-eth0)#ip address 172.21.55.198
   255.255.255.224
```

2 Enter this command to use this interface for inter-GSS communication:

```
GSSM-SECONDARY.cisco.com(config-eth0)#gss-communications
```

3 Use the following command to specify the interface for the GSS to use to initiate the keepalives:

```
GSSM-SECONDARY.cisco.com(config-eth0)#gss-tcp-keepalives
```

4 Enter the following command to specify the default gateway for the primary GSSM:

```
GSSM-SECONDARY.cisco.com(config)#ip default-gateway 172.21.55.193
```

5 Enter the following command to enable the GSSM as the secondary (where 172.21.55.197 is the IP address of the primary):

```
GSSM-SECONDARY.cisco.com#gss enable gssm-standby 172.21.55.197
Note: GSSM database is required only on the primary GSSM and the
  standby GSSM.
Creating database. This may take a few minutes...
Generating certificates
```

```
Deploying certificates for interbox communications.
Generating certificates
System started. (Routing component waiting for configuration data (wait
    a minute).)
```

6 Issue the following commands to check the current status of the secondary GSSM:

```
GSSM-SECONDARY.cisco.com#gss status
Cisco GSS - 1.2(2) GSSM - standby [Mon Aug 29 23:56:50 UTC 2005]
Registered to primary GSSM: 172.21.55.197
Routing component waiting for configuration data (wait a minute). [runmode = 3]
 START   SERVER
 23:52   Config Agent (crdirector)
 23:52   Config Server (crm)
 23:52   Database
 23:52   GUI Server (tomcat)
 23:52   Node Manager
 23:52   Web Server (apache)
```

GSS Secondary GSSM Activation

After logging into the primary GSSM, click the Resources tab, and select Global Site Selectors. As shown in Figure 12-24, the secondary GSSM will show up as INACTIVE. Click the Modify GSS button for the secondary GSSM, and on the next screen select Activate and click the Submit button (see Figure 12-25). The secondary GSSM will then show up as online, as shown in Figure 12-26.

Figure 12-25 *Modifying GSS Secondary GSSM*

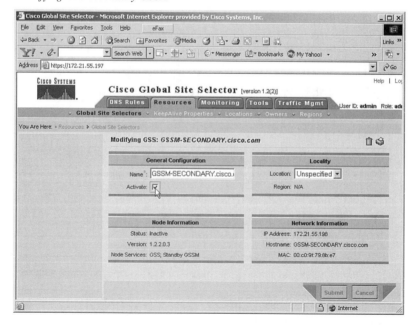

Figure 12-26 *GSS Secondary Online*

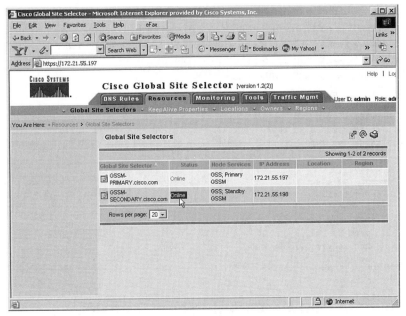

CSS Setup in Primary Data Center

The CSS in the primary data center for the www.roundrobin.com domain has a
VIP address of 172.21.55.205. The client VLAN on the CSS has an IP address of
172.21.55.203, and the server VLAN has an IP address of 80.80.80.203. The server's
IP addresses are 80.80.80.55–59. Example 12-1 shows the content rule and the service
configuration on the CSS in the primary data center.

Example 12-1 *CSS Content Rule and Service Configuration in Primary Data Center*

```
service simple-pri
  ip address 80.80.80.55
  keepalive type tcp
  port 80
  active
owner simple-pri
  content simple-80-pri
    protocol tcp
    vip address 172.21.55.205
    port 80
    add service simple-pri
    active
```

CSS Setup in Secondary Data Center

The CSS in the secondary data center for the www.roundrobin.com domain has a VIP address of 172.21.55.206. The client VLAN on the CSS has an IP address of 172.21.55.204, and the server VLAN has an IP address of 80.80.80.204. The server's IP addresses are 80.80.80.4–9. Example 12-2 shows the content rule and the service configuration on the CSS in the secondary data center.

Example 12-2 *CSS Content Rule and Service Configuration in Secondary Data Center*

```
service simple-sec
  ip address 80.80.80.4
  keepalive type tcp
  port 80
  active
owner simple-sec
  content simple-80-sec
    protocol tcp
    vip address 172.21.55.206
    port 80
    add service simple-sec
    active
```

GSS Setup for the www.roundrobin.com Domain

Before any configuration can be made to the GSS, the DNS servers that are currently authoritative for the www.roundrobin.com domain need to have two NS records pointing to the primary GSSM (172.21.55.197) and secondary GSSM (172.21.55.198).

The screen shots of the GSS GUI on the primary GSSM (see the following section) illustrate the process of configuring round robin load balancing for the www.roundrobin.com domain.

GSS DNS Rule Configuration for www.roundrobin.com

In the DNS Rules configuration, select the Rule Wizard button to allow the GSS to capture the input needed for creating a DNS rule, as illustrated in Figure 12-27.

The specific input required for creating DNS rules is as follows:

- The source address list of the client DNS servers that make a DNS query to the GSS
- The domain list (www.roundrobin.com, *.roundrobin.*, and so on) that would match the configured domain
- The answer groups and the VIP addresses for the domains
- The load-balancing method for returning the A records

Figure 12-27 *GSS DNS Rule Wizard*

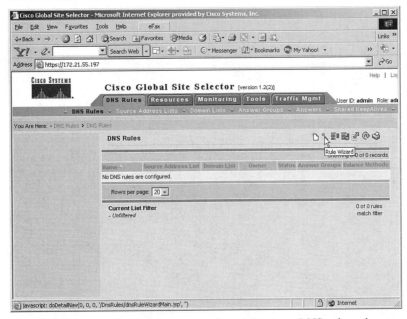

Figure 12-28 shows the steps necessary for setting up a DNS rule and answers using the Rules Wizard.

Figure 12-28 *GSS DNS Rule Wizard Steps*

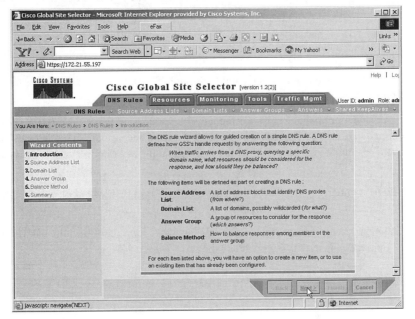

The first piece of input required is the DNS client's source IP address, as illustrated in Figure 12-29.

Figure 12-29 *GSS DNS Rule Source Address*

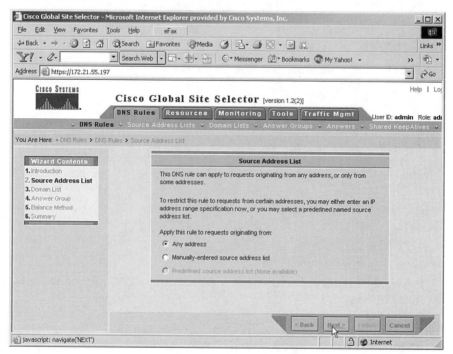

To allow the GSS to accept all queries, any source address is selected, or IP addresses can be entered in manually.

Next, the domain names associated with the DNS rule are entered. Figures 12-30 and Figure 12-31 show how the user inputs the domains used.

After selecting manual entry for the list, the domain list name and the list of domains are entered. In this case study, www.roundrobin.com is the domain that will be used. The owner in this example is the system, which is the default owner on the GSS. This is illustrated in Figure 12-31.

The next entry required is for the answer group. Figure 12-32 shows the Answer Group input screen.

The next screen prompts the user for the answer group name and the answer type. In this example, the answer type is VIP, as shown in Figure 12-33.

Figure 12-30 *GSS DNS Rule Domain Name Manual Entry*

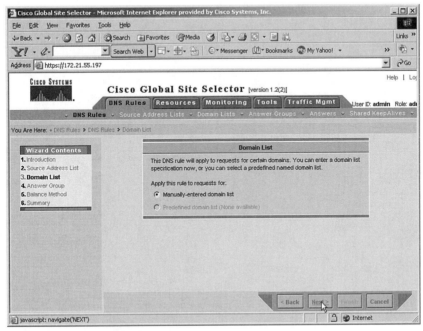

Figure 12-31 *GSS DNS Rule Domain Name*

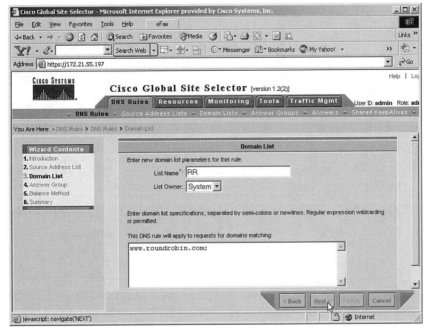

Figure 12-32 *GSS DNS Rule Answer for Manual Entry*

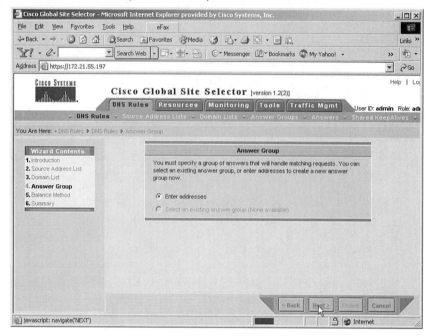

Figure 12-33 *GSS DNS Rule Answer Type and Name*

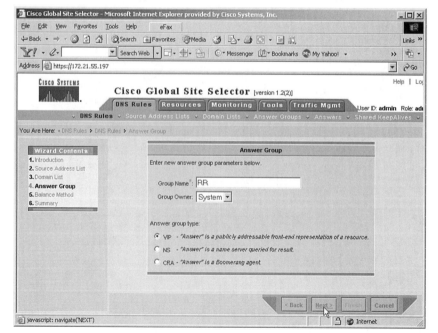

The next screen is where the actual VIP addresses get entered. As shown in Figure 12-34, both the VIP addresses (172.21.55.205 and 172.21.55.206) are entered. The weight and the order (that is, a Weighted Round Robin) would have been used if one VIP had been preferred over the other. However, in this case, the fact that the load-balancing algorithm is Round Robin indicates that the weight and the order are the same. If you are using KAL-AP with the CSS, the load is used to make decisions based on the load on the servers.

Figure 12-34 *GSS DNS Rule Answer Addresses*

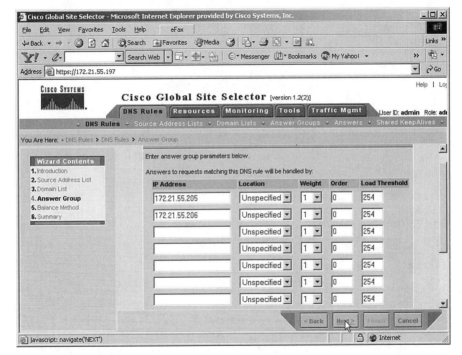

Following the answer input, select the balance method used for returning the VIP addresses. In our example, www.roundrobin.com, the round robin algorithm will be used, as shown in Figure 12-35.

Figure 12-36 shows a summary of the input provided for the www.roundrobin.com domain.

Once the DNS rule has been created, there are three answer group clauses associated to the DNS rule. These act as fallback methods if the first clause becomes unavailable. Figure 12-37 shows the three clauses (two of which are undefined).

Figure 12-35 *GSS DNS Balance Method*

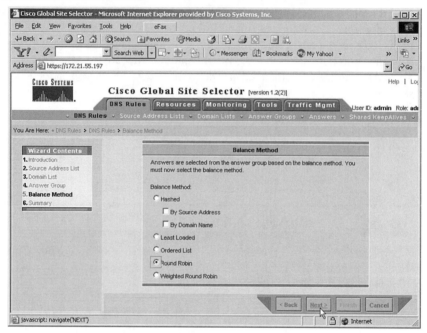

Figure 12-36 *GSS DNS Rule Summary*

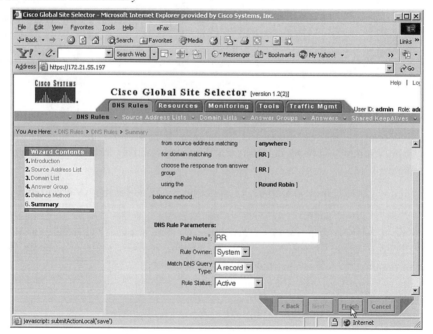

Figure 12-37 *GSS DNS Rule Clauses*

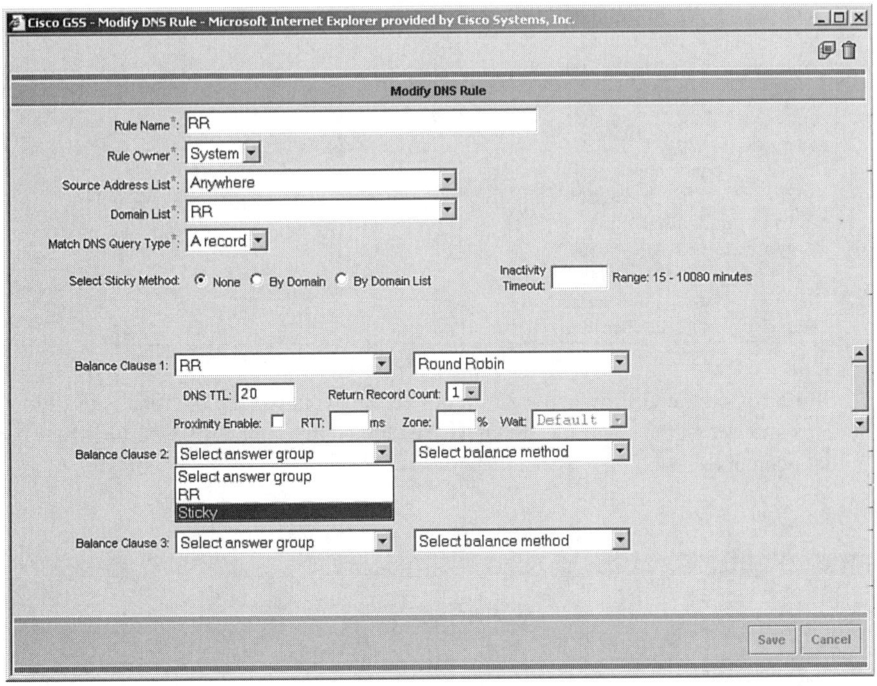

GSS DNS Rule Testing for www.roundrobin.com

As demonstrated in Example 12-3 (from a DOS prompt), when trying to resolve to www.roundrobin.com, the VIP addresses returned should be between 172.21.55.205 for the primary data center and 172.21.55.206 for the secondary data center, even when the primary DNS server is set to be the GSS in the primary data center.

Example 12-3 *DOS Output from Client*

```
D:\Documents and Settings\hkhan>nslookup
Default Server:  dns-sjk.cisco.com
Address:  171.68.226.120
> server 172.21.55.197
Default Server:  [172.21.55.197]
Address:  172.21.55.197
> www.roundrobin.com
Server:  [172.21.55.197]
Address:  172.21.55.197
Name:     www.roundrobin.com
Address:  172.21.55.205
> www.roundrobin.com
Server:  [172.21.55.197]
```

continues

Example 12-3 *DOS Output from Client (Continued)*

```
Address:   172.21.55.197
Name:      www.roundrobin.com
Address:   172.21.55.206
> www.roundrobin.com
Server:    [172.21.55.197]
Address:   172.21.55.197
Name:      www.roundrobin.com
Address:   172.21.55.205
> www.roundrobin.com
Server:    [172.21.55.197]
Address:   172.21.55.197
Name:      www.roundrobin.com
Address:   172.21.55.206
```

Similarly, on the GSS, when we monitor for answers we see the results in Figure 12-38. This shows that the request is being load balanced in a round robin fashion between the two data centers.

Figure 12-38 *GSS Answer Hit Count*

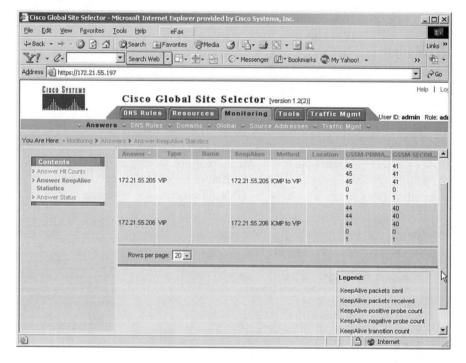

GSS TCP Keepalive for the www.roundrobin.com Domain

The default keepalive on the GSS is ICMP if one is not specified. However, the GSS has the capability to look at the TCP port information and initiate the keepalive based on a TCP handshake. To change the TCP keepalive type for the www.roundrobin.com domain, select the answer in the GSS Answers option under the DNS Rules tab, as shown in Figure 12-39.

Figure 12-39 *GSS TCP Keepalive*

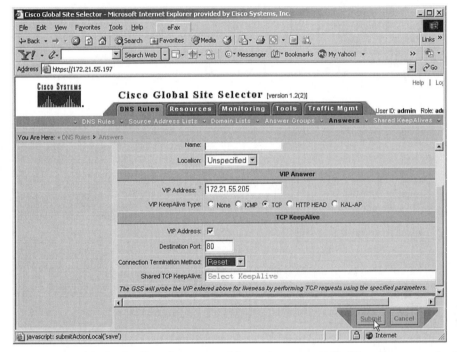

Since the VIP is also listening on port 80, you have to specify 80 as the port on the GSS for the TCP keepalive as well.

The GSS CLI command output in Example 12-4 can also be used to verify the status of keepalives. (This shows ICMP keepalives; the VIPs shown as OFFLINE are not yet configured on the CSS.)

Example 12-4 *GSS CLI Output and show Command for Viewing Keepalive Statistics*

```
GSSM-PRIMARY.cisco.com#show  statistics keepalive icmp all
IP: 172.21.55.206
Keepalive => 172.21.55.206
Status: ONLINE
Keepalive Type: Standard
Packets Sent:              104
Packets Received:          104
Positive Probe:            104
```

continues

Example 12-4 *GSS CLI Output and show Command for Viewing Keepalive Statistics (Continued)*

```
Negative Probe:              0
Transitions:                 1
GID: 92 LID: 2

IP: 172.21.55.207
Keepalive => 172.21.55.207
Status: OFFLINE
Keepalive Type: Standard
Packets Sent:               27
Packets Received:            0
Positive Probe:              0
Negative Probe:             26
Transitions:                 1
GID: 103 LID: 3

IP: 172.21.55.208
Keepalive => 172.21.55.208
Status: OFFLINE
Keepalive Type: Standard
Packets Sent:               25
Packets Received:            0
Positive Probe:              0
Negative Probe:             24
Transitions:                 1
GID: 101 LID: 4
GSSM-PRIMARY.cisco.com#
```

The output in Example 12-5 shows the TCP keepalive status on the GSS.

Example 12-5 *GSS show Command for Viewing TCP Keepalive Statistics*

```
GSSM-PRIMARY.cisco.com#show  statistics keepalive tcp all
IP: 172.21.55.205
Keepalive => 172.21.55.205
Termination Method: Reset
Status: ONLINE
Keepalive Type: Standard
Destination Port: 80
Packets Sent:               99
Packets Received:           33
Positive Probe:             33
Negative Probe:              0
Transitions:                 1
GID: 94 LID: 1
GSSM-PRIMARY.cisco.com#
```

GSS Setup for the www.sticky.com Domain

Before any configurations can be made to the GSS, the DNS servers that are currently authoritative for the www.sticky.com domain will need to have two NS records pointing to the primary GSSM (172.21.55.197) and to the secondary GSSM (172.21.55.198).

The two new VIP addresses for the www.sticky.com domain are 172.21.55.207 for the primary data center and 172.21.55.208 for the secondary data center. The key requirement for the domain is that the client making an HTTPS connection to the site should always make the connection to the first VIP address to which it connected, unless that address becomes unavailable. With the GSS sticky, the applications providing e-commerce services can maintain the same connection to the client when resolving the domain names to the GSS. While some browsers allow client connections to remain for the lifetime of the browser instance or for several hours, other browsers may impose a connection limit of 30 minutes before requiring a DNS re-resolution. This time period may not be long enough for a client to complete an e-commerce transaction. A new DNS resolution can then cause the client to connect to a server other than the original one, and this can disrupt the transaction. DNS sticky helps to ensure that a client completes a transaction if a DNS re-resolution occurs. The GSS collects requests from the client's D-proxies and stores these requests in memory as the sticky database. Requests may be identified by the IP address of the client's DNS server or by a database ID representing a list of D-proxy IP addresses.

The DNS sticky on the GSS can be configured as local or global. With local DNS sticky, each GSS device attempts to ensure that subsequent client DNS server requests to the same domain name and to the same GSS device will be "stuck" to the same location as the first request. DNS sticky guarantees that all requests from a client's D-proxy to a particular hosted domain or domain list are given the same answer by the GSS for the duration of a user-configurable sticky inactivity time interval, assuming the answer is still valid.

With global DNS sticky enabled, each GSS device on the network shares sticky database answers with the other GSS devices on the network, operating together as a fully connected peer-to-peer mesh. Each GSS device in the mesh stores the requests and responses from the client's D-proxies in its own local database, in addition to sharing this information with the other GSS devices on the network. As a result, subsequent client D-proxy requests to the same domain name and to any GSS in the network cause the client to be "stuck" to the same location.

For www.sticky.com, we will be using the local sticky database on the GSS 172.21.55.197. Figure 12-40 shows the screen shot used to enable the sticky database.

In the Mask field, you can enter a global subnet mask for the GSS to use to uniformly group contiguous client DNS server addresses in an attempt to increase the number of clients the sticky database can support. This mask is applied to the client source IP address before accessing the sticky database. The default global mask of 255.255.255.255 is used in this case.

In the Entry Inactivity Timeout field, you can enter a maximum time period for an unused answer to remain valid in the sticky database. This value defines the sticky database entry age-out process. Every time the GSS returns an answer to the requesting client's DNS server, the GSS resets the expiration time of the answer to this value. When the sticky inactivity timeout value elapses without the client again requesting the answer, the GSS identifies the answer as invalid and purges it from the sticky database. The default value is 60 minutes and will be used for the www.sticky.com domain.

Figure 12-40 *GSS Local Sticky Configuration*

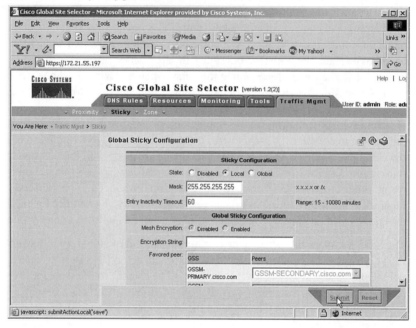

Next, the DNS Sticky rule needs to be enabled in order to use the sticky database based on the domain name, as illustrated in Figure 12-41.

Figure 12-41 *GSS DNS Server Sticky*

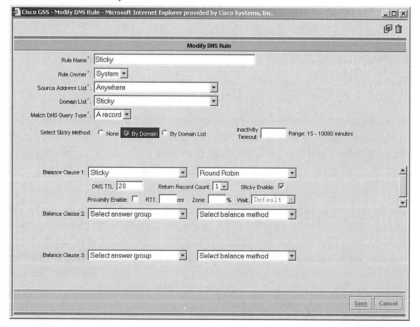

GSS DNS Rule Testing for www.sticky.com

As shown in Example 12-6, when trying to resolve to www.sticky.com, the VIP addresses returned should be either 172.21.55.207 for the primary data center or 172.21.55.208 for the secondary data center, even when the primary DNS server is set to be the GSS in the primary data center. Every time the resolution is done, the client will always be stuck to either the primary or the secondary.

Example 12-6 *DOS Output from Client Using nslookup Program*

```
> server 172.21.55.198
Default Server:  [172.21.55.198]
Address:  172.21.55.198
>
> www.sticky.com
Server:  [172.21.55.198]
Address:  172.21.55.198
Name:    www.sticky.com
Address:  172.21.55.208
> www.sticky.com
Server:  [172.21.55.198]
Address:  172.21.55.198
Name:    www.sticky.com
Address:  172.21.55.208
> www.sticky.com
Server:  [172.21.55.198]
Address:  172.21.55.198
Name:    www.sticky.com
Address:  172.21.55.208
> www.sticky.com
Server:  [172.21.55.198]
Address:  172.21.55.198
Name:    www.sticky.com
Address:  172.21.55.208
```

In the log in Example 12-6, the primary server is set to the GSS in the secondary data center, and the VIP is returned for the content rule in the secondary CSS. Every time the client tries to resolve the www.sticky.com domain, the client will be stuck to 172.21.55.208.

As demonstrated in Example 12-7, the **show sticky database all** CLI command on the GSS displays the Sticky database entry.

Example 12-7 *GSS show Command to View the Sticky Table*

```
GSSM-PRIMARY.cisco.com#show sticky database all
    Client/Group Domain/DL    Rule         Answer         SIT   TTL      Hits
--------------- ------------ ------------ ------------- ----- ----- ----------
   171.69.218.189 www.sticky.com Sticky        172.21.55.208   60    59
5
   Displayed 1 database entry.
```

Figure 12-42 from the monitoring window shows the sticky database entries.

Figure 12-42 *GSS DNS Sticky Stats*

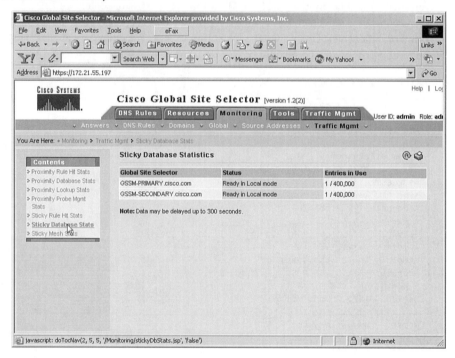

Configuration Details

Example 12-8 *GSS Configurations*

```
! GSSM Primary configuration
GSSM-PRIMARY.cisco.com#sh run
interface ethernet 0
   ip address 172.21.55.197 255.255.255.224
   gss-communications
   gss-tcp-keepalives
hostname GSSM-PRIMARY.cisco.com
ip default-gateway 172.21.55.193
ip name-server 172.21.55.131
no ssh keys
no ssh protocol version 1
terminal length 23
exec-timeout 150
logging disk enable
logging disk priority Notifications(5)
no logging host enable
logging host priority Warnings(4)
```

Example 12-8 *GSS Configurations (Continued)*

```
logging facility local5
tacacs-server timeout 5
tacacs-server keepalive-enable
GSSM-PRIMARY.cisco.com#
! GSSM Secondary configuration
GSSM-SECONDARY.cisco.com#sh run
interface ethernet 0
   ip address 172.21.55.198 255.255.255.224
   gss-communications
   gss-tcp-keepalives
hostname GSSM-SECONDARY.cisco.com
ip default-gateway 172.21.55.193
ip name-server 172.21.55.131
no ssh keys
no ssh protocol version 1
terminal length 23
exec-timeout 150
logging disk enable
logging disk priority Notifications(5)
no logging host enable
logging host priority Warnings(4)
logging facility local5
tacacs-server timeout 5
tacacs-server keepalive-enable
GSSM-SECONDARY.cisco.com#
```

Example 12-9 *CSS Configurations*

```
! CSS Primary Data Center configuration
CSS-Pri-3# sh run
!Generated on 08/31/2005 14:09:26
!Active version: sg0720305
configure

!*************************** GLOBAL ***************************
   ip route 0.0.0.0 0.0.0.0 172.21.55.193 1
!*********************** INTERFACE ***********************
interface  2/1
   bridge vlan 80
interface  2/2
   bridge vlan 52
!*********************** CIRCUIT ***********************
circuit VLAN80
   ip address 80.80.80.203 255.255.255.0
circuit VLAN52
   ip address 172.21.55.203 255.255.255.224
!*********************** SERVICE ***********************
service simple-pri
   ip address 80.80.80.55
   keepalive type tcp
   port 80
```

continues

Example 12-9 *CSS Configurations (Continued)*

```
    active
service sticky-pri
  ip address 80.80.80.55
  port 443
  keepalive type tcp
  active
!************************** OWNER **************************
owner simple-pri
  content simple-80-pri
    protocol tcp
    vip address 172.21.55.205
    port 80
    add service simple-pri
    active
owner sticky
  content sticky-pri
    protocol tcp
    vip address 172.21.55.207
    port 443
    add service sticky-pri
    active
CSS-Pri-3#
```
```
! CSS Secondary Data Center configuration
CSS-Sec-4# sh run
!Generated on 08/31/2005 14:08:29
!Active version: sg0720305
configure

!************************** GLOBAL **************************
  ip route 0.0.0.0 0.0.0.0 172.21.55.193 1
!************************ INTERFACE ************************
interface  2/1
  bridge vlan 80
interface  2/3
  bridge vlan 52
!************************* CIRCUIT *************************
circuit VLAN80
  ip address 80.80.80.204 255.255.255.0
circuit VLAN52
  ip address 172.21.55.204 255.255.255.224
!************************* SERVICE *************************
service simple-sec
  ip address 80.80.80.4
  keepalive type tcp
  port 80
  active
service sticky-sec
  ip address 80.80.80.4
  port 443
  keepalive type tcp
  active
!************************** OWNER **************************
```

Example 12-9 *CSS Configurations (Continued)*

```
owner simple-sec
  content simple-80-sec
    protocol tcp
    vip address 172.21.55.206
    port 80
    add service simple-sec
    active
owner sticky-sec
  content sticky-sec
    protocol tcp
    vip address 172.21.55.208
    port 443
    add service sticky-sec
    active
CSS-Sec-4#
```

Summary

GSLB has become an integral part of the disaster recovery solution for data centers. As more and more applications have requirements for minimum downtime, load balancing devices, such as the GSS, are providing unique features and functionalities to help manage and maintain the load and resiliency between many geographically dispersed data centers. One of the key solutions that the traditional DNS server does not provide is the link between the DNS process and the state of the applications, which the GSS provides in many different scenarios. The case study described the configuration and logical network details for deploying some of the features on the GSS.

In Chapter 13, "IP-Based GSLB Using RHI," we review other GSLB solutions based on IP, as well as the technique of injecting routes in the routing tables to direct traffic.

IP-Based GSLB Using RHI

Today's enterprises have strict requirements for high availability and application uptime that must be met through a business continuance and disaster recovery solution. Multiple data centers provide business continuance, disaster recovery, and load-sharing solutions. Some organizations use the Domain Name System (DNS) for managing business continuance and load sharing between data centers. However, organizations that do not want to make changes to DNS can use Interior Gateway Protocol (IGP)/Border Gateway Protocol (BGP) mechanisms for their business continuance and disaster recovery solutions.

This chapter introduces example topologies that use IGP/BGP for achieving site-to-site recovery and load distribution between data centers. It describes how IGP/BGP can be used to provide load-sharing, disaster recovery, and business continuance solutions and identifies some possible multiple data center scenarios. No change to DNS is required for any of the solutions described in this chapter. All solutions are based on Route Health Injection (RHI) on the Cisco Content Switching Module (CSM) and on IP routing.

Benefits of Using RHI

RHI, which uses the **advertise active** command available with virtual servers, tells the CSM to install a host route in the Multilayer Switch Feature Card (MSFC) on the same Catalyst 6500 chassis only if the virtual server is in *Operational* state. A virtual server is in the Operational state when at least one of the servers in the associated server farm is operational. Extensive probing is available on the CSM to check the health of the server and the appropriate application daemon that runs on the server. No change to DNS is required for solutions using RHI.

Architecture

The architecture described in this chapter uses two data centers with at least one data center connected to multiple Internet service providers (ISPs). The different scenarios discussed are as follows:

- Site-to-site recovery (active/standby data centers)
- Site-to-site load distribution (active/active data centers)

In the active/standby scenario, the traffic flows to the active data center as long as the routes exist for the application servers at the active data center. Traffic is routed to the standby data center only upon failure of the application servers at the active data center.

The active/active scenario includes two different implementations, differing in how the applications are deployed at the two data centers:

- Some active applications are deployed at each data center to provide a logical active/standby configuration for each application.
- All active applications are deployed at both sites.

Active/Standby Site-to-Site Recovery

In an active/standby data center solution, the applications are hosted on both the data centers; however, only one of the data centers is active. In a steady state, all traffic goes to the active data center; traffic is routed to the standby data center only when the active data center fails.

One way to implement an active/standby data center solution is by using the same IP addresses at two different locations within the enterprise network and advertising the IP addresses with different metrics from each location. The metrics determine the path taken by traffic to and from the network clients. This may be preferable to a DNS solution because it avoids the vulnerabilities of DNS record caching. This section describes how you can use BGP to direct clients to the primary site in an active/standby scenario, with no changes required to the DNS entries. The following scenarios are discussed in the site-to-site recovery category:

- Autonomous system (AS) prepending
- BGP conditional advertisements

The first scenario is probably the simplest to implement. The second solution is more sophisticated because the secondary path is advertised conditionally if the primary location goes out of service. To implement any of these solutions successfully, the cooperation of your ISP is required.

Figure 13-1 illustrates a simple topology for implementing site-to-site recovery solutions. The edge routers at both the primary and standby sites are connected to ISPs using Exterior BGP (E-BGP). Also, the two sites are interconnected by a link with Interior BGP (I-BGP) running between sites. The edge routers are running both IGP and BGP routing protocols. It is assumed that the rest of the internal network at both sites is running an IGP protocol and that the IP prefix of interest shows up in the routers at both sites. These routes must be redistributed into BGP so that clients trying to get to this IP address are routed to the primary site as long as the virtual IP (VIP) address is active there.

Figure 13-1 *Multisite Topology for Site-to-site Recovery*

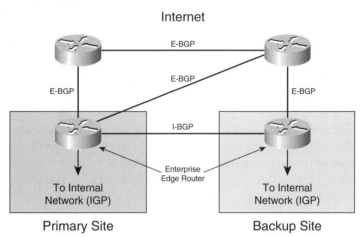

Autonomous System Prepending

The BGP best path algorithm follows a series of steps to determine the best route to a specific destination. One of the steps involves BGP looking at the AS path to select the best route. AS prepending causes AS numbers to be added to an advertised route. The lower the number of the AS in the path list, the better the route is considered. For a disaster recovery solution using an active and standby site, the routes can be prepended with AS numbers from the secondary site. When BGP goes through best path selection, the primary site will be chosen because it was advertised normally without a prepended AS.

AS prepending is suited for enterprises that own an entire block of IP addresses. The other caveat is that Cisco routers allow path selection based on the AS path being turned off, even though the RFC mandates its use for path selection. The following section describes how to use BGP attributes as an alternative to AS prepending.

BGP Conditional Advertisements

Cisco's implementation of BGP allows conditional route advertisement, which can be used for the site-to-site recovery solution. With this method, a certain condition must be met before advertisement occurs. A router at the secondary site monitors a list of prefixes from the primary site, and if the prefixes are "missing" from the BGP table then it advertises a set of specified prefixes. There is no ambiguity because only the secondary site advertises routes. The secondary site learns the list of prefixes from I-BGP between sites.

To make this work, you configure a conditional advertisement on both the primary and secondary sites. The conditional advertisement at the primary site facilitates the conditional advertisement at the secondary site. If the routes are simply redistributed into BGP from IGP and advertised to the I-BGP peer, the secondary site will also advertise the route and this defeats the purpose of conditional advertisement. For this reason, the router at the primary site advertises the prefix to its I-BGP peer with the community set to "no-export." This setting prevents the secondary site from advertising the route to its E-BGP peer. Also, the prefix is only found in the BGP table, so the condition required for advertisement is not met.

The conditional advertisement configuration at the primary site router stops the I-BGP advertisements if both ISPs fail at the primary site. This triggers the conditional advertisement at the secondary site router, which then advertises a more specific prefix. To implement this solution, make sure your ISP allows the advertisement of a block of IP addresses obtained from a different service provider.

Design Limitations

Both solutions advertise the same IP address from a secondary site based on certain criteria. If you do not own a block of IP addresses, your service provider must be willing to accept a route that belongs to a different ISP because the same IP address is being advertised from both sites. If you do own a block of IP addresses, the implementation is straightforward.

Exercise caution when using either of these solutions if the link connecting the primary and standby data centers has limited bandwidth, such as a serial link. Failure of both ISP links from the primary site will cause traffic to be directed to the secondary site through the ISP. The traffic then has to flow over a low-bandwidth link from the secondary site to the primary site, unless the active/standby roles are reversed. However, reversing the roles of the sites may not be desirable if the primary data center is just temporarily disconnected from the Internet. This is critical because the services appliances, such as server load balancers or firewalls, within the data center or site are stateful, so reversing the roles of the sites causes a loss of these session states. This results in the user session getting disconnected. Thus a site role switch should happen when all the servers within a site go down or when the link to the ISP goes down for a long duration.

Implementation Details for Active/Standby Scenarios

To use BGP for site-to-site recovery, the CSM will inject a VIP as a host route into the routing table using RHI. Typically, the data center network is set up as a stub network or a not-so-stubby area. Figure 13-2 illustrates how a route is injected from the data center, advertised into the enterprise core network, and redistributed at the edge router. Solutions differ based on how the routes are advertised from the edge to the ISP. Figure 13-2 also provides an illustration of the routing domains and how the test topology was set up.

Figure 13-2 *Routing Domains for Site-to-Site Recovery*

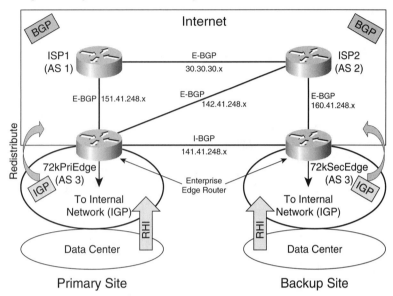

Configuration for the solutions in this section uses the following procedure:

1 Redistribute routes into BGP.

2 Configure filters to selectively advertise routes to BGP peers as necessary.

3 Perform configuration required for the specific solution.

Note that in all the topologies, the primary site is multihomed to two ISPs, which requires using Multiple Exit Descriptor (MED) to send a lower metric with the routing updates to ISP1 and a higher metric to ISP2 from the primary site edge router. In addition, you must set weights to prefer a specific ISP as the next-hop router for outgoing traffic.

AS Prepending

To implement this solution, complete the following steps:

1 Redistribute IGP routes into BGP at both data center sites.

2 Configure route maps or distribute lists to filter OSPF routes if necessary.

3 Configure route maps to perform AS prepending at the secondary site.

Figure 13-3 depicts the topology for AS prepending, which assumes that the routes of interest are injected into IGP using RHI.

Figure 13-3 *AS Prepending*

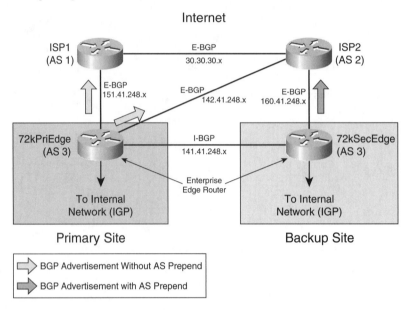

Primary Site Configuration

The two ISP neighbors are in AS 1 and AS 2, and the IP addresses are 151.41.248.129 and 142.41.248.130, respectively. The primary site is in AS 3 and has an I-BGP connection to the router in the secondary site. Example 13-1 shows this configuration (with the remote AS configured as 3).

Example 13-1 *BGP Configuration Example of the Primary Site*

```
router bgp 3
  bgp log-neighbor-changes
  redistribute ospf 1 route-map OspfRouteFilter
  neighbor 141.41.248.130 remote-as 3
  neighbor 142.41.248.130 remote-as 2
  neighbor 151.41.248.129 remote-as 1
  no auto-summary
 !
```

The OSPF routes are redistributed into BGP using the **redistribute** command. A route map is also configured and is used to selectively advertise the routes into BGP. There are different ways that you can do this. This implementation uses the **prefix-list** command. Example 13-2 shows the route maps and the prefix lists.

Example 13-2 *BGP Prefix List Configuration Example*

```
ip prefix-list OspfRoute seq 10 permit 130.34.0.0/16 le 32
ip prefix-list OspfRoute seq 15 permit 20.20.0.0/16 le 32
route-map OspfRouteFilter permit 10
 match ip address prefix-list OspfRoute
 !
```

The **match** statement in the route map matches all the IP addresses in the prefix list and selectively redistributes OSPF routes into BGP. The **ip prefix-list** command is configured as shown in Example 13-2. The first address, 130.34.0.0, is shown for demonstration purposes only. Note that the prefix of interest is 20.20.0.0. This is the prefix that will be advertised from both the primary site and the secondary site with different AS paths. There is no need for AS prepending because this is the primary site.

Standby Site Configuration

The standby site configuration shown in Example 13-3 is similar except for the addition of AS prepending.

Example 13-3 *BGP Configuration Example of the Standby Site*

```
router bgp 3
  no synchronization
  bgp log-neighbor-changes
  redistribute ospf 1 route-map OspfRoutes
  neighbor 141.41.248.129 remote-as 3
  neighbor 160.41.248.130 remote-as 2
  neighbor 160.41.248.130 route-map AddASnumbers out
  no auto-summary
 !
ip prefix-list DR-Applications seq 10 permit 140.36.0.0/16 le 32
ip prefix-list DR-Applications seq 15 permit 140.40.0.0/16 le 32
ip prefix-list DR-Applications seq 20 permit 20.20.0.0/16 le 32
 !
route-map OspfRoutes permit 10
 match ip address prefix-list DR-Applications
 !
```

The configuration for redistribution for the secondary site is similar to the configuration for the primary site. Note that the prefix of interest is 20.20.0.0. As Example 13-3 shows, an additional route map (AddASnumbers) is configured for all outbound advertisements. This route map is used when advertising routes to the neighbor 160.41.248.130. The route map is as follows:

```
route-map AddASnumbers permit 10
 match ip address prefix-list DR-Applications
 set as-path prepend 3 3 3
 !
```

Notice that the **match** command matches the prefix list, and the **set** command prepends the AS. When the route is advertised to the ISP, it shows up with multiple paths. Example 13-4 shows the output from the **show ip bgp** command on the second ISP router. Notice the prefix of interest.

Example 13-4 *BGP Table on the ISP Router Showing Multiple Next Hops for 20.20.20.0*

```
72k-ISP2#sh ip bgp
BGP table version is 47, local router ID is 160.41.248.130
Status codes: s suppressed, d damped, h history, * valid, > best, i - internal,
              r RIB-failure
Origin codes: i - IGP, e - EGP, ? - incomplete
   Network          Next Hop            Metric LocPrf Weight Path
*> 10.10.0.4/30     160.41.248.129           0             0 3 ?
*  20.20.20.0/24    160.41.248.129          20             0 3 3 3 3 ?
*                   30.30.30.129                           0 1 3 ?
*>                  142.41.248.129          20             0 3 ?
*  130.34.248.128/26
                    30.30.30.129                           0 1 3 ?
*>                  160.41.248.129                         0 3 ?
...
```

Three alternate paths show up as a result of dual-homing on the primary site. The prefix advertised from the secondary site has a longer AS path. The best path is indicated by ">" next to the asterisk on the third line and this is the prefix advertised by the primary site without AS prepending.

BGP Conditional Advertisement

Figure 13-4 illustrates conditional advertisement from two different sites.

Figure 13-4 *BGP Conditional Advertisement, Steady State*

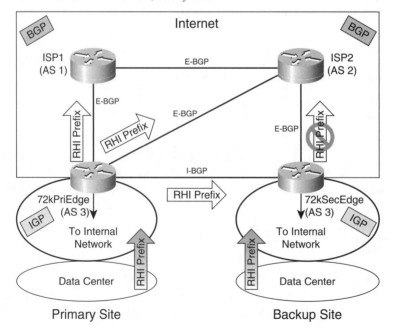

There are two different ways to use BGP conditional advertisement:

- Using the **advertise-map** command
- Using the **aggregate-address** and suppress-map commands

Both of these methods conditionally advertise routes based on the availability of routes in the BGP table. The implementation details for the second method are not discussed in this chapter. The difference between the two methods is that the two IP addresses are the same when using the **advertise-map** command, while they are different when using the **aggregate-address** and **suppress-map** commands. Details of the Cisco BGP conditional advertisement feature can be found at the following web page:

http://www.cisco.com/warp/public/459/cond_adv.html

To implement BGP conditional advertisement using the **advertise-map** command, complete the following steps:

1 Redistribute IGP routes into BGP at both sites.

2 Conditionally advertise the prefix of interest from the primary site into I-BGP.

3 The primary site will advertise the prefix of interest with a longer mask (a more specific route) to the E-BGP peer of the secondary site router if the prefix of interest is not in the BGP table of the secondary site router.

Figure 13-5 illustrates a conditional advertisement solution between the two sites in the event that the ISP links to the primary site fail.

Figure 13-5 *BGP Conditional Advertisement, ISP Failure*

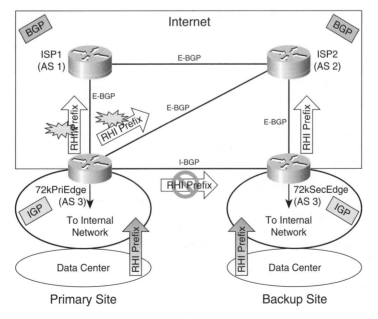

Figure 13-6 illustrates a conditional advertisement solution between the two sites in the event that the servers within the primary data center fail.

Figure 13-6 *BGP Conditional Advertisement, Data Center Failure*

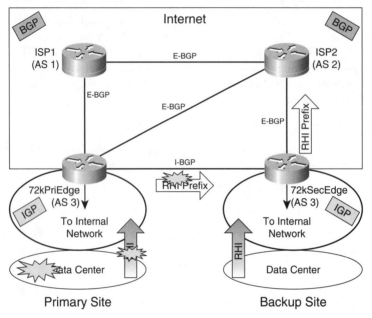

When the topology changes, it takes about 80 seconds for the BGP tables to become stable with default timers.

Primary Site Configuration

Example 13-5 shows the BGP configuration for the primary site. It is recommended to use redundant links for I-BGP connection. The details are not discussed in this chapter because this is a well understood concept. Also, the disaster recovery solutions in this chapter use interface IP addresses rather than loopback IP addresses for E-BGP and I-BGP peering.

Example 13-5 *BGP Conditional Advertisement Configuration Example*

```
router bgp 3
 no synchronization
 bgp log-neighbor-changes
 network 142.41.248.128 mask 255.255.255.192
 network 151.41.248.128 mask 255.255.255.192
 redistribute ospf 1 route-map OspfRouteFilter
 neighbor 141.41.248.130 remote-as 3
 neighbor 141.41.248.130 next-hop-self
```

Example 13-5 *BGP Conditional Advertisement Configuration Example (Continued)*

```
neighbor 141.41.248.130 send-community
neighbor 141.41.248.130 advertise-map ADV exist-map NON
neighbor 142.41.248.130 remote-as 2
neighbor 142.41.248.130 distribute-list 10 out
neighbor 151.41.248.129 remote-as 1
neighbor 151.41.248.129 distribute-list 10 out
no auto-summary
!
```

NOTE   When RHI is used, routes show up as E2 routes in the routing table. With BGP, the specific type of route has to be identified when redistributing routes. However, if prefix lists or distribute lists are used in the configuration, the route type does not matter.

In Examples 13-1 and 13-2, AS prepending was illustrated using the **prefix-list** command. For this configuration, the **distribute-list** command is used for each neighbor to prevent unwanted routes from being advertised. The **neighbor 141.41.248.130 send-community** command advertises the prefix with the community. This community is used at the standby site router to make decisions about advertising the prefix. Because you do not want to advertise this route to the E-BGP peer of the secondary router from the secondary site, set the community to "no-export" using the following commands:

```
route-map ADV permit 10
 match ip address prefix-list Adv
 set community no-export
```

The second route map is as shown here:

```
route-map NON permit 10
 match ip address prefix-list Non
```

The prefix lists, Non and Adv, are as follows:

```
ip prefix-list Adv seq 5 permit 20.20.0.0/16
!
ip prefix-list Non seq 10 permit 142.41.248.128/26
ip prefix-list Non seq 15 permit 151.41.248.128/26
!
```

The prefix of interest here is 20.20.0.0/16.

The distribute list refers to an access list, which has a list of all the prefixes that have to be filtered.

```
access-list 10 deny    3.3.3.0
access-list 10 permit 20.20.20.0
access-list 10 permit 130.34.0.0
access-list 10 permit 142.41.0.0
access-list 10 permit 151.41.0.0
access-list 10 permit 130.34.0.0 0.0.255.255
```

Standby Site Configuration

You must complete similar configuration at the standby site. You must also configure conditional advertisements on the standby site router. Example 13-6 shows the configuration at the standby site router.

Example 13-6 *BGP Conditional Advertisement Configuration Example on the Standby Site*

```
router bgp 3
 no synchronization
 bgp log-neighbor-changes
 redistribute ospf 1 route-map OspfRoutes
 neighbor 141.41.248.129 remote-as 3
 neighbor 141.41.248.129 next-hop-self
 neighbor 141.41.248.129 distribute-list 11 out
 neighbor 160.41.248.130 remote-as 2
 neighbor 160.41.248.130 distribute-list 2 out
 neighbor 160.41.248.130 advertise-map ADV non-exist-map NON
 no auto-summary
 !
```

Remember that route maps, distribute lists, and prefix lists can be used at the secondary site to control redistribution and peer advertisements. The conditional advertisement is provided by the following command:

```
 neighbor 160.41.248.130 advertise-map ADV non-exist-map NON
```

This command advertises the prefix specified in ADV if the prefix is missing from the NON route map. The route map configuration is as follows:

```
route-map NON permit 10
 match ip address prefix-list Non
!
route-map ADV permit 10
 match ip address prefix-list Adv
!
```

The prefix list configuration is as follows:

```
ip prefix-list Adv seq 5 permit 20.20.20.0/24
!
ip prefix-list Non seq 10 permit 20.20.0.0/16
!
```

The prefix in the list, Non, represents the advertisement from the primary. If this prefix is missing from the BGP table, the prefix specified in Adv is advertised. The prefix in Adv is more specific than the prefix in Non.

Example 13-7 shows the configuration for the redistribution of OSPF routes into BGP.

Example 13-7 *Configuration Example of Redistribution of OSPF Routes into BGP*

```
 !
 ip prefix-list DR-Applications seq 10 permit 140.36.0.0/16 le 32
 ip prefix-list DR-Applications seq 15 permit 140.40.0.0/16 le 32
 ip prefix-list DR-Applications seq 20 permit 20.20.0.0/16 le 32
```

Example 13-7 *Configuration Example of Redistribution of OSPF Routes into BGP (Continued)*

```
ip prefix-list DR-Applications seq 25 deny 10.10.0.0/16 le 32
!
route-map OspfRoutes permit 10
 match ip address prefix-list DR-Applications
 !
```

Make sure that you modify the OSPF weight at the standby site when redistributing routes
into BGP so it will not take precedence over a route learned from the I-BGP peer. The
required commands are as follows:

```
route-map OspfRoutes permit 10
 match ip address prefix-list DR-Applications
 set weight 0
 !
```

Example 13-8 shows the BGP tables on the ISP routers.

Example 13-8 *BGP Tables in ISP2 Router with Multiple Next Hops for 20.20.0.0*

```
72k-ISP2#sh ip bgp
BGP table version is 140, local router ID is 160.41.248.130
Status codes: s suppressed, d damped, h history, * valid, > best, i - internal,
              r RIB-failure, S Stale
Origin codes: i - IGP, e - EGP, ? - incomplete
   Network          Next Hop          Metric LocPrf Weight Path
*  20.20.0.0/16     30.30.30.129                        0 1 3 ?
*>                  142.41.248.129       20             0 3 ?
*  130.34.248.128/26
                    30.30.30.129                        0 1 3 ?
*>                  142.41.248.129       12             0 3 ?
*> 142.41.248.128/26
                    0.0.0.0              0           32768 i
*> 160.41.248.128/26
                    0.0.0.0              0           32768 i
72k-ISP2#
```

Note that the standby site does not advertise the prefix of interest as long as the ISP
links to the primary site are up. BGP points to the primary site as the best path. The other
path that was learned on this ISP router was over the link between the two ISPs.

When one ISP at the primary site goes down, the conditional advertisement is not triggered
at the standby site. Example 13-9 shows the BGP table at the second ISP, when one of
the ISPs went down at the primary site.

Example 13-9 *BGP Tables in ISP2 Router After ISP Failure in Primary Site*

```
72k-ISP2#sh ip bgp
BGP table version is 140, local router ID is 160.41.248.130
Status codes: s suppressed, d damped, h history, * valid, > best, i - internal,
              r RIB-failure, S Stale
Origin codes: i - IGP, e - EGP, ? - incomplete
```

continues

Example 13-9 *BGP Tables in ISP2 Router After ISP Failure in Primary Site (Continued)*

```
     Network          Next Hop          Metric LocPrf Weight Path
*> 20.20.0.0/16     142.41.248.129        20              0 3 ?
*> 130.34.248.128/26
                     142.41.248.129        12              0 3 ?
*> 142.41.248.128/26
                     0.0.0.0                0          32768 i
*> 160.41.248.128/26
                     0.0.0.0                0          32768 i
```

Example 13-10 shows the BGP table when both ISP links to the primary site go down.

Example 13-10 *BGP Tables in ISP2 Router After Failure of Both ISP Links in Primary Site*

```
72k-ISP2#sh ip bgp
BGP table version is 102, local router ID is 160.41.248.130
Status codes: s suppressed, d damped, h history, * valid, > best, i - internal,
              r RIB-failure, S Stale
Origin codes: i - IGP, e - EGP, ? - incomplete
     Network          Next Hop          Metric LocPrf Weight Path
*> 20.20.20.0/24    160.41.248.129        20              0 3 ?
*> 160.41.248.128/26
                     0.0.0.                 0          32768 i
```

Active/Active Site-to-Site Load Distribution

For site-to-site load balancing, you must use an active/active scenario in which both data centers host active applications. Applications can be active concurrently or can be hosted in a logical active/standby mode. Logical active/standby mode means that some applications will be active on the first site while those same applications will be in standby mode at the second site. Other applications will be active at the second site while those same applications will be in standby mode in the first site.

Support for logical active/standby mode depends on the capabilities of specific applications and databases. If this mode is supported, you can use IGP mechanisms to route traffic to the data center that is logically active for a specific application.

In an active/active data center solution, the applications are hosted on both the data centers and both the data centers serve client requests. Both the data centers use the same VIP address to represent the server cluster for each application, and the same subnet is advertised to the Internet with BGP. The routing infrastructure directs any client requests to the topologically nearest site. This mechanism is referred to as an Anycast mechanism, and it offers three major advantages:

- **Proximity**—Clients terminate at the closest data center.

- **Site stickiness**—Clients achieve "stickiness" and do not bounce between sites as a result of DNS or Microsoft Internet Explorer shortcomings.

- **Load distribution**—Clients are dynamically distributed between available sites.

Caution	The solutions discussed in this chapter require that the routing infrastructure be stable. *Route flapping,* a rapid fluctuation of routing information, could cause long-lived application sessions (such as TCP) to break.

Active/active load distribution between sites can be divided into two main categories:

- **Load distribution/balancing without IGP between sites**—In this scenario, there is no correlation between the configurations at the two sites from a routing perspective. Each site is independent of each other except for using the same VIP address for the applications. It is sufficient if the same route is advertised from two different sites. This simplifies the design because only internal IGP has to be configured based on how the applications are hosted.

- **Load distribution/balancing with IGP between sites**—The second topology for site-to-site load balancing is similar to Figure 13-6, except that a link is required between sites with enough bandwidth to carry the traffic between the sites. There are subscenarios that can be used to host active applications either based on the subnet or based on the applications. More details are provided in the following sections, later in the chapter:

    - "Subnet-Based Load Balancing Using IGP Between Sites"

    - "Application-Based Load Balancing Using IGP Between Sites"

    - "Using NAT in Active/Active Load-Balancing Solutions"

Implementation Details for Active/Active Scenarios

Each active/active scenario provides disaster recovery and load distribution, utilizing IP Anycast, BGP, IGP, and RHI. Subnet-based and application-based load balancing require a link, which makes it possible to route traffic between sites within seconds if either data center fails.

In the subnet-based design, the two sites are active at the same time, and the clients that get routed to a specific site terminate their connection to the data center at that specific site. If the data center fails at that site, the traffic is routed to the second site through the internal IGP. If the entire site fails, including the edge routers, external clients can still reach the second data center through the external network. The subnet-based implementation also provides a quick way to bring down the site for maintenance.

The application-based design logically partitions the data centers into active/standby sites. If the application environment requires it, the route metrics can be changed in the data center so that a specific VIP is active at one site and is on standby at the second site. This design also helps to load balance traffic for different applications between two sites.

Network address translation (NAT) can be applied to all three designs, but this is not within the scope of the chapter because each implementation of NAT requires design modifications. One application-based active/active design with NAT is covered in the section "Using NAT in Active/Active Load-Balancing Solutions."

OSPF Route Redistribution and Summarization

When redistributing RHI static routes into OSPF, use metric-type 1 for adding the internal cost to the external cost. This is essential in designs with IGP between sites. It is best to summarize the host routes on the MSFC in the same chassis as the CSM. Example 13-11 shows redistribution of static routes using metric type 1 and then summarization of these routes on the same router.

Example 13-11 *OSPF Example of Static Redistribution and Summarization of VIP Subnet*

```
cat6K_1#sh run | beg router ospf
router ospf 1
 log-adjacency-changes
 summary-address 24.24.24.0 255.255.255.0
 redistribute static metric-type 1 subnets
 network 10.0.0.0 0.0.0.255 area 0
 network 10.4.0.16 0.0.0.3 area 0
 network 10.4.1.0 0.0.0.255 area 0
 network 10.6.0.16 0.0.0.3 area 0
 network 130.40.248.0 0.0.0.255 area 0
!
cat6K_1#sh ip route ospf
     140.40.0.0/26 is subnetted, 1 subnets
O IA   140.40.248.128 [110/4] via 10.0.0.129, 01:32:02, Vlan10
     141.41.0.0/26 is subnetted, 1 subnets
O IA   141.41.248.128 [110/2] via 10.0.0.129, 01:32:07, Vlan10
     24.0.0.0/8 is variably subnetted, 4 subnets, 2 masks
O      24.24.24.0/24 is a summary, 00:02:21, Null0
     130.34.0.0/26 is subnetted, 1 subnets
```

The edge router receives the default route from the ISP and propagates it down to the data center MSFC. Example 13-12 shows what the OSPF configuration on the edge router looks like.

Example 13-12 *OSPF Configuration Example from Edge Router*

```
72k-edgePriDC#sh run | beg router ospf
router ospf 1
 log-adjacency-changes
 network 10.0.0.0 0.0.0.255 area 0
 default-information originate
!
```

Notice that in this configuration, the **always** keyword is not used. This means the edge router will advertise a default route in the OSPF domain only if a 0.0.0.0/0 route exists in its routing table.

BGP Route Redistribution and Route Preference

The edge routers distribute OSPF into their BGP process using a prefix list, and each updates its neighbor with these routes (most importantly 24.24.24.0/24).

This is slightly complicated for the edge router in this example, 72kPriEdge. The reason is because 72kPriEdge has links to both ISP1 and ISP2, to which the other edge router, 72kSecEdge, is connected. From 72kPriEdge, use MED to configure a lower metric for the route updates sent to ISP1 than for those sent to ISP2. As a result, ISP2 will always prefer 72kSecEdge for reaching 24.24.24.0/24.

You also have to set the weight for the inbound routes (0.0.0.0/0.0.0.0 routes) so that ISP1 has a higher weight (2000) than ISP2. As a result, 72kPriEdge will use the router at ISP1 for its default (next-hop) router.

BGP Configuration of Primary Site Edge Router

Example 13-13 shows the BGP configuration on the primary site edge router that will be used in all the active/active design scenarios. If there are any changes in this configuration, they will be highlighted in the appropriate design scenario section.

Example 13-13 *BGP Configuration on Primary Site for Active/Active Deployments*

```
72k-edgePriDC#sh run | beg router bgp
router bgp 3
 no synchronization
 bgp log-neighbor-changes
 network 142.41.248.128 mask 255.255.255.192
 network 151.41.248.128 mask 255.255.255.192
 redistribute ospf 1 route-map OspfRouteFilter
 neighbor 142.41.248.132 remote-as 2
 neighbor 142.41.248.132 route-map WEIGHT-IN in
 neighbor 142.41.248.132 route-map ISP2-OUT out
 neighbor 151.41.248.131 remote-as 1
 neighbor 151.41.248.131 route-map WEIGHT-IN in
 neighbor 151.41.248.131 route-map ISP1-OUT out
 no auto-summary
!
ip as-path access-list 2 permit ^2$
!
ip prefix-list OspfRoute seq 10 permit 130.34.0.0/16 le 32
ip prefix-list OspfRoute seq 15 permit 20.20.20.0/24
ip prefix-list OspfRoute seq 20 permit 24.0.0.0/8 le 32
access-list 10 permit 20.20.0.0 0.0.255.255
access-list 10 permit 130.34.0.0 0.0.255.255
access-list 10 permit 142.41.0.0 0.0.255.255
access-list 10 permit 151.41.0.0 0.0.255.255
```

continues

Example 13-13 *BGP Configuration on Primary Site for Active/Active Deployments (Continued)*

```
access-list 10 permit 24.24.24.0 0.0.0.255
!
route-map ISP1-OUT permit 10
 match ip address 10
 set metric 20
!
route-map ISP2-OUT permit 10
 match ip address 10
 set metric 30
!
route-map WEIGHT-IN permit 10
 match as-path 2
 set weight 200
!
route-map WEIGHT-IN permit 20
 set weight 2000
!
route-map OspfRouteFilter permit 10
 match ip address prefix-list OspfRoute
!
```

BGP Configuration of Secondary Site Edge Router

Example 13-14 shows the BGP configuration on the secondary site edge router that will be used in all the active/active design scenarios. If there are any changes in this configuration, they will be highlighted in the appropriate design scenario section.

Example 13-14 *BGP Configuration on Secondary Site for Active/Active Deployments*

```
72k-edgeSecDC#sh run | beg router bgp
router bgp 3
 no synchronization
 bgp log-neighbor-changes
 network 160.41.248.128 mask 255.255.255.192
 redistribute ospf 1 route-map OspfRouteFilter
 neighbor 160.41.248.132 remote-as 2
 neighbor 160.41.248.132 route-map ISP2-OUT out
 no auto-summary
!
ip prefix-list OspfRoute seq 10 permit 140.40.0.0/16 le 32
ip prefix-list OspfRoute seq 15 permit 20.20.20.0/24
ip prefix-list OspfRoute seq 20 permit 24.0.0.0/8 le 32
!
access-list 10 permit 20.20.0.0 0.0.255.255
access-list 10 permit 24.24.24.0 0.0.0.255
!
!
route-map ISP2-OUT permit 10
 match ip address 10
 set metric 20
!
```

Example 13-14 *BGP Configuration on Secondary Site for Active/Active Deployments (Continued)*

```
!
route-map OspfRouteFilter permit 10
 match ip address prefix-list OspfRoute
 !
 !
```

Load Balancing Without IGP Between Sites

Before using the instructions in this section to implement the load-balancing solution without IGP, complete the general configuration described in the previous sections:

- "OSPF Route Redistribution and Summarization"
- "BGP Route Redistribution and Route Preference"

Figure 13-7 illustrates a load-balancing solution without IGP, which is the simplest design discussed in this chapter. In this design, the benefits of IP Anycast can be obtained without making any physical changes to the network environment.

Figure 13-7 *Load Balancing Without IGP*

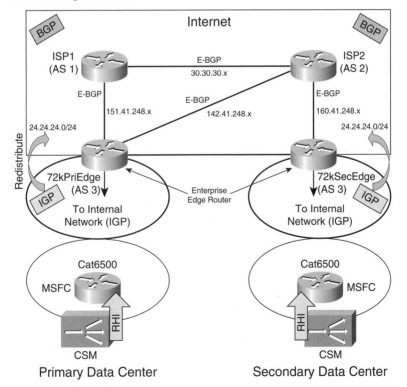

In this design, the CSM is used in both data centers for server load balancing. RHI is enabled so that the CSM injects a host static route into the MSFC on the same Catalyst 6500 chassis. These routes are redistributed and summarized in OSPF. OSPF is redistributed into BGP on the edge routers. The link between 72kPriEdge and ISP2 is only used for redundancy. This shows how to control incoming and outgoing routes in BGP using weights and how to prefer routes using MEDs.

Routes During Steady State

Following is the steady state routes on the ISP1 and ISP2 routers connected to our primary and standby sites.

Example 13-15 *BGP Routes in ISP1 and ISP2 Routers During Steady State*

```
Cat6k-ISP1#sh ip bgp 24.24.24.0
BGP routing table entry for 24.24.24.0/24, version 40
Paths: (2 available, best #1)
  Advertised to non peer-group peers:
  30.30.30.132
  3
    151.41.248.129 from 151.41.248.129 (151.41.248.129)
      Origin incomplete, metric 20, localpref 100, valid, external, best
  2 3
    30.30.30.132 from 30.30.30.132 (160.41.248.132)
      Origin incomplete, localpref 100, valid, external
Cat6k-ISP1#
```

```
72k-ISP2#sh ip bgp 24.24.24.0
BGP routing table entry for 24.24.24.0/24, version 27
Paths: (3 available, best #3, table Default-IP-Routing-Table)
  Advertised to non peer-group peers:
  30.30.30.131 142.41.248.129
  1 3
    30.30.30.131 from 30.30.30.131 (151.41.248.131)
      Origin incomplete, localpref 100, valid, external
  3
    142.41.248.129 from 142.41.248.129 (151.41.248.129)
      Origin incomplete, metric 30, localpref 100, valid, external
  3
    160.41.248.130 from 160.41.248.130 (160.41.248.130)
      Origin incomplete, metric 20, localpref 100, valid, external, best
72k-ISP2#
72k-ISP2#
```

Routes After All Servers on the Primary Site Are Down

Notice in Example 13-16 that the 24.24.24.0/24 routes that point to 151.41.248.129 on ISP1 and those that point to 142.41.248.129 on ISP2 are removed. This is because the primary site edge router stopped receiving routes from the connected MSFC. These changes were triggered by the CSM removing the routes from the MSFC when it determined that the servers were down.

In our testing with minimal routes in the ISP routers, these BGP routes were removed in less then five seconds. Convergence would be higher in a production network.

Example 13-16 *BGP Routes in ISP1 and ISP2 Routers After Primary Site Failure*

```
Cat6k-ISP1#sh ip bgp 24.24.24.0
BGP routing table entry for 24.24.24.0/24, version 42
Paths: (1 available, best #1)
Flag: 0x820
  Advertised to non peer-group peers:
  151.41.248.129
  2 3
    30.30.30.132 from 30.30.30.132 (160.41.248.132)
      Origin incomplete, localpref 100, valid, external, best
Cat6k-ISP1#
72k-ISP2#sh ip bgp 24.24.24.0
BGP routing table entry for 24.24.24.0/24, version 27
Paths: (1 available, best #1, table Default-IP-Routing-Table)
  Advertised to non peer-group peers:
  30.30.30.131 142.41.248.129
  3
    160.41.248.130 from 160.41.248.130 (160.41.248.130)
      Origin incomplete, metric 20, localpref 100, valid, external, best
72k-ISP2#
```

Limitations and Restrictions

The limitations and restrictions you should consider when implementing this design include the following:

- All applications that have VIPs within the announced subnet (24.24.24.0, in the example 13-16) must have front-end/back-end servers in production at both sites.
- A site cannot be easily taken out of service for maintenance. Routes need to be pulled from the BGP routing table for the site to be taken out of service. This can be done using one of the following methods:
  - By changing **router bgp** configurations on the edge router
  - By changing **router ospf** configurations on the edge router or data center MSFC
  - By taking all the relevant virtual servers out of service (**no inservice**) on the CSMs
- Long-lived TCP applications may break due to instability in the routing infrastructure.
- If there is a Firewall Service Module (FWSM) in the data center between the CSM and the MSFC, RHI will not work. Appendix A provides details about the RHI feature.

Subnet-Based Load Balancing Using IGP Between Sites

Figure 13-8 illustrates a subnet-based load-balancing solution with a link between the sites and both edge routers running IGP. This design is an enhancement over the scenario without a link between the sites.

Figure 13-8 *Subnet-Based Load Balancing with IGP Running Between Sites*

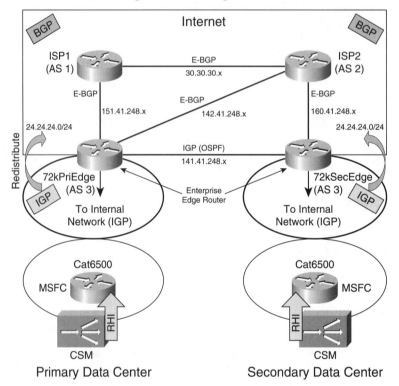

Changing IGP Cost for Site Maintenance

The main advantage of this solution compared to the one without a link between sites is that you can change an active/active design to an active/standby design on the fly by changing the OSPF cost of the link. This allows you to take the secondary data center out of service with a simple IGP cost modification.

For example, if the secondary data center needs to be brought down for maintenance without stopping BGP updates, just increase the OSPF cost on the link connecting the edge router to the internal MSFC. The traffic that comes in from ISP2 to the secondary data center can be forwarded to the primary data center over the link between sites. Internet clients and ISPs are not aware of any route changes. In most environments, this link between sites would have higher bandwidth than the path through the ISP. Example 13-17 shows the configuration for this scenario.

Example 13-17 *IP Routing Table Before and After OSPF Cost Adjustment*

```
72k-edgeSecDC#sh ip route 24.24.24.0
Routing entry for 24.24.24.0/24
  Known via "ospf 1", distance 110, metric 21, type extern 1
  Redistributing via bgp 3
  Advertised by bgp 3 route-map OspfRouteFilter
  Last update from 10.10.0.6 on FastEthernet4/0, 00:10:27 ago
  Routing Descriptor Blocks:
  * 10.10.0.6, from 140.40.248.130, 00:10:27 ago, via FastEthernet4/0
      Route metric is 21, traffic share count is 1
72k-edgeSecDC#
72k-edgeSecDC#conf t
Enter configuration commands, one per line.  End with CNTL/Z.
72k-edgeSecDC(config)#interface FastEthernet4/0
72k-edgeSecDC(config-if)# ip address 10.10.0.130 255.255.255.0
72k-edgeSecDC(config-if)# ip ospf cost 5
72k-edgeSecDC(config-if)#^Z
72k-edgeSecDC#
72k-edgeSecDC#
72k-edgeSecDC#sh ip route 24.24.24.0
Routing entry for 24.24.24.0/24
  Known via "ospf 1", distance 110, metric 22, type extern 1
  Redistributing via bgp 3
  Advertised by bgp 3 route-map OspfRouteFilter
  Last update from 141.41.248.129 on FastEthernet5/0, 00:00:12 ago
  Routing Descriptor Blocks:
  * 141.41.248.129, from 130.40.248.130, 00:00:12 ago, via FastEthernet5/0
      Route metric is 22, traffic share count is 1
```

Routes During Steady State

Example 13-18 shows the steady state routes for all the relevant devices.

Example 13-18 *Routes on Primary and Secondary Edge Routers and the ISP Routers During
Steady State*

```
72k-edgePriDC#sh ip route 24.24.24.0
Routing entry for 24.24.24.0/24
  Known via "ospf 1", distance 110, metric 21, type extern 1
  Redistributing via bgp 3
  Advertised by bgp 3 route-map OspfRouteFilter
  Last update from 10.0.0.6 on FastEthernet1/1, 00:08:57 ago
  Routing Descriptor Blocks:
  * 10.0.0.6, from 130.40.248.130, 00:08:57 ago, via FastEthernet1/1
      Route metric is 21, traffic share count is 1
72k-edgePriDC#
72k-edgePriDC#sh ip bgp 0.0.0.0
BGP routing table entry for 0.0.0.0/0, version 6
Paths: (2 available, best #2, table Default-IP-Routing-Table)
  Not advertised to any peer
  2
    142.41.248.132 from 142.41.248.132 (160.41.248.132)
      Origin IGP, localpref 100, weight 200, valid, external
```

continues

Example 13-18 *Routes on Primary and Secondary Edge Routers and the ISP Routers During Steady State (Continued)*

```
      1
         151.41.248.131 from 151.41.248.131 (151.41.248.131)
            Origin IGP, localpref 100, weight 2000, valid, external, best
   72k-edgePriDC#
   Cat6k-ISP1#sh ip bgp 24.24.24.0
   BGP routing table entry for 24.24.24.0/24, version 18
   Paths: (2 available, best #1)
     Advertised to non peer-group peers:
     30.30.30.132
     3
         151.41.248.129 from 151.41.248.129 (151.41.248.129)
            Origin incomplete, metric 20, localpref 100, valid, external, best
     2 3
         30.30.30.132 from 30.30.30.132 (160.41.248.132)
            Origin incomplete, localpref 100, valid, external
   Cat6k-ISP1#
   72k-ISP2#sh ip bgp 24.24.24.0
   BGP routing table entry for 24.24.24.0/24, version 7
   Paths: (3 available, best #3, table Default-IP-Routing-Table)
   Multipath: eBGP
     Advertised to non peer-group peers:
     30.30.30.131 142.41.248.129
     1 3
         30.30.30.131 from 30.30.30.131 (151.41.248.131)
            Origin incomplete, localpref 100, valid, external
     3
         142.41.248.129 from 142.41.248.129 (151.41.248.129)
            Origin incomplete, metric 30, localpref 100, valid, external
     3
         160.41.248.130 from 160.41.248.130 (160.41.248.130)
            Origin incomplete, metric 20, localpref 100, valid, external, best
   72k-ISP2#
   72k-ISP2#
   72k-edgeSecDC#sh ip route 24.24.24.0
   Routing entry for 24.24.24.0/24
     Known via "ospf 1", distance 110, metric 22, type extern 1
     Redistributing via bgp 3
     Advertised by bgp 3 route-map OspfRouteFilter
     Last update from 141.41.248.129 on FastEthernet5/0, 00:37:05 ago
     Routing Descriptor Blocks:
     * 141.41.248.129, from 130.40.248.130, 00:37:05 ago, via FastEthernet5/0
         Route metric is 22, traffic share count is 1
   72k-edgeSecDC#
   72k-edgeSecDC#sh ip bgp 0.0.0.0
   BGP routing table entry for 0.0.0.0/0, version 27
   Paths: (1 available, best #1, table Default-IP-Routing-Table)
     Not advertised to any peer
     2
         160.41.248.132 from 160.41.248.132 (160.41.248.132)
            Origin IGP, localpref 100, valid, external, best
```

Example 13-18 *Routes on Primary and Secondary Edge Routers and the ISP Routers During Steady State (Continued)*

```
72k-edgeSecDC#
72k-edgeSecDC#sh run int f4/0
Building configuration...
Current configuration : 100 bytes
!
interface FastEthernet4/0
 ip address 10.10.0.130 255.255.255.0
 ip ospf cost 5
 duplex full
end
72k-edgeSecDC#
```

Limitations and Restrictions

The limitations and restrictions you should consider when implementing the subnet-based load balancing design using IGP between sites include the following:

- All applications that have VIPs within the announced subnet (24.24.24.0, in the example 13-17) must have front-end/back-end servers in production at both sites.

- Long-lived TCP applications may break due to instability in the routing infrastructure.

- For RHI to function, the CSM needs to share a VLAN with the MSFC in the same Catalyst 6500 chassis.

- The internal path between the sites should not have any firewalls. If a firewall is present, it should be either a Layer 2 or Layer 3 firewall capable of running IGP (such as OSPF).

Application-Based Load Balancing Using IGP Between Sites

This application-based design is a further enhancement over the subnet-based design. In this design, we move the RHI host route summarization up to the BGP layer on the edge routers. The RHI host route for each application is given a different weight so that some applications are active on the primary site while others are active on the secondary site. You can keep an instance of the application at both sites for backup purposes, as required.

Weights are used on the data center MSFC to control active/standby behavior for the VIP for each application. Local active applications are given a lower metric compared to a remote application. For example, the primary site in this example is primary for 24.24.24.1 and 24.24.24.2, while the secondary site is standby. The secondary site is primary for 24.24.24.3, while the primary site is standby for this route and the associated application.

Configuration on all devices stays the same as in the previous scenario except for the configurations shown in Example 13-19 and 13-20.

Configuration on Primary Site

Following is the OSPF configuration in the primary site in both the MSFC on the Cat6500 where the CSM resides and on the edge router.

Example 13-19 *OSPF Configuration on the Primary Cat6500 and the Edge Router*

```
! Primary Data Center Catalyst 6500
!
router ospf 1
 log-adjacency-changes
 redistribute static metric-type 1 subnets route-map REMOTE-APP
 network 10.0.0.0 0.0.0.255 area 0
 network 10.4.0.16 0.0.0.3 area 0
 network 10.4.1.0 0.0.0.255 area 0
 network 10.6.0.16 0.0.0.3 area 0
 network 130.40.248.0 0.0.0.255 area 0
!
access-list 11 permit 24.24.24.3
!
route-map REMOTE-APP permit 10
 match ip address 11
 set metric 30
!
route-map REMOTE-APP permit 30
 set metric 20
!
! Primary Data Center Edge Router
!
router ospf 1
 log-adjacency-changes
 network 10.0.0.0 0.0.0.255 area 0
 network 141.41.248.128 0.0.0.127 area 1
 default-information originate
!
router bgp 3
 no synchronization
 aggregate-address 24.24.24.0 255.255.255.0 summary-only
 <SNIP>
 no auto-summary
!
!
```

Configuration on Secondary Site

Following is the OSPF configuration in the secondary site in both the MSFC on the Cat6500 where the CSM resides and on the secondary site edge router.

Example 13-20 *OSPF Configuration on the Secondary Cat6500 and the Edge Router*

```
! Secondary Data Center Catalyst 6500
!
router ospf 1
 log-adjacency-changes
 redistribute static metric-type 1 subnets route-map REMOTE-APP
```

Example 13-20 *OSPF Configuration on the Secondary Cat6500 and the Edge Router (Continued)*

```
 network 10.10.0.0 0.0.0.255 area 1
 network 10.14.0.16 0.0.0.3 area 1
 network 10.14.1.0 0.0.0.255 area 1
 network 10.16.0.16 0.0.0.3 area 1
 network 140.40.248.0 0.0.0.255 area 1
!
!
access-list 11 permit 24.24.24.1
access-list 11 permit 24.24.24.2
!
route-map REMOTE-APP permit 10
 match ip address 11
 set metric 30
!
route-map REMOTE-APP permit 30
 set metric 20
!
!
! Secondary Data Center Edge Router
router ospf 1
 log-adjacency-changes
 network 10.10.0.0 0.0.0.255 area 1
 network 141.41.248.128 0.0.0.127 area 1
 default-information originate
!
router bgp 3
 no synchronization
 aggregate-address 24.24.24.0 255.255.255.0 summary-only
 <SNIP>
 no auto-summary
!
!
```

Routes During Steady State

Following is the OSPF configuration in the primary site in both the MSFC on the Cat6500 where the CSM resides and on the edge router.

Example 13-21 *IP Routes in Primary and Secondary Edge Routers During Steady State*

```
! Primary Edge Router
72k-edgePriDC#sh ip route | in 24.24.24
B       24.24.24.0/24 [200/0] via 0.0.0.0, 00:14:45, Null0
O E1    24.24.24.1/32 [110/21] via 10.0.0.6, 00:14:41, FastEthernet1/1
O E1    24.24.24.2/32 [110/21] via 10.0.0.6, 00:14:41, FastEthernet1/1
O E1    24.24.24.3/32 [110/22] via 141.41.248.130, 00:14:41, FastEthernet0/0
72k-edgePriDC#
72k-edgePriDC#
! Secondary Edge Router
72k-edgeSecDC#sh ip route | in 24.24.24
B       24.24.24.0/24 [200/0] via 0.0.0.0, 00:15:17, Null0
```

continues

Example 13-21 *IP Routes in Primary and Secondary Edge Routers During Steady State (Continued)*

```
O E1    24.24.24.1/32 [110/22] via 141.41.248.129, 00:15:13, FastEthernet5/0
O E1    24.24.24.2/32 [110/22] via 141.41.248.129, 00:15:13, FastEthernet5/0
O E1    24.24.24.3/32 [110/21] via 10.10.0.6, 00:15:13, FastEthernet4/0
72k-edgeSecDC#
```

Limitations and Restrictions

The limitations and restrictions you should consider when implementing the application-based load balancing design using IGP between sites include the following:

- Long-lived TCP applications may break due to instability in the routing infrastructure.

- For RHI to work, the CSM needs to share a VLAN with the MSFC in the same Catalyst 6500 chassis.

- The internal path between the sites should not have any firewalls. If a firewall is present, it should be either a Layer 2 or Layer 3 firewall capable of running IGP (such as OSPF).

Using NAT in Active/Active Load-Balancing Solutions

Figure 13-9 illustrates changes in the application-based design required for a NAT-based solution. This option is an enhancement that can be used in all the active/active load-balancing scenarios described in this chapter.

In this example, the VIPs used to represent the applications are private IPs that are NATed one to one to public IP addresses. For example, the private address 24.24.24.1 is NATed to the public address 124.124.124.1. In a production network, the 24.24.24.0 subnet would be in the 10.0.0.0 address space.

NOTE   To implement NAT on a design without IGP running between the sites, you have to use appropriate conditional advertisements when redistributing the configured static route into BGP. Otherwise, traffic may be lost.

All configurations stay the same except for the addition of IOS NAT configuration and the redistribution of the public IP addresses into BGP. For example, in the configuration in the next section, 124.124.124.0 is advertised to the external world by redistributing a NULL0 static route into BGP.

Figure 13-9 *Application-Based Load-Balancing Sites with IGP Running Between Data Centers*

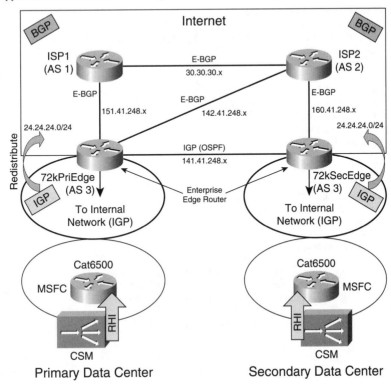

Primary Site Edge Router Configuration

Example 13-22 shows the IOS NAT configuration in the primary edge router. This includes the interface configuration, the one-to-one static NAT configurations, and the BGP static redistribution example.

Example 13-22 *IOS NAT Configuration Example on the Primary Edge Router*

```
interface FastEthernet0/0
 description "To 5/0 72kEdge(IBGP)"
 ip address 141.41.248.129 255.255.255.192
 ip nat inside
 duplex full
!
interface FastEthernet1/1
 description To cat6k-1 f2/26
 ip address 10.0.0.129 255.255.255.0
 ip nat inside
 duplex full
!
```

continues

Example 13-22 *IOS NAT Configuration Example on the Primary Edge Router (Continued)*

```
interface FastEthernet2/0
 description "To 2/13 Cat6k(ISP1)"
 ip address 151.41.248.129 255.255.255.192
 ip nat outside
 duplex full
!
interface FastEthernet3/0
 description "To 2/1 72k(ISP2)"
 ip address 142.41.248.129 255.255.255.192
 ip nat outside
 duplex full
!
!
router bgp 3
 no synchronization
 bgp log-neighbor-changes
 redistribute static
 <SNIP>
 no auto-summary
!
ip nat inside source static 24.24.24.1 124.124.124.1
ip nat inside source static 24.24.24.2 124.124.124.2
ip nat inside source static 24.24.24.3 124.124.124.3
!
ip route 124.124.124.0 255.255.255.0 Null0
!
!
!
```

Secondary Site Edge Router Configuration

Example 13-23 shows the IOS NAT configuration in the secondary edge router. This includes the interface configuration, the one-to-one static NAT configurations, and the BGP static redistribution example.

Example 13-23 *IOS NAT Configuration Example on the Secondary Edge Router*

```
interface FastEthernet3/0
 description "To 3/0 72k(ISP2)"
 ip address 160.41.248.130 255.255.255.192
 ip nat outside
 duplex full
!
interface FastEthernet4/0
 ip address 10.10.0.130 255.255.255.0
 ip nat inside
 duplex full
!
interface FastEthernet5/0
 description "To 0/0 72kPriDC"
 ip address 141.41.248.130 255.255.255.192
```

Example 13-23 *IOS NAT Configuration Example on the Secondary Edge Router (Continued)*

```
 ip nat inside
 duplex full
 !
 !
 router bgp 3
  no synchronization
  redistribute static
  <SNIP>
  no auto-summary
 !
 ip route 124.124.124.0 255.255.255.0 Null0
 !
 !
 ip nat inside source static 24.24.24.1 124.124.124.1
 ip nat inside source static 24.24.24.2 124.124.124.2
 ip nat inside source static 24.24.24.3 124.124.124.3
 !
 72k-edgeSecDC#
```

Steady State Routes

Example 13-24 shows the steady state routes on all the edge devices linked to each other—namely, the primary and secondary edge routers and the ISP1 and ISP2 routers.

Example 13-24 *Steady State Routes on the Primary and Secondary Edge Routers and the ISPs*

```
72k-edgePriDC#
72k-edgePriDC#sh ip bgp 0.0.0.0
BGP routing table entry for 0.0.0.0/0, version 57
Paths: (2 available, best #1, table Default-IP-Routing-Table)
  Not advertised to any peer
  1
    151.41.248.131 from 151.41.248.131 (151.41.248.131)
      Origin IGP, localpref 100, weight 2000, valid, external, best
  2
    142.41.248.132 from 142.41.248.132 (160.41.248.132)
      Origin IGP, localpref 100, weight 200, valid, external
72k-edgePriDC#
72k-edgePriDC#
72k-edgePriDC#sh ip route | in 24.24.24.
O E1    24.24.24.1 [110/21] via 10.0.0.6, 1d10h, FastEthernet1/1
O E1    24.24.24.2 [110/21] via 10.0.0.6, 1d10h, FastEthernet1/1
O E1    24.24.24.3 [110/22] via 141.41.248.130, 1d10h, FastEthernet0/0
72k-edgePriDC#
72k-edgePriDC#
72k-edgePriDC#sh ip route | in 124.124.124.
S       124.124.124.0 is directly connected, Null0
72k-edgePriDC#
72k-edgePriDC#
Cat6k-ISP1#sh ip bgp
```

continues

Example 13-24 *Steady State Routes on the Primary and Secondary Edge Routers and the ISPs (Continued)*

```
BGP table version is 6, local router ID is 151.41.248.131
Status codes: s suppressed, d damped, h history, * valid, > best, i - internal
Origin codes: i - IGP, e - EGP, ? - incomplete
   Network          Next Hop          Metric LocPrf Weight Path
*  124.124.124.0/24 30.30.30.132                        0 2 3 ?
*>                  151.41.248.129        20             0 3 ?
*  142.41.248.128/26
                    30.30.30.132          0              0 2 i
*>                  151.41.248.129        20             0 3 i
*> 151.41.248.128/26
                    0.0.0.0               0          32768 i
*                   30.30.30.132                         0 2 3 i
*                   151.41.248.129        20             0 3 i
*> 160.41.248.128/26
                    30.30.30.132          0              0 2 i
Cat6k-ISP1#
Cat6k-ISP1#
Cat6k-ISP1#
Cat6k-ISP1#sh ip bgp 124.124.124.0
BGP routing table entry for 124.124.124.0/24, version 2
Paths: (2 available, best #2)
  Advertised to non peer-group peers:
  30.30.30.132
  2 3
    30.30.30.132 from 30.30.30.132 (160.41.248.132)
      Origin incomplete, localpref 100, valid, external
  3
    151.41.248.129 from 151.41.248.129 (151.41.248.129)
      Origin incomplete, metric 20, localpref 100, valid, external, best
Cat6k-ISP1#
Cat6k-ISP1#
72k-ISP2#sh ip bgp
BGP table version is 16, local router ID is 160.41.248.132
Status codes: s suppressed, d damped, h history, * valid, > best, i - internal,
              r RIB-failure, S Stale
Origin codes: i - IGP, e - EGP, ? - incomplete
   Network          Next Hop          Metric LocPrf Weight Path
*  124.124.124.0/24 30.30.30.131                        0 1 3 ?
*                   142.41.248.129        30             0 3 ?
*>                  160.41.248.130        20             0 3 ?
*  142.41.248.128/26
                    30.30.30.131                         0 1 3 i
*>                  0.0.0.0               0          32768 i
*                   142.41.248.129        30             0 3 i
*  151.41.248.128/26
                    30.30.30.131          0              0 1 i
*>                  142.41.248.129        30             0 3 i
*> 160.41.248.128/26
                    0.0.0.0               0          32768 i
72k-ISP2#
72k-ISP2#
72k-ISP2#sh ip bgp 124.124.124.0
```

Example 13-24 *Steady State Routes on the Primary and Secondary Edge Routers and the ISPs (Continued)*

```
BGP routing table entry for 124.124.124.0/24, version 3
Paths: (3 available, best #3, table Default-IP-Routing-Table)
  Advertised to non peer-group peers:
  30.30.30.131 142.41.248.129
  1 3
    30.30.30.131 from 30.30.30.131 (151.41.248.131)
      Origin incomplete, localpref 100, valid, external
  3
    142.41.248.129 from 142.41.248.129 (151.41.248.129)
      Origin incomplete, metric 30, localpref 100, valid, external
  3
    160.41.248.130 from 160.41.248.130 (160.41.248.130)
      Origin incomplete, metric 20, localpref 100, valid, external, best
72k-ISP2#
72k-ISP2#
72k-edgeSecDC#
```

```
72k-edgeSecDC#sh ip bgp 0.0.0.0
BGP routing table entry for 0.0.0.0/0, version 25
Paths: (1 available, best #1, table Default-IP-Routing-Table)
  Not advertised to any peer
  2
    160.41.248.132 from 160.41.248.132 (160.41.248.132)
      Origin IGP, localpref 100, valid, external, best
72k-edgeSecDC#
72k-edgeSecDC#
72k-edgeSecDC#sh ip route ¦ in 24.24.24.
O E1    24.24.24.1 [110/22] via 141.41.248.129, 1d10h, FastEthernet5/0
O E1    24.24.24.2 [110/22] via 141.41.248.129, 1d10h, FastEthernet5/0
O E1    24.24.24.3 [110/21] via 10.10.0.6, 1d10h, FastEthernet4/0
72k-edgeSecDC#
72k-edgeSecDC#sh ip route ¦ in 124.124.124.
S       124.124.124.0 is directly connected, Null0
72k-edgeSecDC#
72k-edgeSecDC#
```

```
3500AP#
3500AP#traceroute 124.124.124.1
Type escape sequence to abort.
Tracing the route to 124.124.124.1
  1 55.55.1.1 5 msec 2 msec 3 msec              (ISP1)
  2 151.41.248.129 2 msec 2 msec 3 msec    (Primary Site Edge Router)
  3 10.0.0.6 3 msec 6 msec 2 msec      (Primary Site Data Center)
  4  *  *  *
```

Routes When Servers in Primary Data Center Goes Down

When the servers in the primary data center go down, there are no route changes on either of the ISPs. Client traffic will reach both sites and take the internal path from the primary to the secondary site. Example 13-25 shows the routes in the primary and secondary site edge routers and also a **traceroute** command from client to VIP.

Example 13-25 *IP Routes on Primary and Secondary Site Edge Routers with Primary Site Servers Go Down*

```
72k-edgePriDC#
72k-edgePriDC#sh ip route ¦ in 24.24.24.
O E1    24.24.24.1 [110/32] via 141.41.248.130, 00:00:31, FastEthernet0/0
O E1    24.24.24.2 [110/32] via 141.41.248.130, 00:00:31, FastEthernet0/0
O E1    24.24.24.3 [110/22] via 141.41.248.130, 00:00:31, FastEthernet0/0
72k-edgePriDC#
```
```
72k-edgeSecDC#
72k-edgeSecDC#sh ip route ¦ in 24.24.24.
O E1    24.24.24.1 [110/31] via 10.10.0.6, 00:00:46, FastEthernet4/0
O E1    24.24.24.2 [110/31] via 10.10.0.6, 00:00:46, FastEthernet4/0
O E1    24.24.24.3 [110/21] via 10.10.0.6, 00:00:46, FastEthernet4/0
72k-edgeSecDC#
72k-edgeSecDC#
```
```
3500AP#traceroute 124.124.124.1
Type escape sequence to abort.
Tracing the route to 124.124.124.1
  1 55.55.1.1 6 msec 5 msec 3 msec        (ISP1)
  2 151.41.248.129 2 msec 3 msec 0 msec       (Primary Site Edge Router)
  3 141.41.248.130 6 msec 2 msec 3 msec       (Secondary Site Edge Router)
  4 10.10.0.6 2 msec 3 msec 2 msec      (Secondary Site Data Center)
  5      *   *   *
```

Summary

This chapter introduced the concept of IP Anycast and described how BGP/IGP can be used to provide load-sharing, disaster recovery, and business continuance solutions. The chapter also identified some possible multiple data center scenarios with configuration examples.

All solutions presented in this chapter were based on RHI on the CSM and on IP routing. We discussed sample implementations of both active/standby and active/active data center solutions.

Chapter 14, "Scaling Server Load Balancing Within a Data Center," introduces the concepts, methods, and reasoning behind SLB environments within a single data center. Distribution of applications, use of DNS for same application scalability, and use of RHI are discussed in detail.

PART IV

Data Center Designs

Scaling Server Load Balancing Within a Data Center

Now that we have covered server load-balancing (SLB) functionality and design approaches in detail, we will focus on how a load-balanced environment can be scaled. With the passage of time as the user base increases, the key question that comes up is how to scale an application such that user experience is not compromised. Typically, an application is scaled simply by adding more servers to the load-balanced server farms within the same data center or by replicating the application in another data center. Having the same application exist in two in-service data centers achieves dual purposes—one being scalability and the other being disaster recovery. There are several ways to provide redundancy between data centers. These approaches were discussed in detail in Chapter 13, "IP-Based GSLB Using RHI."

This chapter introduces the reader to the concepts and design methodologies of scaling load-balancing services within a single data center. We will discuss how load-balanced applications can be scaled using DNS or IP and also how they are scaled when server capacity within a load balancer is maximized. In other words, we will cover how the same application is load balanced in two different SLB devices, the approaches to SLB device selection, and the methods of scaling when the servers within an SLB device have reached their maximum capacity or have failed health checks.

Benefits of Scaling Content Switching

The motivations behind scaling content switching within a data center are similar to the motivations for SLB. Scalability and performance are the main reasons behind SLB in general.

Scalability

A server load-balancing device can be fully utilized in connections per second, concurrent connections, probes or health checks to servers, slow path or process-switching performance, or software configuration limits. Once any of the above-mentioned functionality is maximized, another SLB device would have to be deployed.

Performance

Performance of the load balancer in terms of packet switching and raw throughput is another key reason to deploy multiple pairs of SLB devices in the same data center. To overcome performance limitations of the load balancer, one option is to design the SLB device so that only load-balanced traffic passes through the SLB devices. If this does not help, another pair of load balancers can be deployed for a different application or the same application. In the next few sections, we will discuss several design methodologies that can be used to scale SLB environments.

Figure 14-1 shows how multiple factors ranging from throughput, size of configurations, server health checks, and connections per second, to concurrent connections can lead to an SLB device getting oversubscribed.

Figure 14-1 *Scaling Server Load Balancers*

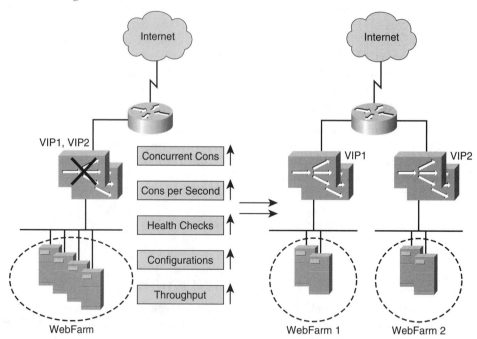

Scaling Methodologies

In this section we will introduce you to some of the design approaches and technologies that can be used to scale within a data center. The key scaling methodologies are distributing applications over multiple SLB devices using smart DNS to distribute the same application traffic over multiple SLB devices and using IP-based Route Health Injection (RHI) to distribute the same application traffic over multiple SLB devices.

Distribution of Applications

Distributing applications across multiple SLB devices is the simplest and the most manageable of all the design approaches. The idea is to segment an existing fully utilized SLB device's configuration with respect to applications. One set of applications will reside in the old SLB device, and a different set of applications will reside in a new SLB device.

In this approach, each application owner would have to service a particular SLB device. Routing infrastructure changes or DNS changes are not required.

Using DNS for Application Scalability

In a situation where the SLB device is overloaded by a single application, distribution of applications will not help. In that case, the particular application traffic will have to be split across multiple pairs of SLB devices. One way to do this is to host the application using different sets of server farms and different virtual IP (VIP) addresses on separate pairs of SLB devices. A smart DNS server (a DNS device that can do health checks and verify availability of the VIP addresses) can be used to distribute the users across the two VIP addresses being hosted on separate pairs of SLB devices.

A typical smart DNS appliance does have source IP-based stickiness or source IP-based hash functionality available that can be used to provide client persistence to a particular SLB device.

Using Route Health Injection for Application Scalability

In environments where the use of DNS is not desired and where the client base is internal, an IP-based load-balancing solution can be used to scale the SLB device. This design requires the application to be hosted using different sets of server farms but same VIP addresses on separate pairs of SLB devices. Based on the availability of the servers, the VIP address will be injected into the routing table of the directly connected Multilayer Switch Feature Cards (MSFCs), the router daughter cards on the Catalyst 6500 Supervisor module. This enables the routes to dynamically be part of the routing domain based on server farm health. This feature is called RHI.

If servers are operational in both SLB devices, then two host-based routes for the same VIP address will show up in the routing domain. As client requests are routed, they will end up at the SLB device closest to them in terms of routing metrics.

Application Distribution Approach

The application distribution approach is fairly straightforward conceptually. It requires the configurations of the SLB device to be split along the lines of different applications or business units. The segmented configuration resides on different SLB devices. The complex part of this approach is to distribute the server resources. The servers belonging to a particular application should have their default gateway pointing to the SLB device hosting that specific application. This becomes difficult when load-balanced servers associated with different applications reside in the same VLAN.

To ensure that load-balanced server return traffic traverses the appropriate SLB device, we can take several measures. These methods range from re-IP addressing and placement of the servers in appropriate VLANs behind the SLB device to redesigning the SLB environment to a one-armed design approach where the physical and logical presence of the application servers does not matter.

Figure 14-2 shows how the application distribution approach scales a maximized SLB environment.

Figure 14-2 *Application Distribution Approach*

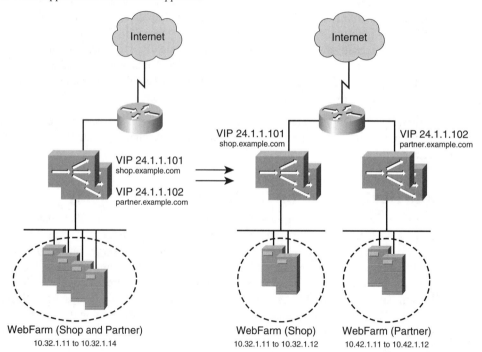

In this example, partner.example.com and shop.example.com resided on the same SLB device. As the usage of the SLB device went to 100 percent, clients started experiencing delays. These delays were resolved by splitting the SLB device configurations into two different units, one hosting partner.example.com and the other shop.example.com.

DNS-Based Scaling Approach

DNS is typically used to load balance applications across multiple data centers. This is known as global site (or server) load balancing (GSLB). Similarly, we can use DNS to perform GSLB within a data center to scale SLB devices.

The DNS-based scaling approach is simple to integrate in most existing infrastructures and can be migrated over time. As shown in Figure 14-3, a pair of global site selectors (GSSs), intelligent DNS service appliances, is deployed within a data center. The GSSs are authoritative for the domains shop.example.com and partner.example.com. These applications are load balanced by the CSM pairs within the data center. Each CSM pair load balances traffic across a local set of servers for the same application.

Figure 14-3 *DNS-Based Scaling Approach*

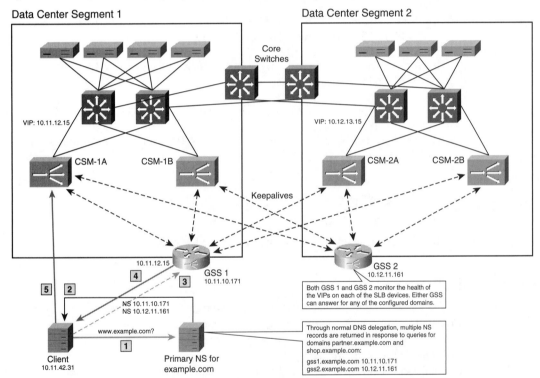

Let's take the example of shop.example.com. The VIP addresses for this are 10.11.12.15 in data center segment 1 and 10.12.13.15 in data center segment 2. The idea is that if any client would like to access shop.example.com, the GSS will respond with the next available VIP, 10.12.13.15 or 10.11.12.15, based on the load-balancing algorithm. The load-balancing methods on the GSS range from simple round robin to static proximity based on the requestor's source IP address. Let's say a client with an IP address in subnet 10.11.0.0 queries the GSS; the response should have the VIP of data center segment 1 unless that VIP is down. The GSS accomplishes that by looking at the source IP of the requestor. If the source IP is that of a client or server in subnet 10.11.0.0, for example, then the answer within the DNS response has the data center segment 1 VIP (10.11.12.15). Following are the steps of DNS resolution:

1 A client with IP address 10.11.42.31 issues a DNS query for shop.example.com.

2 The internal example.com name server (NS) receives the request and responds with both GSSs' IP addresses; that is, 10.11.10.171 and 10.12.11.161.

3 The client sends the request to the first member in the answer list; that is, 10.11.10.171. (If 10.11.10.171 times out, the client queries 10.12.11.161.)

4 GSS inspects the query and finds a match for shop.example.com; the policy configured on the GSS indicates to look at the source IP address of the requestor and respond back appropriately. Static policy configuration is similar to that detailed here:

    a If the source address is 10.11.0.0/16, then respond with 10.11.12.15; if 10.11.12.15 is down, respond with 10.12.13.15.

    b If the source address is 10.12.0.0/16, then respond with 10.12.13.15; if 10.12.13.15 is down, respond with 10.11.12.15.

    c Alternatively, do a source IP hash and balance between 10.11.12.15 and 10.12.13.15.

5 As the client gets the response of the local CSM VIP (10.11.12.15), it initiates the TCP connect to that VIP.

The DNS-based solution meets the requirements of proximity and stickiness to the selected SLB device. The key advantages of the DNS-based approach are:

- Predictable traffic flow
- Ease of management and maintenance of the SLB node

Predictable Traffic Flow

The DNS-based solution is independent of routing protocol issues like flaps (rapid fluctuation of routing information) or slow convergence. The decision about which CSM will be used is made before the session is initiated by the data center client. The SLB node selection is based on the IP address and configured policy. The configured decision will be taken unless the CSM node in the policy is unavailable. Several balancing methods similar to the ones used in SLB devices are available to load balance client DNS requests.

Ease of Management and Maintenance

In the DNS approach previously mentioned, the GSS is configured with the VIP addresses on the SLB devices in all the data center segments. In order to take down an application, services, or the entire SLB node, the process is fairly simple. The service can be easily suspended on the GSS by a click of a button.

RHI-Based Scaling Approach

RHI is a feature on the CSM that can be used for GSLB or for scaling an SLB environment. This IP-based approach works best when the client base is internal or in a controlled routing environment. In this solution, the application is hosted on multiple SLB devices with different servers but the same VIP address.

To enable this feature, the **advertise active** command is used within the virtual server configuration on the CSM. This causes the CSM to install a host route in the MSFC on the same Catalyst 6500 chassis only if the virtual server is in *Operational* state. A virtual server is in the Operational state when at least one of the servers in the same server farm is operational. Extensive probing is available on the CSM to check the health of the server and the appropriate application daemon that runs on the server. For RHI to work, the MSFC and CSM must share a client-side VLAN (VLAN 26 in Example 14-1, shown in the following section).

Hence, when we use this feature on multiple CSMs hosting the same application with the same VIP address, the routing domain will have multiple paths to the same VIP address. The next hop on these host routes will be the *alias* IP address on the CSM. As the user request enters the routing domain, it is sent to the CSM closest to the user based on the routing metrics.

Figure 14-4 shows how the same host-based route of 10.1.32.101 is injected into the enterprise routing domain from both CSMs in both the data center segments. Figure 14-4 shows that client A goes to segment 1, which is closest to it, and client B goes to segment 2, also due to proximity.

Figure 14-4 *RHI–Based Scaling Approach*

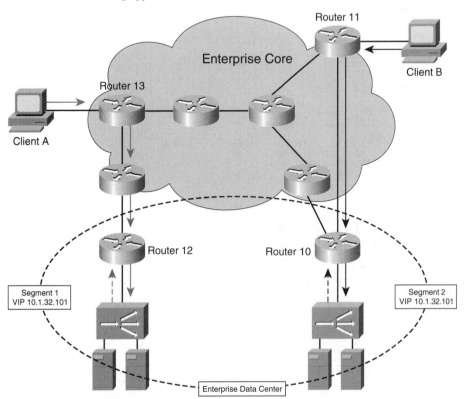

CSM RHI Configuration

Example 14-1 shows a minimal RHI configuration.

Example 14-1 *CSM RHI Configuration Example*

```
module ContentSwitchingModule 4
 vlan 14 server
  ip address 130.34.248.161 255.255.255.192
 !
 vlan 26 client
  ip address 10.16.0.2 255.255.255.0
  gateway 10.16.0.1
  alias 10.16.0.3 255.255.255.0
 !
 probe ICMP icmp
  interval 5
  retries 2
 !
 serverfarm RHI-TEST
  nat server
  no nat client
  real 130.34.248.129
   inservice
  probe ICMP
 !
 vserver RHI-TEST-1
  virtual 24.24.24.1 tcp www
  vlan 26
  serverfarm RHI-TEST
  advertise active
  persistent rebalance
  inservice
 !
 vserver RHI-TEST-2
  virtual 24.24.24.2 tcp www
  vlan 26
  serverfarm RHI-TEST
  advertise active
  persistent rebalance
  inservice
 !
 vserver RHI-TEST-3
  virtual 24.24.24.3 tcp www
  vlan 26
  serverfarm RHI-TEST
  advertise active
  persistent rebalance
  inservice
 !
 ft group 1 vlan 5
  priority 110
 !
cat6K_1#
```

MSFC RHI Configuration and Routes

Example 14-2 shows the configuration on the interface on the MSFC that connects to the CSM.

Example 14-2 *MSFC RHI Configuration Example*

```
cat6K_1#sh run int vlan 26
Building configuration...
Current configuration : 60 bytes
!
interface Vlan26
 ip address 10.16.0.1 255.255.255.0
end
cat6K_1#
cat6K_1#sh mod c 4 vlan id 26 detail
vlan   IP address       IP mask           type
----------------------------------------------------
26     10.16.0.2        255.255.255.0     SERVER
  ALIASES
  IP address      IP mask
  ------------------------------
  10.16.0.3       255.255.255.0
cat6K_1#
```

Example 14-3 shows the static route in the MSFC routing table pointing to the alias on the CSM. An alias is a shared IP address, similar to a Hot Standby Router Protocol (HSRP) group IP address. Figure 14-5 shows how these routes are injected into the routing domain.

Example 14-3 *Dynamic Host Routes Added in the MSFC's Routing Table*

```
cat6K_1# sh ip route static
     24.0.0.0/32 is subnetted, 3 subnets
S       24.24.24.1 [1/0] via 10.16.0.3, Vlan26
S       24.24.24.2 [1/0] via 10.16.0.3, Vlan26
S       24.24.24.3 [1/0] via 10.16.0.3, Vlan26
cat6K_1#
```

Figure 14-5 *32-Bit Route Injection by CSM*

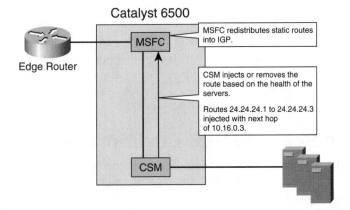

Scaling Beyond Server Capacity

In the preceding sections; we discussed how to scale SLB devices beyond their capacity limits. In this section, we will discuss how to scale the server's capacity within an SLB device. Let's say we have an SLB device with 10 servers configured on it for a particular resource-intensive web-based application. Each server is capable of serving only 100 user sessions concurrently. So at any given time, the SLB environment can service 1000 users—beyond that, if any new user is load balanced to a server, the server becomes unstable.

There are several approaches to resolve this server capacity issue. These solutions range from increasing the server CPU/memory resources to using multiple features on the SLB devices to form a scalable environment. The complex but comprehensive solutions rely on the max connections feature on the real server or virtual server level. The max connections configuration within a real server informs the SLB device that the server can only handle the configured number of sessions concurrently. This protects the real servers from excessive user requests that may in turn cause them to become unstable. The idea is not to disrupt the existing users' sessions.

So, the first step is to detect the max connections on the servers and the second step is to take appropriate action. If the SLB device detects that all the servers in the server farm of a particular application have reached their maximum capacity, any of the following measures can be taken:

- Have a server that will serve a turn-away page or a sorry message to the clients. The user will be informed to return to the site at a later time.

- Send an HTTP 302 redirect to the new clients and send them to another SLB device hosting the same application.

- Deploy the SLB devices in conjunction with a smart DNS appliance like GSS. When max connections are reached, the CSM will inform the GSS to service the user DNS query with a VIP from another CSM.

- Send the user request to another SLB device, but source translate the packet. This ensures that the packet from the second SLB device will traverse the first SLB device. In other words, the session path will be symmetric.

The overall solution can use a combination of approaches to come up with an environment that best services the hosted application.

The case study discussed in this chapter is not a design recommendation but an example of a SLB environment within a single data center that provides for scalability of the SLB device and that of the servers.

Case Study: Scalable SLB Environment

Now that you understand the various design approaches and methodologies for scaling SLB devices and servers, we will start our discussion of how an SLB environment can be designed using many of these approaches.

In this case study, we will test and design a solution around specific application requirements. Again, this is not a design recommendation but an example of a possible solution. Topics covered in this case study include:

- Server and application requirements
- Management and security requirements
- Infrastructure requirements
- DNS-based design
- RHI-based design
- Testing maximum connections

Server and Application Requirements

Server and application requirements for this case study are defined as follows:

- Directly manage the servers from the front end (the client-side network)
- Servers should also be able to initiate sessions for application software and driver upgrades. Server backups have high traffic volume for backing up data.
- Number of servers: 100 per site
- Application should be HTTP based, requiring client persistence.
- Application clients should be allowed to connect to the applications from different regions.
- Data center should be split into multiple segments with branch offices connecting to different segments over dedicated lines.
- HTTP-based probes are essential.

Management and Security Requirements

Security requirements for this case study are as follows:

- Sys logging and SNMP traps from the Catalyst 6509 are needed for the CSM real server and virtual server state changes and fault-tolerant events.
- Commonly configured management services Telnet and Secure Shell (SSH) are needed for access to the command-line interface (CLI) on Catalyst 6509.

Infrastructure Requirements

Layer 2 and Layer 3 infrastructure requirements for this case study are as follows:

- Minimal disruption to the OSPF domain is needed.
- Redistribution of static routes into IGP must be allowed.

- Seamless integration of the CSM into current Layer 2 and Layer 3 infrastructure should be provided.

- Robust failover is needed for servers with dual network interface cards (NICs). Server NICs would be in Active/Passive mode, residing in the same VLAN but connected to different Catalyst 6509s.

DNS-Based Design

The main idea behind this solution is to use a GSS to monitor the SLB devices within the same data center. The GSS responds to the client's DNS queries with the available VIPs based on load-balancing policy. In order to protect against servers being overloaded, the SLB device is configured with max connections for each real server. In order to communicate the server load information with the GSS, the KeepAlive-Appliance Protocol (KAL-AP) is used as the keepalive mechanism between the GSS and the CSM. KAL-AP is a keepalive client/server-based protocol that runs between the GSLB device and the SLB device. When the max number of connections is reached for the entire server farm, the CSM informs the GSS of the unavailability of the VIP by responding appropriately to KAL-AP queries. Figure 14-6 shows the logical view of this solution.

Figure 14-6 *DNS-Based Scalable SLB Environment Using CSM and Maxconns*

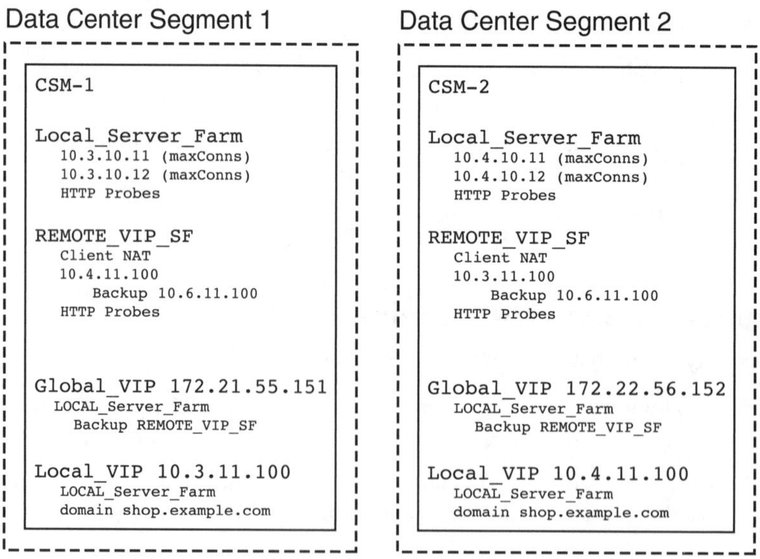

```
Data Center Segment 1              Data Center Segment 2
┌──────────────────────────┐      ┌──────────────────────────┐
│                          │      │                          │
│  CSM-1                   │      │  CSM-2                   │
│                          │      │                          │
│  Local_Server_Farm       │      │  Local_Server_Farm       │
│    10.3.10.11 (maxConns) │      │    10.4.10.11 (maxConns) │
│    10.3.10.12 (maxConns) │      │    10.4.10.12 (maxConns) │
│    HTTP Probes           │      │    HTTP Probes           │
│                          │      │                          │
│  REMOTE_VIP_SF           │      │  REMOTE_VIP_SF           │
│    Client NAT            │      │    Client NAT            │
│    10.4.11.100           │      │    10.3.11.100           │
│      Backup 10.6.11.100  │      │      Backup 10.6.11.100  │
│    HTTP Probes           │      │    HTTP Probes           │
│                          │      │                          │
│                          │      │                          │
│  Global_VIP 172.21.55.151│      │  Global_VIP 172.22.56.152│
│    LOCAL_Server_Farm     │      │    LOCAL_Server_Farm     │
│      Backup REMOTE_VIP_SF│      │      Backup REMOTE_VIP_SF│
│                          │      │                          │
│  Local_VIP 10.3.11.100   │      │  Local_VIP 10.4.11.100   │
│    LOCAL_Server_Farm     │      │    LOCAL_Server_Farm     │
│    domain shop.example.com│      │    domain shop.example.com│
└──────────────────────────┘      └──────────────────────────┘
```

The first configuration to notice in this design is that for each virtual server there are two virtual servers—one local and one global, with both of them using the same server farm. The VIP in the global virtual server is the one used as the answer on the GSS. If a client wants to reach shop.example.com, it will be provided with the global VIP as the answer—172.21.55.151 or 172.22.56.152. The KAL-AP keepalive previously discussed will poll the local VIP on the CSM. This is done to ensure that the CSM only provides the GSS with the health and load of Local_Server_Farm and not the backup server farm.

Let's step through a typical state transition in this solution:

1 In a steady state, clients receive Global_VIPs as the answers, and their requests with the destination IP address of 172.21.55.151 or 172.22.56.152 are routed to the CSM.

2 When MaxConns is hit on the local server pool, the next available CSM is used within the same data center. For example, if the Local_Server_Farm of CSM-1 hits MaxConn, CSM-1 will start using CSM-2. When CSM-1 sends packets to CSM-2, it performs a source NAT. This ensures that the return traffic goes through CSM-1.

3 Notice that the Remote_VIP_SF server farm on CSM-1 actually has CSM-2's Local_VIP.

4 The Remote_VIP_SF acts as a sorry server farm. Within this server farm, we also have a backup server defined—10.6.11.100. In other words, we have two levels of redundancy. The server with IP address 10.6.11.100 only provides turn-away web pages.

5 The backup server of the backup server farm would be used to protect against two CSM pairs being fully utilized. (All servers in the respective application server farm in both CSM hit MaxConn.)

Because this solution is based on DNS, it works for both intranet- and Internet-based clients. In the next section, we will cover the configurations of the CSMs. This should help you better understand the solution. For testing purposes, the RHI value is set to a low number.

CSM-1 Configuration for DNS-Based Solution

Example 14-4 shows the configuration from the active CSM in the first CSM pair. This pair of CSMs exists in data center segment 1.

Example 14-4 *CSM-1 Configuration for the DNS-Based Solution*

```
module ContentSwitchingModule 6
 vlan 50 server
  ip address 172.21.55.141 255.255.255.224
  gateway 172.21.55.133
  alias 172.21.55.140 255.255.255.224
 !
 natpool CNAT2 10.3.11.61 10.3.11.62 netmask 255.255.255.0
 natpool CNAT1 10.3.11.51 10.3.11.52 netmask 255.255.255.0
 !
 probe HTTP_LOC http
  request method get url /csmprobe.html
  expect status 200
  interval 5
```

continues

Example 14-4 *CSM-1 Configuration for the DNS-Based Solution (Continued)*

```
   failed 30
 !
 probe HTTP_REM http
  request method get url /csmprobe.html
  expect status 200
  interval 10
  failed 30
 !
 serverfarm LOCAL_SF
  nat server
  nat client CNAT1
  real 10.3.10.11
   maxconns 2
   inservice
  real 10.3.10.12
   maxconns 2
   inservice
  probe HTTP_LOC
 !
 serverfarm REMOTE_VIP_SF
  nat server
  nat client CNAT2
  real 10.4.11.100
   backup real 10.6.11.100
   inservice
  real 10.6.11.100
   inservice standby
  probe HTTP_REM
 !
 policy GLOBAL_VIP
  serverfarm LOCAL_SF backup REMOTE_VIP_SF
 !
 policy LOCAL_VIP
  serverfarm LOCAL_SF
 !
 !
 !
 vserver V_GLOBAL_VIP
  no inservice
  virtual 172.21.55.151 tcp telnet
  vlan 50
  replicate csrp sticky
  replicate csrp connection
  persistent rebalance
  slb-policy GLOBAL_VIP
  inservice
 !
 vserver V_LOCAL_VIP
  no inservice
  virtual 10.3.11.100 tcp telnet
  vlan 50
  replicate csrp sticky
```

Example 14-4 *CSM-1 Configuration for the DNS-Based Solution (Continued)*

```
   replicate csrp connection
   persistent rebalance
   slb-policy LOCAL_VIP
   domain shop.example.com
   inservice
 !
 !
 capp udp
  secure
  options 10.11.10.171 encryption md5 test
  options 10.12.11.161 encryption md5 test
 !
 ft group 1 vlan 101
 !
```

CSM-2 Configuration for DNS-Based Solution

Example 14-5 shows the configuration from the active CSM in the second CSM pair. This pair of CSMs exists in data center segment 2.

Example 14-5 *CSM-2 Configuration for the DNS-Based Solution*

```
module ContentSwitchingModule 6
 vlan 50 server
  ip address 172.22.56.147 255.255.255.224
  gateway 172.22.56.134
  alias 172.22.56.146 255.255.255.224
 !
 natpool CNAT2 10.4.11.61 10.4.11.62 netmask 255.255.255.0
 natpool CNAT1 10.4.11.51 10.4.11.52 netmask 255.255.255.0
 !
 probe HTTP_LOC http
  request method get url /csmprobe.html
  expect status 200
  interval 5
  failed 30
 !
 probe HTTP_REM http
  request method get url /csmprobe.html
  expect status 200
  interval 10
  failed 30
 !
 serverfarm LOCAL_SF
  nat server
  nat client CNAT1
  real 10.4.10.11
   maxconns 2
   inservice
  real 10.4.10.12
```

continues

Example 14-5 *CSM-2 Configuration for the DNS-Based Solution (Continued)*

```
    maxconns 2
    inservice
   probe HTTP_LOC
 !
  serverfarm REMOTE_VIP_SF
   nat server
   nat client CNAT2
   real 10.5.11.100
    backup real 10.6.11.100
    inservice
   real 10.6.11.100
    inservice standby
   probe HTTP_REM
 !
  policy GLOBAL_VIP
   serverfarm LOCAL_SF backup REMOTE_VIP_SF
 !
  policy LOCAL_VIP
   serverfarm LOCAL_SF
 !
 !
 !
  vserver V_GLOBAL_VIP
   no inservice
   virtual 172.22.56.152 tcp telnet
   vlan 50
   replicate csrp sticky
   replicate csrp connection
   persistent rebalance
   slb-policy GLOBAL_VIP
   no inservice
 !
  vserver V_LOCAL_VIP
   no inservice
   virtual 10.4.11.100 tcp telnet
   vlan 50
   replicate csrp sticky
   replicate csrp connection
   persistent rebalance
   slb-policy LOCAL_VIP
   domain shop.example.com
   inservice
 !
 !
  capp udp
   secure
   options 10.11.10.171 encryption md5 test
   options 10.12.11.161 encryption md5 test
 !
  ft group 2 vlan 102
 !
```

RHI-Based Design

The main modification in this design is to use RHI instead of DNS for Global_VIP availability. The key is that the Global_VIP is the same in both the data center segments. Clients closest to each segment will be routed to the local CSM pair. The health checks and sorry server farm and backup server behavior stay the same. Figure 14-7 shows the logical view of this solution.

Figure 14-7 *RHI-Based Scalable SLB Environment Using CSM and Maxconns*

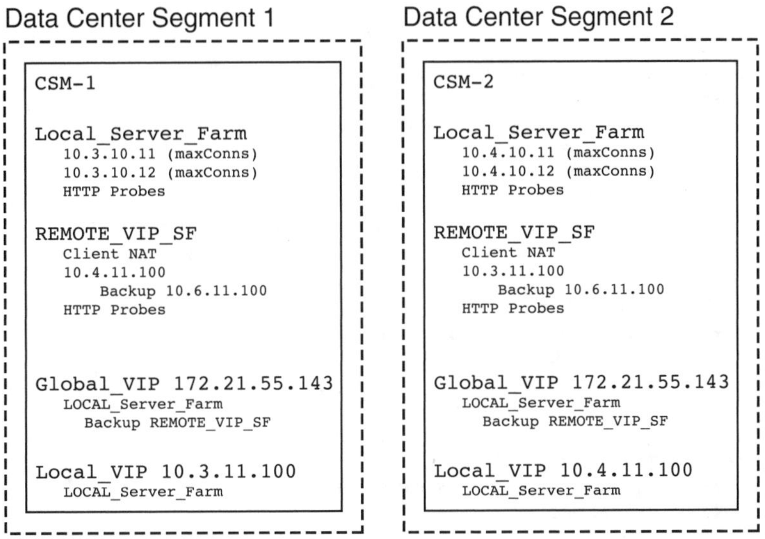

```
Data Center Segment 1              Data Center Segment 2
.----------------------------.     .----------------------------.
|                            |     |                            |
|  CSM-1                     |     |  CSM-2                     |
|                            |     |                            |
|  Local_Server_Farm         |     |  Local_Server_Farm         |
|    10.3.10.11 (maxConns)   |     |    10.4.10.11 (maxConns)   |
|    10.3.10.12 (maxConns)   |     |    10.4.10.12 (maxConns)   |
|    HTTP Probes             |     |    HTTP Probes             |
|                            |     |                            |
|  REMOTE_VIP_SF             |     |  REMOTE_VIP_SF             |
|    Client NAT              |     |    Client NAT              |
|    10.4.11.100             |     |    10.3.11.100             |
|      Backup 10.6.11.100    |     |      Backup 10.6.11.100    |
|    HTTP Probes             |     |    HTTP Probes             |
|                            |     |                            |
|                            |     |                            |
|  Global_VIP 172.21.55.143  |     |  Global_VIP 172.21.55.143  |
|    LOCAL_Server_Farm       |     |    LOCAL_Server_Farm       |
|      Backup REMOTE_VIP_SF  |     |      Backup REMOTE_VIP_SF  |
|                            |     |                            |
|  Local_VIP 10.3.11.100     |     |  Local_VIP 10.4.11.100     |
|    LOCAL_Server_Farm       |     |    LOCAL_Server_Farm       |
|                            |     |                            |
'----------------------------'     '----------------------------'
```

Let's step through a typical state transition in this solution.

1 In a steady state, clients resolve shop.example.com to 172.21.55.143. This is the Global_VIP in both segments of CSM pairs. The client's request is routed by the IGP domain to the segment closest to the client.

2 When MaxConns is hit on the local server pool, the next available CSM is used within the same data center. For example, if the Local_Server_Farm of CSM-1 hits MaxConn, CSM-1 will start using CSM-2.

3 Notice that the Remote_VIP_SF server farm on CSM-1 actually has CSM-2's Local_VIP.

4 Remote_VIP_SF acts as a sorry server farm. Within this server farm, we also have a backup server defined—10.6.11.100. In other words, we have two levels of redundancy. The server with IP address 10.6.11.100 provides only turn-away web pages.

5 The backup server of the Backup server farm would be used to protect against two CSM pairs being fully utilized. (All servers in the respective application server farm in both CSM hit MaxConn.)

Because this solution is based on RHI, it works best for intranet-based clients. In the next section, we will cover the configurations of the CSMs. This should help you better understand the solution.

CSM-1 Configuration for RHI-Based Solution

Example 14-6 shows the configuration from the active CSM in the first CSM pair. This pair of CSMs exists in data center segment 1.

Example 14-6 *CSM-1 Configuration for the RHI-Based Solution*

```
module ContentSwitchingModule 6
 vlan 50 server
  ip address 172.21.55.141 255.255.255.224
  gateway 172.21.55.133
  alias 172.21.55.140 255.255.255.224
 !
 natpool CNAT2 10.3.11.61 10.3.11.62 netmask 255.255.255.0
 natpool CNAT1 10.3.11.51 10.3.11.52 netmask 255.255.255.0
 !
 probe HTTP_LOC http
  request method get url /csmprobe.html
  expect status 200
  interval 5
  failed 30
 !
 probe HTTP_REM http
  request method get url /csmprobe.html
  expect status 200
  interval 10
  failed 30
 !
 serverfarm LOCAL_SF
  nat server
  nat client CNAT1
  real 10.3.10.11
   maxconns 2
   inservice
  real 10.3.10.12
   maxconns 2
   inservice
  probe HTTP_LOC
 !
 serverfarm REMOTE_VIP_SF
  nat server
  nat client CNAT2
  real 10.4.11.100
   backup real 10.6.11.100
   inservice
  real 10.6.11.100
   inservice standby
  probe HTTP_REM
```

Example 14-6 *CSM-1 Configuration for the RHI-Based Solution (Continued)*

```
!
 policy GLOBAL_VIP
  serverfarm LOCAL_SF backup REMOTE_VIP_SF
 !
 policy LOCAL_VIP
  serverfarm LOCAL_SF
 !
 !
 !
 vserver V_GLOBAL_VIP
  no inservice
  virtual 172.21.55.143 tcp telnet
  vlan 50
  advertise active
  replicate csrp sticky
  replicate csrp connection
  persistent rebalance
  slb-policy GLOBAL_VIP
  inservice
 !
 vserver V_LOCAL_VIP
  no inservice
  virtual 10.3.11.100 tcp telnet
  vlan 50
  replicate csrp sticky
  replicate csrp connection
  persistent rebalance
  slb-policy LOCAL_VIP
  inservice
 !
 !
 ft group 3 vlan 103
 !
```

CSM-2 Configuration for RHI-Based Solution

Example 14-7 shows the configuration from the active CSM in the second CSM pair. This pair of CSMs exists in data center segment 2.

Example 14-7 *CSM-2 Configuration for the RHI-Based Solution*

```
module ContentSwitchingModule 6
 vlan 50 server
  ip address 172.21.55.151 255.255.255.224
  gateway 172.21.55.134
  alias 172.21.55.150 255.255.255.224
 !
 natpool CNAT2 10.4.11.61 10.4.11.62 netmask 255.255.255.0
 natpool CNAT1 10.4.11.51 10.4.11.52 netmask 255.255.255.0
 !
```

continues

Example 14-7 *CSM-2 Configuration for the RHI-Based Solution (Continued)*

```
 probe HTTP_LOC http
  request method get url /csmprobe.html
  expect status 200
  interval 5
  failed 30
 !
 probe HTTP_REM http
  request method get url /csmprobe.html
  expect status 200
  interval 10
  failed 30
 !
 serverfarm LOCAL_SF
  nat server
  nat client CNAT1
  real 10.4.10.11
   maxconns 2
   inservice
  real 10.4.10.12
   maxconns 2
   inservice
  probe HTTP_LOC
 !
 serverfarm REMOTE_VIP_SF
  nat server
  nat client CNAT2
  real 10.5.11.100
   backup real 10.6.11.100
   inservice
  real 10.6.11.100
   inservice standby
  probe HTTP_REM
 !
 policy GLOBAL_VIP
  serverfarm LOCAL_SF backup REMOTE_VIP_SF
 !
 policy LOCAL_VIP
  serverfarm LOCAL_SF
 !
 !
 !
 vserver V_GLOBAL_VIP
  no inservice
  virtual 172.21.55.143 tcp telnet
  vlan 50
  advertise active
  replicate csrp sticky
  replicate csrp connection
  persistent rebalance
  slb-policy GLOBAL_VIP
  no inservice
 !
 vserver V_LOCAL_VIP
```

Example 14-7 *CSM-2 Configuration for the RHI-Based Solution (Continued)*

```
  no inservice
  virtual 10.4.11.100 tcp telnet
  vlan 50
  replicate csrp sticky
  replicate csrp connection
  persistent rebalance
  slb-policy LOCAL_VIP
  inservice
!
!
 ft group 4 vlan 104
!
```

Testing Maximum Connections

Both solutions discussed earlier rely on CSM's Maximum Connections feature. In this section, we will discuss some test cases that were performed to verify this functionality on the CSM. Following are the key areas of testing that we will cover:

- TestCase1—The capability of CSM to start using the backup server farm when all the servers in the primary server farm hit MaxConn

- TestCase2—The capability of CSM to fail probes to another CSM that has hit MaxConn

- TestCase3—The capability of CSM to use a backup real server within the backup server farm when the primary server (remote VIP) within the backup server farm goes down

Test Case 1

This test case focuses on CSM's ability to start using the backup server farm when all the servers in the primary server farm hit MaxConn. This test case passed without any issues. As expected, RHI is not stopped when MaxConn is hit. This is because you would want traffic for existing sessions to continue and get routed to the CSM.

After all servers within the server farm hit MaxConn, the CSM does not stop injecting RHI. This is desirable behavior because existing session IP packets still need to be routed to the CSM. Example 14-8 shows an injected static route in the MSFC's routing table. The route stays in the table even when all the servers hit MaxConn.

Example 14-8 *RHI Route in the MSFC's Routing Table*

```
CAT-Native-4#sh ip route static
     10.0.0.0/8 is variably subnetted, 5 subnets, 2 masks
S       10.3.11.0/24 [1/0] via 172.21.55.141
S       10.4.11.0/24 [1/0] via 172.21.55.142
S       10.4.11.100/32 [1/0] via 172.21.55.142, Vlan50
S*    0.0.0.0/0 [1/0] via 172.21.55.130
CAT-Native-4#
```

As expected, after all servers go to a probe-failed state, RHI is removed. Example 14-9 shows the RHI route disappearing from the MSFC's routing table as the servers move to a probe failed state.

Example 14-9 *Servers in a Probe-Failed State and RHI Route Disappearing*

```
CAT-Native-4#
*Jun  9 19:49:53.451: %CSM_SLB-6-RSERVERSTATE: Module 6 server state
  changed: SLB-NETMGT: TCP health probe failed for server 10.4.10.12:23
  in serverfarm 'LOCAL_SF'
*Jun  9 19:49:56.583: %CSM_SLB-6-RSERVERSTATE: Module 6 server state
  changed: SLB-NETMGT: TCP health probe failed for server 10.4.10.11:23
  in serverfarm 'LOCAL_SF'
CAT-Native-4#
CAT-Native-4#sh ip route static
      10.0.0.0/24 is subnetted, 4 subnets
S        10.3.11.0 [1/0] via 172.21.55.141
S        10.4.11.0 [1/0] via 172.21.55.142
S*   0.0.0.0/0 [1/0] via 172.21.55.130
CAT-Native-4#
```

Test Case 2

This test case focuses on CSM's ability to fail probes to another CSM that has hit MaxConn. In this case, the monitoring CSM is CAT-Native-3, and the monitored CSM is CAT-Native-4. The VIP in question is 10.4.11.100. Initially, it's OPERATIONAL in CAT-Native-3. Example 14-10 shows VIP 10.4.11.100 in OPERATIONAL state.

Example 14-10 *OPERATIONAL Remote VIP in CAT-Native-3*

```
CAT-Native-3#
CAT-Native-3#show mod csm 6 reals sfarm REMOTE_VIPS
real               server farm     weight  state         conns/hits
-----------------------------------------------------------------------
10.4.11.100        REMOTE_VIPS     8       OPERATIONAL   0
10.6.11.100        REMOTE_VIPS     8       PROBE_FAILED  0
CAT-Native-3#
```

All servers within server farm LOCAL_SF hit MaxConn in CAT-Native-4. Example 14-11 shows the servers in CAT-Native-4 hitting MaxConn.

Example 14-11 *Servers in CAT-Native-4 Hitting MaxConn*

```
CAT-Native-4#show mod csm 6 reals sfarm LOCAL_SF
real               server farm     weight  state         conns/hits
-----------------------------------------------------------------------
10.4.10.11         LOCAL_SF        8       OPERATIONAL   0
10.4.10.12         LOCAL_SF        8       OPERATIONAL   0
CAT-Native-4#
*Jun  9 19:42:44.463: %CSM_SLB-6-RSERVERSTATE: Module 6 server state
  changed: server 10.4.10.12:0 in serverfarm 'LOCAL_SF' has reached
  configured max-conns
```

Example 14-11 *Servers in CAT-Native-4 Hitting MaxConn (Continued)*

```
*Jun  9 19:42:46.495: %CSM_SLB-6-RSERVERSTATE: Module 6 server state
  changed: server 10.4.10.11:0 in serverfarm 'LOCAL_SF' has reached
  configured max-conns
CAT-Native-4#
CAT-Native-4#show mod csm 6 reals sfarm LOCAL_SF
real                    server farm      weight  state          conns/hits
-----------------------------------------------------------------------
10.4.10.11              LOCAL_SF         8       MAXCONNS       2
10.4.10.12              LOCAL_SF         8       MAXCONNS       2
CAT-Native-4#
```

CAT-Native-3 detects the state in the preceding example and probe fails for VIP 10.4.11.100 (which is, of course, configured as real server in this CSM). Example 14-12 shows the detection of probe failure on CAT-Native-3. Real server 10.4.11.100 is moved into a probe-failed state.

Example 14-12 *Probe Failure on CAT-Native-3 for Remote VIP*

```
CAT-Native-3#
CAT-Native-3#
CAT-Native-3#
Jun  9 12:45:21.719: %CSM_SLB-6-RSERVERSTATE: Module 6 server state
  changed: SLB-NETMGT: TCP health probe failed for server 10.4.11.100:23
  in serverfarm 'REMOTE_VIPS'
CAT-Native-3#show mod csm 6 reals sfarm REMOTE_VIPS
real                    server farm      weight  state          conns/hits
-----------------------------------------------------------------------
10.4.11.100             REMOTE_VIPS      8       PROBE_FAILED   0
10.6.11.100             REMOTE_VIPS      8       PROBE_FAILED   0
CAT-Native-3#
```

If the virtual server on the monitored CSM (CAT-Native-4) was Layer 7, then the probe on the monitoring CSM (CAT-Native-3) *must* be Layer 7 (HTTP head or get).

Also, a ping to VIP still works after MaxConns is reached.

Test Case 3

This test case focuses on CSM's ability to use a backup real server within the backup server farm when the primary server (remote VIP) within the backup server farm goes down. This test passed. The output in Example 14-13 clearly shows the whole solution working.

1 The first four sessions in the connection table in Example 14-13 go to the Local Server Farm.

2 After they hit MaxConn, the next connection goes to the remote VIP of 10.4.11.100.

3 At this point, three additional connections to 10.4.11.100 were generated to max out that CSM's local server farm.

4 Now the next connection from our primary CSM goes to the backup real server of the backup server farm, which is 10.4.10.15.

Example 14-13 shows the CSM configuration with a backup real server within a backup server farm. The example also shows the connection table on the CSM with the six connections described in the preceding list.

Example 14-13 *CSM Configuration with Backup Real Server Within Backup Server Farm and Connection Table*

```
!
 serverfarm LOCAL_SF
 nat server
 nat client CNAT1
 real 10.3.10.11
  maxconns 2
  inservice
 real 10.3.10.12
  maxconns 2
  inservice
 probe TCP
!
 serverfarm REMOTE_VIP_SF
 nat server
 nat client CNAT3
 real 10.4.11.100
  backup real 10.4.10.15
  inservice
 real 10.6.11.100
  inservice standby
 real 10.4.10.15
  inservice standby
 probe TCP
!
CAT-Native-3#
CAT-Native-3#show mod csm 6 conn de
     prot vlan source                 destination        state
-----------------------------------------------------------------------
In  TCP  50   172.21.55.133:12801   172.21.55.143:23    ESTAB
Out TCP  50   10.3.10.12:23           10.3.11.51:8195    ESTAB
      vs = V_GLOBAL_VIP, ftp = No, csrp = True
In  TCP  50   172.21.55.133:12290   172.21.55.143:23    ESTAB
Out TCP  50   10.3.10.11:23           10.3.11.51:8194    ESTAB
      vs = V_GLOBAL_VIP, ftp = No, csrp = True
In  TCP  50   172.21.55.133:11268   172.21.55.143:23    ESTAB
Out TCP  50   10.3.10.11:23           10.3.11.51:8192    ESTAB
      vs = V_GLOBAL_VIP, ftp = No, csrp = True
In  TCP  50   172.21.55.133:11779   172.21.55.143:23    ESTAB
Out TCP  50   10.3.10.12:23           10.3.11.51:8193    ESTAB
      vs = V_GLOBAL_VIP, ftp = No, csrp = True
In  TCP  50   10.21.96.8:3183         172.21.55.143:23    ESTAB
Out TCP  50   10.4.11.100:23          10.3.11.72:8194    ESTAB
      vs = V_GLOBAL_VIP, ftp = No, csrp = True
In  TCP  50   10.21.96.8:3185         172.21.55.143:23    ESTAB
Out TCP  50   10.4.10.15:23           10.3.11.72:8198    ESTAB
      vs = V_GLOBAL_VIP, ftp = No, csrp = True
CAT-Native-3#
```

Summary

This chapter introduced the concepts and design methodologies of SLB services within a single data center. The chapter covered how load-balanced applications can be scaled using DNS or IP, and how they are scaled when server capacity within a load balancer is maximized.

In order to combine all the concepts of device and server scalability from the perspective of the CSM platform, this chapter presented a case study with two different solutions. In order to familiarize you with the CSM configurations and features, the case study detailed the CSM configuration for both solutions and went over some key test cases.

Chapter 15, "Integrated Data Center Designs," introduces the concept of integrated data centers. We discuss several design approaches that utilize content, SSL, and Firewall Services Modules on the Catalyst 6500.

Integrated Data Center Designs

In the previous chapters in this book, we have discussed key aspects of server load balancing (SLB), Secure Socket Layer (SSL) offloading, and global server load-balancing (GSLB) solutions. We have talked about the data center products such as the Content Services Switch (CSS), the Content Switch Module (CSM), the Catalyst 6500 SSL Module (SSLM), and the Global Site Selector (GSS), and discussed how they can be designed and deployed. In this chapter, we will take our discussion to the next level by presenting several integrated design methodologies.

These design approaches are to build integrated data centers primarily by using service modules on the Catalyst 6500. These designs incorporate a Firewall Services Module (FWSM) and demonstrate how security can be integrated with SLB and SSL offload. In presenting the designs, we will include the advantages and disadvantages of each. These designs are not best practice recommendations but potential ways of designing and developing integrated data centers. Data center architects should use the information provided in this chapter and the rest of the book to develop a design customized for the applications being hosted in their environments.

This chapter also includes a case study that provides complete implementation details of one of the design options.

Motivations Behind Integrated Data Center Designs

Integrated data center designs are primarily used to consolidate several smaller data centers into single or multiple larger data centers. Such designs use high-bandwidth service modules on the Catalyst 6500 to provide SLB and firewall services in a scalable fashion. Typically, the integrated service modules are deployed in the distribution layer such that it can be used by all the servers connected to the access switches. In some instances where separate physical devices are required by the security team, use of an appliance-based solution is desired.

Some of the primary motivations behind deploying integrated and consolidated data centers are as follows:

- **Network infrastructure cost savings**—Data center consolidation implies the integration of data center network services, reduction of network devices—whether those be switches or routers—and enhancement where necessary to improve network high availability. In general, consolidation of data centers and integrated data center designs results in direct cost savings in network infrastructure. For example, an integrated data center design enables the enterprise to virtually segment an SLB device to service multiple applications or business units instead of having the different SLB device pair per business unit. Similarly, a FWSM can be deployed in a virtualized fashion such that the same physical firewall can function as multiple logical firewall instances.

- **Data center floor space savings**—Deployment of service modules enables the enterprise to remove stand-alone and appliance-based SLB, SSL offload, and firewall devices. Depending on the size of the data center, this can save hundreds of rack units.

- **Ease of management**—The management of the integrated data center is less cumbersome as the number of network devices decreases. If a Catalyst 6500 is deployed with a CSM, an SSL offload, and a FWSM, then the management of these devices can be centralized to some extent. Still, some modules like the FWSM do require separate management using the VPN/Security Management Solution (CiscoWorks VMS). The status of all modules can be polled from the Catalyst 6500 supervisor, and in the case of the CSMs the status of the real servers can be polled from the supervisor.

  Integrated data center designs also substantially reduce cabling that is otherwise needed to connect the appliances with the infrastructure. Service modules do require power from the Catalyst 6500, but it is significantly less than the power required by separate appliances.

- **Virtualization of network resources**—Virtualization of network resources is another key benefit of integrated data center designs. As the network resources are consolidated, deploying virtualization on a single module or across all the service modules is simpler. Virtualization basically means to logically split the network resource, such as a firewall, into multiple entities dedicated to different departments or business units.

Reviewing the design options covered in this chapter will help you to clearly understand these benefits.

Data Center Design 1: FWSM in the Core and Layer 3 CSM in Aggregation

The first design we will discuss is a fairly common implementation where the FWSMs or appliance-based firewalls exist in the core switches and the CSMs and SSLMs are in the aggregation. This section discusses the topology, design caveats, and configuration details pertaining to this design.

Design 1 Topology Details

The first integrated data center shows a topology with three distinct switching layers—those being core, aggregation, and access. Figure 15-1 displays the logical topology.

Figure 15-1 *Integrated Data Center Design Option 1*

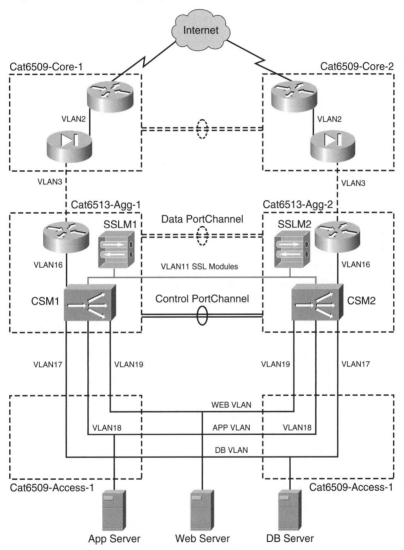

The IP connectivity in this design can be summarized as follows:

- Multilayer Switch Feature Card (MSFC) on Catalyst 6509-Core-1 and Catalyst 6509-Core-2 connects to the Internet. This link is direct or through edge routers.

- Toward the inside, MSFCs connect to the FWSM over VLAN 2.

- FWSM connects to the MSFCs in the aggregation switches over VLAN 3.

- Aggregation MSFC connects to the CSM on VLAN 16.

- All load-balanced server VLANs (17 to 19) exist on the CSM.

- VLAN 11 is the SSLM VLAN on the CSM.
- Connectivity between aggregation and access is Layer 2.

Design 1 Details

Following are some further design caveats and considerations:

- Security details
  - FWSM is deployed in a Layer 3 mode.
  - FWSM is the security perimeter between the untrusted Internet and the trusted data center.
  - Aggregation and access are considered trusted zones.
  - In this design, the security perimeter is not possible between the web, app, and db (database) tiers.
  - In the aggregation layer, some security using VLAN tags on the CSM is possible.
- Content switching details
  - CSM is used in a routed fashion.
  - Server's default gateway is the CSM alias IP address on the server VLANs.
  - Apart from the load-balancing configurations, some extra configuration is needed on the CSM for direct access to servers and non-load-balanced, server-initiated sessions.
  - CSM's default gateway is the HSRP group IP on the MSFC on VLAN 16.
  - Since the MSFC is directly connected to the CSM on VLAN 16, Route Health Injection (RHI) functionality can be used.
  - All to/from traffic from servers, load balanced or non-load-balanced, passes through the CSM.

Design 1 Configuration Details

Example 15-1 shows the partial CSM configuration template used for this design.

Example 15-1 *CSM Configuration for Design 1*

```
!
module ContentSwitchingModule 3
 vlan 16 client
  ip address 10.16.1.12 255.255.255.0
  gateway 10.16.1.1
  alias 10.16.1.11 255.255.255.0
 !
 vlan 11 server
  ip address 10.11.1.2 255.255.255.0
  alias 10.11.1.1 255.255.255.0
 !
```

Example 15-1 *CSM Configuration for Design 1 (Continued)*

```
 vlan 17 server
  ip address 10.17.1.2 255.255.255.0
  alias 10.17.1.1 255.255.255.0
 !
 vlan 18 server
  ip address 10.18.1.2 255.255.255.0
  alias 10.18.1.1 255.255.255.0
 !
 vlan 19 server
  ip address 10.19.1.2 255.255.255.0
  alias 10.19.1.1 255.255.255.0
 !
 !
 serverfarm ROUTE
  no nat server
  no nat client
  predictor forward
 !
 vserver ROUTE
  virtual 0.0.0.0 0.0.0.0 any
  serverfarm ROUTE
  persistent rebalance
  inservice
 !
```

Example 15-2 shows a partial configuration from the MSFC in the aggregation switch.

Example 15-2 *MSFC Configuration for Design 1*

```
MSFC SVI
!
interface Vlan16
  ip address 10.16.1.2 255.255.255.0
  standby 16 ip 10.16.1.1
  standby 16 priority 150
!
```

Data Center Design 2: Layer 3 FWSM and Layer 2 CSM in Aggregation

The second design is an enhancement on the first one. In this design, an FWSM is positioned between the MSFC and the CSM. This firewall in aggregation acts in Layer 3 mode. The mode of operation of the CSM is also changed from Routed mode to Bridge mode. This section discusses the topology, design caveats, and configuration details pertaining to this design.

Design 2 Topology Details

Figure 15-2 displays the logical topology of the second design. The networking infrastructure stays the same as the first design except for an addition of a pair of FWSMs.

Figure 15-2 *Integrated Data Center Design Option 2*

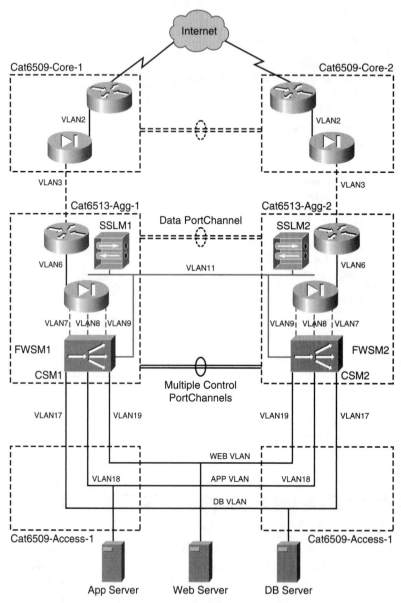

The IP connectivity in this design can be summarized as follows:

- MSFC on Catalyst 6509-Core-1 and Catalyst 6509-Core-2 connects to the Internet. This link is direct or through edge routers.

- Toward the inside, MSFCs connect to the FWSM over VLAN 2.

- FWSM connects to the MSFCs in the aggregation switches over VLAN 3.
- Aggregation MSFC connects to the aggregation FWSM over VLAN 6.
- Aggregation FWSM connects to the CSM over all three DMZ VLANs—VLAN 7, VLAN 8, and VLAN 9.
- VLAN 11 is the SSLM VLAN on the CSM.
- CSM bridges these FW-side VLANs to the server-side VLANs; that is, the following:
  - VLAN 7 is bridged to VLAN 17.
  - VLAN 8 is bridged to VLAN 18.
  - VLAN 9 is bridged to VLAN 19.
- Connectivity between aggregation and access is Layer 2.

Design 2 Caveats

Following are some further design caveats and considerations:

- Security details
  - FWSMs are deployed in a Layer 3 mode in both core and aggregation switches.
  - Core FWSM is the security perimeter between the untrusted Internet and the trusted data center.
  - In this design, the security perimeter is possible between the web, app, and db tiers. This functionality is provided by the aggregation FWSM. This security perimeter applies to both load-balanced and non-load-balanced traffic.
  - Aggregation FWSM's default gateway is the MSFC on VLAN 6.
  - Aggregation FWSM has multiple DMZ VLANs; namely, VLAN 7, VLAN 8, and VLAN 9.
- Content switching details
  - CSM is used in bridged fashion with a distinct bridged VLAN pair per secure segment.
  - Server's default gateway is the firewall primary IP address.
  - Apart from the load-balancing configurations, no extra configuration is needed on the CSM for direct access to servers and non-load-balanced, server-initiated sessions.
  - Because MSFC is not directly connected to the CSM, RHI functionality is not possible.
  - All to/from traffic from servers, load balanced or non-load-balanced, passes through the CSM.

Design 2 Configuration Details

Example 15-3 shows the partial CSM configuration template used for this design.

Example 15-3 *CSM Configuration for Design 2*

```
!
module ContentSwitchingModule 3
!
 vlan 11 server
  ip address 10.11.1.2 255.255.255.0
  alias 10.11.1.1 255.255.255.0
!
 vlan 7 client
  ip address 10.17.1.11 255.255.255.0
  gateway 10.17.1.1
!
 vlan 17 server
  ip address 10.17.1.11 255.255.255.0
!
 vlan 8 client
  ip address 10.18.1.11 255.255.255.0
  gateway 10.18.1.1
!
 vlan 18 server
  ip address 10.18.1.11 255.255.255.0
!
 vlan 9 client
  ip address 10.19.1.11 255.255.255.0
  gateway 10.19.1.1
!
 vlan 19 server
  ip address 10.19.1.11 255.255.255.0
!
```

Example 15-4 shows a partial configuration from the MSFC in the aggregation switch.

Example 15-4 *MSFC Configuration for Design 2*

```
MSFC SVI
!
interface Vlan16
  ip address 10.16.1.2 255.255.255.0
  standby 16 ip 10.16.1.1
  standby 16 priority 150
```

Data Center Design 3: Layer 3 FWSM and Layer 2 CSM in Aggregation

The third design is an enhancement on the second one. In this design, the type and number of networking devices stays the same. The only key difference is the change in CSM design from a bridged mode to a one-armed approach. This section discusses the topology, design caveats, and configuration details pertaining to this design.

Design 3 Topology Details

Figure 15-3 displays the logical topology of the third design. The networking infrastructure stays the same as the second design except that the CSM is now connected directly to the MSFC.

Figure 15-3 *Integrated Data Center Design Option 3*

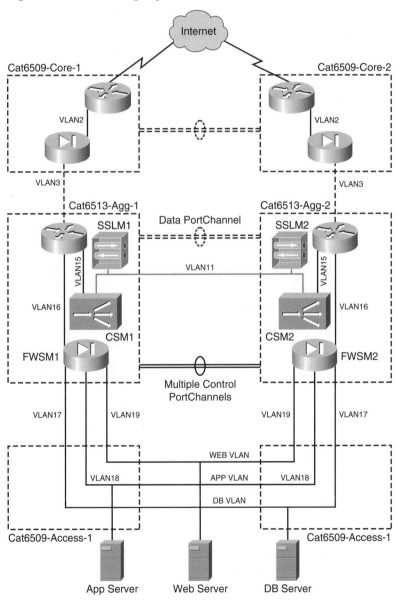

The IP connectivity in this design can be summarized as follows:

- MSFC on Catalyst 6509-Core-1 and Catalyst 6509-Core-2 connects to the Internet. This link is direct or through edge routers.

- Toward the inside, MSFCs connect to the FWSM over VLAN 2.

- FWSM connects to the MSFCs in the aggregation switches over VLAN 3.

- Aggregation MSFC connects to the aggregation FWSM over VLAN 16.

- Aggregation FWSM connects to all the server VLANs—VLAN 17, VLAN 18, and VLAN 19.

- CSM has a single, server-defined type VLAN—VLAN 15—which connects to the MSFC.

- VLAN 11 is the SSLM VLAN on the CSM.

- Connectivity between aggregation and access is Layer 2.

Design 3 Caveats

Following are some further design caveats and considerations:

- Security details
  - FWSMs are deployed in a Layer 3 mode in both core and aggregation switches.
  - Core FWSM is the security perimeter between the untrusted Internet and the trusted data center.
  - In this design, a security perimeter is possible between the web, app, and db tiers. This functionality is provided by the aggregation FWSM. This security perimeter applies to non-load-balanced traffic as well. Since the CSM exists outside of the aggregation FWSM, the VIPs on the CSM are accessible without going through the aggregation FWSM.
  - Aggregation FWSM's default gateway is the MSFC on VLAN 16.
  - Aggregation FWSM has multiple DMZ VLANs; namely, VLAN 17, VLAN 18, and VLAN 19.

- Content switching details
  - CSM is used in one-armed fashion.
  - Server's default gateway is the aggregation firewall's primary IP address.
  - Apart from the load-balancing configurations, no extra configuration is needed on the CSM for direct access to servers and non-load-balanced server-initiated sessions.

— Because the MSFC is directly connected to the CSM on VLAN 15, RHI functionality is possible.

— Only load-balanced traffic passes through the CSM. All other server-initiated or direct access server traffic bypasses the CSM.

Design 3 Configuration Details

Example 15-5 shows the partial CSM configuration template used for this design.

Example 15-5 *CSM Configuration for Design 3*

```
!
module ContentSwitchingModule 3
 vlan 15 server
  ip address 10.15.1.12 255.255.255.0
  gateway 10.15.1.1
  alias 10.15.1.11 255.255.255.0
 !
 vlan 11 server
  ip address 10.11.1.2 255.255.255.0
  alias 10.11.1.1 255.255.255.0
 !
```

Example 15-6 shows a partial configuration from the MSFC in the aggregation switch.

Example 15-6 *MSFC Configuration for Design 3*

```
MSFC SVI
interface Vlan15
  ip address 10.15.1.2 255.255.255.0
  standby 15 ip 10.15.1.1
  standby 15 priority 150
!
interface Vlan16
  ip address 10.16.1.2 255.255.255.0
  standby 16 ip 10.16.1.1
  standby 16 priority 150
```

Data Center Design 4: Layer 3 FWSM and Layer 2 CSM in Aggregation

The fourth design is a further enhancement on the third one. In this design, the type and number of networking devices stays the same except that the FWSM pair on the core switches is not needed anymore. This design is different from the third one, as it uses transparent virtual context on the FWSM. The CSM is still deployed in a one-armed design approach.

The transparent virtual context on the FWSM enables the use of the same physical FWSM pair as multiple virtual firewalls protecting different segments. This approach uses the FWSM in

Bridge mode, thus keeping the MSFC as the Layer 3 termination point of the servers. This section discusses the topology, design caveats, and configuration details pertaining to this design.

Design 4 Topology Details

Figure 15-4 displays the logical topology of the fourth design.

Figure 15-4 *Integrated Data Center Design Option 4*

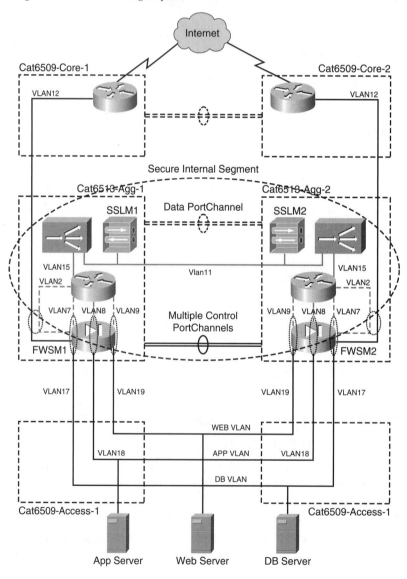

The IP connectivity in this design can be summarized as follows:

* MSFC on Catalyst 6509-Core-1 and Catalyst 6509-Core-2 connects to the Internet. This link is direct or through edge routers.

* Toward the inside, MSFCs connect to the aggregation FWSM over VLAN 12. FWSM merges this VLAN with the aggregation MSFC on VLAN 2.

* Aggregation MSFC connects to the aggregation FWSM over VLAN 7, VLAN 8, and VLAN 9.

* Aggregation FWSM connects to the server VLANs—VLAN 17, VLAN 18, and VLAN 19. Each of these VLANs exist in a different context.

* CSM has a single, server-defined type VLAN—VLAN 15—which connects it to the MSFC.

* VLAN 11 is the SSLM VLAN on the CSM.

* Connectivity between aggregation and access is Layer 2.

Design 4 Caveats

Following are some further design caveats and considerations:

* Security details
  — FWSMs are deployed in a Layer 2 mode with multiple contexts in the aggregation switches.
  — Aggregation switch FWSM provides the security perimeter between the untrusted Internet and the trusted data center.
  — In this design, a security perimeter is possible between the web, app, and db tiers. This functionality is provided by the aggregation FWSM. This security perimeter applies to load-balanced and non-load-balanced traffic.
  — All traffic from all segments passes through the firewall before reaching the MSFC. This makes the MSFC the secure internal segment.

* Content switching details
  — CSM is used in a one-armed fashion.
  — Server's default gateway is the aggregation MSFC's HSRP group IP address.
  — Apart from the load-balancing configurations, no extra configuration is needed on the CSM for direct access to servers and non-load-balanced, server-initiated sessions.

— Because MSFC is directly connected to the CSM on VLAN 15, RHI functionality is possible.

— Only load-balanced traffic passes through the CSM. All other server-initiated or direct access server traffic bypasses the CSM.

Design 4 Configuration Details

Example 15-7 shows the partial CSM configuration template used for this design.

Example 15-7 *CSM Configuration for Design 4*

```
!
module ContentSwitchingModule 3
  vlan 15 server
    ip address 10.15.1.12 255.255.255.0
    gateway 10.15.1.1
    alias 10.15.1.11 255.255.255.0
  !
  vlan 11 server
    ip address 10.11.1.2 255.255.255.0
    alias 10.11.1.1 255.255.255.0
```

Example 15-8 shows a partial configuration from the MSFC in the aggregation switch.

Example 15-8 *MSFC Configuration for Design 4*

```
MSFC SVI
interface Vlan15
  ip address 10.15.1.2 255.255.255.0
  standby 15 ip 10.15.1.1
  standby 15 priority 150
!
interface Vlan7
  ip address 10.17.1.2 255.255.255.0
  standby 17 ip 10.17.1.1
  standby 17 priority 150
!
interface Vlan8
  ip address 10.18.1.2 255.255.255.0
  standby 18 ip 10.18.1.1
  standby 18 priority 150
!
interface Vlan9
  ip address 10.19.1.2 255.255.255.0
  standby 19 ip 10.19.1.1
  standby 19 priority 150
```

Example 15-9 shows the partial FWSM configuration template used for this design.

Example 15-9 *FWSM Configuration for Design 4*

```
!
FIREWALL CONTEXTS
context DB
  allocate-interface vlan7
  allocate-interface vlan17
  config-url disk:/DB.cfg
!
context APP
  allocate-interface vlan8
  allocate-interface vlan18
  config-url disk:/APP.cfg
!
context WEB
  allocate-interface vlan9
  allocate-interface vlan19
  config-url disk:/WEB.cfg
```

Case Study: Integrated Data Center Design

This section covers a data center IP design using a transparent virtual context on the FWSM, Catalyst 6500 Supervisor 720 (Sup720), and the CSS. This design is unique in how the outside (Internet-facing) and inside (internal network) is designed together with Cisco IOS NAT and policy-based routing (PBR). The secure internal segment scheme allows for a secure segment consisting of the MSFC, the SLB device, content engines, and the SSL offloading device. This segment is completely secure and protected from malicious activities from all the DMZs, the inside network, and most of all, the outside network.

The design is highly optimized in terms of data center performance, high availability, and security. It is scalable to address future server farms, secure DMZs, and content switching needs. To ensure protection against active/active scenarios (also known as *split brain,* when both modules become active and forward traffic), separate port-channels are used for data traffic and for control traffic, such as Firewall Module *LAN failover* and Firewall Module *state link*.

The CSS 11506 is set up in a one-armed fashion using a single link carrying a single VLAN. To ensure that the server return traffic goes through the CSS, source IP NAT or PBR can be used. In this design, PBR is utilized.

Figure 15-5 displays the logical topology of the case study in discussion. Notice that this design is similar to design option 4, discussed in the previous section.

Figure 15-5 *Integrated Data Center Case Study Topology*

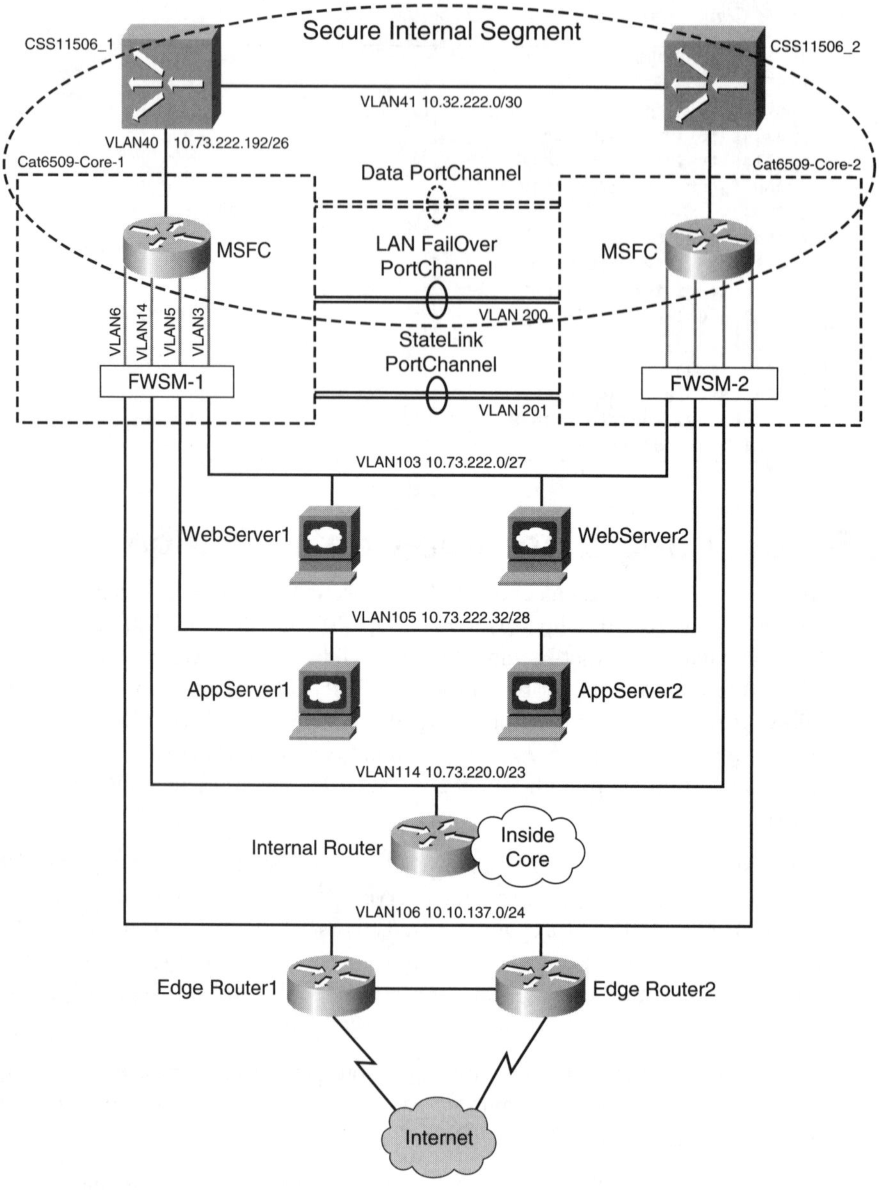

Design Details

The idea behind this design is to use the FWSM on the Catalyst 6500 in a virtual transparent context to create a secure internal segment. Virtual contexts are used not just to virtualize the DMZs and the inside and outside networks, but also to bring Layer 3 for all segments transparently up to the MSFC. In other words, each segment is bridged through the FWSM.

Consider the example of the web DMZ to understand how the environment works. Web servers with IPs in the subnet 10.73.222.0/27 reside in VLAN 103. Their default gateway is the HSRP group IP on the MSFC on VLAN 3, or 10.73.222.1. VLAN 3 has the same subnet as VLAN 103, and both of these VLANs are bridged by the FWSM virtual context, namely dmzweb. On this virtual context on the FWSM, VLAN 103 is configured as the outside network and VLAN 3 is configured as the inside protected network. Access list acl_dmzweb has the packet-filtering policy definition. Similarly, all the other DMZs and the inside and outside networks are configured.

The advantages of this approach are as follows:

- No changes to the server IP addresses or default gateway settings.

- Separate Layer 2 port-channels provide for robust and redundant data and control traffic paths.

- Non-TCP/UDP traffic, such as SNMP, ARP, broadcast, multicast, and so on bypasses the SLB devices.

- Non-load-balanced traffic (backups and so on) bypasses the SLB devices. Care should be taken into consideration making sure these traffic instances do not use the load-balanced listeners on the servers.

- Client IP address is preserved.

- IOS NAT is utilized on the MSFC to provide for easy and manageable NAT functionality.

- Design is scalable for new DMZs and new load-balanced applications.

- Since port address translation (PAT) is used on the SLB device, each server can host multiple applications on different ports.

- The port-listening methodology preserves IP addresses in each DMZ.

- This design can be scaled to multiple SLB or other content devices (such as content engines, SSL offload devices, and so on).

The disadvantages of this approach are as follows:

- Care must be taken in making sure the management and direct access traffic instances do not use the load-balanced listeners on the servers.

- Policy-based routing needs to be configured on the MSFC and may become difficult to maintain. Using port ranges in the PBR ACLs is helpful.

- The application instances on the servers may send redirects to the client on the listener port and not the announce port (the default protocol port). For example, if an application is virtualized on the SLB device as 10.73.222.204:443 but the server listener is on 4433, the server may send a HTTPS redirect to the client on port 4433. Redirect applications should use the default protocol ports—80 for HTTP and 443 for HTTPS.

- Further content rules need to be configured to protect against the above redirects. For example, for production partner applications, two content rules are set up: partner_prod:443 and partner_prod:4433.

- Because of the redirects, firewall rules should allow requests to these port address translated ports.

Table 15-1 shows the various IP addresses and TCP ports used in the design. This table will help you understand the configurations of each device.

Table 15-1 *Real Server IP Addresses and Public and Private Virtual IP Addresses Associated with Each Application (Domain)*

Application Name	Server IP Addresses	TCP Port	Public (NATed) IP	CSS VIP
DMZWeb				
ZLAB staging	10.73.222.3 10.73.222.17	80/443	10.10.137.156	10.73.222.201
Client portal	10.73.222.4 10.73.222.18	8082/4432	10.10.137.22	10.73.222.203
Partner portal	10.73.222.4 10.73.222.18	8083/4433	10.10.137.23	10.73.222.204
DMZApp				
ZLAB database application	10.73.222.35 10.73.222.36			10.73.222.221

Primary CSS (CSS 11506-1) Configuration Details

Example 15-10 provides complete configuration of the CSS 11506-1. This CSS is the primary CSS within the pair. Since box-to-box redundancy (the **ip redundancy** command shown in the configuration) is used, the second CSS is in standby or silent mode.

Example 15-10 *CSS 11506-1 Complete Configuration*

```
!
! CSS11506_1 Configuration
! CustX ZLAB Data Center in San Jose, CA
!
! Version 0.06
! Author: Zeeshan Naseh
! Cisco Advanced Services
!
```

Example 15-10 *CSS 11506-1 Complete Configuration (Continued)*

```
!
configure

!************************* GLOBAL **************************
! Box-to-box redundancy is used
  ip redundancy
! Following CAPP session is needed between the active and backup CSSs for
! the purpose of configuration sync.
  app session 10.32.222.2
  app
  ip route 0.0.0.0 0.0.0.0 10.73.222.193 1

!************************* INTERFACE ************************
interface  2/1
  bridge vlan 40
  description "Link to Cat6509"
interface  3/1
  bridge vlan 41
  description "Redundancy Port"
!************************* CIRCUIT **************************
circuit VLAN40
  redundancy
  ip address 10.73.222.196 255.255.255.192
circuit VLAN41
  ip address 10.32.222.1 255.255.255.252
    redundancy-protocol

!************************* SERVICE **************************
! Production ZLAB Web Applications on port 80. TCP Keepalives are used to
! determine the health of the servers.
service staging_prod_1:80
  protocol tcp
  port 80
  ip address 10.73.222.3
  keepalive port 80
  keepalive type tcp
  active
service staging_prod_2:80
  protocol tcp
  port 80
  ip address 10.73.222.17
  keepalive port 80
  keepalive type tcp
  active
! PATing is enabled for all production web applications.
service client_prod_1:80
  protocol tcp
  port 8082
  ip address 10.73.222.4
  keepalive port 8082
  keepalive type tcp
  active
```

continues

Example 15-10 *CSS 11506-1 Complete Configuration (Continued)*

```
service client_prod_2:80
  protocol tcp
  port 8082
  ip address 10.73.222.18
  keepalive port 8082
  keepalive type tcp
  active
service partner_prod_1:80
  protocol tcp
  port 8083
  ip address 10.73.222.4
  keepalive port 8083
  keepalive type tcp
  active
service partner_prod_2:80
  protocol tcp
  port 8083
  ip address 10.73.222.18
  keepalive port 8083
  keepalive type tcp
  active

! Production ZLAB Web Applications on port 443
service staging_prod_1:443
  protocol tcp
  port 443
  ip address 10.73.222.3
  keepalive port 443
  keepalive type tcp
  active
service staging_prod_2:443
  protocol tcp
  port 443
  ip address 10.73.222.17
  keepalive port 443
  keepalive type tcp
  active
service client_prod_1:443
  protocol tcp
  port 4432
  ip address 10.73.222.4
  keepalive port 4432
  keepalive type tcp
  active
service client_prod_2:443
  protocol tcp
  port 4432
  ip address 10.73.222.18
  keepalive port 4432
  keepalive type tcp
  active
```

Example 15-10 *CSS 11506-1 Complete Configuration (Continued)*

```
service partner_prod_1:443
  protocol tcp
  port 4433
  ip address 10.73.222.4
  keepalive port 4433
  keepalive type tcp
  active
service partner_prod_2:443
  protocol tcp
  port 4433
  ip address 10.73.222.18
  keepalive port 4433
  keepalive type tcp
  active

! Production ZLAB DB App Application on port 17892
service ZLab_db_app_1
  protocol tcp
  port 17892
  ip address 10.73.222.35
  keepalive port 17892
  keepalive type tcp
  active
service ZLab_db_app_2
  protocol tcp
  port 17892
  ip address 10.73.222.36
  keepalive port 17892
  keepalive type tcp
  suspen

!*************************** OWNER ***************************
owner ZLab_web_staging
  content staging_prod:80
    protocol tcp
    port 80
    vip address 10.73.222.201
    add service staging_prod_1:80
    add service staging_prod_2:80
    active
  content staging_prod:443
    protocol tcp
    port 443
    vip address 10.73.222.201
    add service staging_prod_1:443
    add service staging_prod_2:443
    active

owner ZLab_web
  content client_prod:80
    protocol tcp
    port 80
```

continues

Example 15-10 *CSS 11506-1 Complete Configuration (Continued)*

```
          vip address 10.73.222.203
          add service client_prod_1:80
          add service client_prod_2:80
          active
       content partner_prod:80
          protocol tcp
          port 80
          vip address 10.73.222.204
          add service partner_prod_1:80
          add service partner_prod_2:80
active

! In order to catch HTTPS redirects from the Application on the server
! listening port, the content rule for the listening port (in this case 4432)
! is set up. Similar additions need to be made for HTTP content rules also.

   content client_prod:443
     protocol tcp
     port 443
     vip address 10.73.222.203
     add service client_prod_1:443
     add service client_prod_2:443
     active
   content client_prod: 4432
     protocol tcp
     port 4432
     vip address 10.73.222.203
     add service client_prod_1:443
     add service client_prod_2:443
     active
   content partner_prod:443
     protocol tcp
     port 443
     vip address 10.73.222.204
     add service partner_prod_1:443
     add service partner_prod_2:443
     active
   content partner_prod:4433
     protocol tcp
     port 4433
     vip address 10.73.222.204
     add service partner_prod_1:443
     add service partner_prod_2:443
     active

owner ZLab_remoting
   content ZLab_db_app
     protocol tcp
     port 17892
     vip address 10.73.222.221
     add service ZLab_db_app_1
     add service ZLab_db_app_2
     active
```

Backup CSS (CSS 11506-2) Configuration Details

Example 15-11 provides the portions of the configuration of the CSS 11506-2 that are different from CSS 11506-1.

Example 15-11 *CSS 11506-2 Redundancy Configuration*

```
!
! CSS11506_2 Configuration
! CustX ZLAB Data Center in San Jose, CA
!
! Version 0.06
! Author: Zeeshan Naseh
! Cisco Advanced Services
!
!
configure

!************************* GLOBAL *************************
  ip redundancy
  app session 10.32.222.1
  app
  ip route 0.0.0.0 0.0.0.0 10.73.222.193 1


!************************ INTERFACE ************************
interface  2/1
  bridge vlan 40
  description "Link to Cat6509"
interface  3/1
  bridge vlan 41
  description "Redundancy Port"
!************************ CIRCUIT ************************
circuit VLAN40
  redundancy
  ip address 10.73.222.196 255.255.255.192
circuit VLAN41
  ip address 10.32.222.2 255.255.255.252
    redundancy-protocol
```

All services and content rule configurations stay the same as for CSS 11506-1.

Catalyst 6509 Configuration Details

Example 15-12 provides the Layer 2 and Layer 3 configuration details of the Catalyst 6509.

Example 15-12 *Catalyst 6509's Layer 2 and Layer 3 Configuration*

```
!
! Cat6509-Core-1 Configuration
! CustX ZLAB Data Center in San Jose, CA
!
! Version 0.06
```

continues

Example 15-12 *Catalyst 6509's Layer 2 and Layer 3 Configuration (Continued)*

```
! Author: Zeeshan Naseh
! Cisco Advanced Services
!
!
conf t
!
!hostname Cat6509-1
!
!
spanning-tree mode rapid-pvst
spanning-tree vlan 2-202 priority 16384
!
!
power redundancy-mode combined
!
vlan 14
 name inside
!
vlan 114
 name msfcinside
!
vlan 3
 name dmzweb
!
vlan 103
 name msfcdmzweb
!
vlan 5
 name dmzapp
!
vlan 105
 name msfcdmzapp
!
vlan 6
 name outside
!
vlan 106
 name msfcoutside
!
vlan 40
 name css_vlan
!
vlan 200
 name fwsm_heartbeat_link
!
vlan 201
 name fwsm_state_link
!
!
```

Example 15-12 *Catalyst 6509's Layer 2 and Layer 3 Configuration (Continued)*

```
interface Vlan114
 description Inside
 ip address 10.73.221.187 255.255.254.0
 standby ip 10.73.221.186
 standby priority 150
 standby preempt
 standby authentication VLAN114
 no shutdown
!
interface Vlan103
 description DMZWeb
 ip address 10.73.222.29 255.255.255.224
 standby ip 10.73.222.1
 standby priority 150
 standby preempt
 standby authentication VLAN103
 no shutdown
!
interface Vlan105
 description DMZApp
 ip address 10.73.222.45 255.255.255.240
 standby ip 10.73.222.33
 standby priority 150
 standby preempt
 standby authentication VLAN105
 no shutdown
!
interface Vlan106
 description Outside
 ip address 10.10.137.252 255.255.255.0
 standby ip 10.10.137.254
 standby priority 150
 standby preempt
 standby authentication VLAN106
 no shutdown
!
!
interface Vlan40
 description CSS Vlan
 ip address 10.73.222.194 255.255.255.192
 standby ip 10.73.222.193
 standby priority 150
 standby preempt
 standby authentication VLAN40
 no shutdown
!
!
End
```

Layer 2 Port-Channel Configuration Details

The use of port-channels shown in Example 15-13 is one of the key elements of this design. Having separate port-channels for data and control traffic is critical. In order to protect against module failures, members of the port-channel should be in different modules.

Example 15-13 *Catalyst 6509 Layer 2 Port-Channel Configuration*

```
! DATA Port Channel
! Member interfaces GigabitEthernet1/47-48, GigabitEthernet2/47-48
interface Port-channel111
 description DATA Port Channel
 no ip address
 switchport
 switchport trunk encapsulation dot1q
 switchport trunk allowed vlan 1-199,202-4094
 switchport mode trunk
!


! FW LAN Failover Port Channel
! Member interfaces GigabitEthernet1/45, GigabitEthernet2/45
interface Port-channel200
 description FW LAN Failover Port Channel
 no ip address
 switchport
 switchport access vlan 200
 switchport trunk encapsulation dot1q
 switchport mode access
!


! FW Link State Failover Port Channel
! Member interfaces GigabitEthernet1/46, GigabitEthernet2/46
interface Port-channel201
 description FW Link State Failover Port Channel
 no ip address
 switchport
 switchport access vlan 201
 switchport trunk encapsulation dot1q
 switchport mode access
!
```

NAT Configuration Details

Setting up IOS NAT on the MSFC with HSRP redundancy is not trivial. This can potentially result in ARP conflicts and broken NAT. In order to ensure that both the MSFCs work together, you need to turn off gratuitous ARP on the static NAT entry and add static ARPs with gratuitous ARP (**alias** keyword) on both the MSFCs. These ARP should point to the shared MAC address of the HSRP group address. Example 15-14 provides configurations for both one-to-one NAT and also dynamic NAT.

Example 15-14 *Cisco IOS NAT Configuration*

```
!
! One-to-One Static Nat
! For this case study I will use 10.10.0.0 as our public IP space
ip nat inside source static 10.73.222.201 10.10.137.156 no-alias
ip nat inside source static 10.73.222.203 10.10.137.22 no-alias
ip nat inside source static 10.73.222.204 10.10.137.23 no-alias
!
arp 10.10.137.22 0000.0c07.ac00 ARPA alias
arp 10.10.137.23 0000.0c07.ac00 ARPA alias
arp 10.10.137.156 0000.0c07.ac00 ARPA alias


!
! Dynamic NAT
!
! No special measures are needed for dynamic NAT
!
access-list 102 permit ip 10.73.0.0 0.0.255.255 10.73.0.0 0.0.255.255
!
!
ip nat pool nat-public-IP 10.10. 137.157 10.10.137.157 netmask 255.255.255.0
ip nat inside source list 102 pool nat-public-IP overload
!


!
! NAT interface configurations
interface Vlan114
 description Inside
 ip nat inside
!
interface Vlan103
 description DMZWeb
 ip nat inside
!
interface Vlan105
 description DMZApp
 ip nat inside
!
interface Vlan106
 description Outside
 ip nat outside
!
interface Vlan40
 description CSS Vlan
 ip nat inside
!
```

Policy-Based Routing Configuration Details

Example 15-15 provides details of PBR configuration on the MSFC. This configuration is needed to ensure that server return traffic goes back through the CSS 11506.

Example 15-15 *Cisco IOS PBR Configuration*

```
!
! PBR for Production Web Apps
!
access-list 121 permit tcp any eq www any
access-list 121 permit tcp any eq 443 any
access-list 121 permit tcp any range 8081 8083 any
access-list 121 permit tcp any range 4431 4433 any
access-list 121 deny   ip any any
!
route-map FromDMZWebSendToCSS permit 10
 match ip address 121
 set ip next-hop 10.73.222.196
!
!
interface Vlan103
 description DMZWeb
 ip policy route-map FromDMZWebSendToCSS
!

! PBR for Production DB App
access-list 122 permit tcp any eq 17892 any
access-list 122 deny   ip any any
!
route-map FromDMZAppSendToCSS permit 10
 match ip address 122
 set ip next-hop 10.73.222.196
!
interface Vlan105
 description DMZApp
 ip policy route-map FromDMZAppSendToCSS
!
```

FWSM Configuration Details

Example 15-16 provides details of FWSM on Catalyst 6509 configurations. This example provides main system context configuration where redundancy and VLAN configuration of inside, outside, dmzapp, and dmzweb contexts are defined.

Example 15-16 *FWSM System Context Configuration*

```
!
hostname FWSM
ftp mode passive
pager lines 24
class default
  limit-resource IPSec 5
  limit-resource Mac-addresses 65535
  limit-resource SSH 5
  limit-resource Telnet 5
  limit-resource All 0
!
failover
failover lan unit primary
failover lan interface failover vlan 200
failover polltime unit 1 holdtime 15
failover polltime interface 15
failover interface-policy 1
failover replication http
failover link statelink vlan 201
failover interface ip failover 10.32.222.5 255.255.255.252 standby 10.32.222.6
failover interface ip statelink 10.32.222.9 255.255.255.252 standby 10.32.222.10
arp timeout 14400
!
!
timeout xlate 3:00:00
timeout conn 1:00:00 half-closed 0:10:00 udp 0:02:00 icmp 0:00:02 rpc 0:10:00 h323
  0:05:00 h225 1:00:00 mgcp 0:05:00 sip 0:30:00 sip_media 0:02:00
timeout uauth 0:05:00 absolute
sysopt nodnsalias inbound
sysopt nodnsalias outbound
terminal width 80
no gdb enable
admin-context inside
context inside
  description INSIDE
  allocate-interface vlan14
  allocate-interface vlan114
  config-url disk:/inside.cfg
!
context outside
  description OUTSIDE
  allocate-interface vlan6
  allocate-interface vlan106
  config-url disk:/outside.cfg
!
context dmzapp
  description DMZAPP
  allocate-interface vlan5
  allocate-interface vlan105
  config-url disk:/dmzapp.cfg
```

continues

Example 15-16 *FWSM System Context Configuration (Continued)*

```
!
context dmzweb
  description DMZWEB
  allocate-interface vlan3
  allocate-interface vlan103
  config-url disk:/dmzweb.cfg
!
```

DMZWeb Virtual Context

Example 15-17 provides details of FWSM configuration with regard to the dmzweb context.

Example 15-17 *FWSM dmzweb Context Configuration*

```
FWSM/inside# changeto context dmzweb
FWSM/dmzweb#
FWSM/dmzweb#
FWSM/dmzweb# sh run
: Saved
:
FWSM Version 2.2(1)8 <context>
firewall transparent
nameif vlan3 inside security100
nameif vlan103 outside security0
!
hostname dmzweb
fixup protocol dns maximum-length 512
fixup protocol ftp 21
fixup protocol h323 H225 1720
fixup protocol h323 ras 1718-1719
fixup protocol rsh 514
fixup protocol sip 5060
no fixup protocol sip udp 5060
fixup protocol skinny 2000
fixup protocol smtp 25
fixup protocol sqlnet 1521
names
access-list deny-flow-max 4096
access-list alert-interval 300
access-list outside extended permit ip any any
access-list acl_dmzweb extended deny tcp any any range 135 netbios-ssn
access-list acl_dmzweb extended deny udp any any range 135 139
access-list acl_dmzweb extended permit icmp any any
<SKIP>
pager lines 24
icmp permit any inside
icmp permit any outside
mtu inside 1500
```

Example 15-17 *FWSM dmzweb Context Configuration (Continued)*

```
mtu outside 1500
ip address  10.73.222.27 255.255.255.240 standby 10.73.222.28
no pdm history enable
arp timeout 14400
access-group acl_dmzweb in interface inside
access-group outside in interface outside
!
interface inside
!
!
interface outside
!
!
route outside 0.0.0.0 0.0.0.0 10.73.222.1 1
<SKIP>
: end
FWSM/dmzweb#
```

DMZApp Virtual Context

Example 15-18 provides details of FWSM configuration with regard to the dmzapp context.

Example 15-18 *FWSM dmzapp Context Configuration*

```
FWSM/inside# changeto context dmzwapp
FWSM/dmzapp# sh run
: Saved
:
FWSM Version 2.2(1)8 <context>
firewall transparent
nameif vlan5 inside security100
nameif vlan105 outside security0
hostname dmzapp
fixup protocol dns maximum-length 512
fixup protocol ftp 21
fixup protocol h323 H225 1720
fixup protocol h323 ras 1718-1719
fixup protocol rsh 514
fixup protocol sip 5060
no fixup protocol sip udp 5060
fixup protocol skinny 2000
fixup protocol smtp 25
fixup protocol sqlnet 1521
names
access-list deny-flow-max 4096
access-list alert-interval 300
access-list outside extended permit ip any any
access-list acl_dmzapp extended deny tcp any any range 135 netbios-ssn
```

continues

Example 15-18 *FWSM dmzapp Context Configuration (Continued)*

```
access-list acl_dmzapp extended deny udp any any range 135 139
access-list acl_dmzapp extended permit icmp any any
<SKIP>
pager lines 24
logging console debugging
logging monitor debugging
icmp permit any outside
mtu inside 1500
mtu outside 1500
ip address  10.73.222.43 255.255.255.240 standby 10.73.222.44
no pdm history enable
arp timeout 14400
access-group acl_dmzapp in interface inside
access-group outside in interface outside
!
interface inside
!
!
interface outside
!
!
route outside 0.0.0.0 0.0.0.0 10.73.222.33 1
<SKIP>
: end
FWSM/dmzapp#
FWSM/dmzapp#
```

Outside Virtual Context

Example 15-19 provides details of FWSM configuration with regard to the outside context.

Example 15-19 *FWSM Outside Context Configuration*

```
FWSM/inside# changeto context outside
FWSM/outside# sh run
: Saved
:
FWSM Version 2.2(1)8 <context>
firewall transparent
nameif vlan6 inside security0
nameif vlan106 outside security100
hostname outside
fixup protocol dns maximum-length 512
fixup protocol ftp 21
fixup protocol h323 H225 1720
fixup protocol h323 ras 1718-1719
fixup protocol rsh 514
fixup protocol sip 5060
no fixup protocol sip udp 5060
```

Example 15-19 *FWSM Outside Context Configuration (Continued)*

```
fixup protocol skinny 2000
fixup protocol smtp 25
fixup protocol sqlnet 1521
names
access-list deny-flow-max 4096
access-list alert-interval 300
access-list outside extended permit ip any any
access-list acl_out extended permit tcp any host 10.10.137.22 eq www
access-list acl_out extended permit tcp any host 10.10.137.22 eq https
access-list acl_out extended permit tcp any host 10.10.137.23 eq www
access-list acl_out extended permit tcp any host 10.10.137.23 eq https
access-list acl_out extended permit tcp any host 10.10.137.156 eq www
access-list acl_out extended permit tcp any host 10.10.137.156 eq https
<SKIP>
pager lines 24
icmp permit any inside
icmp permit any outside
mtu inside 1500
mtu outside 1500
ip address  65.162.137.250 255.255.255.0 standby 65.162.137.251
no pdm history enable
arp timeout 14400
access-group acl_out in interface inside
access-group outside in interface outside
!
interface inside
!
!
interface outside
!
!
route outside 0.0.0.0 0.0.0.0 65.162.137.254 1
<SKIP>
: end
FWSM/outside#
FWSM/outside#
FWSM/outside#
```

Inside Virtual Context

Example 15-20 provides details of FWSM configuration with regard to the inside context.

Example 15-20 *FWSM Inside Context Configuration*

```
FWSM/inside# changeto context inside
FWSM/inside# sh run
: Saved
:
FWSM Version 2.2(1)8 <context>
firewall transparent
```

continues

Example 15-20 *FWSM Inside Context Configuration (Continued)*

```
nameif vlan14 inside security100
nameif vlan114 outside security0
hostname inside
domain-name innovativemerchants.com
fixup protocol dns maximum-length 512
fixup protocol ftp 21
fixup protocol h323 H225 1720
fixup protocol h323 ras 1718-1719
fixup protocol rsh 514
fixup protocol sip 5060
no fixup protocol sip udp 5060
fixup protocol skinny 2000
fixup protocol smtp 25
fixup protocol sqlnet 1521
names
access-list deny-flow-max 4096
access-list alert-interval 300
access-list outside extended permit ip any any
access-list acl_in extended permit icmp any any
<SKIP>
pager lines 24
icmp permit any outside
mtu inside 1500
mtu outside 1500
ip address  10.73.221.248 255.255.254.0 standby 10.73.221.249
no pdm history enable
arp timeout 14400
access-group acl_in in interface inside
access-group outside in interface outside
!
interface inside
!
!
interface outside
!
!
route outside 0.0.0.0 0.0.0.0 10.73.221.186 1
<SKIP>
ssh 0.0.0.0 0.0.0.0 inside
ssh 0.0.0.0 0.0.0.0 outside
ssh timeout 5
terminal width 80
Cryptochecksum:28565d1c0be731b7c02f18b7c02138fd
: end
FWSM/inside#
FWSM/inside#
```

Summary

This chapter introduced the reader to some key design methodologies for integrated or consolidated data centers. It covered motivations behind data center redesigns, including four distinct designs with different design considerations.

In order to combine all of the design concepts, the chapter ended with a detailed case study of an integrated data center. This case study included all of the configurations on the Catalyst 6500, the CSS, and the FWSM.

CISCO SYSTEMS

Cisco Press

NETWORKING TECHNOLOGY GUIDES
MASTER THE NETWORK

Turn to Networking Technology Guides whenever you need **in-depth knowledge of complex networking technologies**. Written by leading networking authorities, these guides offer theoretical and practical knowledge for **real-world networking applications and solutions**.

Look for Networking Technology Guides at your favorite bookseller

Cisco CallManager Best Practices:
A Cisco AVVID Solution
ISBN: 1-58705-139-7

Cisco IP Telephony: Planning, Design,
Implementation, Operation, and Optimization
ISBN: 1-58705-157-5

Cisco PIX Firewall and ASA Handbook
ISBN: 1-58705-158-3

Cisco Wireless LAN Security
ISBN: 1-58705-154-0

End-to-End QoS Network Design:
Quality of Service in LANs, WANs, and VPNs
ISBN: 1-58705-176-1

Network Security Architectures
ISBN: 1-58705-115-X

Optimal Routing Design
ISBN: 1-58705-187-7

Top-Down Network Design, Second Edition
ISBN: 1-58705-152-4

Visit **www.ciscopress.com/series** for details about Networking Technology Guides and a complete list of titles.

Learning is serious business.
Invest wisely.

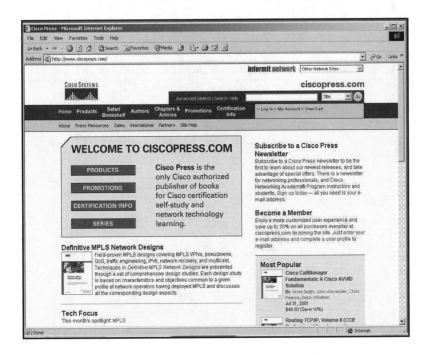
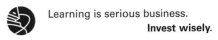

Safari®
BOOKS ONLINE
ENABLED

THIS BOOK IS SAFARI ENABLED

INCLUDES FREE 45-DAY ACCESS TO THE ONLINE EDITION

The Safari® Enabled icon on the cover of your favorite technology book means the book is available through Safari Bookshelf. When you buy this book, you get free access to the online edition for 45 days.

Safari Bookshelf is an electronic reference library that lets you easily search thousands of technical books, find code samples, download chapters, and access technical information whenever and wherever you need it.

TO GAIN 45-DAY SAFARI ENABLED ACCESS TO THIS BOOK:

- Go to **http://www.ciscopress.com/safarienabled**

- Complete the brief registration form

- Enter the coupon code found in the front of this book before the "Contents at a Glance" page

If you have difficulty registering on Safari Bookshelf or accessing the online edition, please e-mail customer-service@safaribooksonline.com.